WRITTEN IN BLOOD

THE HISTORY OF FORT WORTH'S FALLEN LAWMEN

Volume I
1861–1909

By
Richard F. Selcer
and Kevin S. Foster

University of North Texas Press
Denton, Texas

10 9 8 7 6 5 4 3 2 1

Permissions:
University of North Texas Press
1155 Union Circle #311336
Denton, TX 76203-5017

The paper used in this book meets the minimum requirements of the
American National Standard for Permanence of Paper for Printed
Library Materials, z39.48.1984. Binding materials have been chosen
for durability.

Library of Congress Cataloging-in-Publication Data

Selcer, Richard F.
Written in blood : the history of Fort Worth's fallen lawmen / by
Richard F. Selcer and Kevin S. Foster. -- 1st ed.
p. cm.
Includes bibliographical references and index.
ISBN 978-1-57441-295-6 (cloth : alk. paper) --
ISBN 978-1-57441-296-3
(pbk. : alk. paper)
1. Peace officers--Texas--Tarrant County--Biography.
2. Police murders--Texas--Tarrant County.
3. Tarrant County (Tex.)--Biography. I.
Foster, Kevin, 1960- II. Title.
HV8145.T4S45 2010
363.2092'2764531--dc22
2010024002

Cover photo: Fort Worth Police Department, 1901
(Photo by John Swartz courtesy of
Fort Worth Police Historical Association)

DEDICATION

This one's for you, Janet Lee—the best sister a fellow ever had.
— Richard F. Selcer

For my wife, Lisa, and our children, Stephen and Danielle . . . and my other family: the men and women of the Fort Worth Police Department.
— Kevin S. Foster

CONTENTS

ACKNOWLEDGMENTS

So many people to thank, so few words in which to do it! There's a rule of thumb in history: the bigger the book and the more footnotes, the more people there are to thank. That includes colleagues, collectors, librarians, archivists, proofreaders, et al. And when a book like this one has two authors, that doubles the number of folks to thank.

We'll start with the library staff in the Genealogy, History, and Archives Unit of the Fort Worth Public Library: Betty Shankle, Shirley Apley, and Tom Kellam. They dug up obscure documents and photographs, checked our facts on request, and let us into the inner sanctum where the "good stuff" is stored.

Dalton Hoffman and Quentin McGown graciously provided pictures from their vast collections of old Fort Worth images. Ditto for Jon Frembling at the Amon Carter Museum. Susie Pritchett at the Tarrant County Historical Commission is one of those people every Fort Worth historian should know. Not only is she a walking encyclopedia of knowledge on our favorite city, but she knows the collections of the Commission better than anyone.

Robert Smith, who I suspect loves history as much as he loves architecture (his profession), produced the excellent graphics so that, for instance, you can follow Ike Knight's path of murder and mayhem and understand the "dead line" at the Texas and Pacific passenger station. Bob has an amazing talent for taking my crude drawings and transforming them into clear, sharp maps, and floor plans. And he takes pity when it comes to billing starving authors for his time.

Kevin was in contact with several families of fallen officers who were kind enough to share their family stories and documents. And in some cases they also managed to dig up photos of officers whose visages were previously unknown. These include, in particular, descendants of Andy Grimes, Ad Campbell, C. E. Parsley, and John Ogletree. Thanks for trusting us with the memories of your brave ancestors.

ACKNOWLEDGMENTS

The merry gang at UNT Press deserves a Great Big Thanks for accepting the manuscript and working with us, even when I drove them nuts with last-second changes. Director Ron Chrisman had the excellent idea of cutting an over-long manuscript into two parts, thus opening the door for a second volume of *Written in Blood*. Editor Karen DeVinney has now shepherded two of my books through the publishing process. Paula Oates puts on a signing party that puts professional wedding planners to shame. Working with Bonnie Lovell, the assistant editor we dealt with personally, was a marriage made in authors' heaven; she is meticulous and detail oriented but is also a patient, kindly soul.

More kudos to Betty Shankle, without whom this thing would never have gotten indexed.

The Fort Worth Police Historical Association and Combined Law Enforcement Associations of Texas (CLEAT) were all on board every step of the way, even though some of the things about Fort Worth officers that we dug up were not flattering. Special thanks to Terry Baker, retired Assistant Chief of the Dallas County Sheriff's Office, and Ron DeLord, Special Counsel for CLEAT. Both took time out from their real jobs to provide early research help and guidance.

The Tarrant County Sheriff's Office also pitched in, in the person of retired Chief Deputy Hank Pope, unofficial historian of the Office for many years. Thanks to Hank, we were able to fill in some of the gaps in the stories of our fallen sheriffs' officers.

And an all-inclusive *gracias* to all of our friends in Fort Worth history—Donna Donnell, Max Hill, Scott Barker, Hollace Weiner, Clara Ruddell, Art Weinman, and anybody we left out—thanks for your input and support year in and year out. You are a big part of what makes writing Fort Worth history fun.

Personal note: And finally, to my co-author Kevin, thanks for reaching out to me on this project nine years ago and for being patient while your writing partner took *forever* trying to get everything just right. And now, on to Volume 2!

INTRODUCTION TO VOLUME I

The lawman is a mythic figure in Western history distinguished from mere mortals by the badge on his chest. It was that badge, not the gun he carried, that separated him from other men. Most men carried guns; few were defenders of law and order. The symbolic importance of the badge is illustrated by the fact that one of the first actions of the first Fort Worth City Council, on April 22, 1873, was to "prescribe" an official badge for its police force. It was a simple five-pointed tin star. If an officer wanted anything fancier, he had to purchase it himself.[1]

That little tin star gave a man status as well as authority. Law enforcement was considered a higher calling, a concept expressed in frequent references to the brotherhood of the badge. It was part of the mythology surrounding peace officers. Another part of that mythology is that those old lawmen struck fear into the hearts of wrongdoers just by showing up. Texas Ranger Bill McDonald said it best when he said, "No man in the wrong can stand up against a fellow that's in the right and keeps on a-comin'." This particular part of the myth was given new life in 2007 by the president of the National Law Enforcement Officers Memorial Fund when he said, "There was a code of . . . respect, even among the most heinous criminals, that you would never harm a police officer, certainly never kill a police officer."[2] Unfortunately, that claim is not supported by the evidence. Often as not, it was open season on lawmen in the presumed good old days. What has been characterized as a recent "surge" in "cop killings"—seventy in the past five years in Texas alone—is really nothing new.[3] Dying "in the line of duty" has always been normal, so normal that eighty-four Fort Worth and Tarrant County officers suffered job-related deaths in the 149 years between 1861 and 2010.[4]

An officer who died "in the line of duty" was practically guaranteed two things: First, city or county fathers would issue a formal resolution commending the deceased. A copy of those resolutions would be presented to the family. Second, the fallen officer would

Until 1891 Fort Worth police officers wore whatever badge they wanted and could afford; that was the year Marshal J. H. Maddox introduced the first official Department badge. Even after 1891, there was great variety in the design and expense of FWPD badges as many men still preferred to create their own. These two examples represent the disparity: On the left is the simple "star" badge of George Craig (1887–1915); on the right, the 1908 custom-made badge of Captain A. N. Bills (1906–1910). (Craig's badge courtesy of Wayne Craig of Lodi, CA; Bills' badge courtesy of Michael Dunn of Dallas, TX)

receive a first-class funeral befitting a genuine hero. If those early-day affairs lacked the pomp and circumstance of a traditional military funeral, they were nonetheless much more elaborate affairs than the average civilian funeral. In the nineteenth century, services began at the family residence before moving on to the cemetery. After the turn of the century, the services moved to funeral homes or churches. In time, funeral homes almost completely replaced the family residence and the church, becoming one-stop operations that provided undertaking, funeral arrangements, and even ambulance service.

In those early days, lacking a caisson or hearse, officials transported the casket to the cemetery in the "patrol wagon" or else on a buckboard pressed into service for the occasion. The funeral cortege had a police escort and, almost always, an honor guard from the local fire department because historically there was such a close fraternal bond between lawmen and firefighters. City and county offices closed for the day so that officials could march in the cortege. The whole town turned out and lined the route, partly out of curiosity but mostly to salute the deceased. An officer's funeral was a very public occasion. Formal mourning rituals always included (1) the official resolutions published the next day in the newspaper, (2) every officer wearing a black "badge of mourning" plus black crepe on his hat or helmet and sleeve for a period of thirty days, and (3) a "subscription" raised by citizens to ease the transition of the widow or family. These rituals were not written down, but they were nearly sacrosanct nonetheless.

It is what came afterwards that inspired this book: Life moved on as fallen heroes quickly became forgotten heroes. First, deceased officers dropped out of the news; then, they dropped out of the public consciousness. But no more. The tide turned after the tragedy of 9/11. That was when the modern memorial movement was born to honor fallen officers as far back as they could be identified.

Honoring top cops is nothing new. For more than forty years *Parade* Sunday magazine has put out a special annual issue "saluting the year's top police officers" across the nation.[5] But digging into the historical record to identify those long-forgotten men who died in the line of duty is a modern phenomenon. After 9/11, a mass movement was born. Suddenly, communities all over the United States wanted to do something to honor their fallen officers.

In the Lone Star State, the Combined Law Enforcement Association of Texas (CLEAT) in 2008 petitioned the legislature to fund a project that would "go back and track every death [of law officers] in Texas from the beginning of the Republic." The result would be "an official accounting" of every officer—state, county, and municipal—killed in the line of duty, which would "detail the circumstances surrounding each death." CLEAT's interest is job-related as well as historical, but no one disputes the importance of gathering the data.[6]

Locally, the memorial movement has taken three tracks with three separate honor rolls and related monuments. Fort Worth and

**A GREATER FORCE OF LAW
ENFORCEMENT PROFESSIONALS**

The logo of the Combined Law Enforcement Associations of Texas
(CLEAT), founded in 1976 to protect the rights and honor the sacrifices
of Texas lawmen. It is the largest police officers' union in the state today
and also operates the Peace Officers Memorial Foundation. (Courtesy of
CLEAT)

Tarrant County officers are eligible for one or more of the three:
the Texas Peace Officers Memorial in Austin; the Lost Lawman
Memorial, also in Austin; the Fort Worth Police and Firefighters
Memorial. The first includes all duly commissioned officers, even
jailers and posse members. The second is exclusively for sheriffs and
sheriffs' deputies. The Fort Worth memorial includes police but not
county officers (i.e., sheriffs, sheriff's deputies, constables). It is also
the only one to include firefighters. The different groups honored
by each memorial reflect the differing agendas and standards of their
sponsors.[7]

Now, nearly 150 years after the death of the first local officer,
Fort Worth finally memorialized its fallen heroes with a $300,000,
larger-than-life sculpture completed and dedicated in 2009. This
book began as a companion to that memorial—and then some. Of
the eighty-four officers who since 1861 have either died on the job

or as a direct result of illness or injury suffered on the job, this book covers only the first thirteen to die in the line of duty. Obviously, the pace accelerated after 1909. The others will be covered in future volumes. All the fallen did not die on the spot, nor were all the victims of gunplay. The common denominator among these thirteen, besides being local lawmen, is that they all died violently or suffered grievous wounds contributing to their early deaths. Ten were shot, one was stabbed to death, and two died years later as a result of gunshot wounds.

The authors did not limit themselves to members of the Fort Worth Police Department (FWPD) although there would have been a certain logic to such a self-imposed limitation. Instead, we chose to cast a wide net, choosing to include one sheriff and one deputy sheriff, one "special officer," and one county attorney because they were all part of the local law enforcement scene, and it would be unfair to single out only one group of fallen officers. The first group of deaths fit conveniently into an almost fifty-year span. Statistically, that represents one line-of-duty death every three to four years, not bad numbers if we are talking batting averages, but these were human lives, and one death in the line of duty was one too many. There is also the fact that the tragedy of their deaths rippled outward touching the entire community.

Starting in 2002, an ad hoc group known as the Fort Worth Police Memorial Project took on the job of locating and marking the final resting place of every fallen Fort Worth *and* Tarrant County officer. This admirable project quickly became a "magnificent obsession" for Sgt. Kevin Foster. The first challenge, after identifying every last officer who had died in the line of duty going back to the beginning, was to locate each man's final resting place: not as easy as it sounds even when you know what town and what cemetery they are buried in. Ten of our subjects were laid to rest in the Fort Worth area; one in Honey Grove, Texas; one in Hico, Texas; and one in Sarepta, Mississippi. Some of the graves no longer had headstones, and of those with headstones, nothing on any of the stones showed that the deceased had been peace officers who died in the line of duty. So these men were twice victimized—the first time when they were murdered, and the second when they were forgotten. Thanks to the efforts of the Fort Worth Police Memorial

Project and Sgt. Kevin Foster in particular, the graves of eleven of our thirteen are now marked and will stay that way. Two, John York and Dick Townsend, are not marked because it has proved impossible to determine the exact location of their graves although the cemeteries where they were buried are known.

Deciding who made the cut proved more challenging than anticipated. We tried to follow the guidelines of the Fort Worth Police and Firefighters Memorial Committee, but we were forced to refine our criteria as we went along, deciding, for instance, to include county officers (members of the Sheriff's Department and constables), as well as policemen. We still had to make some tough decisions. For instance, originally we included T. I. "Longhair Jim" Courtright, who was a deputy sheriff at the time he died in 1886, but we dropped him because he died as the result of a personal feud not official business. Special officers were a difficult call because they worked as private security officers but were commissioned by the city or county, making them a collateral branch of law enforcement. We included one county attorney because although he was not, strictly speaking, a commissioned peace officer, his job description nonetheless made him part of law enforcement, and he definitely died "in the line of duty."

In the end, we had to make our calls on a case-by-case basis. Among the questions we anguished over: Did a man have to expire on the spot to qualify as a "line of duty" death? What if he was wounded and died weeks or even years later as a result of his injuries? What if he died while doing something improper such as executing an illegal warrant? Is every job-related death, strictly speaking, "in the line of duty"? What if a man died while on duty, but as a result of a perfectly innocent accident? After due consideration, we decided to exclude the whole category of accidental deaths.

Before we could even begin deciding who was in and who was out, we first had to compile a complete list of all local law officers who had died on the job. We were in for a surprise: Our original list of known deaths kept growing as we kept discovering lost or forgotten cases. Neither the Fort Worth Police Department nor the Tarrant County Sheriff's Department has done a very good job of preserving their institutional histories. There was no record of some of these men because the agency they worked for had forgotten them, not intentionally but because of abominable record-keeping over the years. It was not until 1951 that the FWPD even created a permanent identification system to keep track of its officers. Since that date, every officer from captains on down is issued an ID number when he joins the force, and that number remains his through death, retirement, or firing; it can never be issued to another officer. In the old days, officers had badge numbers, but those were recycled as officers came and went. As far as the FWPD was concerned, an officer ceased to exist when he left the force.

The Tarrant County Sheriff's Department, if anything, has been even worse about record-keeping over the years. Typically, all records of the Department went out the door when the old sheriff retired because Tarrant County sheriffs treated Department records as their personal property, and there was no law to prevent them from doing this. When, for instance, Lon Evans retired after twenty-four years as the county's top lawman, he took a substantial chunk of history home with him.

In the absence of institutional records, we had to reconstruct each subject's life from scratch. Old newspapers were the richest source of information on events, with census records filling in the gaps on family history. Unfortunately, newspaper accounts can vary widely from one newspaper to another, and even the reporting of the same event can be inconsistent when the story stretches out over several days. One of the curious things that struck us was that August seems to be a very bad month in law enforcement. Four of the officers in this volume died in the dog days of August. It may just have been coincidence, or it may be that in the days before air conditioning, when the Texas sun was at its hottest, tempers grew short, and men were more likely to snap.

One of the things we learned along the way is that public consciousness of fallen officers lasts about fifteen minutes. In the collective memory decades later, those officers might have sprung from the soil fully formed ready for their date with destiny. Little or nothing was known of their lives before they met their end, of the men who killed them, or of what happened to their families afterwards. These were things the authors wanted to know, and we thought readers would, too. Our approach was to take the broad view of finding out as much as we could about the officers who were killed, the men who killed them, and in some cases even the supporting players that played key roles. That approach required writing more than two dozen mini-biographies. It might be argued that this takes the spotlight away from where it properly belongs—on the victims—but we wanted to tell the full story, which required putting faces on all the principal players.

The stories of the killers were inextricably linked to the officers they killed, and in some cases the relationship between the officer and his killer was a factor in what happened. We had another reason for including the killers, too: There has long been an unwritten rule in law enforcement that "cop killers" would be hunted down and receive the full punishment of the law, no exceptions. The editor of the *San Francisco Chronicle* wrote in 1878, "An officer of a city like San Francisco is frequently called upon to risk his life. . . . His only protection [in case he is disabled or killed] is the knowledge that the law will surely punish anyone who attacks an officer." Closer to home, for many years there was almost a compact between the Dallas DA's office and the Dallas Police Department that "when a cop is killed in Dallas an electrocution is sure to follow." This was made abundantly clear following the death of Officer Robert Wood during a routine traffic stop in 1976. The DA's office was so determined to uphold its end of the compact, it wrongfully prosecuted an innocent man. Justice demands closure, and people want to know what happened to the men who targeted the forces of law and order.[8]

Fleshing out all the principal characters' stories—the killers *and* their victims—caused us a lot of frustration. The sources in most cases proved skimpy. None of these men, officers or killers, left behind memoirs or family papers. Apart from hand-me-down stories, in most cases there was little more than newspaper coverage of the homicide itself plus a brief obituary. Sometimes, the killers were not even deemed worthy of a real obituary, just a simple burial announcement. We had better luck where there was a high-profile trial. The newspaper coverage and trial records (if they survived) proved a goldmine of material. Actual trial transcripts were the exception, however, not the rule. That is because only "courts of record" are required by law to keep transcripts. Municipal and justice of the peace courts are not courts of record, only county and district courts. Even then, court reporters only transcribe their notes of the proceedings when the defendant is convicted; in the case of an acquittal or a mistrial, no transcript. (This is still true today.) Appeals records, where they existed, turned out to be the best source on the trials of our cop killers.

"Trial jackets" (i.e., permanent files) for criminal cases over the years were archived in county-owned warehouses and unused areas of the courthouse. We found in many cases that those trial jackets still existed, at least nominally. When the files were retrieved, however, we were shocked by what they contained. Or rather, what they did not contain. There were no trial transcripts. For some unfathomable reason, most major criminal trials were able to dispense with court transcripts, or at least such records did not become part of the trial jacket. Most official files contained nothing more than collections of subpoenas, capiases (judicial writs or process), warrants, jury lists, and judges' instructions to the jury. Cases that made it as far as the Texas Court of Criminal Appeals provided a much richer source of information, and those cases had the added advantage of being reproduced on-line.

One significant difference in the criminal justice system, then and now, was that before modern sentencing guidelines, juries had the final say. "Twelve good men" decided whether the accused was guilty or not guilty, and in the event of the latter, the punishment. The judge's input into the verdict ended after he instructed the jury, although those instructions might include, for instance, the sentencing range for, say, manslaughter.

The road from popular hero to historical afterthought is an interesting one. Immediately after their deaths, the local newspapers rushed to bestow heroic status on fallen officers. Catchy quotes by a captain or police chief were turned into instant headlines, and no superlative was too over-the-top for editors mourning a fallen hero. Among the honorifics deployed by the Fourth Estate were "the best man that ever carried a club in Fort Worth" and "the Clean-up Policeman," both used to describe Will Campbell after he was gunned down in 1909. The *Fort Worth Record* was the worst at producing wince-inducing hyperbole.[9] Unfortunately, once the initial uproar faded, fallen officers quickly passed from front-page news to family lore, and sometimes those two sources flatly contradict each other. In time, the stories ceased to be of interest to anyone, even family members.

When we started our quest we had to scroll through miles of microfilmed old newspapers, examine crumbling court records, family histories, census reports, and cemetery records. Some of our research took the form of oral history. Dealing with living relatives is a lot different from dealing with old records. Even when we were able to locate descendants, we often found that the families knew even less about their ancestors than we did, and what they did know was vague hand-me-down lore. One descendant that we contacted swore that her lawman ancestor had died from being shot in the back by bank robbers (not true on either count) and took exception to all contrary information, even after we pointed out it came from contemporary newspaper accounts and the appeals record. Her reaction was a variation on the old joke, "Who you gonna believe, me or your lyin' eyes?" Among descendants, family stories usually trump the historical record. On the opposite extreme, we were amazed at some descendants' complete lack of knowledge or even interest in their distinguished ancestors. In time we came to see this as perfectly normal: most people have only the sketchiest idea of who their ancestors were or what they did. Americans typically live in the present, and even with all the marvelous research tools just a keystroke away nowadays, people simply do not care to dig into the past. Most families, however, were genuinely grateful to receive any information we could give them.

The language and attitudes of the late nineteenth and early twentieth century can be quite offensive to modern sensibilities. It was not just the uneducated and the illiterate who were racist and bigoted; judges, lawyers, and editors could be just as bad as the man on the street. They too were products of their time who sprinkled their conversation with such terms as "darky," "black fiend," "nigger," "Chinee man," and "wench." The language cannot be cleaned up without rewriting the record. We opted for historical accuracy rather than political correctness when quoting participants directly, using, for instance, "Negro" and "whore" because their modern equivalents, "African American" and "sex worker," are anachronistic. We hope our modern readers are not offended by contemporary usage.

Similarly, we decided early on to let the chips fall where they may. Our goal was neither to debunk brave men nor to perpetuate heroic legends. These were flawed men. Racism and brutality alternated with courage and heroism in their approach to their jobs. They lived in violent and racist times, and they reflected those times. The fact that an officer of the law was a mite quick to pull his pistol or showed contempt for minorities did not negate the good he did; it just means things have to be taken in context. Whatever their weaknesses and faults, however, because they took on the low-paying, dangerous, often thankless work of protecting their community, they deserve to be remembered. The lives of these thirteen men are a wonderful prism through which we can view law enforcement during a critical era in our history.

We dubbed these early officers "cowboy cops," not because they ever punched cattle but because of the violent, unregimented nature of law enforcement in those days. It took a special kind of man to pin on a badge and go nose-to-nose with hard cases, without any backup and for wages that were less than a drover on the Western Trail made. They were nonconformists: ornery, solitary, self-reliant, macho fellows. This cowboy culture endured well into the twentieth century. The professionalization of law enforcement came only slowly and in fits and starts. The simple truth is, these were not nice men, and while they could be brave, even heroic, they were hardly role models.

Until recently, Fort Worth has lagged far behind other major cities in Texas and across the country when it comes to honoring our fallen law officers. Not only have their stories not been collected in print until now, but Fort Worth is also the last major city in the state to erect a memorial to those heroes. In many other cities there was a movement underway, even before 9/11, to retrieve the stories of martyred peace officers so that future generations can know about them. A number of books in this vein have been written by police officers-cum-historians whose self-appointed mission was to keep alive the memories of the men in blue "who paid the ultimate sacrifice." A second objective was educational in nature, i.e., so that every new generation of officers "can learn from what happened."[10] Unlike CLEAT, we have no desire to use the information we have gathered to lobby for better working conditions for lawmen. We are just telling stories. The result is both a social history and a memorial volume that we hope represents the best of both genres.

We tried to locate pictures of every fallen officer presented here, but ran into a dead end on several of the earliest men: C. C. Fitzgerald, George White, William Wise, and Dick Townsend. None of their pictures, if they ever stood before a camera, have come down to us today. That is sad because we lose a great deal of our ability to connect with them when we have no idea what they looked like. Did Fitzgerald look like a typical big Irish cop? Was George White as youthful and callow-looking as he sounds? Did Dick Townsend look more like a steely-eyed deputy sheriff or a part-time house painter? We may never know.

Richard F. Selcer
Kevin S. Foster
January 2010

PART I

THE FRONTIER YEARS
(1861–1888)

INTRODUCTION

Before the first cattle drive came through, before there was even a town worthy of the name, Fort Worth marked the frontier where civilization ended and "the West began." There was a community around the fort as early as 1853, but law and order was slow in coming. For the next twenty years, the peace was kept by a sheriff who could call on a trio of constables in a pinch. Since there was no town to speak of, there was no need for a municipal law officer, specifically, a marshal. The county lawman (the sheriff) and the precinct lawman (the constable) could easily get the job done. For Tarrant County's first twelve sheriffs, it was a part-time job; the rest of the time they were farmers or cattlemen or shopkeepers. Fort Worth finally got its own law enforcement in 1873 when it was chartered by the state legislature, making it the first town between Dallas and El Paso to have its own marshal.

The sheriff, however, remained the principal local law officer even after Fort Worth had a marshal. His domain was mostly empty prairie plus a handful of settlements such as Birdville and Johnson's Station that dotted the 848 square miles comprising Tarrant County. He had an office in the courthouse, but spent most of his time out of the office rounding up rustlers and horse thieves and chasing stagecoach robbers. He was aided by two or three deputies.

The marshal was not much of a lawman in those early years. Five of the first nine Fort Worth marshals did not finish their terms, either quitting or being driven from office in disgrace. The first to serve his full term was Timothy Isaiah "Longhair Jim" Courtright (1876–79). According to the city charter, the marshal's domain ended at the corporate limits of the city. When he needed backup, the marshal could call on the sheriff and vice versa. The same went for constables. During the time when Fort Worth was a rowdy cow town, marshals really earned their pay during the annual cattle-driving season, roughly from April through October. During those seven months they had to carefully balance their responsibilities, on the one hand keeping the peace while on the other hand not running off the cowboys who filled the city's coffers when they weren't shooting out the lights. After the railroad came to town in 1876, the population exploded, and there was no longer an off-season for the marshal and his men.

The marshal had an office in the city hall that doubled as "police headquarters." He was aided in performance of his duties by a deputy marshal and a handful of policemen (as few as two men or as many as six). Policemen worked twelve-hour shifts, seven days a week, with no sick days and no vacations. They were accountable to both their immediate boss, the marshal, and to the city council, and those two were sometimes at odds.

Both the sheriff and marshal had non-law-enforcement duties. The sheriff sometimes had to conduct foreclosure sales on the steps of the courthouse, and the earliest sheriffs were also the county's tax collectors. The marshal was also the city's chief sanitation officer, responsible for keeping the streets clean of refuse and dead animals. He was also the city's chief dogcatcher, in charge of getting stray animals off the streets.

Sheriffs and marshals and all of their men supplemented meager salaries by collecting fees for performing certain duties, such as serving papers and picking up or delivering "wanted" men to other jurisdictions. Those fees could equal or even exceed their regular salaries so they were a very important part of the job. So was the occasional reward money that came from bringing in a wanted man.

The most junior member of local law enforcement was the constable, whose jurisdiction was the precinct and whose immediate boss was the justice of the peace. When Tarrant County was organized in 1850 it was carved into three voting precincts: Fort Worth, Birdville, and Johnson's Station. Later, additional precincts were created as the county filled up. Before 1876 constables were appointed by the JPs of their precinct; after that date they were elected just like other county officials. Usually the constable was only a process server, but he carried a gun and his job could be dangerous.

In addition to the legally constituted peace officers, there was a class of lawmen who went by the generic title "special officers." They were commissioned by either the county or the city but paid by the business or the institution that employed them. They helped bridge the gap between law enforcement needs and tight budgets.

Special officers wore badges, carried guns, and could make arrests just like deputy sheriffs, policemen, and constables. Some worked as "bouncers" for saloons and variety theaters in the red-light district known as Hell's Half-acre, others as security for the railroads. Their numbers proliferated in the 1880s as the local population boomed, but they were scarcely regulated by either the county or city. Still, since they were duly commissioned officers of the law, we shall consider them full-fledged members of the honor roll of fallen officers.

Until well into the twentieth century, no law officer went through any training before putting on the badge. He learned on the job if he did not quit or get killed first. The only two qualifications were knowing how to use a gun and having a set of brass *cojones*. Thus equipped, a lawman was ready to take on anybody who challenged his authority. Some of those who challenged his authority were even friends and former compadres.

The man with the badge was a law unto himself. He felt no compunction about cracking some drunken cowboy over the skull with a six-gun or shaking down the local gambling fraternity. It was all business as usual. Technicalities such as getting legal warrants before going out to arrest someone, due process, and habeas corpus were regularly ignored. Vagrants and African Americans, for instance, were two classes of people who could be run out of town at any time just because of who they were. Law enforcement not only lacked rules and regulations, it also lacked the equivalent of the modern Internal Affairs Bureau to keep an eye on the boys with the badges. What accountability there was mostly was a by-product of politics. Sheriffs had to answer to the voters in elections every two years. Marshals had to answer to the voters in annual elections, and to the mayor and city council all the time. Sheriff's deputies answered to their boss, the sheriff, and to county commissioners. Policemen answered to the marshal and the council, but too many times those two were not on the same page. In fact, policemen had three masters: the marshal, the mayor, and the city council. The sheriff, by contrast, had much more independence running his office although after every election there was pressure exerted to hire this man or that one as a deputy. And any time between elections there was an opening for a new policeman or deputy, every applicant for the job had his influential supporters. With no standards or hiring criteria, the ultimate decision was always personal and political.

The use of deadly force was the most controversial part of the lawman's job. It was left to an officer's judgment, which meant he could shoot someone for merely aggravating him, engage in gun battles on the street, or blaze away at fleeing perps, innocent bystanders be damned. It all came down to the public's tolerance for mayhem. The good citizens of Fort Worth allowed T. I. Courtright a great deal of latitude during his tenure as marshal (1876–1879). He regularly beat up people and even shot a few with questionable justification. Yet Courtright was no loose cannon. The Fort Worth Police Department (FWPD) would not implement a "deadly force" policy for another fifty-two years. The Tarrant County Sheriff's Office had no equivalent of "Longhair Jim" in terms of either celebrity status or abusiveness. The worst thing Tarrant County sheriffs were accused of was letting prisoners escape.

But the FWPD did a better job of keeping up with the times. In 1887 city fathers established a "permanent police force" trying

Fort Worth City Hall at Ninth and Throckmorton, as it appeared on a postcard sometime after 1900. Constructed in 1892–93, it had four stories plus a clock tower. The impressive Gothic structure housed both the FWPD (first floor) and city jail (basement), and was the scene of a number of jail breaks and mob action over the years. (Postcard, collections of Kevin Foster)

to get away from the practice of reappointing (or not) the entire force after municipal elections every year. Since the marshal came up for re-election every year, the thinking had always been that the marshal's men should likewise work on one-year contracts ("commissions"). In practice, this meant that the entire police force could turn over every year. At the council meeting of October 4, 1887, the Police Committee of Ephraim Daggett, F. J. Farmer, and W. A. Darter submitted its recommendation that a "permanent police force" be created. Their recommendation went nowhere because a majority of the council preferred to keep the police on a short leash and use the power of appointment as patronage.[1]

This first era of law enforcement in Fort Worth and Tarrant County came to a close in 1888. It produced a generation of peace officers who all arrived on the scene about the same time, knew each other well, and dominated local law enforcement for the next thirty years. The group includes some notable figures, such as brothers Walter and James Maddox, William M. Rea, Sam Farmer, Joe Witcher, and "Longhair Jim" Courtright. They put their stamp on local law enforcement, and some even became local legends.

Among the local law enforcement fraternity of this era, five men died in the line of duty. Three were shot up close and in cold blood, one was ambushed, and one was carved up with a bowie knife. One of the victims did not die in Texas, but he was still performing his duty at the time so he deserves a place on the roll of honor. These are their stories.

According to received lore in the Tarrant County Sheriff's Office, this is Sheriff John York, although the daguerreotype is not actually identified as such. (Courtesy of the Genealogy, History and Archives Unit, Fort Worth Public Library)

CHAPTER 1

SHERIFF JOHN B. YORK

August 24, 1861

Felled by "an assassin"?

Tarrant County's first sheriff was Francis Jourdan (sometimes Anglicized to "Jordan"), elected in the first countywide elections on August 5, 1850. Since the little community of Fort Worth would not get its first town marshal for another twenty-three years, the sheriff shouldered all the responsibility for local law enforcement. Jourdan was just a part-time lawman, which was normal in those days. He was a farmer first and peace officer second, spending more time on his homestead near Johnson's Station than at the county seat in Birdville. His two-year term passed without incident, and he gladly turned the office over to his successor in 1852.[1]

That successor was twenty-seven-year-old John York, who before being elected sheriff worked as a farmhand for Jourdan. York was a big man who could manhandle a heavy moldboard plow through the tough prairie sod or wrestle bales of hay onto a wagon singlehandedly. He was Tarrant County's second sheriff.[2] Actually, he was more anointed than elected because no one else wanted the job. His tenure could have been as unremarkable as Jourdan's had he not been the first local peace officer to die in the line of duty.

John B. York was born May 13, 1825, in Tennessee, birthplace of many nineteenth-century Texans, but he did not come directly to Texas from the Volunteer State. His family was part of a vast tide of Americans looking for the promised land, first in Illinois, then Missouri, before finding their way to north Texas. He married Julia Ann Gilmore, daughter of Seaborne Gilmore, on January 26, 1846, in Springfield, Illinois. The capital of Illinois was a small burg of fewer than two thousand people at the time, with three churches, Presbyterian, Methodist, and Episcopal. Abraham Lincoln was soon to become its most famous resident, but the Yorks and Gilmores did not stay around that long. They were off to Missouri. Then in June 1848 they came by covered wagon to north Texas to stake a claim on a parcel of land in the Peters Colony, three miles north of the Trinity. The two families built their cabins on adjacent homesteads, each comprising a 640-acre "headright" that represented more than one man could work profitably. To make ends meet, York hired himself out as a farmhand to Francis Jourdan. Soon after John and Julia arrived in Texas, they started a family, and that family grew steadily in the years that followed.[3]

John York's family history is vague due to an absence of official records and family papers. Even the records and papers that exist conflict on some important points. Strong oral tradition says that Julia gave birth to their first child, a boy, a few months after they arrived in Tarrant County. They named him William only to see him die of unknown causes, a sad start to their new life in Texas. They buried him in a small plot of ground near their homestead, which later became known as the Mitchell-Gilmore Cemetery. A second son was born in 1850 to whom they also gave the name William, a legacy baby so to speak. Through 1856, Julia produced a new child every other year—Antonia in 1852, Oliver in 1854, Texana in 1856—then a sixth child, John B., Jr., came in 1860. Julia was pregnant with the couple's seventh child in the summer of 1861.[4]

The Yorks and Gilmores were among a handful of families already in the area when Major Ripley Arnold and elements of the Second Dragoons came to the confluence of the West and Clear forks of the Trinity River in the summer of 1849 to establish an outpost. The presence of the troops at that location brought a measure of security to the isolated frontier, bringing others to the area.

Running for sheriff in 1852 was not an impulsive decision by John York. He had already shown an affinity for law enforcement by getting elected the county's first constable in 1850. The fact that he ran for public office and won, just four years after arriving in the area, shows not only that he had political ambitions but that he was popular with his neighbors. It did not hurt that he was well connected thanks to his father-in-law, Seaborne Gilmore, elected as the county's first judge in August 1850.[5]

Sheriff York was even-handed and conscientious in performance of his duties. His imposing bulk gave him a natural advantage over smaller men. He did not throw his weight around, but neither did he shy away from using force when necessary. As a rule, he kept the old Colt army revolver he wore in its holster. Being sheriff was more politicking and paperwork than peacekeeping. He was re-elected to another two-year term in 1854 before losing his third race to William Bonaparte Tucker in 1856. Like the Yorks and Gilmores, the Tuckers were one of the First Families of Fort Worth, so there was no shame in losing to Bill Tucker. The Tucker name later adorned several landmarks in the city.[6]

York's duties kept him close to Fort Worth most of the time. The empty western reaches of the county did not need much law enforcement because there was just one road and only a few isolated homesteads between Fort Worth and the Tarrant-Parker County boundary. Fort Worth was far off the "outlaw trail" and too far east of Comanche territory to need a real gunman or an Indian fighter in the position. John York was a regular guy who happened to wear a badge. When he left office in 1856 he was still well regarded. The new sheriff, Bill Tucker, treated the job as a steppingstone to bigger things, and after one term got himself appointed clerk to the district court and subsequently won election as a county judge.[7]

Bill Tucker's swift political rise opened the door for York to re-claim the sheriff's office in 1858. Following his third term, Tarrant County voters were not so much disappointed with his performance as they were ready for change again. In 1860 they chose William O. Yantes over York, but despite being a two-time loser, events conspired to put him back in office a fourth time. In the spring of 1861 the Civil War erupted, and Yantes traded in his badge for a musket and a butternut-colored uniform to serve in the Confederate army. York did not join the first wave of volunteers from Tarrant County, and the decision seemed to be a shrewd political move at the time. His experience and family connections got him appointed by the county court to finish out Yantes' term. At the time he was killed that summer, therefore, he was just the interim sheriff until the next elections came around, and with more of the county's men going off to fight all the time, it is unlikely he would have faced much of a challenge for another full term.

Not much is known about what Sheriff York did during his seven years in office. Perhaps his most notable accomplishment was overseeing construction of the first county jail in 1856, a rough-hewn, one-room log cabin that resembled the guardhouse used by the army when Fort Worth was an actual fort.[8] It was still in use twenty years later. We also know he joined thirty-seven other citizens in 1859 to post a $10,000 bond so that construction could commence on a proper courthouse befitting Fort Worth's status as the county seat. The signatories pledged to build the courthouse without raising taxes.[9]

Over and above being public-minded, Sheriff York had personal reasons for wanting to see the courthouse built. At the time, his office was in a cramped, two-room building on the public square (formerly the parade ground of the fort) that housed all county offices. At least the filthy, malodorous calaboose was detached. Unfortunately, York never got to move into the new courthouse because the Civil War interrupted construction, and he died before it was completed.

York was killed in a confrontation with Archibald Young Fowler in the summer of 1861 that caused Fowler's death, too. It was no "affair of honor," and it is even arguable whether York's death was "in the line of duty" under the circumstances. In fact, everything about the affair is arguable. There are two completely different versions of what happened in a classic case of "he said-she said," except that the "he" and "she" are the descendants of the York-Gilmore and Fowler-Peak families and their supporters. Writing years later, old-timers could not even agree on the basic details of the story: not the date or the cause of the confrontation or where it occurred or the weapons used, or even who killed whom! York-Gilmore partisans refer to the "tragic killing" of John York; Fowler-Peak partisans refer to the "murder" of Archibald Fowler. About the only thing the two sides agree on is that both men died that day. Modern historians have only muddied the water by accepting uncritically either the Fort Worth (York-Gilmore) version or the Dallas (Fowler-Peak) version.[10]

The other principal in the affair was Archibald Young Fowler, Jr., referred to in the records as simply A. Y. Fowler. He was born in

Laurence County, South Carolina, on January 8, 1825, and spent his formative years there before heading for the western frontier in search of the American Dream after his father died in 1840. That search eventually landed him in Texas where he read for the law and hung out his shingle in Austin for a few years before relocating to Dallas. Arch Fowler had become "A. Y. Fowler, Esq." by this time, and he began a rapid ascent up the social ladder.[11]

It did not hurt his standing that on April 27, 1859, he married Juliette Peak, daughter of one of the most prominent families in the town. He was thirty-four years old at the time and she was nineteen. Her father, Jefferson Peak, was a Mexican War veteran and successful merchant in Kentucky when he brought his family down to Texas in 1855 to take advantage of the booming frontier economy. He was also a pillar in the Disciples of Christ church who considered Dallas a field ripe for evangelism. There is no indication that Arch Fowler was one of his converts, however. Juliette had eleven siblings, including one brother, Dr. Carroll Peak who preceded her to Fort Worth by six years, and another, Junius Peak, who would become legendary as a Dallas lawman and Texas Ranger.

Juliette Fowler, the wife of Archibald Fowler, fled back to Dallas and her own family as soon as she could after the death of her husband. She established herself as a "gentlewoman" and philanthropist of Dallas society in the decades that followed. This oil portrait was painted around 1880. (Courtesy Juliette Fowler Homes, Dallas, TX)

Fair Juliette must have been quite a looker because in May 1858 she was crowned Dallas' first "May Queen." Her girlhood was brief, however, because two years later she was married to Arch, living on the wild frontier in Fort Worth, and pregnant with their first child. But her heart remained in Dallas. She never felt comfortable in Fort Worth because it was so rough and violent. Like Julia York, Juliette Fowler suffered the tragedy of losing a child early in her marriage. Arch and Juliette's daughter, Ada, born in February 1860, died nine months later of unknown cause, but by the summer of 1861 Juliette was pregnant with their second child.[12]

Arch Fowler was an excellent lawyer and a real go-getter. The lure of opportunity pulled him westward to Fort Worth where there were fewer lawyers and land aplenty for the homesteader or the speculator. Fowler fell into the second category. When legal business was slow through his law office, he kept busy as a self-styled "general land agent." The combination supported the couple, allowing them to buy a nice house on the corner of Fifth and Rusk. They also had family in Fort Worth. Arch had a brother and sister-in-law (names unknown), and Juliette's brother, Carroll Peak, was the town's physician and helped introduce the newcomers around. Arch was content in Fort Worth but did not turn his back on Dallas. He and his brother-in-law were the local agents for the *Dallas Herald*, and he regularly advertised his law practice in the Dallas newspapers after relocating to Fort Worth.[13]

In Fort Worth, Fowler found a place perfectly suited to his temperament. Mrs. William Crawford, a Yankee transplant who was his contemporary, described it as a town where "men went about wearing pistols and bowie knives openly, and it was a common thing to hear of a man being shot without any notice being taken of it by the authorities."[14] He fit in because he carried a very large chip on his narrow shoulders, probably related to his slight stature. We know he was not a big man because contemporary accounts speak of him being physically manhandled by opponents even before he tangled with Sheriff York. Being on the losing end of such encounters did not inspire any propensity for turning the other cheek, any more than joining the churchgoing Peak family. On the contrary, Fowler had a notoriously short fuse and a disposition that was not improved by a fondness for liquor. He was a pugnacious, hard-drinking lawyer as likely to be a defendant as defense counsel. He was to the legal profession what Doc Holliday was to dentistry. Still, his fellow citizens did not consider him a menace. On the contrary, he was a community leader who moved in the same circles as Fort Worth founding fathers Ephraim M. Daggett, J. C. Terrell, and John Peter Smith. Indeed, Smith started his own legal career by "reading law" under Fowler and after proving himself to his mentor they became partners.[15] Fowler must have been a good mentor because Smith became one of the best title lawyers in Texas, yet when he wrote his "Own Story" in 1901, Smith did not even mention Fowler as an influence in his life. In 1861, they shared an office on or near the public square. There were six other lawyers in the small community of about 500, but the town was growing so there was plenty of work for all. Fowler followed the big-city practice of having business cards printed up and passing them out liberally. He was also a Freemason in Lodge no. 148, transferring his membership over from Dallas.[16]

There is no indication that Fowler owned slaves, but he definitely supported the institution. He was a Southerner through and through, and although a lawyer in good standing in the community, he was not above a little vigilantism when it came to dealing with Yankee-lovers and abolitionists. On the night of July 16–17, 1860, he was one of the "regulators" who strung up William H. Crawford, a recently arrived homesteader from Maine accused of being an abolitionist and "an agent of the underground railroad." Fowler subsequently admitted to a newspaper reporter that he had been a member of a "committee" that spied on Crawford to gather evidence on his abolitionist activities, and while not admitting his own participation in the lynching, Fowler swore an affidavit that another pillar of the local community, Charles Turner, had *not* been present that night, which he could only have done if he had been involved himself. He also sat on the coroner's jury afterwards that refused to call it a lynching. The sheriff at the time was John York. There is no indication of York's feelings about slavery or about the sectional crisis, but he did not enlist to fight for the Confederacy after Fort Sumter, and as the first defender of law and order in Tarrant County, he could not have approved of vigilante justice.[17]

In the fall of 1860 when the secession crisis came to a boil, Fowler served with other prominent local men on a "Resolutions

Committee" that drew up a statement denouncing pro-Union Governor Sam Houston and supporting secession. When Texas seceded from the Union three months later, Fowler helped rally local opinion behind the nascent Confederacy. Still, he was not part of the first wave of eager enlistees who signed up to fight.[18]

How Arch Fowler got crossways with Sheriff York is part of the mystery. Both men were solid citizens in their community. Fowler was no more violent than other men except when he was drinking; then he became combative, but that did not make him a killer. He was one of those men Mrs. Crawford spoke about who went around armed with a bowie knife, which even on the frontier was not normally considered a tool of the legal profession. (But it was not unknown either. Flamboyant California lawyer David S. Terry also carried a bowie knife in addition to his briefcase, and used it to stab a member of the San Francisco Vigilance Committee in 1856.) Fowler's habit coupled with his notoriously bad temper caused fellow citizens to give him a wide berth, although he was never known to have pulled the weapon on either his clients or opponents prior to August 1861. By the same token, Sheriff York is not known to have pulled his Colt revolver before that tragic day.

The date of their fatal confrontation has been variously reported as 1856, 1861, or 1863. Like everything else about the story, the Peaks and Fowlers disagree with the Yorks and Gilmores about the date. We have chosen to go with August 24, 1861, because that is the date given in a Dallas newspaper soon after the event. [19]

There is also disagreement over the cause of the affair. According to Fort Worth lore, it grew out of the long-running political dispute between Birdville and Fort Worth over where to locate the county seat. The winner's future would be assured while the loser would likely wither and die. Birdville won the first round when the legislature designated it as the county seat on August 5, 1850, but Fort Worth residents demanded the matter be reopened, and in 1856 a countywide election supported its claim. The two communities continued to scrap over the honor for four more years before Fort Worth's preeminence was confirmed once and for all in 1860. As Fort Worth resident J. C. Terrell later wrote, "This question cost the life of more than one good man, and [cost] the State in legislation, $30,000."[20] Before it was all over, the "county-seat fight" did cost two men their lives, but they were not John York and Archibald Fowler. In 1856 three Fort Worth partisans killed a Birdville man named Tucker, which was answered when A. G. Walker, editor of the Birdville newspaper, killed John J. Courtney, a resident of Fort Worth. That ended the killing in the county-seat war.[21]

Popular lore to the contrary, the county-seat fight was not the cause since neither John York nor Arch Fowler was a Birdville resident or even supporter, and the timing of the York-Fowler killings, the summer of 1861, was after the county-seat fight had been settled once and for all. By that date, the main things on everyone's mind were secession and civil war, which did not divide neatly along town lines. On those twin incendiary issues, John York's feelings are not known. If he was a Unionist, he was not outspoken about it.

A second Fort Worth tradition attributes the whole thing to male ego, not politics, making it a crime of passion and nothing more. This is the explanation given by Howard Peak, son of Dr. Carroll Peak, who stated that "the occasion was trivial, resulting from over-excitement at a barbecue . . . a few days before." Peak does not specify what caused the "over-excitement," but it is a safe guess liquor was involved. Potent liquid refreshment would have flowed freely at any public gathering, making imbibers even more belligerent than normal.[22]

The most reasonable ordering of the facts starts with the community barbecue at the Cold Spring on Saturday, July 20. The Cold Spring, about a mile northeast of the public square, was a popular gathering place for the community, which held picnics and political rallies under the shade of the nearby grove of trees. The occasion this time was a full-dress military review by eight local companies enrolled in Confederate service. Most of the area's residents were in attendance. It had been an especially hot, dry summer, so there was a long line to dip into the spring. A fence around the spring to keep livestock away also controlled human access to the spring. Arch Fowler grew impatient with the wait and jumped the fence to get down to the water. Sheriff York confronted him and ordered him to the back of the line. When Fowler defied him, York easily manhandled the smaller man, perhaps even tossing him into a "mud hole." Fowler did not take the indignity lightly but jumped up ready to fight. Cooler heads separated the two men and persuaded Fowler to leave. He left but did not forget, brooding over the insult for a month. There may also have been other issues that were eating at him but the record is maddeningly vague.[23]

Fort Worth was a very small town, and the two men could not long avoid each other even if they had wanted to. On August 24, they encountered each other on or near the public square on the north end of town. It is doubtful if Fowler had come looking for his enemy because he was accompanied by his nephew Willie. The feisty lawyer was neither impressed nor intimidated by the Sheriff's badge. He pulled his bowie knife and sprang on the other man, stabbing him repeatedly. York finally managed to unholster his Colt and shot and killed Fowler. At this point Willie pulled a gun from somewhere and fatally shot the Sheriff who clung to life another hour and a half before succumbing. With two bodies lying on the street and a crowd gathering, Willie ran to Dr. Peak for help. The physician did what any relative would have done under the circumstances: he helped the boy get out of town. Willie fled to Missouri where he joined the Confederate army and, according to family tradition, died in the war. The irony is that, as the town's resident physician, Dr. Peak would have been the attending physician for both victims while he was an accomplice to murder after the fact.[24]

These are the bare-bones facts of the story. Everything else is speculation, local lore, or competing family traditions. There are no eyewitness accounts, and the only contemporary account is a secondhand version that has come down to us through the family of John Jay Good, a captain in the Confederate army at the time, who learned of it through letters from his wife, Sue, back home in Dallas.[25]

The death of the county sheriff should have been a major event, but this was wartime. Men were dying by the tens of thousands on distant battlefields, and events on the Texas frontier were beyond the pale so to speak. The lynching of five Unionists at Decatur in 1862 and forty-four Unionists at Gainesville a year later was far more newsworthy, yet even those incidents were not reported nationally at the time. Frontier violence was nothing new, even if one of the victims was the sheriff.[26]

All that was left was to bury the dead and get on with life. There is no record that a great outpouring of grief attended John York's demise. He was quietly buried in the Mitchell-Gilmore family plot next to his infant son, who had become the first occupant of the plot thirteen years before. The modest estate he left was not probated until three years after the war, by which time the family's pain had dulled and the civil courts were functioning more or less normally again. According to Juliette's wishes, Arch Fowler's remains were taken back to Dallas by his Masonic brethren and buried in the Masonic section of the Old Dallas Cemetery, which still exists today as Pioneer Memorial Park. Their children were already buried there, and a place in the same plot was set aside for Juliette. Fort Worth did not hold so much as a memorial service for Fowler.[27]

The sensational double killing might have touched off one of those bloody feuds for which Texas is famous: The York-Gilmores against the Peak-Fowlers with the hatred stoked by the natural rivalry between Dallas and Fort Worth. John York had many friends in Fort Worth, and his father-in-law was of tough pioneer stock, handy with a gun or knife. Arch Fowler had his brother in Fort Worth and four brothers-in-law in Dallas, including Junius Peak. Any or all of these men might have launched a vendetta. Passions in the area were already running high because of the Civil War and fears of a slave uprising. But nobody did anything to turn it into a Hatfields-versus-McCoys feud. Perhaps both families thought there had been enough killing already. More surprising is that there was no coroner's inquest. But the citizens of Fort Worth did not need the formality of an inquest to tell them why two men were dead. With both principals beyond caring and the accused killer of one spirited out of the state beyond the reach of local law officers, there was no sense charging anyone with a crime.

Juliette Fowler and Julia York were the sympathetic victims here. Juliette was a twenty-five-year-old pregnant widow living in a rough, frontier town that had killed her husband. She took his body and fled Fort Worth, never to return. Had she stayed, she might have found a soul mate in Julia York. Ironically, she was sometimes called "Julia" in her hometown. John York's widow gave birth to her seventh child, a girl she named Mary, just a few months after burying her husband. She never remarried, so the six York children who reached adulthood grew up without a father. Her extended family must have supported her since she did not work outside the home, and neither the state nor the county provided pension benefits. Julia was thrown onto the charity of Judge Gilmore, who fortunately was capable of taking another seven persons into his household. Julia and the children continued to live in Tarrant County for the next thirty-four years. Finally, in 1885 the fifty-eight-year-old widow and the youngest of her children packed up and moved to Strawn, Texas, about eighty miles west of Fort Worth. She ultimately settled in New Mexico.[28]

As for Juliette Fowler, five months pregnant at the time her husband was killed, she too was thrown onto the benevolence of her family. She gave birth to a son in December whom she named Archibald Young Fowler, Jr., after his father. The child died before he was a year old, leaving her childless as well as husbandless. The horrific coincidence of not just one but two pregnant widows coming out of this affair only compounded the original tragedy. What had started out as a clash of two proud men escalated into a double killing whose ripples affected two extended families for years to come.

Juliette Fowler never remarried. To fill the hole in her heart, she adopted an orphan boy. Between her husband's investments and the Peak family's wealth, she was set financially, but her physical health and nerves were fragile. She lost her hearing while still in her forties and was in New York City to consult specialists ("the ablest aurists") when she died on June 4, 1889, at the age of fifty-two of complications from an ear infection. The body was returned to Dallas and buried beside her husband and children in the Masonic Cemetery. In her will she left fifteen acres and a "munificent bequest" to establish a home for "white widows and orphans" in Dallas. To later generations, Arch Fowler may have been largely forgotten, but Juliette is lovingly remembered for her munificent generosity.[29]

The real story here is how historical memory works and how two different communities, Dallas and Fort Worth, constructed two very different versions of the event. There are four first-person versions of the affair from the Fort Worth side versus two from the Dallas side, plus long oral traditions on both sides. None of the first-person versions come from an eyewitness. Fort Worth residents Pinkney Holt and Charles Ellis Mitchell were children at the time and did not tell their stories for the record until many years later.

John Peter Smith was an adult at the time and also a Fort Worth resident but did not see the killing and did not commit his recollections of what he had heard about it to paper until forty years later. The fourth version comes from Khleber M. Van Zandt, put down on paper for posterity at the prodding of his daughter in 1929 when he was ninety-two years old. He also got his information secondhand. The common denominator among all four accounts is that this was a personal feud that began with the incident at the Cold Spring and it was Fowler who attacked York in a vicious, unprovoked manner and killed him, losing his own life in the process. Neither Smith nor Van Zandt assign blame, simply saying, "They met on the square . . . , and both men were killed" on the spot.[30]

Smith and Van Zandt also agree that the weapons of choice were pistols, and they say nothing about a third person, the nephew, being involved. But both their accounts are so vague and generic that they sound more like the products of local lore than something that came from personal knowledge or research. Pinkney Holt and Charles Mitchell say that York used a knife and provide other details, including the number of stab wounds (they differ on how many). Holt also mentions a third participant, describing him as Fowler's brother and stating that he finished York off with a shotgun. Until he adds the details about the shotgun and the brother, Pinkney Holt's recollections possess the most verisimilitude of all the Fort Worth accounts.[31]

On the Dallas side, the only two accounts by contemporaries come from Susan Good and Olive Peak. Susan Good's letters to her husband in 1861 constitute the closest source to the affair and are untainted by ties to either family, but she was only passing on the latest news. Initially, she did not know the nature of the "controversy" between the two men or even the name of the second man besides A. Y. Fowler. The other Dallas account by a contemporary was written by Olive Peak, daughter of Dr. Carroll Peak. Olive did not commit her recollections to paper until 1941, and they were shaped by time and family sympathies.[32]

It is an exercise in frustration to try to separate the historical accounts from local lore. Both are hopelessly partisan hewing closely to either the Fort Worth or the Dallas story line. When you pick your city, you've picked your version of the affair. On the Fort

Worth side, Julia Kathryn Garrett's *Fort Worth: A Frontier Triumph* is a collection of oral traditions gathered by the author. According to them, Fowler and another Fort Worth citizen, Hiram Calloway, started things by getting into it at the Cold Spring. After Calloway pushed Fowler over "a bluff," causing him to suffer a broken arm, York intervened in his capacity as sheriff. "A few days later" the sheriff and the lawyer met on the public square and the fatal gun battle ensued. The same oral traditions also say that both men drew their pistols and fired simultaneously.[33] There is no official York-Gilmore family history, but their view would coincide with the "Fort Worth version," namely that Sheriff York was murdered in cold blood by a cowardly assassin.

The Fort Worth and Dallas versions are positive and negative images of the same picture. As told on the east side of the Trinity, the "picnic" [*sic*] took place in Dallas, not Fort Worth; York was the trouble-maker and Fowler, the voice of reason; it was Fowler's job, not York's, to keep order at the spring that day; and York stabbed Fowler, not vice versa. There are three identifiable sources for this version: Peak-Fowler family history, Juliette Fowler's 1889 obituary, and the records of Dallas' oldest Masonic chapter. The family history has come down to us in the form of letters, stories, and a privately printed genealogy. One family tradition says, "York stalked Archer [*sic*]"; another says, "Archibald Fowler was not killed by an assassin's bullet but by a Mr. York, a well-thought-of man . . . ." The genealogy states that Arch Fowler "tried every gentlemanly way to extricate himself from [the confrontation], but in the end he fell to an assassin's bullet." Twenty-eight years after the affair, the *Dallas Morning News*, writing Juliette Fowler's obituary, was equally kind to the deceased and her long-dead husband, even filling out the story with specious dialogue that has Fowler crying out, "For God's sake, don't let him shoot me!" just before being gunned down. In the newspaper's telling, Archibald Fowler was a "typical gentleman of his day, a scholar of superior attainments and a lawyer in the very front rank of his profession." Finally, there is the undated entry in the records of the Dallas Masons that says Arch Fowler was "assassinated," a verb that packs a powerful punch, which is hardly surprising since the departed was a brother Mason and originally a resident of Dallas.[34]

Of the twelve men who held the office of sheriff in Tarrant County between 1850 and 1876, only John B. York left a mark on history. All the others were elected nonentities or Reconstruction-era appointees who were forgotten as soon as they left office. For that matter, John York is only remembered because he died in a sensational double killing, the only Tarrant County sheriff to die in office in more than 150 years of history. That also makes his name the first on the honor roll of local officers who died in the line of duty.

John York's final resting place, once known as Mitchell-Gilmore Cemetery for the family whose relatives were its main occupants. As a private cemetery, it eventually fell into disrepair and all but one marker disappeared—including John York's. Today, it lies behind the Fort Worth Grain Exchange (not pictured) in an overgrown area between two sets of railroad tracks. (Photograph by Richard Selcer)

CHAPTER 2

DEPUTY MARSHAL CHRISTOPHER COLUMBUS FITZGERALD

August 25, 1877

An Irish Cop with Attitude

The second local peace officer to die in the line of duty was Christopher Columbus Fitzgerald, mostly remembered as C. C. Fitzgerald, who joined the little community on the Trinity after it was incorporated as a city in 1873. Far removed from the Emerald Isle, homeland of his ancestors, Fitzgerald decided to put down his roots in north Texas. By this time Irish cops were already a cliché in law enforcement, and not just in big cities like Boston, San Francisco, and Chicago. Tombstone had Marshal Dave Neagle; Cochise County, Arizona, had Sheriff Johnny Behan; and Wichita, Kansas, had Marshal Michael Meagher during this era. The Irishman remembered today only by a pair of initials and a last name became one of the stalwarts of the first Fort Worth police force.

As Fort Worth grew from a rude hamlet into full-fledged town, it needed a municipal police force. "Wild and woolly" may be an overused term, but it describes Fort Worth to a T in the 1870s. Those were dangerous, unsettled times. The decade started off with a rash of grisly murders that echoed all the way to Austin. As if that were not enough, the town also experienced more than its share of non-lethal mayhem. In August 1870 a bunch of rowdies made the town's new dentist do an impromptu jig in the middle of Main to a tune played on six-guns. A deputy sheriff looked on and did nothing. The Austin newspaper harrumphed that a "strong dose of militia law" was needed "up on the Trinity."[1]

It was not troops but a regular police force that was needed. That finally came after Fort Worth was incorporated by an act of the state legislature on March 1, 1873. Before that, Fort Worth had only an *ad hoc* marshal who performed all the duties of the office without the legal standing. In the very first municipal elections in April 1873, voters elected Edward S. Terrell as the first marshal. Terrell had come to the region thirty years earlier as a trapper, endured Indian captivity, then after the army arrived in 1849 went into the saloon business. Thereafter, he remained a saloon man first and a lawman second. Many of the people he had to ride herd on were also customers at his First and Last Chance Saloon.[2]

Columbus Fitzgerald learned law enforcement under Ed Terrell, Fort Worth's first marshal who hired the town's first police force in April 1873. Terrell had come to the area in 1843 and stayed around long enough to be included in this Charles Swartz photo of "Six Early Pioneers" sitting in front of the county courthouse sometime after 1900. "Cap'n Ed," in his seventh decade, is seated front row, middle with cane. (Courtesy of the Genealogy, History and Archives Unit, Fort Worth Public Library)

On April 12, 1873, just a week after the first elections, the new city council passed Ordinance No. 27, establishing a police force of four officers to assist Marshal Terrell in keeping the peace inside the city limits. Officers worked 24/7 during cattle season, which stretched from April through October, but had time on their hands the rest of the year. Seven months into the job, Ed Terrell quit. We don't know who served the rest of his term, but T. M. Ewing stepped into the position of marshal as a result of elections in April 1874. He did not last any longer than his predecessor, quitting in November 1874. Waiting in the wings was Columbus Fitzgerald, Ewing's deputy marshal, who won a special election on December 1 to be the marshal until the next regular election. He posted the required performance bond two weeks later, giving Marshal C. C. Fitzgerald title to the office for the next twelve months. He was barely twenty-five, had lived in Fort Worth less than a year, and been a policeman for just eight months. Whether he was ready for the responsibility of being town marshal was questionable, but he was on top of the world.[3]

Fitzgerald's victory in his first run for public office was heady stuff and gave him unrealistic expectations about his future in politics. Like so many of his fellow townspeople, Fitzgerald was part of the flood of newcomers pouring into the area in 1873–74 in anticipation of the coming of the railroad. Being a newcomer was no impediment to elected office, and political ambition seemed to run in the Irishman's veins.[4]

He had not come to Fort Worth alone. Christopher Columbus Fitzgerald was the son of Asa N. and Mary E. Fitzgerald. The father was a Protestant preacher known to his parishioners as "Parson Fitzgerald" or sometimes "the Son of Thunder" for his bombastic sermons.[5] Early Fort Worth resident Howard W. Peak has described him as "a very devout but eccentric man." The Reverend occupies a unique niche in Fort Worth history as the man who spotted a panther reposing on one of the main streets in 1875, thus giving birth to the legend of "Pantherville."[6]

The Fitzgeralds had come to north Texas in 1865 or '66 fleeing the heavy hand of Reconstruction in Georgia. Asa and Mary arrived with six children and continued to add to their brood after settling down in the county. In 1874 they sold the farm and moved into

The Fitzgerald family is best known in Fort Worth history not for law enforcement but for being the source of the "sleeping panther" story; it was started by Rev. Asa N. Fitzgerald in 1873 when he reported seeing the creature on one of the city's streets; the parts about it being asleep and on Main Street were added later. Ever since, the recumbent panther has been the city's preeminent symbol, pictured here on Belknap Street, the courthouse plaza. (Photograph by Richard Selcer)

town. Asa may have been an ordained minister, but he considered himself a "capitalist" even while he preached the gospel.[7]

Christopher, the third of the Fitzgerald children, was born in 1849. There is no way of knowing what his family called him, but he went down in history as "Columbus" or " C. C." never "Christopher" Fitzgerald.[8] Reverend Fitzgerald was a man of the cloth who also happened to be a confirmed bigot when it came to race. In 1873 he was charged with an unspecified violation of the (Federal) Ku Klux Klan Act, which could have meant anything from merely being an open member of the Klan to participating in "night riding" and other terrorist acts.[9] In any event, the son seemed to have inherited the father's bigotry because as a lawman, Columbus Fitzgerald quickly earned a reputation as a terror to local blacks. He was an unreconstructed Rebel who believed that there were "good blacks" and "bad blacks," and the difference was whether they knew their place and did as they were told.[10]

Any career ambitions Fitzgerald had in law enforcement suffered what could have been a fatal blow on November 29, 1874. It was a Sunday evening, and the young policeman had been summoned to quell a disturbance in the African American section of town. Up until just a few months before, that would have been the job of Hagar Tucker, the town's black "special policeman," but he had not been rehired after the April elections. Now, without any backup, Officer Fitzgerald unwisely decided to take on the combatants singlehandedly. He got the worst of it, suffering painful head injuries, and the perps escaped. The groggy policeman made his way back to headquarters to get his injuries, which were not life threatening, treated, but it was an embarrassing comeuppance just the same. Charles Mitchell, a young white resident at this time, recalled many years later that the town's "Negroes" knew their place—"the Ku Klux Klan saw to that." The next morning, the chastened policeman with help from Sheriff Tom James brought in one of the rowdies, thus restoring some of his pride, but this was not the last time Officer Fitzgerald would be on the losing end of a confrontation with African Americans.[11]

Fitzgerald's time in the marshal's office came to an end in April 1875. He stood for re-election, but in a four-way race among himself, Tom Redding, N. M. Maben, and Henry P. Shiel, Shiel won. Following the example set by his predecessors, he resigned before his term was up, leading to another special election in October 1875. This time the job went to Tom Redding who was subsequently suspended for "disgraceful conduct" and forced out of office. Not until T. I. Courtright became marshal in 1876 was some stability imposed on the marshal's office. None of these men were professional lawmen; they were amateurs who were more or less handy with a gun and needed a job. Courtright, the most distinguished among the group, was an army scout-turned-farmer-turned-jailer-turned-lawman.[12]

Through all the comings and goings, one of the few constants on the force was Deputy Marshal Fitzgerald. The title "Deputy Marshal" meant that he was second-in-command. "Fitz" provided the only stability in a department that was constantly in upheaval, performing his job conscientiously regardless of who was marshal of the month.

When municipal elections rolled around in April 1876, it was only natural that he felt he had a rightful claim to the office. He threw his hat into the ring as one of five candidates for the job. When he came in second behind Courtright, he was understandably disappointed. It did not help that he had lost by just three votes out of 369. This is the election that launched the legend that came to be known as "Longhair Jim" Courtright.[13]

Fitzgerald's consolation prize was being reappointed deputy marshal, a decision that was made by the city council, not the new marshal. Courtright would have picked a different man to be his No. 2. The election results soured the relationship between the marshal and deputy marshal. When Fitzgerald was the top man in 1874–75, Courtright had been only the turnkey at the jail. Now Courtright was top man, and the two officers had to try to work together because the city council said so. Most voters probably agreed with the *Standard* when it said that Fort Worth was the big winner. "We will wager cigars," said the newspaper, "that Fort Worth has the two best Marshals [*sic*] in Texas."[14]

Fitzgerald was the kind of deputy any marshal should have been glad to have beside him, the very model of a first-rate peace officer who was experienced, did not imbibe "intoxicating liquors," was "always at his post," and "not afraid to take on any man."[15] Unknown to either man, a whirlwind was coming down the tracks toward the sleepy, little burg, and Courtright was going to need all the backup he could get. In July 1876 the Texas and Pacific railroad finally reached Fort Worth, three years after it started across the prairie from Dallas. Fort Worth was now a "terminus town." There would be no more snoozing panthers in the street, but plenty of other wildlife would appear. Besides cowboys and buffalo hunters, swarms of gamblers, con men, railroad section hands, and drummers would descend on the town. ("Drummers" were the itinerant sellers who hawked their wares on every block, driving the regular shopkeepers and city fathers to distraction.) Life was about to get a lot more exciting, and dangerous for the good people of Fort Worth.

For a time at least, the odd couple of law enforcement worked together to keep the peace. It took every man on the force to subdue the rowdy elements that treated Fort Worth as one big red-light district. Courtright got along well with the cowboys because he was willing to tolerate a little hell-raising so long as nobody got hurt. He was not even above bending an elbow at the bar with the boys. Fitzgerald was no pal of the cowboys, but he was no hardnose either. According to the *Democrat*, he demonstrated "patience and firmness" without being overbearing. He lacked the talent of "Longhair Jim" with a six-gun, but he had just as much true grit.[16]

Being a teetotaler and wearing a badge did not make "Paddy" Fitzgerald a saint. On the contrary, he indulged in a little gambling on the side to supplement his meager salary and had no scruples about skinning suckers. He even ran his own keno game at one of the saloons when things were quiet about town. Fitzgerald's greatest weakness was his temper; when his Irish was up, you did not want to get in his way, and forget turning the other cheek. In September 1876, D. C. Brown accused him publicly of running a crooked keno game with a partner known as "Keno George." The offended pair went looking for their accuser and "delivered a few daisies" [i.e., they pounded on him]. It took the intervention of Marshal Courtright *and* Sheriff Joseph M. Henderson to stop the two-on-one brawl and hustle all three men to jail.[17] The marshal also took away Fitzgerald's badge, not for the gambling but for the brawl. For all practical purposes, Fitzgerald had been suspended, but without the benefit of due process. Fitzgerald did not take his punishment well, setting up a political rematch between the two men in 1877.

Apparently, the voters were also less than happy with incumbent Courtright's job performance. Ten challengers threw their hats into the ring, more than in any other city race to that point. This time Fitzgerald finished fifth. Apparently his voter approval had peaked in 1876, making him one of those public figures that the more people get to know them, the less they like them. In three runs for public office, he had won, come in second, and then fifth. The city council obligingly reappointed him to be deputy marshal for another year.

Fitzgerald and Courtright shared something else besides a keen yearning to be marshal; they were both volunteer firemen with the M. T. Johnson Hook and Ladder Company. Almost by tradition, the two jobs, lawman and fireman, have attracted the same kind of men. It may have been the excitement, or the public esteem, or just a high-minded sense of duty that drew them. We know Fitzgerald answered the fire bell more than once because the *Democrat* praised him as "a valiant fireman," and when he died their obituary described him as a "young fireman," not a policeman.[18]

Fitzgerald's second tour as deputy marshal lasted only four months. He was shot and killed on Saturday night, August 25, the result of a sporting dispute that he intervened in, albeit not in an official capacity. It started the day before at the weekly horse races at the Cold Spring racetrack just across the river north of town. The track was a favorite gathering place for the town's men folk, both black and white, who entered their own horses and placed gentlemanly wagers on other horses. It also attracted more than its share of outsiders with phony names and nefarious designs. One of those who raced his horse there on occasion was notorious outlaw Sam Bass. Considerable sums of cash and trade goods changed hands on race day, and the parties involved did not always agree on the outcome. When that happened, gentlemanly wagers could turn into nasty disputes.

At the afternoon races on August 24, V. H. Igo, who ran a shipping firm in the same building as the Transcontinental Hotel on the public square, made a bet with C. D. Elson, a barkeep at D. W. C. Pendery's Sample Room, a popular watering hole owned by one of Fort Worth's pioneer settlers. Both men had taken a little time off from work that day to play the ponies, and Igo did not have any cash on him, so he put up his buggy as collateral. He lost. The next evening Elson took off his apron and went to collect the debt. He intended to come back with either the cash or the buggy. Perhaps anticipating trouble, he took along backup: Sam Shannon and Frank P. Quarles, both newcomers to town, and Washington Davis, a twenty-five-year-old black man who worked as the porter at the saloon. Before coming to Fort Worth, Davis had been the servant of Catherine Davis and family in McLennan County. There is no indication that he had ever been anything more than a day laborer, so he may have been dragooned by his boss into going along. Ironically, the man who was at the center of what followed was the one participant with no dog in the fight.[19]

The other two whites are another matter. Sam Shannon was proprietor of the fashionably named Delmonico's Restaurant on Main, directly across the street from Elson's saloon. Quarles is the cipher of the group. Nothing is known of him before this incident except he was accused in Tyler, Texas, in 1874 of trying to scam the post office. The grand jury investigated but declined to indict him, which the newspaper called "the best vindication of his character" and "gratifying to all who are interested in having justice done." How these four came together on this occasion is unknown, but it is clear that they were armed and meant business.[20]

They found Igo in the stable behind the hotel, but he was not alone. Columbus Fitzgerald was with him, apparently by coincidence not by intent. He was not on duty at the time, nor was he armed. That did not prevent him from getting into the middle of what occurred next.[21]

Elson got right to the point, demanding the buggy, which Igo refused to give up, claiming that it had not been part of the bet. Before they could pursue this line of argument, the focus of the confrontation shifted from Elson and Igo to Davis and Fitzgerald. Davis said something, and Fitzgerald, who considered blacks beneath contempt, took exception. The Irish Terror of Fort Worth's black community was not about to take any sass from a porter. Fitzgerald stepped in close and cuffed the other man. Davis reacted, striking the Irishman full in the face with his fist. Fitzgerald flew into a rage and, as the newspaper later put it, the only thing that prevented him from "annihilating the Negro on the spot" was the timely intervention of the others present.[22] After they separated Fitzgerald and Davis, the Irishman stormed off to get his gun, and Davis fled in the opposite direction. Nobody was thinking about the horse-racing debt now.

A little later, an armed and still angry Fitzgerald spied the object of his fury lurking behind Delmonico's Restaurant. Davis was still in the company of Elson, Shannon, and Quarles, but when he saw the Irishman coming he ducked behind a barn. Fitzgerald gave chase. As the officer rounded the corner, Davis turned and pulled a pistol, firing one shot. The bullet struck Fitzgerald in the lower abdomen, passing completely through his body. Still standing, the mortally wounded officer returned fire, getting off three shots at close range, none of which hit Davis. Shannon, Quarles, and Elson grabbed Fitzgerald to prevent him from firing again.

The sound of the gunfire echoing through the business district brought Officers A. N. Woody and fellow Irishman J. W. O'Connell on the run. They took charge of the crime scene, directing bystanders to take Fitzgerald inside and fetch medical help on the double. They also arrested Davis and friends and hustled them off to jail. A Justice of the Peace was rousted out of bed and after hearing the facts, released Shannon and Quarles on $200 bond each, but he denied bond to either Elson or Davis. The stage was set for them to take the fall in subsequent legal proceedings.[23]

Fitzgerald was laid out on the floor of the City Drug Store, where Drs. W. P. Burts and Julian T. Feild examined him. They only had to walk a block to get to the drugstore from their office. The doctors pronounced him in critical condition and deemed his chances of surviving extremely slim. They directed that he be taken to his father's residence at the corner of Houston and Weatherford so he could be made more comfortable in however much time he had left. Someone went to find the Reverend Fitzgerald and bring him home.

As it often did, the public's attention initially focused more on the perpetrator than the victim. A crowd gathered outside the drugstore and vowed to take quick action if Fitz died. A reporter for the *Democrat* talked his way into the county jail and interviewed Davis in his cell. The black man adamantly denied shooting Fitzgerald, insisting he did not even own a gun. His denial suggested a potential legal defense strategy since he had no gun in his possession when arrested. Officers O'Connell and Woody had no time to conduct an investigation because they were called to the scene of another affray on Houston Street, and they had no sooner jailed the perpetrators of that disturbance than they were called to the scene of yet a third affray. It seemed another "black devil" had assaulted a white shopkeeper and escaped. It was a busy Saturday night in Fort Worth![24]

Columbus Fitzgerald clung tenaciously to life for thirty hours, doped up with morphine, and passing in and out of consciousness. Death finally relieved him of his suffering on Sunday night. He succumbed about midnight with his father and doctors hovering at his side. Early the next morning, the city's fire bells were put to work tolling the news, thus starting a new tradition of ringing the bells whenever an officer died. The fact that Columbus Fitzgerald was also a volunteer fireman probably had more to do with it this first time than his status as an officer of the law. Alarmed citizens rushed out of their houses thinking there was a fire somewhere in town.[25]

Nor did Officer Fitzgerald's death and funeral pass unnoticed otherwise. On the contrary, it was a major civic event. Fort Worth had a sizable and close-knit Irish population that would all have turned out, plus there were his father's parishioners and all his fraternal brothers among firemen and lawmen. They would have all wanted to honor him.

The funeral was held late Monday afternoon, after the worst of a summer's day's heat had passed. Members of the M. T. Johnson Hook and Ladder Company, not the Fort Worth Police Department, took charge of things. The funeral cortege left Reverend Fitzgerald's home about four thirty with firemen escorting the wagon that served as a hearse. Following close behind were about thirty or forty buggies and carriages full of somber citizens. The procession, stretching out for six blocks, proceeded to Pioneers Rest Cemetery on Samuels Avenue where Reverend W. W. Brimm of the First Presbyterian Church preached what was reputedly a very emotional graveside service.[26]

The reaction to the killing of Officer Fitzgerald was a mixture of shock and outrage. He was the first lawman killed locally since John York in 1861. Reverend Brimm, in an editorial in the newspaper the day after the funeral, pinned the blame as much on the racetrack as on the murderer. He listed all the vices that sprang from horse racing, including, "profanity, gambling and drunkenness . . . and general corruption," apart from murder. He ended his diatribe by calling on the authorities to put an end to organized racing in the city. A slightly different commentary on the situation in Fort Worth came from the *Galveston Daily News*, which sniffed righteously that, "There are many roughs [up] there and much thieving is going on."[27]

Yet the reaction was surprisingly muted. The *Fort Worth Standard* did not even call the shooting a "murder," but described it obliquely as a "difficulty, which resulted in the death of Columbus Fitzgerald." And at the next regularly scheduled meeting of the city council, which should have occurred on Tuesday evening (August 28) and occasioned public testimonial to the fallen officer, only one alderman even bothered to show up. No meeting, no testimonial.

Obviously, the proper assignment of guilt and blame was not entirely clear in the public mind.[28]

Nonetheless, the criminal justice system worked fast in those days. The county attorney wasted no time bringing the accused to trial, probably fearing vigilante justice if he delayed. On Wednesday, the grand jury indicted Elson, Quarles, and Davis for murder. The record does not show why Shannon was not indicted along with the rest. Elson, considered the ringleader, was tried first, in the District Court of Judge J. A. Carroll. On Friday, August 31, between fifty and sixty Fort Worth citizens were summoned to the courthouse for jury selection. They were sworn in, and winnowed down to twelve in voir dire. Of those rejected, "twenty-four had scruples, nine were challenged by the defense, two by the state, thirteen had opinions, one was prejudiced, two, biased, three excused, and two disqualified." The trial commenced the following morning with the state presenting its case first.[29]

When the proceedings ended, C. D. Elson was a free man. To the surprise of most observers, he was found "not guilty." No record of the trial exists and the local newspapers did not report the reason(s) for the verdict, but apparently the gentlemen of the jury accepted the defense's argument that Fitzgerald had struck Davis first and did not consider "sassing" the officer justification for assault. There was also the fact that Fitzgerald had armed himself and come looking for trouble, seemingly with every intention of doing bodily harm to Davis. Add to that the awkward facts that the state could not find the murder weapon, much less place it in Davis's hand, and the prosecution's case falls apart. It did not help that the state chose to try Elson first. Calling him the instigator was one thing; proving it was something else. The prosecution never said that Elson actually shot the officer, just that he instigated the trouble. This was not County Attorney Sam Furman's finest hour. The acquittal of Elson threw his whole strategy into disarray. He moved to drop all charges against Quarles and asked for a continuance in Davis' case. It was a stunning turn of events for the family and friends of Columbus Fitzgerald.[30]

Washington Davis was never brought to trial. Worried that the Fitzgerald clan might seek justice on their own terms, he hurriedly packed up and left town. Like so many black men in this era, he becomes almost invisible in the public records. He seems to have drifted northward into the Oklahoma Territory where people did not question a man's background too closely, regardless of his color. In 1878 the veil parted: He was charged with murder by the U.S. district attorney for the Western District of Arkansas at Fort Smith, but the trial never went to court. After that he dropped completely out of sight.[31]

Sam Shannon and Frank Quarles also did not hang around town long. The Irish by reputation have a long memory for insults and personal slights. Elson's two pals were afraid of getting a bullet in the back some dark night. They were not cowards, but they were not willing to tempt fate either. Besides, the grand jury might decide to ignore the JP's lead and indict them anyway. Shannon was partners in the restaurant with his wife, and they had managed to accumulate a little nest egg from the business. Early on Monday morning he packed a valise, hurried to the bank and drew out all their money, some $400, then hopped the first train to Dallas. He did all this without consulting Mrs. Shannon, only leaving her a note telling her to meet him on Tuesday at the European Hotel in Dallas. Presumably, they would walk away from the restaurant. Mrs. Shannon followed her husband's directions and showed up at the European Hotel the next day. He was gone, but had left her another note, telling he planned to take their hard-earned money and disappear forever. He asked for her forgiveness and advised her to forget him. She returned to Fort Worth, heartbroken, and pawned the one thing of value she had left, a gold watch. Then she bought a train ticket to Pennsylvania where her parents lived. She was never heard from in Fort Worth again, but Sam seems to have resurfaced nearly ten years later in Dallas. A "Sam Shannon" was working for the Missouri Pacific Railroad during the Great Southwest Strike of 1886. He was one of the workers who went out on strike, and when they tried to block the rails, a train plowed into them. Shannon was badly injured with head wounds and a mangled arm. He was refused treatment in the railroad's hospital. Fortunately for him, the staff at the city hospital did not take their marching orders from the railroad, and they treated him. His arm had to be amputated, but the attending physicians said he would recover. If he did recover, he either left town or kept a low profile thereafter.[32]

When Frank Quarles left town he also headed east but did not stop until he reached Kingston, Texas. There he opened the Cotton Exchange Saloon with a partner and did well with a little help from the city marshal. When a young, muckraking newspaper editor began lambasting their little operation, they administered a beating to make him back off. A short time later the editor left town, and Frank Quarles lived the rest of his life in anonymity.[33]

As for Columbus Fitzgerald, history has been kinder to him than life ever was. While his dying was anything but heroic and the justice system failed him, in death he was transformed into a sympathetic figure. As the years passed, the unflattering facts of the case were replaced by something more palatable to those who like their lawmen always on the side of right. Some sixty years after the event, Fort Worth newspaperman Delbert Willis would paint the Irish cop as the victim of a cold-blooded ambush and his murderer as a "crazed Negro."[34]

If Columbus was not the most sympathetic figure, his family certainly deserves our sympathy. The previous summer, Columbus' brother, John Henry Fitzgerald, had lost his oldest son when the boy choked to death on uncooked corn. Then came the death of Columbus. Less than two weeks later and little more than a year after the death of John Henry's son, Asa Fitzgerald lost his sixty-four-year-old wife, Mary, to consumption (tuberculosis). The grief-stricken Reverend was left to try to make sense of this series of tragedies.[35]

The man who was city marshal when Columbus Fitzgerald was killed is curiously absent from the whole story. "Longhair Jim," the legendary "two-gun marshal of Fort Worth," reputedly a wizard at dealing with drunken cowboys and hard cases, might as well have been on Mars while his deputy was being killed. He only enters the picture after Elson and Davis were locked up when he took the precaution of posting a score of armed guards around the jailhouse to discourage any lynch mob from trying to short-circuit the judicial process. Why he did not promptly transfer his prisoners to the county jail, routine procedure in felony cases, is a mystery. Courtright issued no public statements paying homage to his deputy or offering condolences to the family. Descriptions of the funeral do not even mention his name. "Longhair Jim" Courtright was missing in action.

As for the lynch mob that gathered at the scene of the killing that day, their ardor seems to have cooled as quickly as it arose, suggesting again that there was more to the story than what appeared in the newspapers. Ordinarily, Davis being a black man *and* a cop-killer would have been sufficient to provoke vigilante action. The fact that "John Lynch" did not march on the jail, suggests that there was not much sympathy for Columbus Fitzgerald in the saloons and on the street corners of Fort Worth. This is particularly remarkable when we compare it to what happened with Jim Toots in 1892 (chapter 6) and Bill Thomason in 1906 (chapter 9). They were both cop-killers who came within a whisker of being lynched.

Columbus Fitzgerald's ultimate fate was to be not just forgotten but misunderstood by later generations of Fort Worthers. Though buried in Pioneers Rest Cemetery in the midst of ten other family members, all of whom lived and died in Fort Worth, his tombstone gives an incorrect birth date (1859) and incorrectly calls him the "first city marshal of Fort Worth."[36] What we need to remember about Officer Fitzgerald is that he was representative of that legendary, nineteenth-century law enforcement type: the rough-and-ready Irish cop. He went about his job as he saw it by his own light—not always by the book, but effective for the most part. The difference is that Columbus Fitzgerald was not a "flatfoot" in Boston or some other civilized Eastern city but on the dusty streets of frontier Fort Worth.

Officer Fitzgerald is buried in Pioneers Rest Cemetery, Fort Worth's oldest public cemetery. The nice granite marker was put down years later by person or persons unknown, but presumably family member(s) who did not know the date of death and believed (incorrectly) that Fitzgerald had been the "1st City Marshal of Fort Worth." (Photograph by Kevin Foster)

The gated entrance to the cemetery is on one of Fort Worth's oldest streets, Samuels Avenue. (Photograph by Richard Selcer)

George White was a deputy under Marshal Sam Farmer at the time he was killed, but Farmer could not have prevented the tragedy. In fact it is questionable if the Marshal even knew what the freelancing deputy was up to that day, serving warrants in Arlington. (Courtesy of J. R. Taggert, Lohman, MO)

CHAPTER 3

DEPUTY MARSHAL GEORGE WHITE

August 2, 1879

"All that was left of a hero boy . . ."

When is a police officer justified in using "deadly force"? Today that question is a weighty legal and ethical issue. In nineteenth-century Texas the answer was simple: an officer's decision to draw his weapon was circumscribed only by his own good judgment. There are always two sides to every question, and this one is no different. An officer who hesitated to reach for his gun in a tight situation was likely to wind up dead, and since officers usually operated without backup, it was critical to get control of any situation right out of the gate. The unwritten rule was "shoot first and ask questions later." On the other hand, a trigger-happy lawman might inspire fear, but he would also quickly wear out his welcome.

In April 1879 Sam Farmer was elected Fort Worth marshal, starting a new era in the city's law enforcement history. The T. I. Courtright era was over after three terms in office although "Longhair Jim" would not be riding off into the sunset any time soon. In the weeks after Sam's election, he went through the usual routine of selecting four or five men to serve as his police force for the next twelve months. One of those was nineteen-year-old George White, who despite his youth was appointed "deputy marshal," making him second-in-command. George took to law enforcement like a colt takes to a field of clover—until fate intervened.

George H. White was born in Pike County, Alabama, on December 7, 1859, to Enoch and Amanda White.[1] His father was a poor dirt farmer who moved west with the frontier, starting in Georgia before coming to Alabama and finally Texas. By the time the family settled in Upshur County, Texas, George had four siblings, and the family continued to multiply in the years following as they moved yet again, this time to Rusk County, Texas. By 1877, George had fled the farm and was living in Fort Worth working as an agent for sewing-machine-salesman S. C. Bradford and living under Bradford's roof.[2]

Sometime after 1877 George made the acquaintance of R. C. McPhail who also sold sewing machines. Mr. and Mrs. McPhail were twenty-five years older than George and childless, and soon they were treating George like a son. Around 1879, after an eighth child was born to the Whites and they took in two boarders to help make ends meet, George packed up and went to live with the McPhails. He now considered them his adoptive family, and they had similar feelings for "Georgie," as they called him.[3]

That was the same year that George White joined the barely six-year-old Fort Worth Police Department (FWPD). Although this was his first job in law enforcement, he was hired as deputy marshal, the second position in the chain of command, just below the marshal. Starting so close to the top suggests that he had pull with either Marshal Sam Farmer or the city council that had to sign off on all police appointments. He was also a volunteer fireman, not a surprising development since firemen and policemen were practically blood brothers. He was accepted as "one of the boys." He was unmarried, but he had found all the family he needed in the McPhails, and all who knew the blended family considered George "a most affectionate and devoted son" even though they were not his birth parents.[4]

To make ends meet, George worked part-time as "special constable" (i.e., bailiff) for the Tenth District Court. Since the court only met in March and July it was a job he could easily fit into his regular duties as deputy marshal. Besides, being selected by Sheriff Joseph M. Henderson and Judge J. A. Carroll was a testimonial to his status as an up-and-comer. Serving as Judge Carroll's bailiff while a deputy marshal was not considered a conflict of interest. He also added to his portfolio by doing process serving for the Sheriff even though he lacked a regular deputy sheriff's commission. The legal details did not worry him because in his own mind he was both a deputy marshal *and* a deputy sheriff. He was just grateful that both Sam Farmer and Joseph Henderson had taken a fatherly interest in him.[5]

On the downside, White's budding law enforcement career did not earn him much of a living, even juggling two or three jobs. His salary as a deputy marshal was only $50 per month, and working part-time as a bailiff only fattened his pay when court was in session. The lack of financial security on top of his relative youth explains why he was not married or even engaged to one of the local lasses. He could not afford marriage and, besides, there was no rush; he was just starting his career. The future was bright for "one of the best and most efficient officers" on the force.[6]

White's strong sense of duty did not make him a particularly religious man. Any Sundays he got off from his law enforcement duties were spent at the horse races. It is doubtful if he ever darkened a church doorway, especially since he was a lifelong bachelor. Fortunately, church attendance was not a prerequisite for police work. A man only had one day off a week; how he used that day was his business.

In the late 1870s local law enforcement was facing a crime wave that included the Sam Bass gang plus too many horse thieves and cattle rustlers to count. While public attention focused on Bass's dramatic stagecoach and train robberies, officers also had to contend with the common garden-variety rustlers and thieves who could be just as dangerous as the better known "poster boys" on the sheriff's bulletin board.

The biggest horse thieves in north Texas up to this date had been John Allison Goldsmith and Bill Hawkins. Their lengthy run of thefts, arrests, and escapes finally ran out in 1876. Their downfall started with being arrested by the Wise County sheriff and lodged in the Decatur jail. The pair had several outstanding warrants in Fort Worth, so the sheriff wired Sheriff Joseph Henderson of Tarrant County to come get them. Henderson sent three men, two deputies, Elliott and Ferguson, and a civilian named Hardcastle to drive the buckboard. They went up to Decatur and collected their prisoners, put them in irons, and started home. On a deserted stretch of road, they jumped their guards and escaped. Hawkins was never heard from again, but Goldsmith was foolish enough to stay in the area. Nearly a year later, Sheriff Henderson got a tip that Goldsmith was at his brother's just east of Birdville. He dispatched three heavily armed deputies led by White Collins to bring the fugitive in. They took him in custody, clamped him in irons, and threw him on a horse to bring him back. About a half-mile east of the Trinity on the Denton Road, Goldsmith spurred his horse and tried to get away. They drilled him in the back. A JP was summoned from Denton, and Collins gave him a perfunctory account of what had happened. The coroner labeled it justifiable homicide and went home. The deputies tossed the body on the roof of a nearby cabin so the family could come retrieve it, and returned to Fort Worth.[7]

This was the way horse thieves were supposed to be dealt with: no nonsense and summary justice. Goldsmith's flight had saved the citizens of Tarrant County the cost of a trial and the state of Texas the cost of incarceration. White Collins was the man of the hour.

Unfortunately, Goldsmith's fate did not serve as an exemplary warning to other would-be horse thieves. The crime wave continued. Fort Worth and Dallas officials decided that Arlington, midway between the two cities, was the headquarters of a horse-stealing ring. Suspecting and proving it, however were two different things. Sheriff Henderson spent more time on cases of horse theft than any other category of crime. Complicating the problem was the fact that a lot of men on the frontier bought and sold horses based on little more than a handshake; no paperwork was ever filed. As long as buyer and seller were both happy, there was no need.

At the end of July 1879, Henderson was informed that a mare belonging to O. C. Storm was in the possession of a local "turfman," Charlie McCafferty, one of a trio of brothers who made their livings trading and racing horses all over the South. The mare had been reported stolen by Storm on July 9.[8] The Sheriff could only presume that either McCafferty had stolen the horse or was in possession of stolen property.

This is where being a small-town lawman had its benefits; Henderson knew all the locals well, including Charlie McCafferty. McCafferty was not an easy man to get along with, but he was no horse thief. He was a prickly fellow who in later years had a reputation for being a mite quick on the draw with both knife and gun. In this case, however, he seems to have been an innocent party. Still, Henderson had to follow up on the complaint. Curiously, it was not Storm who swore out the warrant but John Shaddy, whose exact role in the affair has been lost in the historical record, but he was definitely the man who started the wheels turning. The bench warrant, issued by Justice of the Peace A. G. McClung named "John Smith" as the accused and ordered the Sheriff to seize the horse, too. "John Smith" was merely a legal convenience, not an actual person, used by a judge who was either too lazy or in too big a hurry to get all his facts straight. The main thing was to bring in the horse thief, whoever he was, and return the horse to its rightful owner; the rest would be sorted out in court. In a small town like Fort Worth, a judge could dispense with a lot of the legal niceties taught in law books.[9]

Deputy Marshal George White got the job of bringing in the accused even though he was a Fort Worth policeman and Arlington was not in his jurisdiction. But that did not seem to matter; he was still an officer of the law and he did not mind doing a favor for the sheriff. Henderson, for his part was happy to let the gung-ho young deputy ride out to Arlington to serve a minor warrant. Early on the morning of August 2, White picked up the warrant from Judge McClung and set out for Arlington. He did not anticipate any trouble because, as he told a friend, he intended to take in the horse races at the Arlington track before coming home. He did not explain how he would do that with a horse and possibly a suspect in tow. What may have seemed a routine process-serving job, however, would turn out to be anything but.

The warrant's enigmatic "John Smith" was actually Tom Alford, one of four brothers with a history of thumbing their noses at the law. The Tennessee-born Alfords—Tom, George, Mace, Zach, and father Robert—had come to north Texas some years before, establishing themselves on the rich prairieland between Dallas and Fort Worth. Supposedly they were homesteaders and stockmen, but their circle of friends seemed to include more "noted desperadoes" than sodbusters, and one or more of the boys was always in trouble with the authorities. Most recently they had been linked to a series of horse thefts in the area. There was no hard evidence pointing to them but plenty of suspicion. In the summer of 1879, twenty-seven-year-old William Thomas "Tom" Alford was barely eking out a living as a horse trader, farmer, and "timber man." George Alford was twenty-four and described as "a poor boy who has no wealth or family ties" to keep him on the straight and narrow and "no social position, or influential friends to screen and protect him." Little is known about the last two brothers except that Mace and George were twins, and Mace was a hothead who followed his siblings' lead. Tom, Mace, and George homesteaded a piece of land next to their father's place.[10]

How much of this background Charles McCafferty knew at the time he acquired the horse is unknown, but as a law-abiding citizen he would have wanted to do the right thing, so he wrote to Tom Alford explaining the problem. The letter prompted Alford to come to see him bringing a bill of sale for $17.50 that seemed to prove his hands were clean in the matter. But Alford did not stop with proving his own innocence; he solicitously advised McCafferty not to give up the horse to anybody who could not produce the proper paperwork. He also promised to "make it all right" with McCafferty should the animal be "proved away from him," an offer that is almost incomprehensible if indeed Alford were as innocent as he claimed. He was either the world champion when it came to being neighborly or else worried about what would come out if a thorough investigation were conducted. In either case, Good Neighbor Tom Alford soon got the chance to back up his generous offer after McCafferty was obliged to surrender the mare to John Shaddy who was acting on behalf of O. C. Storm.

So on Saturday, August 2, Deputy White headed out to Arlington to serve Tom Alford, accompanied by Charles McCafferty as private citizen. Although they could have taken the train to Arlington Station, they chose to make the trip by road with White riding horseback and McCafferty driving a buggy. They intended to have Alford in the Tarrant County jail before the day was over, and then a judge could sort things out after that. Before setting out, White hastily scratched the name "Tom Olferd" [sic] on the warrant next to "John Smith."[11]

When they reached Arlington, White and McCafferty went straight to Robert Alford's place where they ran into George Alford.

They casually asked for his brother Tom without revealing that they had a warrant for his arrest, and George Alford hospitably offered to take them to the brothers' homestead where they would find Tom. By the time they arrived there it was noon, and the Fort Worth pair seemed in no hurry to collect their man and start back. On the contrary, they were too cagey by half, accepting the Alford brothers' invitation to stay for supper. Clearly, Tom and George suspected nothing, which suggests that they were either the dumbest horse thieves ever, or completely innocent and therefore not on guard. While George got busy cooking, McCafferty and Tom talked horse business, and Deputy White bided his time. He had concocted a scheme to lure Tom away from his brother so that George would not be able to interfere when he sprang the arrest warrant. But his plan seemed to be unraveling after Tom and McCafferty struck a deal whereby Tom would give the aggrieved turfman another horse, thereby fulfilling his promise to make things right. This may have satisfied McCafferty but it did not satisfy the law, and it definitely did not satisfy George White who had no intention of riding out to Arlington and back for nothing. He was determined to collect his fee.

While all this was going on, a party of men rode up to the farmhouse, among them Mace Alford and William Lytle on their way to hunt squirrels. The odds had suddenly changed dramatically. George White had good reason now to regret his dalliance at the Alford's farm. He had no desire to take on the Alford clan and their friends. Adding to the awkwardness of the situation, Mace Alford was George's fraternal twin, and it was hard to tell the two apart even for people who knew them. And neither White nor McCafferty had ever seen either of them before.

The time passed agreeably enough, and White seemed to catch a break when Tom Alford offered to go back with them to his father's place to pick out the replacement horse for Charlie. Then luck took another sharp veer when Mace Alford announced he was coming along. The four men set out with Tom Alford riding White's little gray quarter horse and the two Fort Worth men riding in the buggy. McCafferty had a full stomach and was looking forward to getting a new horse, so he was happy. Deputy White was tense and trying to figure out how he was going to take Tom Alford into custody without stirring up a firestorm. As soon as they were out of sight of the brothers' farmhouse but still about half a mile from "Old Man Alford's," White decided enough chicanery; it was time to take the direct approach. He stopped the buggy and revealed his identity, simultaneously pulling his pistol to get the drop on them. He informed Tom he was under arrest and showed him the warrant. McCafferty, who was not too happy with the way things had suddenly turned, followed White's orders to bind Tom's wrists and tied his ankles together under his horse's belly so he could not escape. When Mace tried to interfere, White pointed his pistol at him and said, "Shut your mouth or I'll do it for you!"

Since Mace was not under arrest, White did not try to stop him from riding away. However, Mace vowed, "Young man, you'll pay for this!" before whipping his horse to a gallop. Letting Mace go was one more mistake that can be charged to George White that day. He had certainly committed gaffes a more experienced officer would never have committed. One cannot help but think if Deputy White Collins had been the lead officer that day the situation would never have spun out of control. The old saw comes to mind about never sending a boy on a man's errand.[12]

As soon as Mace Alford was gone, White and McCafferty continued on their leisurely way. They only got another quarter of a mile before trouble caught up with them. It had not taken Mace long to round up brother George and Bill Lytle, and the three put the spurs to their horses to get back in record time. Making no attempt to sneak up on their quarry, they galloped up hollering "Halt!" when they were close. The commotion spooked Tom Alford's horse, and the animal acted like it was going to bolt despite his efforts to control it. White presumed his prisoner was trying to make a break for it. He ordered McCafferty to stop the buggy and leaped out with his pistol drawn. The three pursuers rode up with their own guns out, and Tom Alford shouted, "Shoot him, Mace, shoot him!"

George Alford chimed in "Shoot!"

Then an old-fashioned shootout erupted. George White and Bill Lytle were the first to open fire, shooting at each other almost simultaneously. But Lytle had a shotgun against White's six-shooter, and he could hardly miss at that distance. The blast peppered White with twenty-five or thirty pellets, most of them striking him in the belly and groin.[13] The impact knocked him off his feet. Mortally wounded though he was, he continued to fire from the prone position rising up on one elbow to aim. He was far from done. He put a slug in Lytle's groin, knocking him from his horse into the bushes alongside the trail. White turned his fire on the two Alford brothers who had managed to corral Tom's horse and were trying to untie Tom. Despite his awkward position and the excruciating pain, there was nothing wrong with George White's aim. He winged Tom in the shoulder, and at that point the Alfords had had enough. George and Mace fled leaving Lytle and Tom Alford to their fates. White gamely fired his last two shots at the retreating pair, and the furious gun battle was over. It had taken only a couple of minutes from start to finish. Charlie McCafferty, because he was unarmed and was not an officer of the law, had not participated. No one would ever publicly criticize him for staying on the sidelines. As soon as the shooting stopped, however, he helped White into the buggy and whipped the horse for the village of Arlington, two miles away. Tom Alford and Bill Lytle were forgotten in the urgency to get White to a doctor. Lytle lay where he had fallen. Tom managed to work himself free from his bonds then rode off looking for medical help for himself. In a one-sided gun battle, George White had severely wounded two men and driven off two more. More incredibly, he had done it after being mortally wounded. His judgment may have been flawed that day, but there was nothing wrong with his courage.

When the Deputy and McCafferty arrived in Arlington, White refused treatment until he could send the following telegram to Sheriff Henderson:

> *Come down at once and catch the wounded thieves. Am mortally wounded, shot through the thigh by one of the Alford horse thieves. Wounded them both. Tell my folks, and bring Dr. Beall.*[14]

His strong sense of duty made him notify his superior even though he believed he was as good as dead. But his constitution proved as strong as his sense of duty, and he clung to life. It was now four o'clock in the afternoon, but the day was far from over.

McCafferty did what he could to make White comfortable, giving him plenty of water because thirst can torment a badly wounded man. A half-hour after White's telegram went off, McCafferty sent another reiterating that White was mortally wounded and pleading for help.

At the other end of those telegrams, Sheriff Henderson wasted no time rounding up a first-class posse of Marshal Sam Farmer, Constables George Ware and Jake Riggle, and Dr. Elias J. Beall. They decided they would get there faster if they took the 5:00 p.m. train to the Arlington station. Mr. and Mrs. McPhail accompanied them. By the time they arrived, White had been made as comfortable as possible in a private home. About ten o'clock that night, Mrs. McPhail sent this telegram back to anxious friends in Fort Worth:

> *I don't think White mortally wounded, but very painfully hurt. He got two of his men after he came down; one will die.*[15]

Dr. Beall, was less sanguine about his patient. He was Fort Worth's only physician with a degree from a recognized medical college, and as a surgeon in the Civil War he had seen plenty of gunshot wounds. He decided to treat the patient where he was rather than try to get him back to Fort Worth. The McPhails, frantic with worry, hovered by the bedside.[16]

In the meantime, the two unscathed Alford boys had returned to the scene of the crime. They picked up Bill Lytle and beat a hasty retreat to their father's place where they were soon joined by sympathetic friends. Tom Alford had apparently not been hurt too badly because he kept going. Mace Alford soon made himself scarce as well. Alford père and George, however, were still at the farmhouse when the Fort Worth posse, reinforced with Arlington men, rode up. The occupants of the farmhouse did not put up a fight when they barged in and placed George Alford under arrest. They stayed around long enough to watch Bill Lytle breathe his last at 1:00 a.m. Then they left and took their prisoner back to Arlington.

Their first stop in Arlington was not the jail but the house where George White was fighting for his life. He was surprisingly alert when George Alford was brought, and as soon as he caught sight of the prisoner he declared, "That's one of the roosters that shot me!"

Alford protested unconvincingly, "You are mistaken; I was not there."

"I fired my two last shots at you as you ran off through the bushes," retorted White.[17]

They took Alford away and locked him up in the Arlington cala-boose until an "examining hearing" could be held. That took place two days later when County Attorney W. S. Pendleton stood before a judge and presented the state's case against George Alford. It was a pro forma proceeding. Bail was set at $1000, which for the Alford family was the same thing as no bail. George Alford would cool his heels in jail until the next grand jury met. At this point, the charge was "assault to murder." At the examining hearing, George White made a dramatic appearance, carried in on a cot to give his testi-mony in person. That testimony was recorded and later introduced as evidence at George Alford's trial. White was able to add little to what Charlie McCafferty had already said in court, but his presence was worth a dozen witnesses or a thousand pages of testimony. This was a man who was still at death's door.

Two parts of White's testimony would prove crucial: He admit-ted that he had never seen any of the Alfords before that afternoon and therefore could not distinguish George Alford from his twin brother; and he stated that after he was hit he fired seven shots from his six-shooter without bothering to explain how under the circumstances and in the short time the shootout lasted, he was able to reload. The latter seemed an insignificant point at the time. After all, the witness was in pain and doped up on morphine. Both points would prove to be very important at the trial.[18]

The fact that White could even make it to court was taken as a promising sign that he might recover, and for several days he did seem to be holding his own. His family and friends took hope. "George was tough," they said. "He was going to make it." It was a false optimism. His intestines were shredded, and Dr. Beall, with all his skills, was unwilling to perform surgery to remove the pellets. Absent modern antibiotics and intensive hospital care, he was living on borrowed time. Beall probably knew that; he had seen hundreds if not thousands of soldiers during the Civil War similarly wounded and knew the odds.

Every change in George White's condition was news. The *Fort Worth Democrat* provided its readers with daily updates received via telegraph. On August 5, the newspaper reported, "White's condition is very favorable, and with proper and careful treatment he will worry through." The following day the *Democrat* was still optimistic: "White will recover." Astute readers might have noted that none of these optimistic reports were attributed to Dr. Beall. The newspaper also reported the rumor that "a certain physician of this city" was treating Tom Alford on the sly at some unidentified hideout. It all sounded quite conspiratorial and was complete nonsense, but it made great copy.[19]

For the better part of a week, Fort Worth Marshal Sam Farmer spent almost as much time in Arlington—checking on the patient, talking to George Alford—as he did in Fort Worth. Every evening he caught the last train to Arlington and stayed the night, coming straight back to his office the next morning. This was the fierce loyalty of a concerned friend but also a brother officer.

White's condition took a sudden turn for the worse on Thursday night (August 7–8). He developed a high fever, became delirious, and had trouble breathing. A second doctor was called in, T. A. Cravens, who announced that his lungs were filling with fluid causing respiratory failure. One must read between the lines of the newspaper reports to understand the reasons for his dramatic and rapid decline. It was not the actual gunshot wounds that were killing him, at least not directly. In fact, his recovery from the shotgun pellets had been showing real progress in the first twenty-four hours. Thus the optimism. What Drs. Beall and Cravens did not understand, for all their skill and experience, was the complications that would soon set in, leading ultimately to multi-organ systemic failure. White had lost a significant amount of blood initially, and without a transfusion, shock would have set in, depriving the major organs of blood. Among the first organs to shut down would have been the kidneys, causing toxins to begin to build up in the body, which would lead to rampant infection. The standard medical practice of giving the patient liquids by mouth, probably a mixture of alcohol and morphine, would only have made things worse because, in his weakened state, the liquids would have been aspirated into the lungs, leading to bacterial pneumonia within seventy-two hours. Without antibiotics, the infection would have entered the bloodstream, spreading throughout his body. The final piece of the medical puzzle would have been the location of the gunshot wounds—in his abdomen. The shotgun pellets would have destroyed the muscles of the abdominal wall, releasing dead tissue into the bloodstream, thereby further burdening the already overworked kidneys and hastening the onset of renal failure. The accumulation of all this bodily trauma and organ damage would have been too much even for a young, healthy man to overcome. During George White's final five days, even as he seemed to be rallying, his body was actually shutting down. Without antibiotics, intravenous fluids, and kidney dialysis, George White was a goner. This is the medical explanation for how George White could seem to be on the road to recovery one day and dead just twelve hours later.[20]

The patient breathed his last just before dawn on Friday, August 8. His adopted mother was by his side at the end, murmuring endearments that he could not hear while tears streamed down her face. Also present was Dr. Cravens who had taken over from Dr. Beall sometime during the previous six days. Mostly the treatment had consisted of little more than maintaining a bedside vigil since there was nothing in either his repertoire or little black bag to help. Afterwards, Cravens submitted an un-itemized bill of $40 to the county for his services. The request for payment was dutifully noted in the minutes of commissioners' court in November 1879, but there is no record the bill was ever paid.[21]

On August 8 the body was prepared for burial and placed on the evening train to Fort Worth. An escort composed of his "step-parents," public officials, and fellow officers escorted the body. That same day, friends and colleagues in Fort Worth began taking up a collection to defray funeral expenses since they knew neither the county nor city covered such contingencies.

Funerals in those days took place quickly because without refrigeration and with the state of the embalming arts, corpses soon started to ripen. The only solution was to get the deceased in the ground as soon as possible. George White's funeral took place the next day, but that was plenty of time for word to get around the small town. The service was at the McPhail residence on Weatherford, and following the wishes of the deceased, it was "conducted under the auspices of the Fort Worth Fire Department." White, it would seem, considered himself a fireman first and a police officer second, although he had died performing his duties as a deputy marshal. Following tradition, the city's fire bell was tolled announcing the public funeral. No one had to ask for whom the bell tolled. An impressive cortege escorted the body from the McPhails' to Pioneers Rest Cemetery. Fire Chief Walter Maddox served as parade marshal. A year later he would be elected Tarrant County sheriff, showing once again the close relationship between firemen and peace officers. The hearse was at the front of the cortege followed by the carriage holding the family. The M. T. Johnson Hook and Ladder Company and the Panther Engine Company furnished an honor guard. Carriages full of friends and well-wishers brought up the rear. At the graveside, the Reverend W. W. Brimm of First Presbyterian Church said "a few appropriate remarks."[22]

The next day the *Democrat* offered the following eulogy:

All that remained of a mother's joy,
And all that was left of a hero boy,
Was lowered in a desolate grave.
Many a tear was shed,
Many a sigh was heard.[23]

With George White barely cold in the ground, attention turned to George Alford. The charge against him was upgraded to murder just as soon as the grand jury met. The case was assigned to district court, meaning County Attorney W. S. Pendleton would prosecute. Tarrant and Parker counties were part of the same judicial district at that date, so Judge A. J. Hood of Weatherford was the presiding judge. The accused seemed to have no trouble engaging defense counsel. His defense team was the respected Fort Worth firm of Edward Hovenkamp, J. M. Thomason, and Henry M. Furman. They immediately filed a series of motions seeking to get the case tossed out on technical grounds. First, they attacked the arrest warrant, pointing out that it had been issued for "John Smith" not Tom Alford, Alford's name was misspelled "Olferd," and there was no description of the wanted man. They also raised questions about the deceased's status as a lawman. At the time White executed the warrant he was not an officer of the court. As a member of the Fort Worth Police Department he had no jurisdiction in Arlington, and since he had never been sworn in as a deputy sheriff, he was not therefore authorized to execute the warrant in question. On the morning of August 2, Sheriff Henderson simply handed him the paperwork and told him to bring in Tom Alford. The casual way the warrant was served would not have mattered if White had not gotten into a gun battle that resulted in criminal assault and murder, which brought the lawyers swarming around like bees on a honeycomb. Furthermore, White's title, "deputy marshal," was not recognized by the State of Texas, and not even Marshal Sam Farmer's testimony that White was a "regularly sworn in" deputy marshal altered that fact. The trial had not even started and already the state's case against George Alford was looking bad.[24]

The county attorney argued that such technicalities were nit-picking, but that argument was not going to win a conviction. Criminal cases were often lost on such nitpicking details. The state could not even produce a signed commission proving that George White was a duly constituted officer of the FWPD. Apparently his commission had gotten lost or misfiled if he ever had one. Now there was only Sam Farmer's word for it. Once again, sloppy paperwork had taken a bite out of the state's case. If George White had not been a duly appointed officer of the law, then the arrest of Tom Alford was illegal.

White's testimony at the preliminary hearing was introduced into evidence by the prosecution. Now the holes in that statement, specifically, not knowing Tom Alford on sight and how many shots he had fired in the gun battle, were gleefully exploited by the defense. The county attorney had not attempted to clean up White's statement at the hearing, merely entered it into the record. Now that statement was turned on the prosecution. If it had been a true "dying declaration," it would have been given a lot more latitude, but since George White lived long enough afterwards to be deposed or even to modify his statement upon further reflection, it did not have the weight of a dying declaration in a court of law.

It finally took the connivance of Judge Hood to save the state's case. He did not do anything illegal, but in his instructions to the jury, he completely ignored the question of the defendant's "right of resistance to illegal arrest." When the jury retired to begin its deliberations, jurors had to balance their sympathy for the victim with the letter of the law. First they had to decide whether George Alford was a murderer or a wrongly accused man whose only "crime" was defending himself against arbitrary and unlawful arrest. They finally came down on the side of the victim, disregarding all the legal technicalities to answer the question with their hearts: Deputy White had been killed in the line of duty.

What was not so easy to set aside was the matter of the "remarkable resemblance" between the defendant and his brother Mace. The defense had posed the question, "How does the state know *which* Alford brother to charge with murder?" The answer: it doesn't. Defense counsel backed that up with George White's own testimony. The jury could not help but wonder whether the state even had the right man on trial. Here again jurors gave the benefit of the doubt to the victim. Twelve good men convicted George Alford of murder even in the face of strong evidence to the contrary. The outcome was not surprising since the victim had been a likable young deputy and, as the appeals court subsequently noted, "but few [accused] persons come clear [i.e., are acquitted] before Tarrant County juries."[25]

The defense appealed the verdict to the State Court of Criminal Appeals, which reversed the decision, mainly on the grounds that the arrest warrant had been invalid and that White was not properly authorized to execute *any* warrant that day. After knocking the legs out from under the state's case, the Court ruled that trying to execute an unlawful arrest warrant was what provoked the shootout, and therefore George Alford was not criminally liable for defending himself *nor* his brother Tom for trying to escape. The Court of Criminal Appeals ordered George Alford released, thereby delivering a judicial TKO to the prosecution and to George White's memory. The lawman-hero had become a de facto vigilante. The state did not attempt to retry Alford.

In the court of public opinion, however, George White remained a genuine hero who had died in the line of duty. During his brief tenure as a lawman, he had served not wisely but well. The Appeals Court's ruling that he was not "an officer of the law" at the time he was killed did not lessen him in the eyes of his fellow citizens. The missteps that led to his death were air-brushed out of the picture.

Making the whole thing more tragic, it was all so unnecessary. The deaths of two men, a murder charge against a third, and two family names blackened, all resulting from a questionable bill of sale for the inconsequential sum of $17.50. But then this was Texas where horseflesh and legal ownership of same had always been matters of life and death.

If the state could not get George Alford, it would go after Tom Alford—not that he did not deserve it. The Tarrant County grand jury indicted him on October 3, 1879, for horse stealing. The animal in question was the same little mare than had caused George White's death two months earlier. The district court, Judge A. J. Hood again, issued a writ of capias on February 21, 1880, but by then Alford had skipped the county. Additional writs followed on November 18 and December 5, 1882. The man charged with executing these latest warrants was Tarrant County Sheriff Walter P. Maddox who accomplished what George White had not been able to do, bringing in Tom Alford on December 21, 1882. A JP court set bail at $1,200, which he promptly posted with the help of friends. Two months later County Attorney Pendleton asked the district court to dismiss all charges because Charlie McCafferty had moved out of the county and could not be located. Thus, the horse-stealing accusation that had started the whole affair ended not with a bang of a gavel but with a fizzle.[26]

That should have been the end of it, but the Alford boys could not seem to stay out of trouble. On January 10, 1883, George and Tom were arrested yet again, this time accused of starting a fire at the Arlington home of Kenneth Anderson Newton then using the ensuing confusion to steal a trunk containing $300 in gold coins and greenbacks. The indictments that followed said Tom had masterminded the scheme but George had executed it, delivering the loot to his brother. The boys knew about the trunk and its contents because their sister Susan was married to Newton's son, and the opportunity was there because Newton's place was just seven miles from the Alford farm. According to the indictment, they set the fire on the night of November 4, 1882, then absconded with the trunk while Newton and his neighbors were putting out the blaze. Adding a surreal quality to the crime, apparently George had stolen a horse to carry off the trunk.[27]

The whole thing was almost too fantastic to be believed, which explains why the case proved difficult to prosecute. But the county attorney was not discouraged from taking another run at the Alfords, perhaps hoping the third time would be the charm. He found himself playing a weak hand again. Neither the trunk nor the money had been recovered, and no one had actually witnessed the crime being committed. On top of that, both Alfords had alibis for the night of November 4. With no witnesses and no evidence, the state's case was entirely circumstantial, and it seemed to many observers that the it was not facts but a personal vendetta against the defendants that was driving the prosecution.

The case was heard in the Seventeenth District Court with R. E. Beckham, the former mayor and county judge of Fort Worth, presiding. By the time the case came to trial in 1885, most of the state's twenty-five witnesses were either scattered or unable to recall crucial details. County officials seemed almost obsessed with getting the Alfords this time. When witnesses proved problematic, County Attorney V. R. Bowlin asked for a continuance. His successors continued to ask for continuances in the forlorn hope that someone—anyone—would come forward. The case remained open until January 22, 1913, long after there was the least chance of prosecuting it. County Attorney Ben Baldwin finally put it to rest, dismissing all charges. The Alfords had been in and out of the legal system for thirty-four years without ever being convicted of anything. Every case against them was derailed on legal technicalities. If George White had known all this back in 1879, perhaps he would never have volunteered to serve that first warrant.[28]

Postscript

A few years ago, when names were being gathered for the Fort Worth Police and Firefighters' Memorial, the old controversy was resurrected, i.e., whether George White's was a "line of duty" death. The same old arguments deployed by the state and the defense at George Alford's trial were revived, but this time the adjudicator was the Memorial committee, which came down on the side of Officer White. He finally got a measure of justice.

George White's case illustrates the gray area that nineteenth century peace officers operated in and the casual attitude they often took toward procedure. Men like George White and Joseph M. Henderson believed that a badge was all the authority they needed to bring in the bad guys. Bench warrants and proper jurisdiction were just legal formalities. Public opinion largely accepted this way of doing things. It was only when the lawyers got involved that problems arose. Buckley B. Paddock, editor of the *Fort Worth Democrat*, delivered a "State of the City" address in May 1876 that had a lot to say about law and order. Speaking for his fellow citizens, Paddock assured Marshal Courtright and his men that it was not necessary for them to have a warrant in hand or even personally witness a crime in order to place a man under arrest. All they needed was the word of a "creditable person" that a crime had been committed. And if they needed any help carrying out their duties, they could always follow the English common law practice of summoning a posse comitatus. The only warning Paddock laid down for the men with the badges was that officers should never usurp the "judicial powers" of the courts. He concluded, "The law protects the officer fully in the discharge of his duty, and will only hold him responsible for a malicious infraction of his powers."[29]

The average citizen never thought to question the authority behind the badge until something went terribly wrong. Then the courts had to try to clean up the mess and dispense a measure of justice that satisfied both the letter of the law and the sentiments of the community. In George White's case, everybody lost.

George White is buried in Pioneers Rest Cemetery, all alone with no family around him because he was living apart from his family and a bachelor when he died. This marker was installed by the Fort Worth Police Officers Association in 2002. (Photograph by Kevin Foster)

CHAPTER 4

DEPUTY MARSHAL WILLIAM T. WISE

October 2, 1884

Tis done, a noble soul is sent
To the land of Heavenly Glory;
A brave detective low is laid
By hands all red and gory.[1]

Five years passed before another local officer died in the line of duty. Once again the case involved a question of jurisdiction: What business does a Fort Worth deputy marshal have joining a Mississippi manhunt? That deputy marshal was William Wise who became the first Fort Worth or Tarrant County officer to die while performing his duties in another state. His death in Mississippi on October 2, 1884, rippled through the ranks of lawmen back home impacting the careers of legendary Fort Worth officers T. I. Courtright and William Rea.

Courtright's tenure as city marshal had ended in 1879, and the voters rejected him when he made one more run in 1881, but he was still part of the close-knit law enforcement fraternity. In October 1884 Marshal Rea tapped him to be acting marshal while Rea went to Mississippi to help track down William Wise's murderer. Courtright's temporary appointment received the council's blessing at the same October 7 meeting where the council granted Rea a two-week leave of absence to go to Mississippi. He was on an eastbound train the next morning.[2]

Why the city marshal of Fort Worth felt obliged to join a Mississippi manhunt and why city fathers gave him permission is one of the more curious stories in the history of Fort Worth law enforcement. Rea wanted to catch Wise's killer for personal as much as professional reasons. The Deputy's widow was the Marshal's favorite niece, Dora James, and he was not going to sit by idly while the killer was free. Law enforcement in those days was often a family affair (see the Earps), making it important to know who the outlaws *and* the in-laws were.

William Terry Wise was born November 2, 1861, in Johnson County, Texas, where his parents had moved from South Carolina. By the time he was eighteen, young Bill was living on his own in Johnson County engaged in farming. The nearest "big city" was Fort Worth. On December 21, 1882, he married eighteen-year-old Dora James of Tarrant County, born Dora Alice Boydston on November 24, 1863. Despite her youth, Dora was already a widow when they wed, having married J. T. James in 1879. James was killed before they had been married even a year, whereupon she returned to her family until marrying Wise. William and Dora had a daughter on August 11, 1884. whom they named William Virgia after her father, calling her "Willie." She would be not even two months old when her father was killed and Dora was widowed for the second time in her young life.[3]

William Wise may have been a rookie cop, but he was not just any rookie. He was the Fort Worth Police Department's (FWPD's) first plainclothes detective, which was not an official rank at the time but a position created just for him by Marshal Rea, his wife's uncle. The family connection explains how young Bill was able to make the jump from farming to law enforcement and start out as the second-in-command in the Fort Worth Police Department.

The only description we have of Deputy Wise comes from the fanciful "Ballad of Dock [*sic*] Bishop," a ditty composed in 1886 to memorialize not the victim but the man who did the dirty deed! The ballad describes Wise in almost effeminate terms, as having "soft, brown, shining eyes, [with] gold brown hair o'er-lying." We are told nothing about his height or build, only that his face showed "daring courage," which was sufficient to redeem him as a man's man.[4]

This reputed picture of Doc Bishop, ca. 1884, shows an undistinguished young man who looks more like a simple farmer than a cold-blooded killer. Looks can be deceiving! (Collections of Kevin Foster)

The rookie had a lot of responsibility resting on his shoulders. For whatever reason he did it, Bill Rea was breaking new ground when he created the position of detective. There is no record that he consulted the city council first, but as a company man Rea would probably have run it past the council's three-man police committee. As a growing city, Fort Worth needed something more than another cop walking another beat. More to the point, his nephew needed a job and Fort Worth needed a detective. The 1885–86 city directory shows that it was no secretive, in-house move, listing William Wise as a "detective" in the Department not merely a "deputy marshal" as the newspapers were calling him.[5]

Wise thus became one of a new breed of Western lawmen. The position of detective was relatively new to the West, signaling the growing importance of the investigative side of law enforcement. The old days when the town marshal knew virtually every "hard case" in his jurisdiction ended when frontier towns became full-blown cities full of anonymous strangers. In the New West, law enforcement demanded smarts as well as toughness and a personal acquaintance with everyone in the community.

At a time when every other man on the force was required to wear the blue uniform, Bill Wise was Fort Worth's first "plain-clothes" officer. His exact job description, if he ever had one, is unknown. Judging by contemporary newspaper accounts, however, there was not a lot of investigative work to be done at this early date. By and large, crime in small-town Fort Worth was still pretty uncomplicated. His principal job was delivering "wanted" prisoners to other jurisdictions or bringing back wanted men from other jurisdictions to Fort Worth. Historically, that had been the sheriff's job, but Wise gave the FWPD that same capability for the first time. The officer who drew such a job had to be sharp and capable of working independently. Fortunately, Bill Wise had a good head on his shoulders and was a quick study. His uncle must have been proud of him.

In September 1884, Detective Wise delivered a murder suspect to Oxford, Mississippi, "on requisition" (extradition). It was a routine job up to the point where he handed his prisoner over to Lafayette County Sheriff P. E. Matthews. Then opportunity knocked when Matthews invited the Fort Worth lawman to join a manhunt already in progress for a pair of no-goods wanted for murder and rumored to be hiding out nearby. What convinced Wise to throw in was the reward money, a share of which he stood to collect if they got their man.

The "wanted" men were Doc Bishop and Robert Lamar, accused of killing brothers William and Evans Harmon at Dallas, Mississippi, on January 16, 1884. On top of the potential reward money, Wise had a second reason for hanging around: two long-time Texas fugitives, John B. Swofford and Allen Marksbury, were reportedly in the neighborhood. That pair had been on the lam from Texas since 1877, wanted in Bosque County for the murder of J. G. Dixon on July 21, 1876. After being tried and sentenced to hang, they escaped and had not been seen around Texas since. Now, rumor placed them in Hancock County, Mississippi, and since there was a reward of $250 on each fugitive's head, Wise thought he would stick around and maybe collect three rewards.[6]

Later chroniclers would claim that Wise believed Bishop and Lamar to be the same pair as Swofford and Marksbury under different aliases, but that explanation does not hold water because Bishop and Lamar were well-known by their Mississippi neighbors.

Wise was not doing anything unethical trying to collect multiple rewards. On the contrary, he was careful to follow the letter of the law by furnishing all the necessary paperwork. He could only arrest the two Texas fugitives in Mississippi with the cooperation of the authorities there, and he could only secure their cooperation if he brought the necessary "requisition papers" from Texas. That is why he initially told Sheriff Matthews he had to go back to Texas before he could join the Bishop-Lamar manhunt. He was also motivated by the larger reward on Swofford's and Marksbury's heads. Bishop and Lamar were the sideshow for him.

As it turned out, Swofford and Marksbury were not in Mississippi, and Wise made a return trip to Texas for nothing. He did not learn this until he was back in Mississippi, making him all the more determined to get some return on the time and effort he had invested, so he joined the Bishop-Lamar manhunt in progress.

The joker in the deck was Doc Bishop, a far more dangerous character than either Swofford or Marksbury. Twenty-seven-year-old Bishop had been born in Manor County, Alabama, on October 27, 1857. He grew up to be a strapping man, six-foot-two inches tall and tipping the scales at over 200 pounds. His dark eyes bored into anybody he turned his attention on, and with his coal-black hair parted down the middle and the black clothes he habitually wore, he looked very much like an undertaker. He even wore black boots, which he kept highly polished. All in all, he was an impressive specimen of manhood and not to be trifled with. Anyone who crossed him did so at their own peril.

In 1884 the blight of civil war and reconstruction still lay heavily on northern Mississippi. Times were hard and money was scarce, but Mississippians made the best of what they had, enjoying simple pleasures such as community hoedowns. One night the citizens of Sarepta held a square dance attended by everyone who had a pair of dancing shoes and could get there. One of those in attendance was Abner Cearley, a big, strong man who was likeable when sober but mean as a snake when he got a few drinks under his belt. On the night of the dance, he had been drinking all day, so he was looking to kick up his heels and raise a little Cain, too.

Another attendee at the square dance was Doc Bishop who was popular with the local girls despite his occasional boorish ways and habitually dressing all in black like an undertaker. On this particular night he was dancing with one of the prettiest girls in Sarepta when they do-si-doed past Ab Cearley, who took a notion to pick a fight, spitting a stream of tobacco juice onto Bishop's shiny boots. Doc ignored the insult until Cearley did it again, splattering tobacco juice this time on his boots and pants both. Bishop forgot all about dancing and challenged the other man to step outside. They did, and the ensuing melee ended with Cearley flat on his back, a bullet from Bishop's pistol through his shoulder. At that point, Bishop was willing to drop it, but not Cearley. He would not be satisfied until he had his revenge, which is how those Southern blood feuds usually got started. A few weeks after the dance, on January 16, Bishop went to the general store in Dallas accompanied by his cousin Jim Bishop and a friend, Robert Lamar. Who should be there at the same time but Ab Cearley. Both men initially expressed a willingness to put the feud behind them, sealing the truce with a handshake.

After the Bishop party exited the store, however, things took a bizarre turn. The Bishops and Lamar started firing their pistols into the air for no apparent reason. The noise drew Cearley outside and he was struck by one of the shots. Fearing that they had killed him, the three shooters jumped on their horses but before they could ride off they noticed the victim was not dead, just wounded in the leg. They dismounted and were headed back into the store when two brothers, William and Evans Harmon, arrived on the scene.

The Harmons were not allies of either side and tried to intervene, beseeching the Bishop men to get back on their horses and leave. Taking offense at their uninvited interference, the Bishops and Lamar now opened fire on the Harmons who had only one small pistol between the two of them. Even that did them no good. The three shooters fired indiscriminately, hitting each of the Harmons in the head and bystander Alexander Harrison in the face. There were now four men on the ground.

Doc Bishop and Bob Lamar decided to leave before the law arrived while Jim Bishop, to his credit, stayed behind to do what he could for the wounded men. The Harmons were beyond help. Harrison would live. Bishop and Lamar were now fugitives from justice. They went into hiding, staying with friends or relatives for a night or two before moving on to their next hideout. Weeks went by, and local law officers were no closer to catching them.

That was when Detective William Wise showed up in town and introduced himself to Sheriff Matthews and was invited to join the manhunt. Wise hurried back to Austin, Texas, to get extradition papers for Swofford and Marksbury, then for some unfathomable reason he came back to Mississippi posing as a wealthy Texas cattle buyer. The only possible reason for the charade was not to alert Bishop's and Lamar's friends to avoid the sort of legal complications that had arisen on previous occasions when Texas lawmen went out of state to get their man. Sometimes Texas officers took their man by main force riding roughshod over legal formalities.[7] As a result, fugitive-chasing Texas lawmen were not always welcome in other states, and the Texans were leery of announcing their presence when they arrived.

Another part of Wise's masquerade was lodging with John A. Matthews, an English-born resident of Sarepta who was eccentric and may or may not have been related to the Sheriff. All things considered, Wise's charade as a rich Texas cattleman and his choice of roommates were not well calculated to keep a low profile. Still, his modus operandi seemed to work at first. After only a few days in town he believed he had won Jim Bishop's confidence and persuaded him to betray his cousin in return for a share of the reward money.

Having given up on Swofford and Marksbury, Wise was hoping to bring in Bishop and/or Lamar singlehandedly and collect all the reward money for himself. He would not even have to share it with his superiors back in Texas. Yet he continued to commit one mistake after another. Apparently he had never heard the old saw that two can keep a secret *if one of them is dead* because he let his roommate in on his plan. The Englishman agreed to help capture Bishop and Lamar, probably for the same reason as Jim Bishop – the reward money. Together Wise and Matthews devised a plan to have Jim Bishop deliver a bottle of whiskey, heavily drugged, to his cousin. After Doc Bishop was out cold, Wise would swoop in and seize him. As they refined their plan they borrowed from the story of Hansel and Gretel: Wise would track Jim Bishop to Doc's hideout by following scraps of newspaper dropped by Jim along the trail. The plan was too clever by half, with Wise putting too much trust in Jim Bishop to betray his blood kin for "thirty pieces of silver." As events played out, it was never clear whether Jim Bishop was a pawn in Wise's game or a co-conspirator with his cousin in a murder scheme.

On the night of October 2, Jim Bishop began his ride to his cousin's hideout, carrying the whiskey and the newspaper. Wise came along behind, following the paper trail, never suspecting that the paper trail led not to Doc Bishop but to an ambush. Five miles southeast of Sarepta on a narrow, country road that wound through the red clay hills, he was bushwhacked by someone hiding in the woods. Folks living nearby heard a volley of gunfire, then a man's scream. Their testimony afterwards would mention both shotgun blasts and pistol shots. When Detective Wise did not show up in town the next day, concerned citizens sent to Oxford for the sheriff.

Even before organizing a search party, Sheriff Matthews sent the following telegram to Tarrant County Sheriff Walter Maddox:

Oxford, Miss.–October 3–I am reliably informed that W. T. Wise was waylaid and killed in an adjoining county, last night. Body not found. P. E. Matthews, Sheriff

Matthews and his posse made a thorough search of the wooded area where the shots had been heard. One sharp-eyed member of the group noticed clods of freshly turned red clay beside a log that his horse had stepped over. He dismounted to investigate, brushing away the dirt and leaves from the suspicious-looking spot. Underneath he found a freshly dug grave. The posse halted, broke out shovels, and got to work. It only took a few moments to unearth the mangled, bullet-riddled corpse of William Wise, buried just two feet below the surface. They returned to Sarepta with the body wrapped in a blanket but without a single suspect in custody.

After a pro forma inquest ruled that Wise had been murdered, the body was placed in a rough pine box for interment in the Sarepta Cemetery. A perfunctory service took place the next day. William Wise deserved better, but apparently, no one cared about honoring the dead officer or going to the trouble of shipping the corpse home for a proper burial.

Three days later, still with no clues and no suspects, Sheriff Matthews sent another telegram to Fort Worth, this one addressed to Marshal William Rea, Detective Wise's boss:

Oxford, Mississippi, Oct. 7, 1884—W. M. Rea, City Marshal, Fort Worth; W. T. Wise was killed October 2. His body was found on the 3rd and buried at Sarepta on the 4th. Don't know particulars, but he is supposed to have been murdered for his money. Two parties arrested, but turned loose for want of proof. Come at once.
P. E. Matthews, Sheriff

Matthews' second telegram is remarkable for its inaccuracies and unanswered questions. First, the claim that Wise was murdered for his money, making it a simple highway robbery, was preposterous. Second, who the two men under arrest were and why they were suspects in the first place called for some explanation. Instead, the telegram revealed a criminal investigation that was completely clueless. Marshal Rea decided that the only thing to do was go to Mississippi in person and conduct his own investigation. He would have to tread lightly if he hoped to have the full cooperation of the local boys when he got to Calhoun County.

Meanwhile, the Bishops and Lamar were having their own problems. Despite their status as local boys versus Wise the outsider trying to hunt them down, they found themselves on the wrong side of popular sentiment. An intense manhunt was still underway when Marshal Rea, accompanied by several of his deputies, arrived a few days later. "Longhair Jim" Courtright was not among those deputies although Rea would have been glad to have him. Unfortunately, Courtright at this time was facing extradition to New Mexico to answer murder charges for two coldblooded killings in May 1883. In the middle of October, while Courtright's pal and mentor was in Mississippi chasing down Bill Wise's killers, a New Mexico sheriff and a pair of Texas Rangers showed up in Fort Worth with an arrest warrant for "Longhair Jim."[8]

Back in Mississippi, the Lone Star visitors were soon on chummy terms with local lawmen, but to the public they remained "the men from Texas," slightly mysterious and all business. In the years that followed, local lore transformed them into fearful vigilantes or even bogeymen. Rea and his boys brought some of it on themselves

Chief William Rea as he appeared in 1901. This legend in Fort Worth law enforcement may have looked like Santa Claus, but he was tough as nails. Seventeen years before this photo was taken, Bill Wise was Rea's nephew-in-law and chief deputy. It is no surprise that Rea made it a personal challenge to bring Doc Bishop to justice. (Collections of Kevin Foster)

by eavesdropping on private conversations in saloons, listening at the windows and doors of Bishop relatives, and even breaking down doors at night to question the owners at gunpoint and search the premises. These were unconventional methods for Bill Rea who was known back home as a law-abiding officer, but these were extraordinary circumstances and the Fort Worth men could not just hang around Sarepta hoping something turned up. They were working on a deadline and were determined not to return home empty-handed when their time was up.

In the end, it may have been the Texans' brutal methods that did the trick, turning up the heat until the Bishops and Lamar finally turned themselves in, reportedly as worried about their families' safety as their own. All three suspects steadfastly denied that they had murdered Wise. Despite their protestations, they were arraigned and held without bail for trial.

All three men had multiple charges hanging over their heads— first for the Harmon brothers and then for William Wise. They were tried separately in the Circuit Court for Calhoun County. Jim Bishop went first, charged with two counts of murder plus being an accomplice in another (Wise's). He was acquitted on all charges, although the verdict outside the courtroom was "guilty," not for committing murder but for betraying his cousin to the Texas detective.[9]

Robert Lamar was tried next and convicted of murder in the Harmon case, but the conviction was appealed and eventually overturned on technical grounds. The state chose not to retry him. As for Doc Bishop, in his first trip through the justice system, he too was acquitted of murdering the Harmons.[10]

He still had to answer for the murder of William Wise, and that trial did not have a happy ending for him. Either he drew a tougher jury his second time around or it took the state three tries to pin Wise's murder on somebody. It did not help that the first trial was still fresh in the public's mind and that the defendant was now being characterized as "a dangerous and criminally inclined man."[11]

Doc Bishop's second trial got underway on March 12, 1886. The prosecution's leading witness was John Matthews, who revealed the details of the plan to capture Bishop. In rebuttal, the defense produced witnesses who testified that Doc was at home "under the bed" [sic] that night, so he could not have been involved in any killing. Following an intense legal battle stretching over four days, the jury took just four hours to find Bishop guilty of the murder of William Wise. They had not bought his alibi or the supporting witnesses' testimony.[12]

After the judge read the verdict, he asked Bishop if he had anything to say before sentence was pronounced. When the defendant remained silent, the judge intoned the classic pronouncement in such cases: "Doc Bishop, you will be hanged by the neck until you are dead, dead, dead, and may the Lord have mercy on your soul."[13] The execution date was set for April 16, 1886, but that date came and went while the appeal process was playing out. After the appeal was denied, the date of execution was reset for July 3, 1886. Only a pardon or stay of execution from the governor could save Bishop now, and no one anticipated either of those.[14]

On the night before the execution, Doc finally accepted his fate and found religion. At his request he was baptized into the Episcopal Church for remission of his sins. The "new" Doc Bishop thanked his friends for their support, as well as his attorneys, the jailer, the sheriff, and the sheriff's deputies; in fact, he had a few kind words for everyone involved in the case except the victim! He then wrote a final letter, which did not become public until several days later. In it, he revealed that he had tried to kill himself in jail by taking an overdose of morphine, but when that failed he prepared himself for the gallows. He did not reveal who had slipped him the morphine or how he had survived the suicide attempt, nor did he insist on his innocence for the umpteenth time.[15]

The Calhoun County Board of Supervisors scheduled a public hanging, which was still the norm in the deep South. The spot that was selected was in a valley two miles west of Pittsboro where the Pittsboro and Big Creek roads intersected. The site, at the head of a little hollow, was a natural amphitheater with tree-covered, earthen banks on three sides surrounding a gallows of large, squared timbers special-built for the occasion. A brand-new hemp rope hung from the crossbeam. When July 3 arrived, more than 2,000 people assembled to witness the hanging of Doc Bishop. They watched in silence as the drama unfolded. Just before the appointed hour, a small, open wagon came down the Pittsboro Road. In it rode the Calhoun County sheriff, his deputies, and the shackled prisoner. It also held the black-draped wooden coffin in which Bishop would soon be laid to rest.[16]

Dismounting from the wagon, Sheriff Scott Hardin led the way up the steps of the scaffold with Doc Bishop following. The prisoner's hands were tightly bound, but he had not been hooded yet. When he reached the platform, Bishop was positioned over the trap door where he stood staring out at the crowd while the final arrangements were made. There was an attending minister, of course, who prayed for the forgiveness of the sins of all present, but especially Doc Bishop. Then the prisoner was allowed to say a few last words. He stepped to the front of the platform and said his farewells in a firm voice. One last time, he thanked all those who had befriended him and said he felt no malice toward any of the officers who had brought him to that place. With almost his last breath, Bishop declared that he was innocent of the death of Detective Wise, that he would not even know the officer if he were to appear before him at that instant. But Bishop did confess to another, unrelated murder: a man in Alabama whose death had never been linked to him until now. It was a strange confession, to say that he was innocent yet not innocent.[17] Having said his piece, he stepped back onto the trap and nodded to the sheriff.

That officer, as designated executioner, slipped a black hood over the prisoner's head, then placed the noose around his neck and snugged the knot up under one ear so that it would snap his neck when he dropped. The crowd seemed to hold its collective breath as Sheriff Hardin raised the hatchet over the taut rope where it stretched across a stump to the trap door mechanism. At 1:44 p.m. Hardin swung the hatchet high over his head and brought it down on the rope. Nothing happened; the sturdy hemp resisted the dull blade. He hesitated a moment, then took a second mighty swing, which did the job. The trap door swung free, and Bishop's body shot downward until it jerked to a stop with the sound of a sharp *snap*. The body twisted slowly in a circle with barely a twitch—a smooth execution that caused no undue suffering.[18]

A last bizarre twist was added to the story after Bishop's body was cut down and placed in a coffin. According to local lore, a woman dressed all in black came out of the crowd accompanied by a couple of men and asked the sheriff for the rope used in the hanging. "I was the wife of Detective W. T. Wise, and these men are my brothers," she explained. Apparently, Dora had come all the way from Texas to witness the execution and wanted to take a memento home with her. Wise-Boydston family lore, however, says that the rope and some of her husband's clothes saved by Sheriff Hardin were sent back to the widow in Texas via Bill Rea. Dora carefully placed the items for safekeeping in a trunk, which a subsequent daughter avoided like the plague. Either way, the episode makes a morbid finale to the hanging of Doc Bishop.[19]

But it does not wrap up the Doc Bishop story. In death he achieved some sort of perverse fame as the first white man *legally* hanged in the state of Mississippi since the Civil War.[20] Public opinion also underwent a sea change after his death, perhaps related to the successful appeals of his two co-defendants, Jim Bishop and Bob Lamar. The townspeople of Sarepta began to believe that perhaps poor Doc had been wrongly convicted after all, that his reputation as a "dangerous man," not the evidence, had gotten him hanged. A local citizen, Dottie Moore of Pontotoc County, even composed a folk song, "The Ballad of Dock Bishop" in a variation on the more famous "Ballad of Sam Bass" and "Ballad of Jesse James." At least Dottie Moore's ode did not attempt to portray its subject as a tarnished hero or a good-boy-gone-bad. Doc Bishop's "Ballad," with its seemingly endless verses on his trials and tribulations, would be frequently sung at community gatherings for the next fifty years. It is still known today although no longer sung.[21]

Swofford's and Marksbury's names never came up again in connection with Detective Wise's mission to Mississippi. In the years that followed, their connection to the case became so muddled as to permit a variety of explanations, none of them conclusive. The pair remained at large for a few more years before being captured separately in Texas. They had probably never left the state.[22]

Neither the execution of Doc Bishop nor the capture of Swofford and Marksbury closed the book on William Wise's murder. That did not happen for another forty years. On June 3, 1923, John A. Matthews, the Englishman whom Wise had taken into his confidence, was lying on his deathbed and feeling the need to confess his past sins. Principal among those was the murder of William T. Wise. The conscience-stricken Englishman claimed to have been the bushwhacker that night so long ago. He was the unseen figure standing in the shadows, drawing bead on the Detective as he rode past. Unfortunately for the record, Matthews did not explain why his deathbed confession did not completely exonerate Doc Bishop.[23]

Wise's death left Dora a widow for the second time in her twenty-one years. Not only did she have a new infant, but she had no education or job skills; all she knew how to do was "keep house" for her husbands. She could expect no help from the city. At this date, Fort Worth officers were still treated as independent contractors, meaning no pensions or death benefits. Not even Dora's Uncle Bill could soften the hearts of city fathers; it was nothing personal, just the way business was done. Ever resourceful, Dora found the best pension plan possible—another husband. On August 15, 1887, she married thirty-nine-year-old Peter P. McDaniel, himself a widower with five children, who owned a farm in Johnson County. But apparently there was no room for Willie in the McDaniel household because the girl was sent to live with the Boydston family in Cleburne, and they raised her.[24]

Years passed before William Wise finally got some respect, although it was misinformed. A 1942 write-up in the Calhoun City, Mississippi, newspaper described him as "a famous detective," which he was not. For the most part, modern writers who have revisited the crime out of historical curiosity have repeated the old stories without shedding any new light on the case.[25]

The final chapter in William Wise's story was not written until 2002. After he was interred in Sarepta and his widow remarried and moved away, he was forgotten by his hometown. Deputy Wise was not "resurrected" until historians Ron DeLord and Kevin Foster began researching his story for the National Law Enforcement Officers Memorial. Finally, in June 2002, representatives of the Fort Worth Police Department traveled to Sarepta lugging a granite tombstone to install on the grave. A rededication ceremony on June 29 was attended by some 200 locals in addition to two Fort Worth officers and newspaper reporters from near and far. One of the Fort Worth officers said, "The only family he [Wise] has left today is us—police officers."[26] Carved on the new tombstone were these words:

FORT WORTH DEPUTY MARSHAL

W. T. WISE

KILLED IN THE LINE OF DUTY

OCTOBER 2, 1884

William Wise, first detective of record in the Fort Worth Police Department, finally had a fitting memorial.

William Wise's grave marker in Sarepta, Mississippi, was not put down until 2002 by a team of Fort Worth officers who drove the whole distance, taking the headstone with them. The decision had already been made to let the deceased officer stay where he was rather than disinterring him and bringing him back to Fort Worth for re-interment. (Photograph by Kevin Foster)

CHAPTER 5

DEPUTY SHERIFF DICK TOWNSEND

April 3, 1886

"Massacre" at Buttermilk Junction

April 3, 1886, was the single bloodiest day in Fort Worth law enforcement history. Three officers were shot down, one of whom died. The injuries of the others certainly shortened their lives. The fact that the "enemy" was the Knights of Labor, not a gang of criminals, and that the three officers were working as hired guns for Jay Gould's Missouri Pacific Railroad, does not change the fact they were duly commissioned peace officers shot in the line of duty.

The railroad strike that erupted in Texas in the spring of 1886 involved every law enforcement agency in the state before it was over. Fort Worth was one of the centers of the maelstrom that sucked in both big and small fish: Marshal Bill Rea, Sheriff Walter Maddox, and "Longhair Jim" Courtright were some of the big fish; Dick Townsend was one of the small fry.[1]

Outside his small circle of family and friends, thirty-two-year-old Townsend was a relative "nobody" at the time of his death. It took being gunned down during Fort Worth's first organized labor strike to make him a "somebody." Unlike many of his contemporaries who wore a badge, Dick Townsend was not a tough guy. He had never worked as a hired gun, nor was he connected to any of the town's saloons as an owner, dealer, or bouncer, which is not to say he was a saint. He had been hauled into the mayor's court a time or two for illegal gambling, but always as one of the small fry who were assessed nominal fines and released.[2] By 1884 such youthful indiscretions were in his past. Now, he worked in the family business and was a reserve officer with the Fort Worth Police Department (FWPD), waiting for a full-time position on the force to open up. There was no training required to be an "extra" police officer as they were called; it just meant being willing to work for the occasional paycheck, filling in when needed while hoping to get on full time. Truth be told, Townsend was more comfortable with a paintbrush in his hand than a six-gun, and this was the main reason he was not a full-time lawman.

Richard W. Townsend had been born in Logan County, Kentucky, in 1855, the son of James T. and Matilda E. Townsend. His father was a farmer, and Richard had two older brothers, James T., Jr., and Walter B., and a younger sister, Lily. His brothers fought for the Confederacy in the Civil War and came home to the family farm afterwards. When Kentucky struggled during Reconstruction, the family pulled up stakes and moved. They were living in Tarrant County in 1870 with sixty-year-old James, Sr., still farming and forty-year-old Matilda keeping house. Sometime during the next decade papa died. None of the boys had any hankering to be dirt farmers, so Walter packed up and left while Jim and Dick settled in town in Matilda's house at Pecan and Sixth. Neither boy married, although by 1880 Jim was thirty-six and Dick, twenty-five. The boys ran a "sign and ornamental painting" business out of Matilda's house, and since Fort Worth was booming there was plenty of business. They made enough money to live comfortably, but a policeman's salary would still have been a step up for Dick because in addition to the regular pay, there were the fees and occasional outside work.[3]

Dick Townsend seems to have eschewed romance and fraternal organizations in favor of business and family. He did join Fort Worth's volunteer hook-and-ladder company, whether out of a sense of civic responsibility or simply seeking camaraderie is impossible to say. What is certain is that as a volunteer fireman he rubbed elbows with career lawmen like Columbus Fitzgerald and "Longhair Jim" Courtright. It may have been their examples that inspired him eventually to put on a badge. In the meantime, he was drawn into

Courtright's tight circle of friends, even aiding the ex-marshal in his dramatic escape from Fort Worth in October 1884.[4]

By the spring of 1886 Dick Townsend still had not made the leap into law enforcement. He may never have done so, but as tension escalated in the railroad strike, he was pressed into service as a deputy sheriff, joining an assortment of fellow citizens who out of political beliefs or simple desire for a paycheck, signed on to preserve law and order. His rural roots and independent streak made him naturally conservative. Sheriff Maddox deputized the volunteers to augment his overworked regular boys, posting them in the rail yards and around the two train stations (Union and T&P). Dick Townsend was no "scab"—he was a workingman—but he had signed on to do a job, and he intended to do it.

Neither the railroad nor the lawmen that protected its property were too popular about town. The Missouri Pacific was a vast system whose Texas division was known as the Missouri, Kansas and Texas Railway or simply "the Katy." It owned more than 600 miles of track statewide and employed thousands of workers. Fort Worth was one of two centers of the railroad's Texas operations (the other was Marshall). It also happened to be a blue-collar town with nearly a thousand Katy employees living there. The Knights of Labor union represented the interests of the workers against Gould and his minions. The Knights had come to Texas in 1882, and by 1886 there were 213 locals comprising "District Assembly 78," the fourth largest collection of locals in the country. Times were so flush for the union that the Fort Worth local had plans to construct a two-story, brick union hall on lower Rusk and published a union newspaper, the *Labor Educator*.[5]

By the spring of 1886, the union was ready to square off in a war to the death against the powerful Gould interests. Union organizers had been slipping into Fort Worth for months, and the local chapter was collecting an arsenal for an expected clash with scabs or the authorities or both. In April the *Fort Worth Gazette* observed nervously, "The Knights of Labor seem to be stronger than the law in Fort Worth."[6]

While Jay Gould stayed in New York, the local Katy management took a hard-nosed attitude toward the strike. Both sides settled into a tense standoff in the Fort Worth rail yards. Every regular police officer and sheriff's deputy was on duty around the clock, mostly as backup for the railroad's hired guns. Facing them were scores of strikers, every one of them armed and presumably willing to use his weapon.[7] Katy management persuaded Judge R. E. Beckham to issue an injunction prohibiting any member of the union from trespassing on railroad property. Its effect was to move the strikers out of the yards onto the surrounding street and raise the tension level another notch, but the stand-off continued. The laborers' strategy was to blockade all rail traffic into or out of the city to force the railroad to negotiate. As the hostility escalated, Sheriff Walter Maddox, with no more than four or five regular deputies assisted by a small army of deputized citizens, leaned on men he knew he could rely on if shooting erupted: Marshal Bill Rea and ex-marshal "Longhair Jim" Courtright.

On April 3, word came down that Katy officials planned to break the blockade by moving a loaded freight train through the city. The train chosen was the regular coal run from the "Hodge" station (North 23rd Street) in north Fort Worth to Alvarado, south of the city. Learning that the strikers planned to stop it on its way through the city, Sheriff Maddox directed Courtright to collect a detail, meet the train at the city limits on the north side, and escort it all the way down the line to Alvarado. Since the New Mexico charges against "Longhair Jim" had been dismissed in 1885, he had been back in Fort Worth running his private detective agency and occasionally picking up a fee by assisting other lawmen. When the strike came in 1886, he was appointed a deputy U.S. Marshal by Dallas' William Lewis Cabell, Marshal for the Northern District of Texas.[8] He was ready therefore when pressed into service by Sheriff Maddox who felt that a strong show of force was the best way to deter any potential attack on the train. He gave Courtright a free hand to pick his own men and swore them all in as deputies. Their sole job was to protect Katy property, but their Tarrant County commissions meant that technically they were not Katy employees. They took their orders from Courtright who took his orders from Walter Maddox. Courtright and his squad might be riding the same train with the Katy guards, but the two groups were in no way coordinating their actions. This lack of cooperation would come back to haunt all involved.

Sheriff Walter Maddox, looking fit and quite dapper in retirement, years after the Great Strike of 1886. During the strike, Maddox was in charge of local law enforcement, deputizing Dick Townsend and the others who were ambushed at Buttermilk Junction. This was one episode in a long law enforcement career for Maddox. (Courtesy of the Genealogy, History and Archives Unit, Fort Worth Public Library)

Courtright's appointment was not well received by many among the city's working men. They saw the once-popular ex-marshal as a union-buster and goon for the railroad. In response, Mayor John Peter Smith sniffed that "people who violated the law had no right to choose who arrested them." Courtright disregarded the criticism and set about gathering a posse of men he could rely on. The rail-road would have its own train guards, but Courtright did not plan on needing them. His seven bravos would be enough.[9]

Dick Townsend was one of those seven. The rest of the squad consisted of Constable William Hale; Deputy Constable Joe Witcher; fireman Charles H. Sneed; and policemen James W. Thomason, John J. Fulford, and Rowan "Bony" Tucker. In modern parlance they would be described as an "inter-agency task force," but what they really amounted to were "Friends of Jim." Each of them was personally known to Courtright, which is why he knew he could depend on them in a pinch.

From one through seven they were all good men, although not all were veteran officers. Dick Townsend was completely "green," but he was solid. Joe Witcher was a veteran lawman with a scrappy reputa-tion, a member of the Fort Worth Police Department since October

1879. He came from the old school of law enforcement, making up the rules as he went along, answering only to his conscience and occasionally to the city council. Over the years, he had put several blots on his record, including an "aggravated assault and battery" charge that he pleaded out, and more seriously, the assassination of saloon man John Galloway in 1884, which was not prosecuted because witnesses who would testify against him were lacking.[10]

Thirty-year-old Rowan Bonaparte "Bony" Tucker was the son of Judge William Bonaparte Tucker. Junior was exceptionally well-educated by the standards of the day, having attended Mansfield College, and he was a member of the Masons. Therefore it was a surprise to his family when he chose law enforcement over business or the professions. His first law enforcement job was as a deputy sheriff (1878–1884) then he moved over to the Police Department where he seemed to have found a home. Tucker was no trigger-happy gunslinger, but a steady, reliable officer.[11]

Thirty-one-year-old James W. Thomason was a native Louisianan who had come to Fort Worth in 1867. He joined Sheriff Walter Maddox's department in 1880 at the age of twenty-six, then jumped to the Police Department in 1883. He was still a policeman in April 1886 and showed every intention of making a career out of law enforcement. Already he had earned a statewide reputation as "one of the most fearless of peace officers." His fellows regarded him as a man of "unquestioned nerve" who nonetheless was always careful when it came to "handling bad characters." He had never lost a prisoner and never been assaulted by anyone in his custody. His most visible attributes were his bulk, 180 pounds of solid muscle, and habitual cheerfulness. Unfortunately, he was not above squeezing gamblers for a little payola on the side.[12]

Twenty-nine-year-old William Hale had been constable of Precinct No. 1 since 1884, but he was more than just a paper-pushing flunky. He got his start in law enforcement in 1880 as a deputy marshal under Sam Farmer with the Hell's Half-acre red-light district as his beat. He was not afraid to stick his nose into trouble. Seven months into the job, he had tried to intervene in a dispute between two of the district's black denizens and was shot in the face for his efforts. His wounds did not keep him from returning fire, however, and he wounded one of his assailants. Only then did he stumble off to seek medical help for himself. He retired from the police force a year later to become a clerk with the Pacific Express Company, but he soon returned to law enforcement in the less dangerous capacity of constable. Still, having earned his "purple heart," he was just the kind of man "Longhair Jim" wanted at his side if the lead started flying.[13]

John Fulford was the rookie of the group, having been a police officer less than a year. But at thirty-eight years of age, he was also the old-timer in the group and, with a wife and three children, the only other family man besides Courtright. Still, he was every bit as game as the rest. Fulford was the rare officer who managed to live on his police salary alone. Not for him a second job as hired gun or bar bouncer.[14]

The Tennessee-born Sneed was the odd man in the group because he had no experience whatsoever as a lawman. He had never worn a gun or a badge for a living, and he had certainly never been in a shootout. Ordinarily those gaps in his resume would have made him suspect as a deputy, but Courtright had taken the young man under his wing. All Charlie Sneed had ever wanted to be was a fireman, which led him to the M. T. Johnson Hook and Ladder Company and the acquaintance of "Longhair Jim" in 1878. He was considered an "expert" and "efficient" volunteer fireman with ice water flowing in his veins, and also a "clever gentleman," whatever that meant. Courtright obviously had enough faith in him to put him on his escort detail, although he was just twenty-two years in April 1886. Sneed may have been a neophyte deputy, but his place on the squad was not as odd as it might seem. The bonds between firefighters and lawmen have always run deep because both groups are public servants who regularly put their lives on the line for their fellow citizens. When Charlie Sneed pinned on a deputy's badge, the others accepted him because they knew he could "always be depended on when he is wanted."[15]

This "magnificent seven" were brimming with confidence, convinced that their mere presence on the train would overawe any potential troublemakers. Theirs was the natural hubris of men of action, but it also made them careless. There was not a rifle among them; each man was armed only with a six-gun because, as one later explained, "We were not dreading any trouble."[16]

J. W. Thomason (top) and Charlie Sneed (bottom, right) were fellow deputies of Dick Townsend on the Buttermilk Junction train. Unlike Townsend, both men survived and enjoyed long careers in public service. Sneed's photograph is ca. 1896 when he was with the Fort Worth Fire Department. Thomason's photograph is from the 1901 Fort Worth Police Annual (Sneed photograph from Jim Noah Collection courtesy of David Griffin of Fort Worth Fire Deptartment; Thompson photograph courtesy of Fort Worth Police Historical Association)

They might have been more concerned had they seen what others observed that morning. At 10:00 a.m., about the time the blockade-busting train was leaving the yards for Hodge, three men carrying Winchester rifles set out at a trot across the Santa Fe tracks heading west toward Main. A little later, four more men headed purposefully down Main toward the South Side, all four likewise armed with Winchesters.[17]

Knowing nothing about these mysterious armed parties, the Courtright men made their preparations for a little train ride reflecting the absolute confidence of their leader. What should have given the ex-marshal pause, however, was the fact that his bravos were not veteran lawmen. Their law enforcement resumes were alarmingly light. There was a house painter (Townsend), a process server (Hale), a fireman (Sneed), and a green-as-grass rookie (Fulford). Perhaps equally troubling, both Fulford and Sneed were dues-paying members of the Knights of Labor.[18]

The company guards were all local men, too, led by Anderson C. Brandon who had been deputized for the duration of the strike by Marshal Bill Rea. His crew included O. F. "Frank" Darby, J. W. Pemberton, and Joe Witcher who had also been deputized as "special officers" by the city of Fort Worth. Like Courtright's squad, they were also lightly armed. In fact, there was not a single Winchester on the train, just thirteen men armed with revolvers. It was a clear case of poor planning and lack of anticipation, a damning indictment of leadership on the law and order side.

The engine and caboose made an uneventful run up to Hodge where it picked up the coal train and headed back to Fort Worth. At the northern city limits, the train stopped just long enough to pick up Courtright and company. They boarded there rather than in the Katy rail yards to avoid provoking the mob of strike supporters. Courtright placed a man atop each coal car and with the rest, crowded into the locomotives' cab.

Coming back through Fort Worth, the coal train hurried through the rail yards, not stopping at Union Depot. Ordinarily, it would have at least slowed to a crawl through the city, but the guards' plan was to dash right through, not giving the mob a chance to hold them up. When the train got beyond the city limits on the south side of town without trouble, everyone on board breathed a sigh of relief.

About two miles south of town, at a bucolic spot known as Buttermilk Junction (or Buttermilk Switch), where the Missouri Pacific tracks crossed those of the Fort Worth and New Orleans, trouble caught up with them. The train reached the junction about 12:45 p.m. As it approached, the engineer noticed that the switch used to set the right of way had been turned the wrong direction. He would have to stop to change it back. The officers in the cab with him were less interested in the switch than in the group of four men standing behind a pile of ties on the west side of the tracks. They were doing nothing particularly threatening, but there was another group of five lounging on the side of a gully about 100 yards east of the tracks, and they were armed with rifles. That put unidentified, potentially hostile, parties of men on both flanks.

The engineer halted the train, and Courtright told him to stay put while the lawmen investigated. He and the three men in the cab with him (Sneed, Tucker, and Thomason) walked up the tracks to check things out while Townsend, on top of a coal car, stayed where he was, covering the other men on the ground. Courtright's crew marched up to the pile of ties and placed the group of men there under arrest for tampering with railroad property (and probably for being union men).

The arrested men did not seem particularly chagrined at being arrested; on the contrary, they were sullenly defiant. Courtright ordered them back to the train and Townsend kept them covered on the way. Since nobody had thought to bring along any shackles, the prisoners were on good behavior, but it seemed unlikely they would try anything with Townsend looking down from his perch, six-gun in hand.

As Courtright and company were advancing on the second group all hell broke loose. They had left the roadbed and were crossing the open field when Courtright ordered the men on the hillside to surrender, which had the opposite effect than what he intended. Instead of surrendering meekly, they opened fire on the lawmen with no warning. Since the train was directly behind Courtright's party, it was in the line of fire. Dick Townsend, silhouetted against the sky as he covered the men coming up the other side, was the first man hit. He never saw it coming. A .45-60 Winchester slug tore into his back, passing completely through his left lung. The bullet's force spun him half-around before he pitched off the car and landed on his back. Townsend lay on the ground without moving. As soon as the four prisoners saw him fall, they bolted into the brush.[19]

Courtright's party returned fire, but their six-shooters were no match for Winchesters. The action escalated into a full-blown fire-fight as the four escapees found rifles somewhere and opened up from the front and west sides of the train. Twenty-one men were now blazing away at each other. Bullets filled the air like an angry swarm of bees, except that whenever one hit it was followed by a groan rather than a mild yelp of pained surprise. Officer Hale later stated that the bushwhackers were using heavy-caliber ammunition: ".45-60 revolvers [sic] and Winchesters," which they handled "rapidly and well."[20]

The lawmen found themselves caught in a deadly crossfire—outflanked and outgunned. A newspaper reporter had once called "Longhair Jim" Courtright "the luckiest man in the west," someone who could "play hazard with fate and win." It seemed Courtright's luck had run out, and he was taking his crew down with him. They had certainly gotten the worst of it so far, and not just because they were lightly armed; they were out in the open with bull's-eyes painted on them. Instinct took over. They dropped and tried to press themselves into the ground, hoping there were no marksmen among the bushwhackers, but unwilling to risk it by making a dash for the train. In their exposed position it was only a matter of time before they started taking casualties.[21]

John Fulford was the second victim after Dick Townsend—hit twice. He was on his back when one of the heavy-caliber rifle slugs passed through both thighs, shattering bones. He cried out in pain and rolled, which is when another round hit him in the abdomen ranging upward. Even with those horrific injuries he stayed in the fight, emptying his pistol at the bushwhackers before dragging himself to the engine and hoisting himself up into the cab. There he reloaded and continued to blaze away at anything that moved on the hillside. He could not tell if he hit anything; he was just trying to keep them at bay. The third victim was Charlie Sneed, who took a bullet in his jaw near one ear that passed completely through his face obliterating teeth, bone, and muscle, leaving him choking on his own blood. Now, of the deputies on the ground, only Courtright and Thomason remained unhurt. The Winchesters were winning the battle hands down. If the lawmen did not do something fast, it would be a massacre.[22]

In the locomotive's cab, where Fulford was still in the fight, the engineer and fireman ignored him, hugging the bloody floor praying that the hail of bullets would miss them. Mr. Nicewarmer, the fireman, looked up long enough to see another man pull himself painfully into the cab. It was Dick Townsend, seemingly resurrected from the dead. The desperately wounded officer ordered Nicewarmer to take his pistols and use them.

After what seemed an eternity, the company guards had finally joined in, firing away from their perch atop the coal cars. Since the heaviest fire was coming from the hillside, Brandon and his boys directed their fire in that direction. Like Courtright's deputies, they were unable to get a clear shot at the men behind the pile of ties on the other side.

Suddenly, Bony Tucker did something straight out of a dime novel. He had been crouching down beside the engine since the shooting started; now he took off sprinting up the west side of the train, using it as cover against the hillside shooters while blazing away at the men behind the railroad ties, not expecting to hit anything but just to make them keep their heads down. He intended to overrun the shooters behind the ties and disarm them, thereby putting an end to the murderous crossfire. Miraculously, he was not hit, but when he got in front of the train and was out in the open he suddenly had second thoughts. He threw himself to the ground but kept firing.

The massed revolver fire from the train at last began to take effect. Nicewarmer, between squeezing off shots with Townsend's revolvers, risked a peek out of the cab and thought he saw three of the bushwhackers get hit. (It was only two.) The bullet-riddled party of lawmen was showing more fight than the bushwhackers had expected.

Neither side was willing to call off the dogs just yet, however. Two accomplices of the wounded bushwhackers picked up their rifles and continued firing. If the riflemen had pressed their advantage they could have completed what they had begun, although it would have cost them more casualties. Instead, they seemed to lose their stomach for the fight, and after what seemed like an eternity but was in reality no more than fifteen or twenty minutes, they ceased firing and withdrew as mysteriously as they had appeared, escaping into the Sycamore Creek bottom. They took their wounded with them, leaving the bloodied train guards to gather up their own wounded and hightail it back to town.

The "Battle of Buttermilk Junction" was over. One survivor later estimated the number of shots fired during the fifteen-to-twenty-minute firefight at "not less than 100." By comparison, the OK Corral shootout in 1881 took only thirty seconds and seventeen shots were fired.[23] The whipped train guard felt no shame about abandoning the field of battle; the men were just glad to be alive. They loaded their wounded in the caboose and backed the train all the way to the Katy roundhouse, the engineer tugging on the whistle the whole way.[24]

Back in safe surroundings they told their tale of ambush and murder to Sheriff Maddox and Katy officials. No one doubted for a minute that the bushwhackers had been strike sympathizers if not actual members of the Knights of Labor. Sheriff Maddox quickly assembled a posse and galloped out to the junction, but the site was deserted. One of the local newspapers would report that the posse found a body on the hillside, but that was incorrect. All they found was blood-soaked ground and spent shells.

The three wounded officers were still alive when the train got back to town. They were quickly rushed to the nearby hospital. Attending physicians did not expect Townsend or Sneed to live, but they held out hope for Fulford. At 6:00 that night Dick Townsend died.

As soon as the first posse returned from Buttermilk Junction, Sheriff Maddox organized a full-scale manhunt for the five men identified as the Buttermilk Junction bushwhackers: Thomas Nace, a switchman with the Katy; John R. Hardin, a carpenter; and Henry O. Henning, John May, and Charles Dalton, whose backgrounds prior to the spring of 1886 are unknown. Only Dalton among the five was a Fort Worth resident. The rest seem to have arrived in town about the time of the strike and were affiliated in some unspecified capacity with the Knights of Labor. Tom Nace got his name in the newspaper on March 6 after discovering the body of a gambler who apparently had committed suicide in the rail yards, but otherwise, the five had kept a low profile. Their presence in Fort Worth at this particular time, with scant evidence of gainful employment or other ties to the city, suggests that the Fort Worth Five were what the anti-union newspapers called "outside agitators."[25]

Besides these five, there was a sixth, unidentified suspect in the ambush at Buttermilk Junction, distinguished by having just one arm although this handicap had not prevented him from working a Winchester during the gun battle. Afterwards, the sheriff's posse found a farmer living nearby who said that a one-armed man had tried unsuccessfully to talk his way into his home. Although the stranger appeared to be seriously wounded, the farmer had turned him away.[26]

That first posse may have come back empty-handed, but the manhunt scouring the town did considerably better, bagging Tom Nace that same day. He was not been hard to find since he had a bullet in his leg and a shattered femur.[27] His friends had slipped him back into town long enough to drop him off at his house before making their own getaway. His wife summoned Dr. James L. Cooper, a jack-of-all-trades physician, druggist, and surgeon whose office-residence happened to be nearby. Cooper did what he could to dress the nasty wound and left after being sworn to silence. About 4:00 p.m., officers showed up on Nace's doorstep and pushed their way into the house. They found him lying helplessly in a world of pain and placed him under arrest despite the protestations of his wife. After an inexplicable two-hour delay, he was booked into the county jail and placed in the infirmary.

Hardin, whom John Fulford identified as the man who had shot him, was last seen hightailing it into the cedar brake bordering Sycamore Creek, and was subsequently charged with being the leader of the bushwhackers. The mysterious one-armed man was identified the next day as Frank Pierce. Word on the street was that he had died from his wound soon after the battle, but the authorities were skeptical of the rumor.[28]

That night a committee of the Knights concerned about the fate of Tom Nace called on Sheriff Maddox. They told him they had heard rumors that a lynch mob would be coming for Nace. Maddox assured them that the prisoner would be safe but would still answer to the law for what he had done.[29]

It was a tense Friday evening for Fort Worth fathers, trying to keep their city from exploding into a full-blown labor war. The next morning the *Dallas Morning News* and *Fort Worth Gazette* competed to see which could be the most alarmist. The Dallas paper said, "The city presents a scene of war." The Fort Worth paper said, "The issue is not now between the railroads and the strikers, but between law and anarchy." Gunfire crackled throughout the city during the night. Policeman Jesse Smith found himself on opposite sides with a longtime friend. The friend "got his leg shot off," and Smith stood guard over him and a jail full of other arrestees that night. Sympathy for wounded strikers was in short supply.[30]

The lamps burned bright at city hall all night as Mayor John Peter Smith and the council met to decide their next move. Their options were limited. The city was a ticking time bomb, and all it would take was one wrong move to set it off. They needed to separate armed posse men and strikers before a general firefight erupted. The regular lawmen did not inspire much more confidence either. They were eager for payback because one of their own had been killed. Dick Townsend had been a friend as well as a brother lawman. Somebody on the council suggested sending for the state militia, and they quickly passed a resolution to that effect. Getting the militia mobilized and on the scene, however, was something else. By law, the approval of the governor was required before the militia could even be called out. The council could only hope Governor Ireland was in Austin and could be persuaded to issue the necessary orders. Mayor Smith composed a telegram outlining the city's dire situation in just four sentences:

Fort Worth, Tex. April 3
John Ireland, Governor

We are threatened with serious trouble here. The presence of one or two companies of rangers or state militia would prevent a riot. Can you furnish the troops? Answer.

J. P. Smith—Mayor

The telegram went out. All they could do now was wait. The Governor's reply came back at 10:30 p.m. saying troops were coming from Austin, Sherman, Decatur, Cleburne, and Dallas. This was a full-blown military mobilization to handle a full-blown insurrection. The main thing was, help was on the way. Governor Ireland, concerned that it might take a day or two for the militia to arrive, sent a follow-up telegram advising the Fort Worth council that the nearest troop of Texas Rangers had also been ordered to the scene.[31] Until all the reinforcements arrived, however, it would be up to Sheriff Maddox and his men to keep the lid on, no easy job considering the fevered pitch of emotions in the city.

The rumor mill worked overtime churning out conspiracy theories and sensational scenarios. One rumor going around on the evening of the third was that strike supporters were going to clean out all the gun stores in town and burn Union Depot to the ground. Another rumor had it that the union men were going to run every "scab" out of town at gunpoint. To stay in touch with their troops, both sides set up a signal to bring their supporters on the run if a pitched battle erupted anywhere in town. Sheriff Maddox's men were to listen for the fire bell to ring three times while the strikers appropriated an idle Santa Fe locomotive and planned to use its whistle to summon the troops. By one count 2,000 armed men were on the city's streets on the night of April 3–4. So-called "citizens' committees" roamed freely placing anybody who was a stranger in town or believed to be an agitator under arrest. The county and city jail were soon full. Deputized citizens armed with an assortment of rifles and shotguns were posted at Union Depot to guard the gateway through which armed reinforcements would come. Rumors of a planned arson attack on the station turned out to be baseless, but the rumors certainly seemed plausible. It was that kind of night. The phantom arsonists might have been deterred not by the armed deputies but by the blue norther that blew in late Friday.[32]

Union Depot remained quiet until 1:00 a.m. Saturday when a train from Dallas arrived carrying two squads of Texas Rangers commanded by Captains C. F. Cook and A. J. Houston. Texas' finest were a welcome sight. Never before had Cowtown residents been this glad to see a train full of Dallas folks descend on their city. Some of those same citizens had cursed Governor Ireland two years earlier when he sent the Rangers to Fort Worth to arrest "Longhair Jim." Now their tough, reassuring presence was cause for celebration. The

Rangers would later become famous for their motto, "One riot, one Ranger," but on this occasion, seventy Rangers seemed barely sufficient to keep the peace in Fort Worth.

Two hours behind the Rangers came the first trainload of soldiers carrying the Dallas Light Guard and the Hibernian Rifles. Their arrival drew a ragged cheer from the tired deputies on the platform. The Dallas boys were followed a few hours later by the Grayson (County) Rifles coming down from Sherman. All day Sunday (April 4), additional troops poured into the city—two companies of infantry from Austin, an artillery battery from Dallas, another infantry company from Decatur—until Fort Worth became a "veritable military encampment."[33] The artillery battery alone demonstrated that the Governor and his advisors took this domestic disturbance very seriously. If necessary, they were prepared to blast buildings and mobs into smithereens.

More Rangers arrived by train Sunday morning and by that night the forces of law and order were firmly in control. The next day, the *Dallas Morning News* estimated the total number of Rangers and soldiers to be no fewer than 500. The *Fort Worth Gazette* on the same date reported 288 Rangers and soldiers patrolling the streets augmented by "more than one hundred" armed citizens. Someone who still had a sense of humor commented, "So many uniforms and brass buttons are a rare spectacle in Fort Worth."[34]

A bevy of high-ranking state officials, including Attorney General John Templeton, the Adjutant-General of the Texas Rangers, and a brigadier general and a colonel of the State Guard, arrived in town on the heels of the troops. They came to add weight to the Governor's get-tough stand: "The authority of the State has been invoked, and the authority of the State will be rendered. . . . If force is presented it will be met with force!" Texas had never before experienced civil strife on this level.[35]

Three days after Buttermilk Junction, sheriff's deputies arrested N. M. Lovin, a "deputy master workman" with the Katy, but more importantly, the "head and front" of the Knights of Labor in Fort Worth. Authorities believed Lovin was the ringleader of the strike and therefore the brains behind the ambush. They charged him with being "an accessory before the fact to the murder of Richard Townsend."[36]

John Hardin, Frank Pierce, and Henry Henning were still on the loose, although posses were scouring the countryside and telegrams had been sent to every city in Texas. At the courthouse, safely removed from the seething atmosphere on the south end of town, Judge R. E. Beckham convened the grand jury for an unusual Sunday session. He charged grand jurors to do their duty by bringing the murderous thugs to justice. Three days later, they returned an indictment for Thomas Nace charging him with first-degree murder. They also indicted Henning and Hardin in absentia for murder and inciting a riot. They did not indict Lovin at this time because he had not been identified as one of the bushwhackers and so far they could not tie him to the fugitives. But he continued to cool his heels in jail while the authorities figured out what to do with him.[37]

The city took time out from civil insurrection long enough to put Dick Townsend in the ground. The funeral was held just twenty-four hours after his death; there was no official period of mourning and arrangements were minimal because the town was in virtual lockdown. Besides, many considered him a hired lackey and strike-breaker. As a result, Townsend was interred with less fanfare than any officer in Fort Worth history. A small service was held at Matilda's house at 2:30 on Sunday afternoon. She and his brother Jim were the only family Dick had in town. Then the body was transported to Pioneers Rest Cemetery with members of the town's hook-and-ladder company leading the cortege. Marshal Rea and two former marshals were among the pall-bearers. There is no indication that Jim Courtright was one of those former marshals; no indication either that Sheriff Maddox was there. The poor turnout among lawmen is easily explained by that fact that every able-bodied officer was on duty. One tradition that was upheld was ringing the big fire bell to mark the passing of another lawman martyred in the line of duty.[38]

Dick Townsend was laid to rest in block no. 3, lot no. 38, right next to his father, James Townsend, the first of the family to pass away and be buried in Pioneers Rest. A temporary marker was put up until something larger and more fitting could be placed over Dick's grave. The interment of five other Townsends would make block 3 virtually a family plot in the years to come, yet no one got around to properly marking Dick Townsend's grave for the next

123 years. In fact, it is fair to say his grave was "lost" for most of that time.[39]

Obsessed with reporting the civil insurrection, Dallas and Fort Worth newspapers barely covered the funeral. What passed for an obituary in the *Dallas Morning News* simply said, "His death has cast a gloom over the entire law-abiding portion of this city." Newspapers on both sides of the Trinity gave more coverage to the good news that Officers Sneed and Fulford were resting easily and expected to recover.[40]

By Monday, April 5, life was returning to normal in Fort Worth, or as normal as it could be with hundreds of soldiers patrolling the streets. Scheduled trains were once more going in and out of Union Depot, but each one carried armed guards. However, no more attempts were made to interfere with rail traffic. Also on Monday, Governor Ireland arrived in town to show the state's concern over recent events. He stayed less than twenty-four hours, but during his visit he "consulted" with military and civilian leaders, railroad management, and even the Knights of Labor. Satisfied that peace had been restored and local government was working, he returned to the capital.

The next day, the militia companies pulled out. Captain Samuel A. McMurry and thirty Rangers stayed on for a few more days, but the strike was basically over. As if to confirm it, Jay Gould, who had been following events from his offices in New York, announced that the strike was over that same day.[41] What remained was to identify all the instigators and bring them to justice. The Katy put a $1,000 reward on the head of each of the Buttermilk Junction bushwhackers. The State of Texas sweetened the pot with additional dollars. Things were so quiet on the streets of Fort Worth that ten of the Texas Rangers posed for a photograph in front of Union Depot, rifles held casually and six-shooters strapped to their waists. In a few days they, too, would be gone.[42]

The job of keeping the peace was once again in the hands of Sheriff Maddox and Marshal Rea. On top of his regular duties, Maddox was also expected to bring the Buttermilk Junction bushwhackers to justice. So far he had one man in custody and five names posted on wanted bulletins: Frank Pierce, John May, John R. Hardin, Henry O. Henning, and Charles Dalton. Since they were all outsiders he did not expect they would find any locals to hide them, but that cut two ways because it also meant they had no ties to the community to keep them in town. Despite all the posses he sent out and the substantial reward money being offered, not a single useful lead came in. The earth seemed to have opened up and swallowed the bushwhackers. Still, the dragnet did not come up completely empty: The authorities arrested special officer T. L. Rowland, a night watchman with the Katy and a member of the Knights, charging him with "inciting strikers to open acts of violence." Rowland would not be the last lawman accused of "sailing under false colors" in this affair. The fact that law enforcement was going after its own shows how deeply divided the town was.[43]

Maddox was not one to give up, even if the railroad was anxious to close the book on this one. It took him more than three months, but he finally caught up with Henry Henning, hiding in plain sight on a farm in Itasca. Based on a tip, Hill County deputies swooped in and arrested him. He might never have been caught if he had not bragged to another man about shooting Dick Townsend. Henning was transferred to Fort Worth where he joined Tom Nace as a guest of the county. On July 31, Sheriff Maddox issued a statement saying he was confident that he would soon have Pierce and Hardin in custody, but the rumor on the street was that both fugitives had skipped the state.[44]

Henning sat in jail for the next six months. At the beginning of 1887 his lawyers filed a writ of habeas corpus petition. On January 15 Judge R. E. Beckham held a hearing on that motion in Seventeenth District Court. It marked the first time since the events of April 1886 that most the principals were reunited. The memory of Dick Townsend was frequently invoked. As the first open forum on the affair, the hearing drew more interest than most murder trials. The crowd was packed in so tight they pressed up against the railing at the front of the courtroom. Sitting at the defense table, Henry Henning hardly looked the part of a cold-blooded killer or radical anarchist. He was a slender, unusually pale man who looked like he had never done a day of hard labor in his life, raising the question, if not a railroad laborer then what was he doing in Fort Worth in April 1886? And furthermore, why was he dressed in rough workman's clothes now? All the other principals in this little legal drama were wearing standard courtroom attire—starched shirt, tie, and coat. His appearance did not match his clothes. He was also distinguished by bright red hair and matching handlebar mustache that he nervously tugged during the proceedings.[45]

Judge Beckham granted the petition and issued the writ of habeas corpus. At the subsequent hearing, the testimony of the Buttermilk Junction officers, describing how they were ambushed and cut down one by one, proved mesmerizing. After both sides presented their witnesses and made their arguments, Beckham denied the relief requested in the habeas corpus motion; Henning would continue to cool his heels in the county jail until his trial. It was apparent to those following the proceedings that Henning's fate was sealed if the jury went by the evidence alone and furthermore that the judge was not going to give him any breaks.[46]

Henning's case did not come to trial until June 1887. The reason it took eleven months was not because the defense was trying to delay things. Defense counsel had been ready to do battle for months, but the state took its own sweet time. County Attorney R. L. Carlock charged Henning with first-degree murder, dropping the riot-related charges. He announced he would be trying the case himself. Basically, every other criminal case would go on the back burner until this one was decided.

Considering all the pre-trial publicity and strong sentiment on both sides, the trial was remarkably brief. Proceedings opened on June 14, a Tuesday, with jury selection. Three venires of sixty men each and another of twenty had to be examined before a dozen jurymen were selected. The last was seated just before 5:00 p.m. A large crowd of spectators hung on every word all day. The testimony phase commenced the next morning at 8:30. The state's case took all day; the defense got their chance on the sixteenth. It went to the jury Thursday afternoon.[47]

It was at this point that things went off script. The prosecution and probably most if not all the spectators expected a quick verdict. Hours passed. Then the foreman sent word to Judge Beckham that they had found the defendant guilty but were hopelessly deadlocked, 10–2, over the punishment—whether hanging or life imprisonment. Beckham refused to declare a mistrial and ordered them to "make another effort" to reach agreement. Three-and-a-half hours later, they finally reached a unanimous verdict. It was nearly midnight, but Henning was brought to court to hear the clerk read the verdict: "We the jury find the defendant, Henry Henning, guilty as charged in the indictment and affix his punishment at confinement in the penitentiary for ninety-nine years."

"So say you all?" asked Beckham formulaically, and each juror answered in the affirmative.[48]

Henning's lawyers wasted no time filing a notice of appeal, and continued filing motion after another. Their first motion for a new trial was based on an affidavit by Frank Darby, one of the company guards in the Buttermilk Junction fight, stating that "the Sheriff's party" [i.e., Courtright's men] had opened fire first. Called before the judge and questioned closely, Darby denied making any such statement although the defense presented a sworn affidavit. After Darby recanted his written statement, Judge Beckham ordered a "thorough investigation" to determine if there was a case for "perjury and the subornation of perjury." In the end he was satisfied that it had all been a simple "misunderstanding."[49]

Undaunted, defense counsel filed new motions. They finally exhausted the appeals process in December 1887 just in time for Christmas. Henning's early Christmas gift from the Court of Criminal Appeals in Tyler was a denial of his motion for a new trial. The case returned to district court where he was sentenced to spend the rest of his life in the penitentiary. He arrived at Huntsville on December 22 to begin serving his sentence. At this point, his defense counsel conceded defeat; they did not even attempt to approach the governor about a pardon.[50]

Tom Nace's journey through the criminal justice system was even more drawn out than Henry Henning's. He was originally set to stand trial with Henning in early 1887, but legal maneuvering got their cases separated and delayed his trial until the fall of 1887. In the interim he remained locked up in the county jail. The case of the *State of Texas v. Tom Nace* finally got underway in Seventeenth District Court on October 3. Jury selection was the first big hurdle because public opinion in Fort Worth was so polarized. On the first day, an unusually large venire of 100 men was present, but even that pool had to be supplemented the next day before twelve men could be seated.

Unlike Henning with his rough dress and sullen demeanor, Nace since his arrest had become something of a sympathetic figure. He had a wife and child who were staying in town for the duration and were regular visitors at the jail. Word even got around, probably thanks to the defense, that his unfortunate wife and child were destitute. There was also some doubt that he would live long enough to go to trial because he was in frail condition, the result of his leg wound from Buttermilk Junction. The injured limb was not improving while he languished in the jail infirmary. Six months after he was shot, a team of doctors performed surgery in the infirmary, amputating the leg "at the upper third of the thigh." The sympathy meter swung further his way after it was reported that the patient had "withstood the painful operation" manfully.[51]

On the first day of his trail, Nace made a dramatic entry into court, on crutches and trailed by his wife and child. If it was a defense ploy, it worked. There were audible murmurs of sympathy for the threesome. During the next four days he sat quietly at the defense table, looking resigned to his fate. To those who had followed Henning's trial, Nace's trial felt like déjà vu: the prosecution followed exactly the same strategy and presented exactly the same evidence as they had when Henning was in the docket.[52] It seemed reasonable to expect the same verdict. However, after four days of testimony and hours of deliberation, the jury could not reach a verdict. Four jurors held out for a murder conviction, while another four were just as stubborn for acquittal. The judge declared a mistrial, and both sides began preparing for a second round. Tom Nace went back to his cell.

The second trial was put on the docket twice in the spring of 1889, and both times it was continued. Finally, in September, the defense successfully sought a change of venue to Hood County, where the community was not so deeply divided on the case. When 1890 arrived and Tom Nace seemed no closer to trial than he had been a year earlier, his Fort Worth supporters held a "benefit ball" to raise money for his defense. The fact that they could openly raise money for his defense fund shows again what a blue-collar town Fort Worth was. The blue bloods of Quality Hill on the western edge of town might have the money and the political clout that came with it, but they could not buy a compliant jury.[53]

Nace's long-delayed trial finally got under way in the Granbury courthouse on March 24, 1890. What followed was anticlimactic. The whole thing lasted just two days from seating the jury to the verdict of "not guilty." As the *Dallas Morning News* reported, Tom Nace was "honorably acquitted" of all charges. Since the newspaper had a Fort Worth office, this was not just Dallas sneering at their neighbors to the west. This simple report represented nearly a complete reversal of public opinion in Fort Worth since the events of April 3, 1886. The Dallas editors skirted the cold-blooded ambush and the shooting down of three officers. The newspaper explained the cause of the trial this way: "The case grew out of troubles originating in the great railroad strike in the spring of 1886." Dick Townsend and the other victims of the ambush were conveniently omitted.[54]

The length of time Tom Nace's case spent in court does not mean all the loose ends were tied up. The cases of Frank Pierce, N. M. Lovin, John Hardin, and Charles Dalton were still open, and Pierce and Lovin would never be brought to justice. The former, despite being badly wounded at Buttermilk Junction, eluded the dragnet and dropped out of sight. Although they did not have a clue where he was, officials did not forget about him. Four years later Fort Worth authorities were still claiming that he would "soon be in the clutches of the law." Instead he kept slipping through their fingers.[55] The law had Lovin in its clutches, but he was released on a writ of habeas corpus after the initial uproar died down, meaning that some JP thought he had a reasonable chance of proving he was innocent and did not pose a risk to society. The county attorney ultimately dropped all charges against him for "being complicit" in the murder of Dick Townsend and "inciting a riot." He left Fort Worth never to return. Two years later he was reported killed in the Indian Territory by confederates in a whiskey-smuggling operation. Lovin, it seemed had never been anything more than a bushwhacker and hired gun. Ironically, the authorities could forgive him sooner for that than for being a socialist or union organizer, neither of which he ever was.[56]

That left John May, John Hardin, and Charles Dalton, all three named in the April 4 indictments. May, like Frank Pierce, turned into a ghost; he was never captured and not even indicted *in absentia*.

He turned up in Waco eight years later, once again involved in a railroad strike, this time against the Pullman Palace Car Company of Chicago. He had joined the American Federation of Labor and was working at the time as a fireman for the Cotton Belt Railway. The Pullman strike was not any more successful than the 1886 strike had been, but in Texas at least violence was averted. After that, he seems to have dropped off the face of the earth. He may have been the most dedicated union man in the group.[57]

Hardin and Dalton eluded authorities for years. Even after Fort Worth and Tarrant County authorities had given up the chase, the "detective service" of the Katy Railroad and its parent, the Missouri Pacific, continued to doggedly pursue them. Tantalizing reports came in occasionally, none of which panned out until 1888. The long arm of the railroad finally caught up with Charles Dalton in St. Louis, Missouri, on March 13, 1888. St. Louis was a major railroad center but more than that, it was a solid union town thanks to all the ethnic Germans who called it home and therefore a good place for a union man on the run to hide. Chief Katy detective Thomas Furlong tracked down Dalton and found him working quietly as a streetcar conductor. He notified the St. Louis police who made the pinch and turned the fugitive over to Furlong. The Detective and his prisoner were back in Fort Worth on March 19. Having the man in jail known as "the murderer of Special Officer Richard Townsend" was newsworthy even in Dallas.[58]

The Tarrant County jail would be Dalton's home for the next twelve months while he waited for his case to come to trial. His lawyers filed the usual writ of habeas corpus and, predictably, relief was denied. Defendant was obviously a flight risk. A trial date was finally set, April 15, 1889, in Judge R. E. Beckham's court. The trial went smoothly, and three days after it started the jury returned a verdict of "not guilty." That verdict was one more sign of the sea change that had occurred in public opinion since April 1886. If twelve ordinary citizens did not completely buy the defense that Charles Dalton was innocent, they did not have any great sympathy for the railroad and the lawmen who had been its goons either. [59]

John Hardin was the last of the Buttermilk Junction seven to be brought in. Between 1886 and 1890 he was variously reported in Canada, California, and Mexico, always one jump ahead of the law despite a $200 reward on his head. Tarrant County Sheriff J. C. Richardson, who entered office in 1888, kept Hardin's file active even after Governor Sul Ross withdrew the reward offer. The big break came in July 1890 when Richardson received a telegram from his counterpart in Brunswick, Georgia, saying he had "Richard Hardin" in custody and inquiring if he was the man wanted for murder in Texas. Richardson answered that *J. R. Hardin* was wanted here, and that brought this reply: "J. R. Hardin arrested here. Come at once." Sheriff Richardson hurried to Georgia with the necessary requisition papers and returned with his man. In April 1891, almost exactly five years after the Buttermilk Junction ambush, Hardin went on trial charged with first-degree murder. To the complete surprise of the authorities, who had opted for capital murder over manslaughter, the jury found him "not guilty."[60] Ever since Henry Henning's conviction, a pattern had emerged that every defendant was found "not guilty" by Fort Worth juries. This was not what the authorities had anticipated and not what they wanted to see.

Five years after the event, the final count for the Buttermilk Junction Seven was one in prison (Henning), three never brought to justice (May, Lovin, Pierce), and three acquitted (Nace, Hardin, Dalton). This was not a good accounting for the champions of law and order. The men who were bushwhacked at the Junction had every reason to believe that the perpetrators would be brought to justice and that Tarrant County juries would go hard on them. After all, no political philosophy or collective action justifies cold-blooded murder. What the champions of law and order forgot was that Fort Worth was at heart a working-class town with strong union sympathies. Despite the testimony of the men who were bushwhacked and other solid evidence, the accused who went to trial were acquitted three to one, and this despite the fact that the men they shot up were duly commissioned officers of the law, not some company goons. Dick Townsend's family and the survivors of the train guard might have wondered why not one of the bushwhackers paid for his crime with his life.

The fates of the two badly wounded survivors of the Buttermilk Junction shootout were completely different. Charlie Sneed's ghastly facial injuries never healed properly, and he lived out the rest of his life disfigured and in chronic pain. John Fulford's injuries were less severe and after a full recovery he resumed his career with the FWPD. During his convalescence, however, he received no disability pay from the county or the city. Only a fund-raising drive by the *Fort Worth Gazette* in the name of his wife and children allowed him to get through it.[61]

Dick Townsend, Charlie Sneed, and John Fulford were lawmen doing their job when they were gunned down on the bloodiest single day in Fort Worth law enforcement history. If justice consists of finding and punishing the guilty, it cannot be said that any of these three got much justice. It is hard to say why. The best guess is that they may have been defending law and order, but they were also serving the interests of a hated robber baron. The irony is that the victims could be so quickly forgotten but not the event. As the *Dallas Times-Herald* said four years later, "Never while history lasts will the people of Fort Worth forget that Saturday afternoon."[62]

"Longhair Jim" Courtright certainly had good reason to remember it. His preparations and dispositions before the Battle of Buttermilk Junction were inept. After getting the train back to Fort Worth he completely dropped out of the picture for the rest of the strike. He may have hoped that if he kept a low profile, his role in the fiasco would be forgiven, as earlier transgressions had been. Not this time. A Congressional subcommittee of the House of Representatives came to Fort Worth later that same month to conduct hearings. Courtright was one of the key witnesses, and he did not help himself with his testimony. He was a witness again at the trial of one of the bushwhackers in January 1887 where he embarrassed himself again. He finally went out in a blaze of glory on the night of February 8, 1887.[63]

The FWPD did not forget the Battle of Buttermilk Junction either. Its lingering effects rippled through the Department long after the echoes of the last shots had faded. Two weeks later, Marshal Rea asked for the resignation of Officer John W. Coker on the grounds that Coker was a member of the Knights of Labor and that on April 3 he had put his loyalties to the union ahead of his sworn duty as an officer, specifically by refusing to fire on strikers. Rea said he had no use for a man "who will not fire at men who are attempting to murder his comrades," suggesting that Coker was not only a traitor but a coward. Since Coker had not been at Buttermilk Junction and there was no clash of arms back in Fort Worth during the events of April 3–6, it is hard to figure out what Rea was referring to, but upon reflection he rescinded his order. John Coker retired from the police force in 1916 after a thirty-year career.[64]

Dick Townsend's fate is saddest of all. When the Fort Worth Police Officers Association came to honor him 120 years later, they found that nobody knew where his final resting place was. The original newspaper stories did not say where he was buried, and none of the city cemeteries have any record of him. It is as if he never existed. Officer Townsend still lies in an unmarked grave, the only fallen officer in this work who can truly be called "forgotten."

The Townsend family plot—block 3, lot 38—in Pioneers Rest Cemetery. If indeed Dick Townsend is buried here, his grave is not marked today, and there is nothing in the cemetery's records to show it. He is probably lying in the grassy area between the rock (lower part of photograph) and the next marked grave to the north (brother James T. Townsend) (Photograph by Kevin Foster)

PART II

BLACK AND WHITE JUSTICE
(1889–1909)

INTRODUCTION

> *To many Negroes, police have come to symbolize white power, white racism and white repression. And the fact is that many police do reflect and express these white attitudes. The atmosphere of hostility and cynicism is reinforced by a widespread perception among Negroes of the existence of police brutality and corruption, and of a 'double standard' of justice and protection—one for Negroes and one for whites.*
> — Kerner Commission Report, 1968[1]

The report of the Kerner Commission investigating racial violence in America in the 1960s pointed the finger at the nation's police as one of the main causes of that violence. If the Kerner Commission had been transported back to Fort Worth at the turn of the century, they would have found race to be at the root of many law enforcement problems then, too.

The majority of Fort Worth citizens did not feel like they had a race problem, however. Fort Worth's minorities were quiescent and comprised a relatively insignificant part of the population. An unofficial census count in 1890 reported 90 percent of the population was "white American," 6 percent was black, and 4 percent was "white foreign [born]," a catchall category that included both Europeans and Mexicans. The latter were considered "white" under Texas law although that legal technicality did not prevent them from being discriminated against. Chinese in Fort Worth at this time were so few that they were not even counted. Twenty years later Mexicans and Chinese still barely registered as a demographic.[2]

These were good years for the city in terms of growth and development. The population climbed from roughly 20,000 in 1890 to 27,000 in 1900 to 73,000 by 1910.[3] Other positives were all the new brick buildings in the business district, new suburbs, and waves of newcomers putting down roots. The staging of the Texas Spring Palace in 1889 and 1890 marked the arrival of Fort Worth as a regional metropolis and "gateway city" to west Texas. Not even a brush with bankruptcy at the end of the century could slow Fort Worth down.

Urban growth brought slums, like Battercake Flats, between the bluffs and the river on the north edge of town and Irish Town on the eastern edge of the red-light district known as Hell's Half-acre. All three areas—Battercake Flats, Irish Town, and the Acre—were breeding grounds for crime with the Acre still the worst. No longer a cowboys' playground, it was turning into a skid row where murder, suicide, drug abuse, vagrancy, and muggings outpaced gambling and prostitution as the most popular pastimes. In the old days when the Acre had been the cash cow of the local economy, authorities had taken a tolerant attitude toward the shenanigans there. Now, however, with the Acre reduced to a blighted ethnic and racial ghetto, its shenanigans were no longer tolerable.

The growing population created more work for the police. In the early 1890s the Fort Worth Police Department (FWPD) numbered sixteen men, twelve of them walking beats. This remarkably low ratio of police to population was a badge of pride not a sign of cheapness. One promotional publication bragged, "The fact that Fort Worth requires only sixteen men on her police force is an excellent recommendation for the moral standing of her 33,000 [*sic*] people." Yet only a few years later, the police chief was begging the city council for more men and advising citizens to "rise up en masse and demand that the council provide additional police protection." The biggest criminal class was not thieves or murderers or rapists but vagrants, a catchall category for drifters and the jobless, particularly minorities.[4]

In a perfect world, the police force would have reflected the ethnic and racial makeup of the population, but the FWPD and Tarrant County Sheriff's Department were 100 percent Anglo. The city's minority population (blacks, Mexicans, and Chinese) was concentrated in Hell's Half-acre and Irish Town, which the police treated as one big ghetto and the residents as a lawless sub-culture. Blacks, as the largest minority, were most likely to be the targets of bias and prejudice. Dealing with race and ethnic issues was something new for the men with the badges. Fort Worth's population may have been 90 percent white in 1890, but it had been 99 percent white previously. Officers were predisposed to see every African American as a criminal or at least a potential criminal, and conventional wisdom was that a strong dose of the billy club and the six-shooter was the only way to handle "those people." Steady growth in the black population and a spike in crime at the turn of the century brought more aggressive policing of minority neighborhoods. Bullying tactics and blatant racism alienated people whose only crime was the color of their skin and produced a sullen resentment towards the boys in blue.

Racism in the FWPD made news in 1896 when the city council tried to commission a black officer for the first time in two decades. White officers openly rebelled against the appointment of Ed Loving as a "special officer" for Douglass Park, the city's new African American park. The council appointed him anyway, but the hard feelings among both blacks and whites were not soon forgotten.[5]

Aside from racial attitudes, the transformation of the FWPD into a more professional force made significant strides during these years thanks to the work of officers like Sam Farmer. Farmer was the "father" of the modern Department, serving as marshal for two long stretches: 1879–1883 and 1887–1891, a total of eight one-year terms. In 1889 Marshal Sam drew up the Department's first comprehensive code of conduct, a landmark in the history of the FWPD. That was seven years after Dodge City, Fort Worth's twin city on the other end of the Western Cattle Trail, drew up a set of "Police Regulations" addressing such issues as drinking on duty, filling out paperwork, and wearing the badge in plain sight.[6]

Farmer's "Rules and Advice to the Police Force" had no standing in law, but carried all the weight of any directive from the Chief. Most important, the rules represented a sharp departure from the traditional way of doing things. The new do's and don'ts for FWPD officers can be summarized as follows:

1) *No "loafing" in saloons or doorways or leaning against lamp-posts when you are supposed to be patrolling.*

2) *Be under no "special obligation" to anyone* [e.g., proprietors of saloons, gambling joints, dance halls]

3) *Use no more force than absolutely necessary to make an arrest.*

[This was the first step toward establishing the modern policy of "deadly force," i.e., that "a police officer may use deadly force when his own life or the lives of others are in mortal danger."]

4) *Never make an arrest merely because someone is "saucy towards you."*

5) *Be familiar with all applicable laws and ordinances and know the difference between civil and criminal statutes.*

6) *Carry a "memorandum book" for keeping a written record of all actions taken in the line of duty.* [Such notebooks even today are still accepted as legal evidence in court trials.]

7) *Be "cheerful and cooperative" with fellow officers and the police chief at all times.*

8) *Do not use offensive or abusive language toward prisoners when making arrests; a "manly officer" never "maltreats" or strikes his prisoner maliciously.*

9) *Make preventing crime equally important as making arrests after the crime.*

10) *Wear six-shooters out of sight, and only use them in self-defense; anything "more than that is illegal."*

11) *Be a goodwill ambassador of the city, not just an enforcer of the law; this means directing out-of-town visitors to their destination, answering citizens' questions, getting to know the people on your beat, and at all times being courteous and cordial.*

Before the end of the century, the FWPD was wrestling with modern problems that would have mystified early marshals such as Ed Terrell and Tom Ewing, namely, drug abuse and juvenile delinquency. The two problems were unrelated in the beginning except insofar as they were both byproducts of rapid urbanization. For most of the Western era, the only "controlled substance" lawmen had to worry about was liquor. The worst offenders were jailed until they sobered up, then assessed a small fine and sent on their way. Everything changed after hard drugs arrived on the scene. Now officers had to deal with the "drug fiends" and heightened criminal activity associated with opium and cocaine.

The first "problem drugs" for law enforcement were laudanum, the preferred "sendoff" for prostitutes tired of living, and opium, introduced in the West by Chinese immigrants. Cocaine made a splash only after opium first raised public concerns. In 1901 Marshal Bill Rea told a reporter for the *Fort Worth Register* that of the eight female inmates currently in his jail, five were "habitual users" of cocaine who turned tricks to feed their habit. That sort of report led the city council the following year to pass a "cocaine ordinance" prohibiting the "sale at retail" of opium or any of its derivatives, *but* the ordinance did not address the problem of drug use.[7]

Officials routinely stereotyped drug users, linking the Chinese with opium and blacks with cocaine. "Only the Chinese seem capable of preparing opium," said a Dallas alderman, and the newspapers regularly referred to "Negro coke fiends" and "dope-crazed Negroes."[8]

Juvenile delinquency was another new problem that frustrated traditional law enforcement methods. In the early days, an officer finding a kid on the street for no good reason late at night either ordered him home or escorted him home personally. Then the occasional incident became a chronic problem. In March 1897 the city council passed a curfew ordinance that made it unlawful for any person under the age of sixteen to be out on the streets unsupervised after 9:00 p.m. from March 1 to September 30, or after 8:00 p.m. from October 1 to the end of February. The fine for violating this curfew was ten dollars assessed the young person and $25 assessed the parent or guardian. Police were authorized to arrest juvenile violators and place them in jail until a parent or guardian came and got them. This well-intended ordinance made the policeman responsible not just for bringing in genuine criminals but also for being juvenile officers. In a few years the problems of illegal drugs and juvenile delinquency merged as city fathers began to note an alarming connection between drug usage and "the youth of this city."[9]

Another harbinger of modern times was the increasing attention given to what is known today as "media relations." Official concern was evident as early as 1886 when Sheriff Walter Maddox sat down with a reporter from the *Dallas Morning News* to relate how he and Marshal Rea had faced down a mob intent on breaking "Longhair Jim" Courtright, the ex-marshal-turned-gun-for-hire, out of jail. Before that, the city marshal had only worried about what the voters thought around election time or what the council thought the rest of the time. "Spinning" stories and polishing their image with the press were not things most lawmen worried about. But as the nature of the job changed, the man who wore the badge had to know how to maintain cordial relations with the Fourth Estate. Bill Rea was Fort Worth's first media-savvy marshal. He even gave "exclusives," such as his November 10, 1898, interview with a *Fort Worth Gazette* reporter to discuss a recent "inside job" at a popular hotel where the robber had cleaned out the safe, then proceeded to "blow [the loot] by having a howling good time." As the wily lawman knew, giving the occasional exclusive helped forge a good working relationship with the press.

Bill Rea sandwiched two tenures in office around Sam Farmer and James H. Maddox. All three were reformist marshals who helped create a modern, professional force. Jim Maddox succeeded Sam Farmer in 1891, carrying on a family tradition in law enforcement, but he was blazing new territory when he promised "a revolution in police affairs."[10] The two biggest problems as he saw things were financial oversight and discipline on the force. For too many years, the cop on the beat had done pretty much as he pleased in spite of Sam Farmer's vaunted maxims. Maddox vowed to put an end to that laissez-faire attitude. He was determined to be a real police chief, not just a figurehead appointed by the council.

One of his first directives was that policemen take care of their Fort Worth duties first before gallivanting off on some manhunt to earn reward money. The city's underpaid officers had long given bounty hunting priority over their regular duties because they could earn more for bringing in a single wanted man than for walking a beat for months. And Marshal Sam Farmer had been one of the worst of the reward chasers, even gallivanting off to Mexico.[11]

Maddox served a total of six terms as marshal before handing the office back to Bill Rea. The judgment of history is that the "Maddox Revolution" turned out to be more of a detour than a radical change of direction for the FWPD, which is not to say he was a failure. The voters elected him to another term in 1905.

That 1905 municipal election represented a watershed in FWPD history because it made Jim Maddox the last elected "city marshal." Two years later, the city adopted the commission form of government, which among other changes made the marshal's job appointive rather than elective. The city marshal was reduced to being police chief, a demotion the city's newspapers had seen coming for years by referring to Bill Rea as "Chief." Henceforward the city's top cop would answer to the Board of Commissioners, which had replaced the old city council.[12]

The first Police and Fire Commissioner was George Mulkey, elected in the spring of 1907. Mulkey tapped Jim Maddox to be his Police Chief, and the old veteran was easily approved by the full Board. An era in local law enforcement had ended, but Maddox, who had already served nine terms as city marshal, was a creature of habit. He never got used to the new title. In Ike Knight's first murder trial in 1908, Maddox prefaced his sworn testimony by saying, "I am City Marshal of Fort Worth." No one bothered to correct the old lawman, so he went on record a year after the changeover as "City Marshal."[13]

Jim Maddox represented the last connection to the old frontier lawmen such as T. I. Courtright, Sam Farmer, and Bill Rea. These were men who defined the law as well as enforced it, and who answered to the voters directly at the annual municipal elections. In the days before rule books, uniforms, and high-tech crime-fighting, the city marshal was a man to be reckoned with. When the title shrank, the size of the man filling the office of top cop also seemed to shrink. On the other hand, the new century demanded a new law enforcement model: the Police Commissioner-Police Chief partnership that would take Fort Worth into the 1920s.

Changes in the police force during this era were not limited to the top man. The force structure was also in transition from the days when the marshal and two or three pals maintained law and order to a new organizational model with a complex chain of command and division of labor involving two or three dozen officers.

When the twentieth century dawned, the marshal was assisted by a "deputy marshal" (a.k.a. assistant chief of police). Below them were two captains, one for the day shift and one for the night shift, and below them were sergeants and beat cops. The latter still included both foot patrolmen and mounted officers. After 1884 there were also plainclothes "city detectives," numbering four by 1901. The chief of detectives reported directly to the marshal/chief, placing him on a par with the assistant chief. This was the regular force.

Below the regular force were the various auxiliary positions: the "turnkeys" at the jail, the patrol wagon drivers, "police clerks," and pound keepers. Also among the auxiliaries was a reserve known as "extra officers" or "relief officers." Their role model was "Longhair Jim" Courtright, who had started his law enforcement career as a humble turnkey before being elected to the first of three terms as city marshal in 1876.

"Special officers" were not part of the regular force but were still a crucial element of local law enforcement in the same way as private security firms are today. They held their commissions from the city but were paid by the private firms for whom they worked. It was always understood that they were "second-class" officers. They worked as private security for theater owners, railroads, and saloons among other businesses. Special officers wore badges and even uniforms, carried guns, and could make arrests. Only in terms of pay and lines of authority were they different. They represented an extension of the Police Department that did not cost the city a dime in additional salaries.

This then was the FWPD's chain of command around the turn of the century, prior to the changeover to the commission form of government.

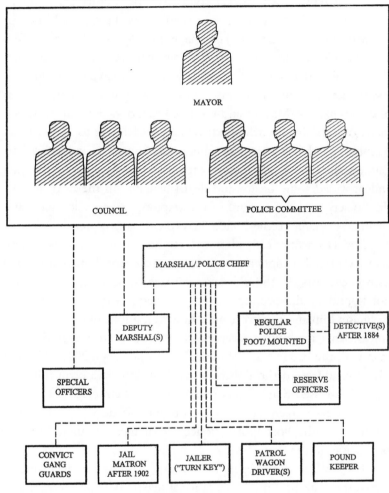

FORT WORTH POLICE DEPARTMENT, ca. 1873 -1907

MAYOR

COUNCIL

POLICE COMMITTEE

MARSHAL/ POLICE CHIEF

DEPUTY MARSHAL(S)

REGULAR POLICE FOOT/ MOUNTED

DETECTIVE(S) AFTER 1884

SPECIAL OFFICERS

RESERVE OFFICERS

CONVICT GANG GUARDS

JAIL MATRON AFTER 1902

JAILER ("TURN KEY")

PATROL WAGON DRIVER(S)

POUND KEEPER

DRAWN BY: ROBERT CULLEN SMITH AIA

The organizational structure of the Fort Worth Police Department from the city's beginnings (1873) until 1907 when the changeover was made to the commission form of government. The Police Committee advised the council on all matters police-related. All members of the force reported to the marshal who was also the police chief *except* "special officers" who owed their appointments to the council. The whole thing was a byzantine organizational structure, but it worked (mostly)! (Drawn by Robert Cullen Smith, AIA)

As the size of the Department grew, old-fashioned camaraderie was no longer sufficient as the glue holding the force together. It had to be replaced by worker solidarity where officers saw themselves less as knights errant than as regular "working Joes." In keeping with this new working-class image, Fort Worth officers in 1896 took the historic step of creating a fraternal organization, the Fort Worth Police Benevolent Society. It was more than a social club but less than a labor union; it was closest in purpose to fraternal organizations like the Masons and Odd Fellows, organizations to which many officers already belonged. While not claiming to represent all members of the Department, much less engage in collective bargaining, the FWPBS still assumed the role of spokesman for the men and provided some health and death benefits. In the next decade, the Society took on a more of the trappings of a trade union and changed its name to the Police Benevolent Association.[14]

The Department that existed at the dawn of the twentieth century placed a higher premium on professional standards than its predecessors. In the old days, the lawman as knight-errant was not bound by the ordinary rules of society; carrying a gun and a badge set him apart. Increasingly, however, public officials and their constituents no longer accepted the specious argument that the man with the badge was above the law. In January 1907, Chief Jim Maddox addressed the Police Benevolent Association on this subject. He stressed that officers must conduct themselves at all times "as first-class citizens, both while on and off duty," so that they might make the Fort Worth Police Department "a model for the other cities in the State."[15]

The FWPD also began networking with other departments across the state beyond the occasional telegram or phone call. The big change came in 1905 when it joined the Texas State Bureau of Information. For a modest fee of $25 per year, Fort Worth officers could access the Bureau's criminal files in Austin. The TSBI institutionalized cooperation for the first time, making it harder for criminals to flee justice across jurisdictional lines. This system would pay big dividends in the future as use of automobiles spread through the underworld.[16]

Despite advances in professionalism, even after the turn of the century, the FWPD remained a mixture of the old and the new.

Officers still worked under a commission, not an employment con-tract, signing an "oath of office" upon joining the force. It was a boilerplate document with places for the officer's name, the date, and a notary's signature. The most anachronistic part of the oath was a requirement that the signee had never participated in a "duel," which was aimed not so much at eliminating the sort of thing that occurred between distinguished gentlemen like Alexander Hamilton and Aaron Burr in 1804 as what happened between bravos like "Longhair Jim" Courtright and Luke Short in 1887. Hamilton and Burr calmly and ritualistically paced off ten paces in a forest glade and fired one shot each at the other. Courtright and Short squared off on Main Street and one pumped five or six shells into the other, then spent the night in jail waiting to see if a lynch mob was going to show up.

Another holdover from the old days was getting around either on horseback or foot. In some cities the police were adopting the bicycle and the internal combustion engine, but in Fort Worth, Joe Witcher, a night captain, continued to make his nightly rounds on his faithful horse, "Old Baldy," as he had for nearly twenty-five years. He would trade in his six-shooter for an automatic, but he was not about to get rid of "Old Baldy." And after hitching posts disappeared from downtown streets, he began tying the animal to the nearest telephone pole. And a horse still the most reliable form of transportation in an emergency. In 1906 when a couple of bruis-ers in the Acre got into it, the police got a call to come quick. Officer Sid Waller already had his horse saddled and tied up outside headquarters. He dashed out the door, leaped on his trusty steed and got to the scene in time to break up the fight before any serious damage could be done.[17] But the days when an officer and his horse were a team were numbered.

During these same years, the Tarrant County Sheriff's Department operated under a different set of rules and standards. While Sam Farmer, Bill Rea, and Jim Maddox were modernizing the FWPD, the Sheriff and his boys continued to patrol the back roads of the county, on the lookout for cattle rustlers and horse thieves mostly. Occasionally, they took time out to chase down some fugitive from justice. Sheriff's deputies also assumed primary responsibility for the small but growing townships like Mansfield and Arlington that dotted Tarrant County, providing backup for the local constable in those communities. These things had not changed much since the days of Sheriff John York.

NORTH FORT WORTH (1902–1909)

Shortly after the turn of the century, a new group of officers joined the mix of local law enforcement in Tarrant County. They were the members of the North Fort Worth Police Department. North Fort Worth was the latest municipal entry in the county, chartered by the legislature in 1902 as an independent township. There had been a community north of the Trinity on the banks of Marine Creek for years, but the incentive to incorporate came only in 1902 with the construction of the giant Swift and Armour meat-packing plants. Incorporation was nothing more than a legal ma-neuver to create an instant "company town" with all the advantages that entailed for the meatpackers. The meatpackers were followed by the stockyards company, which controlled the area around the two plants and also operated as a law unto itself. Until finally an-nexed by Fort Worth seven years later, North Fort Worth existed as a separate municipal entity with its own mayor, council, and police force.[18]

The packing plants and stockyards attracted a crowd that was easily as rough as the cowboys who used to trail herds through town on the way up north to Kansas. There was plenty of work and money to be made, although most of the jobs were what we call "entry-level" today. Oscar Montgomery spent his first sixteen months in North Fort Worth working for Swift and Company, and Dick Howell was the second man hired by Swift during construc-tion. Both soon left the company to enter law enforcement.[19]

Law enforcement in North Fort Worth during the few years the town existed was in the capable hands of the three amigos: Richard D. Howell, Fred Claypool, and Oscar R. Montgomery—as rough-and-ready a trio as ever put on badges in Texas. Their professional and personal relationship is reminiscent of Oklahoma Territory's legendary "Three Guardsmen," but their adventures were not nearly so thrilling. The North Fort Worth trio's story started after thirty-two-year-old "Uncle Dick" Howell was elected North Fort Worth's first town marshal on December 2, 1902. He promptly hired Claypool and Montgomery as his deputies. Together, they rode herd on the raucous cowboys and packing plant workers for the next four years, working nonstop night and day, sometimes pulling twenty-four hour shifts. Howell could usually be seen patrolling the streets late at night because he had to keep the same hours as the saloons and gambling houses that were the principal sources of trouble.[20]

He left the marshal's office in 1904 to go to work as special agent for the Fort Worth and Denver City Railway. The job came with shorter hours and better pay. Howell may have taken off the badge, but he did not desert his pals. He continued to help them keep a lid on North Fort Worth. It was not hard; the town was small enough to walk from one end to the other in a matter of minutes.

The tenure of the three amigos would later be remembered as "heroic days" because of the extraordinary job they did under the most trying circumstances. North Fort Worth scrimped on the budget in every way possible, so the Police Department had a one-cell jail and no patrol wagon, just a "none-too-fast" horse and buggy that the three relied upon to answer calls. If the call happened to be a free-for-all, and they had too many arrests to transport to jail all in one trip, they would take their prisoners in relays. Two of the officers would take one bunch to the jail while the third stayed behind to guard the rest.[21]

In a pinch, the North Fort Worth police could call on the "special officers" employed by the stockyards company and the meatpackers to help keep a lid on the town. But not always. Subduing "drunk and disorderlies" on Exchange Avenue was one thing; dealing with labor conflicts was something else. On such occasions, the interests of the public and the soulless corporations could be at odds. Fortunately, labor violence was practically unheard of in Fort Worth during those years, so the regular police and the special officers maintained a good working relationship.

When North Fort Worth was annexed by Fort Worth in 1909, most of its former officers were hired by the FWPD, including, most notably, Oscar Montgomery and Dick Howell.

The image of C. L. "Lee" Waller from 1891 FWPD group montage out of the studio of David Swartz. Waller's swarthy, unconventional features and curious love-hate relationship with blacks raised questions about his bloodline. Could it be that he was mulatto or half-Indian? (Courtesy of the Genealogy, History and Archives Unit, Fort Worth Public Library)

CHAPTER 6

POLICE OFFICER LEE WALLER

June 30, 1892

"Boys, I'm a goner . . . ."

Lee Waller was a typical nineteenth-century Western lawman: a farm boy who did not care that much about the law but did want something better out of life than being a dirt farmer. He took a round-about route to police work, but once he put on the badge he discovered he had a natural talent for it. It was a tough business, and he was a tough guy—the kind who did not concern himself with such things as civil rights and racial equality. However, he was a good partner and a stand-up guy, and those things counted the most among his fellow lawmen.

C. L. "Lee" Waller was born in Williamson County, Texas, on October 28, 1866, and while still a boy he moved with his parents to Hamilton, in Hamilton County, where his father, Sidney Waller, took a job as town marshal. He had three siblings, two brothers and a sister, of whom he was closest to younger brother A. S. (Sid, Jr.). Both would eventually follow their father into law enforcement. But before they found their niche, Lee went to work at twelve as water boy on a railroad construction project. In 1890, at the age of twenty-two, he moved to the "big city," joining his brother and sister in Fort Worth. Without any law enforcement experience, he was hired by the Police Department as a beat cop. Brother Sid joined the Department two years later as a patrol-wagon driver.[1]

If Lee Waller wanted to make his father proud, he succeeded. After just two years, he had an enviable reputation among his fellows as one of the "nerviest" men on the force and "a man of exceptional

133

habits." He was an employer's delight. His first boss, railroad con-
tractor J. H. Hamilton, "loved him like a son," and his second boss,
Fort Worth Marshal Jim Maddox, "loved him as a brother." Lee
was a man of abstemious habits—a teetotaler who also eschewed
tobacco, making him an oddity among his peers. His partner was
Henry C. Townes, and the two of them over the course of two years
together, worked every beat in the city.[2]

His personal life was something else. He was unmarried, living
with his married sister. As far as family and friends knew, he did not
even have a girlfriend. What he did have, however, was a dark secret:
Lee Waller was keeping a black woman, Lou Davis, as his paramour.
Davis was a well-known prostitute in the Hell's Half-acre district
on the south end of town, so it is not hard to imagine how a beat
cop might make her acquaintance. There is some evidence that the
relationship began even before he joined the force, that it may have
even been a factor in his decision to put on the uniform. Either way,
it posed an ethical and professional dilemma.[3]

One would expect a white man with an intimate relationship
with a black woman to be the least bigoted man around, but as
South Carolina's Strom Thurmond would prove a few decades later,
there is no logic to racial bigotry. A man can live one life publicly
and another privately. And Waller would probably have shared the
opinion of another South Carolina contemporary, Governor Cole
Blease, who believed it was the nature of every African American
woman to want sex all the time; therefore, giving it to them just
made them happier than otherwise, and a corollary to that was that
they could never be raped. While earning a reputation as the biggest
racist on the force, Officer Lee enjoyed the favors of Lou Davis, at
least until she sent him packing sometime before June 1892. After
that, the potential for trouble arising from hard feelings increased
geometrically once he was assigned to the Acre.[4]

Lee and Henry were assigned to the Hell's Half-acre beat on
June 20, 1892. They were not particularly worried about their personal safety, but they knew that they were now walking the toughest beat in the city, an area described as "a disgrace to civilization";
they would be careful. The fact that this was Lou Davis's haunts
only complicated things. During the next week, Waller did not cross
paths with his former paramour although he may well have been

looking for her. Townes, who was aware of Waller's secret, kept his mouth shut and followed his partner's lead. The Tennessee-born Townes was no bigot, just a good partner. Thirty-three years old, he had joined the Department at the same time as Lee Waller; he received badge no. 14 while Waller received no. 13. Like Waller he was a promising officer who got the Acre beat because his superiors considered him capable of handling the city's toughest beat. Although nine years older than Waller, he tended to follow the younger man's lead.[5]

Tuesday, June 28, 1892, was a warm summer evening as the two officers made their rounds. The Acre was unusually quiet, and their shift passed without incident until about eleven o'clock. Then things began to liven up with the kind of mayhem and bloodletting that was a familiar occurrence in the Acre but usually not on a week night.[6]

As they walked south on Rusk, they checked out the low dives and side streets where trouble typically erupted in the Acre. At the intersection of Twelfth, their attention was attracted to Curry & Watkins' Saloon at 110 East Twelfth. A boisterous crowd enjoying the pleasant evening had spilled out onto the sidewalk, and it was the kind of crowd that always attracted the attention of police. Tom Curry and Henry Watkins ran what the newspapers called a "Negro dive" that was a frequent target of police raids. Waller and Townes decided to check it out. The former stuck his head inside and, hearing a "loud disturbance" out back, went through the saloon to the alley. A few moments later, he came up the side of the building driving two people ahead of him. One was Lou Davis, a "notorious Negro woman" to the police. Her companion was Jim Burris, likewise black and a self-styled "sport" who ran a gambling joint in the Acre.[7]

Burris was twenty-five years old, about five-foot-nine inches tall, weighing 152 pounds, light-skinned with a prominent purple birthmark on one cheek that did not inhibit his boisterous personality. He was unmarried, had only six months of schooling, and his habits were described as "intemperate." He bore at least four knife scars on his body, the products of a lifetime of brawling. He was what was known in white Southern parlance as a "cigarette dude" or "zip coon," neither of which was complimentary. Still, he might have gone through his entire life without attracting much attention if he had not gotten into a jam with "the Man" on this night. When the local newspapers subsequently transformed him into a celebrity, they used stereotypical "zip coon" terms to describe him: "ginger-cake-colored . . . dresses well . . . a shrewd Negro." They also added a not-so-subtle jab at his masculinity, saying he had a "feminine laugh." To Fort Worth police and his fellow gamblers alike, Burris was known as "Jim Toots," and that is the name by which history remembers him.[8]

As they emerged from the alley onto Twelfth, Waller already had his "bond book" out preparing to write up Davis or Burris or both, presumably for "disturbing the peace." But the biggest strike against them aside from their color was that they were known as "bad actors" among Fort Worth police, and that by itself was sufficient for Waller to write them up.

White officers regularly roughed up notorious African Americans without giving it a second thought, but that was not what was bothering Waller on this occasion. It was the shameless display they were putting on. They were nuzzling each other, and Toots had one arm draped provocatively across Davis' shoulders. Waller resented the black man taking such liberties with a woman he considered his own. And Davis was throwing it in his face. He ordered the pair to break it up and told Burris to stand to one side while he addressed Davis. He accused her of making a "racket" and ordered her to go on home or else he would arrest her for solicitation. When she began back-talking, he dropped the veneer of formality. It had now become personal, and that did not bode well for either Davis or Burris. If the woman had meekly accepted "Mister Lee's" dressing down, she could probably have walked away and gone about her business.[9]

Waller took one more stab at being the good cop. "I ought to arrest you both," he snapped, leaving the door open for them to beg him to give them a break.

Burris answered first. "What for, Mister Lee? I have not done anything," he protested. It was the wrong thing to say and the wrong tone to say it in.

Waller rounded on Burris. "Dry up!" he snarled. "I don't want to hear [anything] from you."

Too angry or too proud to see the red flags, Toots repeated his question, and Waller repeated his answer. The policeman also pulled out his billy club and brandished it to emphasize the point.

Toots stood his ground. "You ain't going to do a f- - - ing thing to me with that club!" he said.[10]

In Waller's world, no policeman had to stand for being cursed and mocked by a couple of "Ethiopians," as the newspaper subsequently dubbed them. He took a step toward Toots, whereupon Townes, who had been watching the whole thing, tried to jump between them. He was too late. Waller had already cracked Toots "a hard lick" across the skull. The latter was not seriously hurt, and he lunged toward Waller. Now Townes and Davis were both trying to get between them. Bleeding from his head wound, but ready to go ten rounds, Toots cursed the policeman. "No God-damned, brass-buttoned son-of-a-bitch," he said, was going to treat him that way. He asked sarcastically if Waller was "going to play Jesse James" (i.e., go gunslinger). As a matter of fact, that was exactly what Waller had in mind. The final straw was when Toots said to the crowd gathered around, "If he stays on this beat, I'll get even with him for hitting me." There was no way Waller could let such a threat in front of so many witnesses go unanswered.[11]

Both Burris and Waller were guilty of making a bad situation worse. But that is not the way it would be reported. The Fort Worth and Dallas newspapers afterwards put all the blame on Toots for what followed, saying he was the first one to pull a gun. The Dallas paper would even quote him as telling Waller, "You go to hell! Keep away from me or I'll blow a hole through you!" It is obvious they got their information from Townes and probably other members of the Fort Worth Police Department (FWPD), and all concerned just as obviously backed up their brother officer. Townes told a Fort Worth reporter the next day that Toots started the gunplay. The truth is, Toots was not armed at the time and so could not have pulled a gun first even if he wanted to.[12]

Waller was armed and pulled his gun, but not before Burris, taking advantage of Townes' intervention, took off running down the street. Realizing their perp was getting away, Townes pulled out his own pistol, and both officers opened fire in the general direction of the fleeing black man. "We pumped lead at him as rapidly as our guns would work," Townes told a newspaper reporter matter-of-factly afterwards, adding that Toots had to have been "badly wounded" by their fire. On the contrary, the target made a clean getaway, suffering not so much as a scratch. The Dallas newspaper the next day estimated that "over thirty shots" had been discharged, an impossible number, but what is true is that both officers emptied their pistols heedless of innocent bystanders in the line of fire. Fortunately, no one was hit by all the flying lead, probably because the Acre's denizens were smart enough to hit the ground at the first shot. After Townes had time to reflect on how his statements might sound, he amended his story, saying that someone else had also opened fire on Toots, which Townes opined would "explain" any bullet holes in the Negro. "But who did it I can't say," he added lamely.[13]

Hours later, after the bloody night had finally ended, the biggest question would be who started it. Officer Townes was no help. Every time he opened his mouth, he made things worse. Even if he had stuck to the facts, his version of events was suspect because he was Waller's partner. On top of everything else, he had good reason to try to justify his own feckless actions in the affair. Additional eyewitness testimony provided little help establishing the sequence of events because it was contradictory. And forensic science of the time was too primitive to fill in the gaps. None of that mattered to white readers of the *Fort Worth Gazette*. For them, there was not the slightest doubt who started it. As the *Gazette* explained it, "Toots" was guilty of "hugging the Negro woman" and "back-talk[ing]" the officers while Waller was a "brave young officer." That version would remain the official one until the trial when it would be shot full of more holes than Lee Waller. [14]

That night, however, there was just one version: that of the police. As far as the boys in blue were concerned, Jim Toots had declared war on the FWPD, and they were not going to stop until they had arrested or killed him. Ignored in the effort to put the spin on things was the testimony of a (white) bystander who had overheard Waller telling his partner that night, "Toots was interfering with my woman." It was damning testimony, and it would never be heard in court.[15]

After Toots disappeared down the street the two officers gamely gave chase. No blood had been shed so far, but there would be blood for sure if they caught their man. Meanwhile, reports of what had happened began spreading through the town, bringing other police to the crime scene as well as the curious.

As soon as he put some distance between himself and his pursuers, Toots began plotting his revenge. His head ached, but his pride hurt more. To even things up, he needed a weapon and allies. He had little problem finding either since guns were as common as pool cues in the Acre, and there was no shortage of men with a grudge against the police. He quickly enlisted two accomplices: his twenty-six-year-old cousin, Horace Bell, and twenty-eight-year-old Willie Campbell, alias Will Ford, also African American. Bell was a barber and Campbell, a day laborer. Because Bell lived with Campbell's sister, Polly, this had now become a family affair as well as a blood feud. Bell put it this way: "No damned sonovabitch policeman can run over my cousin."[16]

The next order of business for Toots and friends was to arm themselves. They went to Lou Overton's Saloon, an African American establishment at 1306 Rusk and tried to talk the owner out of the piece he kept behind the bar. Overton flatly refused, telling Campbell, "I wouldn't let my own brother have my gun." Unwilling to take "no" for an answer, they adopted a different stratagem: Toots tried to slip behind the bar and grab the pistol when Overton was not looking, but the barkeep caught him and ordered all three out. Undaunted, they went back to Curry & Watkins' Saloon, using the back alleys to avoid running into police. When they arrived, they found Waller and Townes gone, and the little dustup between Toots and Waller the hot topic of conversation among the joint's patrons.[17]

Curry's clientele were naturally sympathetic to Toots. Many had suffered similar indignities at the hands of Fort Worth's finest over the years. Toots harangued an audience on the sidewalk, vowing to kill "those [two] brass-buttoned sons of bitches." As he told it, they had not given him "an even break." With the crowd egging him on, he waxed more brazen. No way, he declared, were those two going to "walk their beats and live." Chimed in Bell and Campbell, "Toots, we'll see that you [get] an even break!"

Leaving his two companions at Curry's place, Toots continued his quest for a weapon. At some point he crossed paths with Officer Tom Snow of the FWPD who was unaware of the recent dustup and proved to be an incredibly agreeable fellow under the circumstances. Snow confided that he kept an old double-action revolver behind the bar at Ridgeway's, a nearby saloon-grocery store where he moonlighted as a bartender. Toots showed up at the saloon a few minutes later asking for the pistol from the bartender on duty that night, Jim Rushing, another member of Fort Worth's finest. Rushing was suspicious and refused to turn it over. Toots stormed out but returned a few moments later with Snow who said Toots could borrow the weapon. What story Toots gave to Officer Snow to elicit his cooperation is unknown, but it must have been a doozy. The only explanation is that Snow knew nothing about the earlier confrontation and believed that Toots wanted it for protection against his own kind—or else, the simplest explanation: money changed hands. However it came about, Jim Toots was now armed with a six-shooter, presumably loaded. The sequence of events that produced this outcome would severely compromise the prosecution's case when it came out in court later.[18]

Happy to be "heeled" and thus on an equal footing with his opponent, Toots next went home to treat his throbbing head. He figured he had the rest of the night to finish his business with Waller. He was only a couple of blocks from home, which is where he was a few minutes later, soaking his aching noggin in a water barrel, when Waller and Townes showed up looking for him. While he hid behind the water barrel they searched the boardinghouse, and as they departed he heard one of them say, "We'll kill the damned sonovabitch [later]!" As soon as Waller and Townes were gone, Toots hopped the backyard fence and headed up Fifteenth more determined than ever to have it out with Waller. [19]

What already seemed like a long night had actually taken only about an hour. That was still plenty of time for the city to be in an uproar. There was an unofficial police dragnet underway in the Acre and word had gotten back to Marshal Jim Maddox at police headquarters in city hall. Maddox was concerned enough to take a walk over to the Acre to check out the situation for himself. Perhaps the reports had been overblown. As he strolled down Rusk he saw no signs of a brewing war on the streets. He was just passing Twelfth when he ran into Horace Bell and Willie Campbell coming back from Ridgeway's Saloon where they had just missed Jim

Toots. When Maddox came up they were trying to bully one of the district's bawds into giving them her pistol. She resisted, and they were loudly cursing her when Maddox intervened. He told them to "hush up and go home" or he would "run them both in." They did not volunteer what they wanted the pistol for, and he did not see any need to detain them. He last saw Bell and Campbell going west on Twelfth. The last thing he heard them say was, "We'll get the sons of bitches yet," but he dismissed it as an empty threat.

Unbeknownst to Maddox, preparations for a full-scale war were going on. Waller and Townes had enlisted reinforcements for what they anticipated would be a showdown when they caught up with Toots. They found willing allies in Special Officers Frank Bryant and Charlie Ware and two others, unnamed. The six of them split up into two parties and fanned out across the Acre. Waller, Townes, and Bryant headed for George Holland's Variety Theater in the 1100 block of Main, an odd destination under the circumstances since Toots was unlikely to be at a whites-only establishment. If they intended to wet their whistles, they were violating Police Department

Chief J. H. "Jim" Maddox was on his first tour of duty as head of the FWPD when Lee Waller was murdered. He loved Officer Waller "as a brother," and was the last man Waller spoke to the night he was shot. Maddox subsequently ordered a period of official mourning in the Department in Waller's honor. (Courtesy of the Genealogy, History and Archives Unit, Fort Worth Public Library)

policy about drinking on duty. Bartender Hill Deering noticed them come in, but would testify later that he did not serve them. The threesome did not hang around long, and right after they left, Toots and his pals came in. Toots had his pistol visibly stuck in his belt. He and his pals did not stick around long either before going back out the same door they had come in, heading up Eleventh toward Rusk. Since Holland's had a strict policy of "No Negroes . . . except for train porters," it is a mystery how they even got inside.[20]

At this point, both armed parties—policemen and blacks—were hunting for each other, and neither was in any mood to settle things peaceably. As the drama moved toward the final act, it was a little after midnight, now June 29. Somewhere along the way, Toots' party had been joined by a fourth man, George Davis. Why his three companions chose to join Toots' vendetta was not just about black solidarity. Each of them had been personally abused by the Fort Worth police or else had friends who had been. That was part of life for young black men. Toots was simply the spark that ignited their fury. By the same token, Waller and friends were not just gunning for Jim Toots; they wanted to teach the entire African American community of Fort Worth a lesson. Waller was simply the headmaster—and a notorious racist. The two parties were on a collision course. They finally caught up with each other on Rusk, almost in the epicenter of the Acre.

Waller, Townes, and Bryant were walking south from Eleventh on the west side of the street. Toots and company were coming north up the east side of the street with a mob of sympathizers behind them. As the officers reached the middle of the 1200 block,

(opposite page) This graphic shows the movements of the principals on the night of June 30, 1892. The night's events started in front of Curry & Watkins' Saloon on Twelfth Street and covered several blocks in the Acre before ending in the middle of Rusk Street between Twelfth and Thirteenth. The final shootout is depicted by the converging dotted lines, with the policemen coming from the north and the Toots group advancing from the south. (Courtesy of Robert Cullen Smith, AIA)

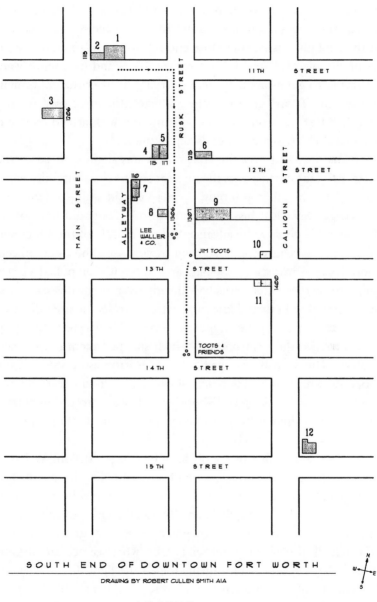

SOUTH END OF DOWNTOWN FORT WORTH

DRAWING BY ROBERT CULLEN SMITH AIA

LEGEND:

1 HOLLAND'S VARIETY THEATER
2 HOLLAND'S SALOON
3 FIREMEN'S CENTRAL HALL
4 SALOON
5 SALOON AND GROCERY

6 SALOON
7 CURRY AND WATKINS
SALOON (COLORED)
8 LOU OVERTON'S
SALOON (COLORED)
9 SOUTHERN LIVERY STABLES

10 LOTTIE FREEMAN'S HOUSE
11 T.E. RIDGWAY'S SALOON-GROCERY
12 JIM TOOTS' BOARDING HOUSE

they sighted their opponents just crossing Fourteenth. Initially, they thought the blacks might be trying to get away. Like a pack of hounds sighting a coon or opossum, they speeded up. All that was on their minds was getting close enough to wreak some havoc on the uppity blacks. They did not realize Toots and his friends were not trying to get away; they were hurrying to meet the policemen. By the time Toots' group reached Thirteenth, the crowd trailing them had lost the stomach for confrontation with armed cops and dropped back. Toots and friends kept coming.

Toots only had eyes for Waller who was slightly ahead of the other two. He veered across the intersection to close with him while Bell and Campbell, continuing up the east sidewalk, sought cover. George Davis lost his nerve and ran off. Toots did not notice. He pulled his pistol as he advanced to the middle of the street and opened fire, catching the policemen by surprise. The three officers stood frozen, surprised by the blitz attack. None even pulled a pistol until after two or three shots had already been fired. Realizing that he was standing in the middle of the street, Toots squatted down as he continued pulling the trigger. The policemen were now taking fire from "two different points," which snapped them out of their paralysis. This was all observed by Lou Overton as he stood in the doorway of his saloon. He practically had a front-row seat. He had watched Toots "walking and shooting" his way into the middle of the street and then as his pals opened up, and finally as the policemen began shooting back.[21]

Each of Toots' first two shots found its target, striking Waller in the body. Meanwhile, he continued firing, emptying his pistol. The officer had been too slow to draw his pistol, and now he was caught in a crossfire as Bell, Campbell, and Toots all concentrated their fire on him. Badly wounded but still game, he gave as good as he got, although all of his shots went wild. After what seemed an eternity, Officers Townes and Bryant finally joined the fight, firing as fast as they could pull their triggers. There were now six men blazing away at each other on Rusk Street, making this the first full-scale gun battle on a public street in the city's history. Toots' one-man charge seemed to inspire his side as much as it unnerved the policemen. All three officers' fire was surprisingly ineffective. This was not the Earps going up against the Clantons and friends.

144

Later, the timeline of the gun battle would come into question. Lou Overton would testify that the first shots came from "the gate" of the Southern Stables at the southeast corner of Thirteenth and Rusk, and that shots continued to come from there for the brief duration of the gun battle, evoking images of the legendary shootout at the O.K. Corral some ten years before. But Overton was the only witness who pinpointed the stables as the source of any shots, so he was probably mistaken. Bystanders caught in the crossfire were less interested in O.K. Corral analogies or who started it than in getting out of the line of fire. They dropped to the ground or scattered for cover.[22]

The gun battle was over in less time than it takes to tell. Some sources put the number of shots that had been fired at thirty-five, using the simple calculation of six men firing six pistols. Incredibly, only one person had been hit by all this flying lead—Lee Waller. He was either the unluckiest man in the world or the primary target of all three shooters on the Toots side because he took three hits: one in each shoulder and one in the lower abdomen. None of the bullets packed enough of a wallop to pass all the way through his body, but he was still in a bad way. The entry wounds tell the story. One of the shoulder wounds was in the front and the other in the back, suggesting that the first one spun him around, which is when the second bullet struck him. The fact that the abdomen wound was also a frontal wound completes the picture. The first slug hit him in the abdomen; the second slug struck him in one shoulder, spinning him around; the third slug struck him in the other shoulder.[23]

One thing was obvious: Fort Worth's finest had lost this gun battle badly. They allowed the bad guys to get the drop on them and outshoot them. Their only consolation was that Officer Waller, though grievously wounded, was still alive and, more impressively, still standing. Whether he survived remained to be seen. It had been less than an hour and a half since Waller and Toots had first faced off in front of Curry & Watkins' Saloon.

Toots did not hang around to admire his handiwork. As soon as he fired his last bullet he took off down Rusk. Officer Bryant followed momentarily, leaving Townes to secure the scene and look after Waller. Toots flagged down a jitney driven by Henry Lynch, who had observed the gunfight from Overton's Saloon. Now

Lynch would provide the getaway vehicle for Jim Toots, quite innocently as he later told it. The jitney was last seen speeding east on Front. The police suspected Lynch of being in on the ambush since he was African American, and it was unlikely a white driver would have picked up an armed black man running down the street. When they located him later, they brought him in for some tough questioning.

Back at the scene, Bell and Campbell wisely split up, each making his getaway on foot. Campbell ran east on Twelfth until he reached Irish Town where he knocked on Lottie Freeman's back door. She hid him, then early the next morning she went to the house of a friend, Jacksie [sic] Rucker, and asked her to keep a small pistol for her. It did not take long for the conspiracy of silence in the black community to unravel. Somebody tipped off the police about the hidden pistol, and they had no trouble tracing it back to Freeman. Her story was that she had found it in her backyard and knew nothing about Willie Campbell or the shootout the night before. It was this sort of lying and uncooperativeness that convinced Fort Worth police that they were dealing with a conspiracy whose purpose, if not to kill police, was to hide the killers and help them get out of town.[24]

In the immediate aftermath of the shootout, pandemonium reigned at the crime scene. People emerged from the nearby saloons and bawdy houses to gawk. Lee Waller was the object of everyone's attention. Although covered with blood and obviously in severe pain, he still stood erect and rock steady, holding an empty pistol in his hand. Looking around and seeing that it was all over, he turned and limped west on Thirteenth. Henry Townes walked beside him supporting him. As they walked, concerned citizens came up to offer encouragement. When they reached Main, the pair turned north although St. Joseph's Infirmary, originally the Missouri Pacific Hospital and the city's only medical facility, was in the opposite direction. The wounded policeman's objective was the Central Fire Hall on Main Street midway between Twelfth and Eleventh. He limped along supported by Townes. No vehicle stopped to give them a lift.

En route, a *Gazette* reporter joined them who had been eight blocks away at the Pickwick Hotel when the shooting started, having sprinted the entire distance to get to the scene, only to arrive after the shooting was all over. So he fell in with Townes and Waller, asking the latter to "tell me about it, Lee."

Waller responded gamely, even though he had three bullets in him. "Oh, I'm afraid you'll have to say, old boy, that I'm a goner. Take me somewhere; I'm awful sick." Just as they reached the fire hall, he clutched Townes' arm and said, "Henry, go after him." These and other words that Waller uttered in the immediate aftermath of being shot would later be used by the defense to show that there was bad blood between the officer and Jim Toots.[25]

H. C. "Henry" Townes, Lee Waller's partner the night he was killed, had to feel a certain amount of guilt over his less-than-heroic performance that night, although his brother officers never publicly blamed him for his passivity. (From 1891 FWPD group montage courtesy of the Genealogy, History and Archives Unit, Fort Worth Public Library)

147

At the fire hall, the firemen laid Waller out on a cot and cut his bloody clothes off. While they administered opiates and tried to dress his less serious wounds, somebody went for the doctor. While waiting for his arrival, Waller held court for the steady stream of fellow officers and well-wishers who came by. He asked that his mother and sister be brought to him, but otherwise he seemed to have only one thing on his mind. To the cops crowded around he issued an incendiary charge that is quoted only in part at the beginning of this chapter. "Boys," he said, "I'm a goner. Get that Nigger!" If his brother officers took those words as his last will and testament, there would be a race war on the streets of Fort Worth that night. Fortunately, they were not his last words. Turning to Captain William Lightfoot he said, "Cap, he got me. Can you catch him?" And when Chief Maddox arrived after the opiates had kicked in, he was still coherent: "Chief, he pumped me full, and I guess I'm done for, but I let him have the best I had." No one after any of these statements needed to ask whom Waller was referring to although he never identified his assailant by name. The timing and wording of none of these statements met the legal definition of a "dying declaration" although the prosecution would try to use them as such at Burris' trial.[26]

It did not matter at this point. The chances of any of the three African American suspects ever seeing the inside of a courtroom were pretty slim. If apprehended by angry whites that night, they were more likely to be strung up to the nearest lamppost. Word was already out that Toots was the ringleader and had been gunning for Waller. A black porter at the Pickwick told the *Gazette*'s reporter that it was common knowledge among his people that "Jim Toots was goin' to kill [that policeman]." Waller's shooting more than anything in recent memory put whites and blacks on a collision course. Whites began talking about a "Negro conspiracy" against the police, and some talked of using a rope. The rhetoric went up after the *Gazette* labeled Toots "an assassin," a term Americans had become familiar with thanks to the recent wave of anarchist assassinations in Europe. The *Gazette* declared ominously the next day, "There will be only one course pursued if the Fort Worth people get hands on him—this can be surmised."[27]

Back at the fire hall, everyone breathed a sigh of relief when Dr. William A. Duringer arrived and took charge of the patient. He had been practicing medicine for twelve years, the last seven in Fort Worth, and this was one of the worst cases he had seen. His first order was to get his patient to the hospital. Waller was fading in and in and out of consciousness as he was loaded onto a buckboard for the short trip. The Doctor jumped on and they took off to St. Joseph's, a ten-minute ride. Waller's two brothers, Sid and John, and his sister, Mrs. H. C. Chase, caught up with him there. Dr. Duringer was able to do a more thorough examination at the hospital, and the results were not encouraging. The shoulder wounds were minor compared to the perforated intestines and the bullet lodged somewhere near his backbone. Without surgery there was no way of telling how much damage had been done or exactly where the bullet was. He had to weigh two equally unappealing options: ignore the patient's critical condition and operate immediately, or not operate and face the risk of sepsis and/or peritonitis setting in. He was reminded of the similar wound suffered by President James Garfield a decade before where doctors had tried to operate without sufficient information, only succeeding in killing the President in the process. In the end he decided to postpone surgery, make Waller as comfortable as possible and see if his condition stabilized by morning. He informed the ever-present *Gazette* reporter at 2:30 a.m. that Waller's wounds were "as bad as can be."[28]

Throughout the rest of the night and all the next day, police officers and city officials trooped through the hospital to inquire about the patient and offer condolences to the family. The *Gazette* called the hospital regularly to get updates. Waller clung stubbornly to life, but even heavily sedated with opiates he still suffered the kind of excruciating pain that comes with gut wounds. While the city was caught up in the manhunt, Lee Waller was fighting for his life.

News of the shooting echoed through the city like a fire bell in the night, bringing the white male population boiling out onto the streets in full vigilante mode, armed with pistols, shotguns, and Winchester rifles. A few also carried ropes. They targeted blacks and were not too choosy about who they caught in their dragnet. The police and sheriff's men were also out in force. The problem was, no one knew where to find the three fugitives, and the city's black residents were not talking. Angry armed men scoured the town chasing phantoms and terrorizing black residents.[29]

Jim Toots was Public Enemy No. 1, but police wanted his two pals also. They made their first arrest at 4:00 a.m. when they found Willie Campbell hiding out in a "Negro dive" near Fifteenth and Calhoun. A helpful customer pointed him out to Officer J. J. Garrett who made the collar. By the time the patrol wagon came, a white mob had gathered and only a show of force by police and a fast getaway prevented a lynching on the spot. An hour later, police burst into Henry Lynch's home and pulled the hack driver from his bed.[30]

After daybreak, mounted posses fanned out into the countryside. Marshal Maddox led one bunch in person although technically he was outside his jurisdiction. Meanwhile, the manhunt in town continued. Groups of officers and newly deputized citizens went from door to door in the "Negro district" searching every shanty and boardinghouse. No black resident was above suspicion and none was immune to being stopped on the street and questioned. Several reports came in during the day of Toots sightings but none panned out. Officers rotated off duty periodically to snatch a little rest and get something to eat. One group of deputies just back from the Acre reported that black residents were starting to "act very ugly."[31]

Later in the day, a policeman rushed into the Marshal's office to report that "the brute [Toots]" had been cornered in a shanty near Sixteenth and Calhoun. Ten men piled into the patrol wagon and rushed down there where they found other officers already on the scene surrounding a frightened-looking black man. They had been searching the shanty, which turned out to be Polly Campbell's, when they noticed a suspicious-looking hole in the canvas ceiling. They piled up furniture until they could climb up to shine a lamp through the hole, but still they could see nothing. They finally decided to tear the roof off from the outside, whereupon the object of their search crawled out and surrendered meekly. He was black, and a crowd of armed whites who had been standing on the street watching assumed it was Jim Toots. The two sides, police and mob, were at a standoff when the patrol wagon pulled up. The lawmen threw their prisoner into the back of the wagon and took off for the county jail where they rushed him upstairs to a cell. Only after he was locked up did someone correctly identify him as Horace Bell. That meant two down and one to go.[32]

Citizens who considered themselves part of the manhunt were not going to be satisfied waiting for the authorities to bring in Jim Toots. An "immense crowd" of at least 1,000 gathered at the courthouse to hear agitators harangue them from the steps. The speakers confined themselves to denouncing the Acre and its denizens, but others in the crowd favored action. At nine thirty the crowd drifted over to the jail on the west side of the square where they milled about uncertainly.[33]

When nervous sheriff's deputies looked out the windows, they saw "a mob of infuriated humanity" on the lawn. Either the crowd had doubled in size or nervous reporters magnified the threat because the *Gazette* would report "no less than 2,000," all loudly calling for the man they thought was Jim Toots. "Hang him, hang him!" they howled. "Turn him loose and we'll fix the damn nigger!" Sheriff J. C. Richardson displayed remarkable courage, going outside to tell them the prisoner was not Toots but Toots' cousin. That quieted them for the time being, but it was impossible to say what they would do if the fugitive was not brought in soon. They might settle for any black man in the jail.[34]

Although there was no howling mob, at the hospital the situation was also tense. Dr. Duringer was doing everything he could for the patient. He even called in Drs. William P. Burts and Julian Feild to consult about the best course of treatment. They all agreed surgery was imperative and must be done immediately before the patient sank any further. At 9:00 a.m. Wednesday, Lee Waller went into surgery. Duringer operated, assisted by his two colleagues. First, they dug the .38 caliber slug out of each shoulder then turned their attention to the wound just below his navel. Once they opened Waller up, they found his intestines perforated in twelve places and massive internal bleeding. They sewed him back up; there was nothing more they could do. Waller had three bullet holes in him, had lost massive amounts of blood, been cut open and sewed up, and spent three hours on the operating table. It was a miracle he was still alive at all. Friends and family began the final deathwatch Wednesday afternoon.[35]

Waller's parents reached Fort Worth from Hico on Wednesday. They could not be notified until that morning when the telegraph office in their small community opened. They caught the first train but did not get to the hospital until Waller was out of surgery. Sid Waller, Sr., was a "manly-looking gentleman" with a full gray beard who was anything but sentimental. Still, he broke down crying upon seeing his son in a hospital bed pale and semi-conscious. Mrs. Waller, just as grief-stricken, remained in the background for the duration, barely noticed by all the men gathered around her son's bed.[36]

Lee Waller lingered through Wednesday, showing amazing stamina. He finally died at 7:00 a.m., Thursday, June 30. The *Gazette* reported that he "peacefully passed away." He had rallied slightly following surgery then passed in and out of consciousness for another fifteen hours. During lucid moments he bid farewell to the familiar faces gathered around. He finally slipped into a deep coma just minutes before death took him. At the end, his father and siblings were at the bedside, but not his mother.[37]

Final arrangements had been commenced during the death-watch, which turned out to be a good thing because the family did not want to stay in Fort Worth any longer than absolutely necessary. They made that clear to the Marshal and to city officials. Lee Waller's final wishes were to be buried in the family plot at Hico. There was a train leaving town shortly before 1:00 p.m., and the Wallers intended to be on it.

Two hours after Lee Waller was pronounced dead, the body was taken away by an undertaker to be prepared for burial. Everything that had to be done was telescoped into the next four hours. No public event in the city's history was ever planned and carried off so quickly. A barber donated his services to give the body a shave and haircut, then it was laid out in an elegant rosewood casket placed on view in the undertaker's chapel. Friends and well-wishers had until noon to pay their final respects. The word got around quickly in a close-knit community like Fort Worth. There was no time to set a police honor guard at the casket, but every member of the force came by to pay his final respects.

City fathers did not waste time either. At noon, the council, meeting in emergency session, issued a public statement that Lee Waller had "come to his death at the hands of a cowardly assassin . . . while in the discharge of his duty." The wording carefully finessed any awkward questions about the circumstances leading up to Waller's death. One floor below where the city council met, another meeting took place at the same time in Marshal Maddox's office. An *ad hoc* committee of senior officers decided it would be proper for a uniformed escort to accompany the body on its last trip through Fort Worth. The Marshal gave permission to use the patrol wagon as a hearse so as soon as the meeting broke up, officers got to work draping the team and the wagon in funereal black. Maddox also issued a directive that for the next thirty days every officer was to dress in mourning, wearing a "badge of mourning" on his left breast, a black armband on his left arm, and black crepe on his helmet. This was the first time in Fort Worth history that such emblems had been worn.

What was missing in all the arrangements was a memorial service. There was no time for one before the family whisked the deceased out of town. It was only by scrambling around in a near-panic that a funeral procession could be organized to escort the body to Union Depot.

At 1:00 p.m. the cortege was lined up in front of Fire Station No. 1. The grapevine had done its job so a large crowd was on hand to pay final respects. The order of the procession was organized on the spot as participants arrived. The patrol wagon-hearse led the way. From somewhere, the Police Department had come up with a large wreath to lay atop the casket. Six members of the Department designated as pallbearers (Marshal Maddox, Peyton Maddox, Frank Darby, Rufe James, John W. Coker, and Walter Townsend) came next. Henry Townes, a "touching and pathetic figure" at this point, got the "honor" of standing at rigid attention on the rear step of the wagon. The rest of the procession came along behind the hearse in this order: a police honor guard led by two assistant chiefs, followed by city and county officials, then members of Waller's Odd Fellows lodge, and finally a contingent of volunteer firemen. The firemen had brought along their one and only fire engine draped in the same black crepe as the hearse. Their participation was a gesture of solidarity with the Police Department since Waller had never been a fireman. The Waller family was strangely absent from the funeral cortege.

As the procession stepped off, the bell atop the fire station began tolling out the death knell. The cortege cut over from Rusk to

Main and turned down Main toward the train station. People lined the sidewalks along the entire route. As the hearse passed, the men respectfully doffed their hats while the women bowed their heads and wept. When the cortege reached Union Depot, they found the Waller family waiting. As a courtesy, the Fort Worth and Rio Grande Railway had delayed the regularly scheduled train. The pallbearers unloaded the coffin and carried it to the platform where it was opened one last time for the family to say their good-byes. Then it was sealed and loaded into a baggage car. The family plus Officers Townes and J. W. Pemberton who were accompanying the body piled into a passenger car, and after a blast of the whistle, the train pulled out.

The FWPD still had one more thing to do to honor its latest fallen hero: publish a set of appropriate "Memorial Resolutions" in the newspaper. A committee of four officers drew them up, and the *Gazette* published them on Friday, July 1. This is what they said:

Whereas it has been our sad misfortune to lose our brave and efficient fellow officer, C. Lee Waller, who came to his death at the hands of a cowardly assassin on the night of the 28th day of June [sic], 1892, while in the discharge of his duty, and

Whereas, in life he was an example of all those traits of character that constitute a true man and courageous officer, faithful to his friends, firm in his convictions of right and wrong, tender and true to those near and dear to him, and fearless in the efficient discharge of his duty; therefore

Resolved, that words are inadequate to express our feelings over the cowardly and murderous manner of his death at the hands of a damnable and cowardly murderous assassin; and

Resolved, further, that we hereby mutually pledge ourselves to use all the power of the law and all our energy and perseverance to bring his murderer to the "bend of that crooked road where the wicked find their way barred by the gates of justice."

Resolved, that we hereby tender to his bereaved family, who were so tender and loving to him in his last hours on earth, our sincere sympathy in their deep trouble, with the assurance that there is a sorrow Whereas nearly as great as their own rankling in our hearts

*over the death of one we loved in life and whose name will ever be
a tender memory to us,*

*Resolved, that an appropriate badge of mourning be worn by the
officers and members of the police force for a period of thirty days
in memory of our deceased brother officer.*

*Resolved further, that a copy of these resolutions be furnished to the
family of our late brother officer.*

This was hardly the first time the Department had published
such resolutions, but this time they set some sort of record for the
number of times a murderer was called "cowardly." And although
Officer Waller had died "in the line of duty," that fact did not trigger
any financial obligation on the part of the city to the deceased or to
his survivors. The book was officially closed on Lee Waller.

Toots remained free for another week, far too long as far as
furious whites were concerned. They had to be content with making sure the two blacks in custody did not escape justice. Starting
on Wednesday night, thirty or more armed white men maintained
a round-the-clock vigil on the jailhouse lawn to be sure nobody
got into or out of the place without their knowledge. There was a
lot of talk about town of bypassing formal judicial proceedings and
stringing up Bell and Campbell to the nearest tree. Keeping the
vigilantes in check were the determined officers of the Police and
Sheriff's Departments who could see among the faces in the crowd
on the lawn their friends and neighbors. Marshal Maddox spoke for
his men when he told a *Dallas Morning News* reporter, "You can say
[to your readers] that if I capture [Toots] and get started for the jail
with him I hope nobody will attempt to stop me."[38]

On Thursday, the stakes in the manhunt were raised when the
city council announced a $250 reward for Toots. Private parties put
up another $225. Then a few days later Governor James Hogg sent
word that the state would kick in another $250, bringing the total
reward up to $775. "Dead" or "alive" was not specified.[39]

The initial outpouring of grief for Lee Waller was genuine. Most
people accepted the newspaper reports that he had been gunned
down in cold blood by a "Negro assassin." But in the days following, two opposing schools of thought began to emerge: A few

citizens, not just blacks, spoke up in Jim Toots' defense. For their temerity, they faced the full fury of any officer who happened to hear them. On Thursday, just hours after the city had bid farewell to Lee Waller, Special Officer Frank Bryant was at his job in one of the Acre's whites-only saloons when a customer said that he was personally acquainted with Toots and knew him to be a "perfect gentleman." Bryant, still feeling guilty about his own inglorious part in the gun battle, laid his coat and pistol aside and decked the loudmouth. When the man stood up and complained that the only reason he did not fight was because Bryant was still armed, the Officer raised his arms to show he had no other weapons on him. The barfly then sucker-punched him. Unhurt, Bryant administered a thorough thrashing. That same day in another part of town, well-known cattleman and gambler Nat Kramer lit into a black waiter at the Pickwick Hotel who dared to exult, "Toots got his man!"[40]

The manhunt continued full throttle. Even routine patrolling by police and sheriff's deputies was suspended for the duration. Virtually every officer was either riding with one of the mounted posses roaming the countryside or else chasing down leads inside the city. They combed the Trinity River bottoms, conducted house-to-house sweeps through the "Negro quarter," posted every bridge out of the city, and even rode out to Hurst to check out a report that the little black community there might be hiding him. Authorities were especially vigilant in the city's rail yards to prevent Toots from hopping an outbound freight train. Police furnished railroad security people with a description of Toots, and no train pulled out of the yards without first being searched. The authorities were confident they had every route out of town covered.[41]

Whenever news of a Toots sighting was received at headquarters, a flying squad was dispatched to check it out, and most of the time a newspaper reporter tagged along. A pack of news hounds hung around the courthouse and city hall hoping for a break, keeping a horse saddled and ready. Some wild goose chases were a bigger waste of time than others. The Itasca sheriff wired Tarrant County Sheriff Richardson that he had Toots in custody, but when Richardson went there in person, the hapless black turned out to be the wrong man. The purported suspect was grateful not to have been lynched *before* Richardson got a look at him.[42]

The public followed the manhunt with the sort of fervor usually reserved for a war or a hot political race. Many citizens called
or came by headquarters to offer advice. One female reader of the
Gazette declared that if the authorities would just promise publicly
that Toots would not be "mobbed," he would probably surrender
peaceably. Her letter was printed on Saturday, July 2 and like all the
other suggestions, had no effect on police operations.[43]

While all this was going on, the object of the manhunt was lying low. On the night of the shooting, Toots' first hideout had been
the home of a black farmer east of town. After being ordered to
leave, he spent the next two nights in Colonel Richard M. Wynne's
outhouse, hidden by a black servant. Since Wynne was a diehard
ex-Confederate and a respected lawyer, he could hardly have been
pleased when he learned later what sort of guests his servants were
sheltering. Ironically, Wynne had built his career as a criminal defense lawyer but of white clients. Late Saturday night, Toots slipped
away from his outhouse hideaway into the West Fork river bottoms,
intending to strike the Texas and Pacific tracks outside city limits,
hop a passing train, and get to Mexico.

The fugitive stowed away in a boxcar on a westbound train.
When it reached Big Spring, 250 miles west of Fort Worth, he left
his hiding place and went into town looking for food and water.
That was when Howard County Sheriff John D. Birdwell noticed a
suspicious stranger in his town and tailed him back to the train yard.
Any black man in Big Spring was unusual, and one who had arrived
in town in such an unconventional way was doubly suspicious. The
fact that the Sheriff had recently been informed there was a Fort
Worth cop-killer on the loose with a $775 reward on his head made
him especially vigilant. Birdwell followed the stranger back to his
boxcar and arrested him without incident. When searched, Toots
had three dollars and two "large revolvers" on him. Under questioning he admitted he was trying to get to Mexico because a lynch
mob was after him back in Fort Worth. He was particularly anxious
that the Tarrant County Sheriff come for him, "not any of the city
police."[44]

Lodged in the Big Spring jail, Toots was big news to the locals. A reporter from the town's only newspaper came to interview
him and found him eager to tell his story. That jailhouse interview

would appear in the *Fort Worth Gazette* on July 9. No surprise, it was considerably different than the story being told by Fort Worth authorities. According to Toots, it had all started when he mistook Waller for Special Officer Charlie Ware, who was "after him for some cause" that he did not bother to explain. Toots, as he told it, had been minding his own business on the night of the shooting when Waller and Townes came up and started harassing him and Lou Davis. When Waller threatened to run him in, he did nothing more than protest that he did not deserve to be arrested, which was when the officer cracked him over the head with his "baton"—hard enough to knock him to the ground. Toots played possum until the two officers moved on, then he went looking for a gun—but only to defend himself if he met them again. When he subsequently overheard them planning to kill him, he was forced to take action. He hurried over to Curry & Watkins' Saloon seeking safety among his own people, and while standing outside the saloon, the two officers and their friends had come along and without warning started shooting at him. His first thought was to escape, but as he fled for his life he fired several shots back over his shoulder. He knew one of his shots hit Waller but did not wait to find out how seriously. He had left the city and made his way up to Texarkana where he threw away the pistol, replacing it with two others. He only stayed around Texarkana long enough to write the letter to Sheriff Maddox, then resumed his flight by hopping a T&P freight train at Gordon and riding it to Big Spring.[45]

This was Toots' story. That first jailhouse interview would serve as a dress rehearsal for the self-defense argument he would use at his trial. The story had more holes in it than a box of doughnuts, but he would stick to it. Most readers of the *Gazette* were certainly not persuaded. The *Dallas Morning News* reported the next day that there were "hot-headed people in Fort Worth" who vowed that Toots would never make it trial, or even to jail; a lynch mob would see to that.[46]

Toots' letter to Marshal Maddox, postmarked Texarkana, arrived in Fort Worth the same week its author was arrested (July 3–9). In it, he asked the Marshal to "give him justice" and "place him aright before the newspapers." He swore he had only been defending himself when he shot Waller. Maddox informed the local newspapers about the letter but also said he believed it had been written in Fort Worth by Toots' accomplices and sent to Texarkana to be mailed from there. The intention was to send the manhunt in the wrong direction.

Toots' story began falling apart even as he was relating it. The first discrepancy was why he had hopped a train going north if, as he said, he was trying to get to Mexico. Second, the presumed murder weapon (a .38 caliber, double-action revolver) had turned up Friday, July 8, not in Texarkana but in Fort Worth in possession of a black woman who lived in the Acre near the intersection of Sixteenth and Jones. A tip told police where to find it, and Officer Sebe Maddox went down there to check it out. Sure enough, the woman had the pistol but claimed to have found it in her backyard. While searching her shack, Maddox also discovered a small savings bank, which he appropriated as evidence. The two items strengthened the case against Toots and also the theory that he had been aided in his escape by accomplices. The gun was the same caliber as the two slugs dug out of Waller, and witnesses identified it as the weapon Toots used the night of the shootout. The savings bank was also connected to him. Detectives theorized that Toots had gone to the house to hide after the shooting and while there had sent for it to get running money. The legal case against Jim Toots was getting stronger by the day, which was good news for those who hoped to avoid a lynching.

On Sunday, July 10, the capture of Jim Toots was the biggest topic of conversation among men exiting the churches. Some of the talk was definitely contrary to what they had just heard from the pulpit about love and forgiveness. Marshal Maddox was not in church that morning. He had taken some officers and gone to Big Spring to take Toots into custody. Before they started back, Maddox examined Toots' noggin looking for signs that he had been whacked over the head by Officer Waller on the night in question. Any telltale injuries would have supported the contention of Toots' supporters that Waller had provoked the whole thing. What Maddox found was that there was "not a scratch or swollen place about his head; no sore nor anything to indicate he had been struck on the head."[47]

Maddox and his men started back as soon as they had their man in custody. The hard part would come when they got back to Fort Worth. They stopped over in Weatherford Sunday night and caught the first train out the next morning, detraining just outside of the city limits. Maddox had wired ahead for a "private conveyance" to meet them at a designated spot and drive them into town by a back road so that they could avoid any hostile reception waiting at the train station. Once in town they changed again to a streetcar for the last few blocks and slipped Toots into the county jail through the back door without the public being any the wiser. Sheriff J. C. Richardson had an empty cell waiting for the prisoner. It was as neat an operation as local authorities had ever pulled off. For the next couple of days, in fact, people on the street argued over whether Toots was even in town or not![48]

The grand jury of the Forty-eighth District Court indicted Jim Toots on a charge of first-degree murder with Bell and Campbell as accomplices. The three were tried separately, however, with the two accomplices going first. Why the state chose to go to the extra trouble and expense of three trials is not clear. At the very least, Bell and Campbell could have been tried together. The county attorney may have hoped to use the threat of their own punishment to persuade Bell and Campbell to turn state's evidence against Toots. No doubt, that is what their legal counsel advised them. Judge S. P. Greene appointed Sam Furman and Ray Bowlin to represent them, an absolute necessity since both men were illiterate and callow in the ways of the law. Furman and Bowlin were veteran criminal defense lawyers, and both had formerly served as county attorneys. This was going to be a high-profile case, and Greene wanted the defendants to have the best representation they could get.

Eight months would pass before any of the defendants saw the inside of a courtroom. In the meantime, the city's black and white communities squared off in the battle for public opinion. Many whites were ready to skip the courtroom folderol all together and go right to the hanging. Most black citizens felt that the defendants were being railroaded because of their race. When the trial phase finally started on March 9, 1893, passions were still running high. Because of the intense feelings and all the publicity the case had received, an unusually large venire of 120 men was summoned—all of them white, of course.[49]

Horace Bell was up first. His trial lasted three days. The jury was empanelled and testimony commenced on the first day. The state put a parade of police officers on the stand who testified about what a fine officer Lee Waller had been and how Bell and his pals had conspired with malice aforethought to assassinate him. The defense seemed to be angling more for the jury's compassion than for a "not guilty" verdict. If so, they were disappointed. The jury brought in a verdict of guilty late in the day on March 11 and sentenced Bell to ninety-nine years. The defendant did not betray any emotion when the sentence was read, but his attorneys immediately announced they would be moving for a new trial.[50]

Even while Bell was being tried, the county attorney's office was making preparations for Campbell's trial. That opened on March 10 in Judge Greene's court with jury selection. The testimony phase commenced the next day. Not counting Sunday, the trial continued for the next three days with the jury bringing in its verdict on March 14. The county attorney had figured that it might take as long as a week to try Campbell, but the defense did not put up that much of a fight. Since the two defendants were locked up in the same cell, they had plenty of time to discuss their cases. Campbell could not have been encouraged when he learned of Bell's fate. The good citizens of Fort Worth showed surprisingly little interest in the proceedings apart from following it in the newspapers. They had gotten on with their lives in the nine months since Officer Waller had been murdered, which considerably lowered the chances of a lynching. Campbell also got the benefit of the doubt in the verdict—guilty but sentenced to only fourteen years in the penitentiary as compared to the ninety-nine years that Bell had gotten.[51]

The decks were cleared now for the state to go after Jim Toots. Since he was charged with first-degree murder, his trial promised to be a more complicated proceeding than those of his co-defendants. The case turned on whether Waller at the time he was shot was "in the discharge of his duties" or on a personal vendetta against Toots. The crucial question was not whether Jim Toots had fired the fatal shot but whether it was cold-blooded murder or self-defense. That was what the all-white jury would decide. The county attorney's office began the preliminaries even before trying Toots' accomplices. In the middle of February they ordered that a "special venire" of unusual size be summoned for jury selection on March 9. No date was set for the trial yet.[52]

Toots' defense faced a daunting challenge trying to prove their client "not guilty by reason of self-defense." They made a critical decision to have the defendant take the stand in his own behalf, risking cross-examination, so that he could appeal directly to the jury. In the event, they found they had badly miscalculated Toots' ability to elicit sympathy. His high-pitched voice and cocky attitude coupled with the disfiguring birthmark on his face won him no friends on the jury.

Yet the state's case was hardly ironclad even with the race issue on its side. The prosecutor, County Attorney Oscar W. Gillespie, had to establish "beyond all reasonable doubt" that it was Toots who had shot Waller that night, not Bell or Campbell. This makes the order the trials were placed on the docket obvious: by the time Toots came to trial, the state had already convicted his buddies as accomplices. Justice demanded that someone pay the severest penalty for Officer Waller's death, and the only person left was Toots. The betting was the jury would give every benefit of the doubt to the state, even with its weak case.

Still, the prosecution had its work cut out for it. Absent eyewitness testimony that Toots had fired the fatal bullet, Gillespie fell back on the defendant's repeated threats against Officer Waller. He also sent a parade of uniformed officers to the witness stand to show that Waller was a good officer just doing his job. Officer Townes was the prosecution's star witness because he had been at Waller's side the whole night including during the final gun battle, and as a policeman he had virtually an unimpeachable reputation. The final piece of the state's strategy was to establish the obtuse legal doctrine known today as the "law of parties," whereby all those involved in the commission of a crime are equally responsible before the law. That meant Toots was still guilty of murder even if the fatal bullet had been fired by one of his pals that night.[53]

The prosecution presented its case from March 22 through the 24th. The first day was taken up with jury selection and preliminary legal maneuvering by both sides. The prosecution rolled out its big guns on the second day: Officers Henry Townes, Frank Bryant, Jim Rushing, Jim Mann, Tom Snow, and Hill Deering; Captain William Lightfoot, and Chief Jim Maddox. Their final witness for the day was saloon man Lou Overton who not only was able to testify about the defendant's frantic attempts to get a weapon but also had a front-row seat to the final shootout. Every seat in the gallery was filled, and the spectators hung on every word of testimony. A significant number of spectators were blacks who occupied their own section separate from the whites, but no attempt was made to bar them from attending and since there was no balcony or back entrance, they came and went through the same door as whites.[54]

The state wrapped up its case on Friday morning, March 24, then it was the defense's turn. Since the prosecution called rebuttal witnesses, the proceedings ran well into the evening. The defense attacked the credibility of Officer Waller and other officers, which in the case of Waller was not hard to do. Flawed or not, the state's case had white public opinion on its side. Waller may have been a racist and a bully, but he was a white officer of the law. The betting in the courtroom was not whether the jury would find Toots guilty but whether they would sentence him to life in prison or the gallows.[55]

The trial records are skimpy, so there is no telling how fairly the proceedings were conducted. Judge Greene had an upstanding reputation, and Oscar Gillespie was not known to be racist. Still, no jury of that day represented a fair cross-section of the community since both blacks and women were excluded. The Toots jury was under pressure by the white community to find the defendant guilty. Judge Greene carefully instructed them before sending them off to their deliberations. He read twelve pages of highly technical charges to the jury that covered all relevant points of law and explained their options on each point. On Saturday morning the jury brought in its verdict: "We the Jury find the defendant Jim Burris, alias Jim Toots, guilty of Murder in the first Degree and assess his punishment at death."[56]

From here on, the fates of Horace Bell, Willie Campbell, and Jim Toots diverged. Bell and Campbell were delivered to Huntsville by Sheriff E. A. Euless on February 8, 1894.[57] Meanwhile, Toots' life hung by a thread. His original lawyers had fumbled the ball by not requesting a change of venue at the very beginning. Perhaps they had counted on the public's short memory to ensure their client a fair trial in Fort Worth. Now his only hope was an appeal for a new trial. His court-appointed lawyers handed off the appeal to James W. Swayne, a former city-attorney-*cum*-state-senator, who filed the necessary paperwork on March 27, 1893. Swayne listed eight reversible "errors" in his motion. The case came up before the Texas Court of Criminal Appeals, which upheld the verdict in April 1895. Sheriff Euless began making preparations for an execution, but Swayne was not done yet. He went back to Judge Greene and filed a motion at the end of 1895 noting that he had turned up "much [new] testimony bearing upon the case" which justified a new trial. He cited three things specifically: Lee Waller's dying statement, which had been presented to the jury only in part; the unrevealed testimony of one of the state's witnesses that Waller had stated to him that night that he intended to kill Toots; and the affidavit of another witness to the shooting that contradicted the state's version of events. For these reasons, counsel "prays that your honor will . . . grant said Toots a new trial." In a matter of days, Greene responded that after a "careful review" of defense counsel's petition plus the facts of the case and the court stenographer's trial notes, he could find nothing to justify reopening the case. Petition denied.[58]

James W. Swayne before becoming judge of the 17th District Court (1909) was a respected lawyer and public figure in Texas who took on unpopular clients, like African American cop-killer Jim Toots. This is Swayne's official portrait when he was a Texas state senator, 1891–92. (Collections of Kevin Foster)

With his execution scheduled for Friday, December 13, Jim Toots' dance with the legal system appeared to be about over. The next dancing he would do was at the end of a rope. But James Swayne had one last trick up his sleeve. He had anticipated that Judge Greene would turn down his petition for a new trial and he was already working one last angle to save his client's life. Even before Greene's decision came down on December 4, he had petitioned the Governor for a "commutation of sentence," meaning to set aside the sentence, not the verdict. He hoped to get Toots' death sentence commuted to life imprisonment by making a personal appeal to Governor Charles A. Culberson. Swayne had been law partners with the previous Governor, James Hogg, so Hogg's successor and protégé, Culberson, could hardly refuse to see him. Swayne went to Austin in November 1895 to make his case. After listening to the Fort Worth lawyer's impassioned arguments, Culberson agreed to convene the board of pardons and, following their recommendation, he included Jim Toots in his annual "Christmas commutations," thus saving Toots from the gallows, not quite at the last minute, but close enough to make it a near thing. (The seasonal proclamations were a popular tradition with Texas governors.) On December 21, Swayne received the good news via personal telegram from the Governor, and prisoner Toots reported to Huntsville on January 4, 1896, to begin serving his life sentence.[59]

James Swayne was an outstanding lawyer, and his political connections were invaluable, but it took more than a personal appeal and impassioned arguments to save Jim Toots. Governors do not overturns jury verdicts lightly, especially in a case such as this one. Culberson's office also received a petition signed by more than 1,000 Fort Worth citizens, black and white, pleading for Toots' life. Also working in the condemned man's favor, the Governor was following in the footsteps of his predecessor, who had set an elevated standard for executive compassion. The Toots case was Culberson's first opportunity to make a strong statement of his own. In the years following, the Governor would earn a reputation as a reformist executive, banning prizefights and setting aside land for the state's first African American college, but it all started here.[60] One final part of the equation was that Culberson had strong Fort Worth connections of his own, having married a local girl, Ellie Harrison, in 1887 and beginning his law practice in the city. He knew the racial climate in Fort Worth firsthand and how the system worked around the Tarrant County courthouse. He never would have taken the action he did if he had not seen something amiss in the case.

Jim Toots proved to have more lives than a cat. He received a full pardon seven years later during the holiday season from Governor Joseph Sayers who, like Culberson, was a progressive with a reputation as "a man of integrity."[61] One week before Christmas 1902 he pardoned Toots, but unlike Culberson, he set down his reasons in black and white for all to see.

PROCLAMATION
By the
Governor of the State of Texas

No. 6935
To All To Whom These Presents Shall Come
Whereas, at the March Term, A.D. 1893, in the District Court of Tarrant County, State of Texas, Jim Burris, alias Jim Toots, was convicted of the offense of murder and sentenced to the death penalty; and
Whereas, he was first condemned to be hanged but upon the petition of a thousand or more of the representative citizens of Fort Worth, commuted defendant's sentence to imprisonment for life; and
Whereas, he was tried during the prevalence of great excitement and the fact that he was a Negro, had killed a white man and policeman of Fort Worth, while apparently in discharge of his official duties, erected so deep a prejudice against defendant as to preclude a fair and impartial trial. . . .[62]

The proclamation laid out all the sordid details of Waller's grudge against the convicted man, thereby placing a large share of the blame for what followed on the officer. None of these details had been admitted into evidence at the trial. What had appeared to be a simple case of bushwhacking at the time now looked like a personal vendetta hiding behind the shield of the uniform and the badge. It seems hard to believe that Waller's fellow policemen at the time were completely unaware of his intimate involvement with Lou Davis. If, as seems likely, they did know the truth, then they closed ranks in a conspiracy of silence to protect the reputation of a dead brother officer and to spare the feelings of his grieving family.

Sayers buttressed his decision by citing the opinions of eight distinguished members of the legal profession drawn from both major political parties, five of them sitting jurists, who all agreed that Jim Toots had not received a fair trial. Their testimonials were consistent that a miscarriage of justice had occurred.

> *From former County Attorney Jim Swayne: "Justice should be done an unfortunate Negro, who if he had been a white man would never have been indicted."*

> *From the Hon. C. M. Templeton: "I am convinced had a white man killed under the same circumstances that surrounds this killing by Toots, that he would either come clear, or have received a short term in the penitentiary."*

> *From the Hon. Sam B. Tomlinson: "From the time that Jim Toots killed Waller in this good hour, I have felt that the facts in the case would not warrant a conviction for murder, but barely a case of manslaughter."*

> *From the Hon. J. M. Moore: "Had Toots been a white man, I do not think he would have been convicted at all."*

> *From the Hon. C. R. Nowlin: "From my own knowledge of the facts, I do not believe that he was guilty of more than manslaughter."*

> *From Judge T. L. Nugent: "I have no hesitancy in saying that my sense of injustice of the extreme verdict rendered in that case is so great, that it's execution would, in my judgment, be judicial murder."*

> *From the Hon. W. P. McLean: "I have formed a decided opinion that the infliction of the death penalty will be little short of judicial murder."*

> *From the Hon. Sam G. Hunter: "I do not believe Toots was guilty in reality of more than manslaughter."*[63]

These were some of the leading lights of Fort Worth at the time, and their testimonials show that at least some *white* public officials recognized the fundamental inequity of the Jim Crow legal system, even if they were powerless to change it. Also supporting a pardon was former governor James Hogg.[64]

After being pardoned, Jim Toots briefly returned to Fort Worth, but as the notorious "colored slayer of Policeman Lee Waller," he got the cold shoulder in both the black and white communities. It took only a few days of being persona non grata to convince him to leave town for good. He told friends he was moving to Houston to "begin life over again." He was not heard from around Fort Worth for the next six years, then turned up in El Paso in 1909, where he was reportedly dying of "paralysis." District Judge James Swayne, who had been Toots' defense counsel at his trial and who still had friends in the black community, was informed that "there was no prospect" he would ever recover. That was good news for most Fort Worthers.[65]

Thereafter, public memory faded and Jim Toots became part of local lore, dimly remembered when remembered at all. A 1912 *Fort Worth Star-Telegram* story called him the "famous Negro bandit," a far cry from the small-time gambler that was the real Jim Toots.[66]

As for Lee Waller, it is not exactly accurate to say he was fondly remembered. Years later, the hometown newspaper could not even get his name right, calling him "Lee Walker." But in the most important area, reputation, he did all right. Waller's reputation was bulletproof to all the revelations that came out after his death. Waller family members made no public comment on Toots being pardoned in 1902 or the damage the governor's press release did to the family name. Officer Waller's reputation as a martyr to the cause of law and order was secure.[67]

As for the other principals in the case, none was ever able to resume his former life. Willie Campbell died in Huntsville on January 23, 1896. Horace Bell also died there on November 27, 1903. No cause of death is listed in prison records for either man. Huntsville was hard on a man, especially a black man. They got the dirtiest jobs and the most lashes with the strap. A long sentence was often a death sentence.[68]

Jailers with a macabre sense of humor posed Jim Toots on the gallows of the Tarrant County jail in 1895, anticipating that soon enough he would be there for real. As it turned out, Toots was sentenced to prison instead and eventually pardoned by the Governor. The photograph has survived however, confusing subsequent generations of Fort Worth historians to no end. (Courtesy *Fort Worth Star-Telegram* Collection, Special Collections, University of Texas at Arlington Library, Arlington, TX)

Lou Davis is not known to have changed her wanton ways. She dropped out of sight, reportedly moving to Dallas after the legal system in Fort Worth finished with her. Being the one-time concubine of a white policeman never got her any breaks with the men in blue later, and probably would have made her life harder if she had stayed around Fort Worth.

Henry Townes' time in the spotlight lasted longest. He had been the principal witness in the trials of all three defendants. After recounting the events of that night more times than he cared to, he went back to his beat, retiring in 1902 after a long, honorable career. Whether he ever got past the "survivor's guilt" he felt for not doing more that night is impossible to say. He was a charter member and first secretary of the Fort Worth Police Benevolent Society in 1896. Six years later, at the age of forty-three, Chief William Rea withdrew his name from the annual list of officer appointments for reasons that were never explained. Since the veteran cop was not accused of anything inappropriate or illegal, he probably got caught in the political crossfire between the Chief and the city council. In any event, a twelve-year career thus came to an abrupt end. He was never involved in another shootout after the night of June 28, 1892.[69]

In an ironic postscript, Lee Waller's death actually benefited his brother, Sid, who had been unable to get onto the police force before but was now hired to drive the patrol wagon after the current driver moved up to take Officer Waller's place. Nobody objected to this bit of nepotism, and Sid Waller went on to a long career on the force, climbing steadily through the ranks to patrolman, mounted officer, night sergeant, city detective, and ultimately captain. He became a charter member of the Police Benevolent Society, which did much to help officers. Looking back on his career after he retired, he was proudest of the fact that "no officer ever accompanied him on a call and received an injury or wound." What he should have been ashamed of was following in his brother's footsteps as a racial bigot who abused his authority over blacks. The two leading Fort Worth and Dallas newspapers put it more politely at the time of his death:

"Sid had many dealings with Negroes."

Fort Worth Star-Telegram

"Sid Waller had a singular aptness in the management of the turbulent Negroes of the city."

Dallas Morning News[70]

Lee Waller had proudly worn badge no. 13 without giving a thought to the superstitions associated with that number. After his death, however, bad luck seemed to attach itself to the "hoodoo badge," causing some in the Department to believe there was a "Toots Curse" on it. The career of the next man who died while wearing it, Andrew Grimes, became exhibit A for that theory.

Lee Waller's grave in the Hico, Texas, cemetery gives no hint of the controversy surrounding his death. The family took him out of Fort Worth as quickly as possible, not even allowing a memorial service. (Photograph by Kevin Foster)

This picture of Officer Grimes, sporting the 1891 official eagle badge, was taken on the steps of city hall. Grimes was a burly man with a chip on his shoulder who never learned how to defuse a situation. (Courtesy of Fort Worth Police Historical Association)

POLICE OFFICER ANDREW J. GRIMES

May 12, 1902

Unlucky Badge No. 13?

The day after Lee Waller was shot, while he was still fighting for his life, another Fort Worth Officer, J. J. Garrett, told a *Gazette* reporter, "About the only thing going on in the criminal world is killing policemen." It certainly must have seemed that way because in addition to Waller, two Dallas police officers had been gunned down on the street. Fort Worth officers began patrolling in pairs and taking extra precautions, such as "While one makes an arrest, the other backs him," explained Garrett. Then the officer added, with a little too much bravado, "I don't think it would be an easy thing for anybody to get the drop on me, for I am generally prepared for any break of that kind."[1]

Perhaps Fort Worth policemen really did become more cautious after Lee Waller's death, or maybe it was just luck that a full decade would pass before another officer was killed in the line of duty. Since the Fort Worth Police Department still did not provide any job training for its officers before sending them out on the street, one has to believe it was more a matter of luck than anything else.[2]

The next death in the line of duty was Fort Worth police officer Andrew J. Grimes, a bear of a man over six feet tall and weighing more than 220 pounds. He had been born in Wayne County, Tennessee, on April 30, 1863, coming to Fort Worth in 1884. During the next fourteen years the only job he was on record holding was driving for a Fort Worth laundry service. He married Ellen Katie Grant on August 25, 1887, and one year later to the month their son, Roy Larkin Grimes, was born. When Katie died on January 16, 1889, Andy remarried, to Mrs. J. L. "Lula" Parker, a widow who earned a living as a seamstress and dressmaker. Lula Parker was a good wife who also made a good mother for young Roy. Ten years later the happy little family was living at 416 Evans. Because at this time the city provided no insurance coverage for its officers, he used his own money to take out two policies, a $2,000 accidental death policy and a burial policy. He was one of the very few officers who planned for such contingencies. Having already lost one wife and with a son to provide for, he was more concerned about such things than most of his fellow officers, who were not family men.[3]

His career in law enforcement began inauspiciously in 1898 as a "special officer" at Frank DeBeque's Standard Theater. Opened in 1897 on the southeast corner of Rusk and Twelfth, it had a mixed reputation: On the one hand it was called "the best vaudeville theater in Texas"; on the other, it was also known as "the hottest spot in Hell's Half-Acre." DeBeque had taken over in 1897 and may have been responsible for transforming its image from the latter to the former. Just outside the front door was where Lee Waller had been gunned down in 1892. Now, customers coming in the Rusk Street entrance walked over the name written in tile on the floor. Inside, they could hang out at the impressive bar, take in the shows in the auditorium, or sit under the stars in the wine garden out back. A private entrance on the south side admitted the high rollers.[4]

Part of cleaning up the image of the Standard was hiring a full-time officer to be on duty every night. DeBeque hired Andy Grimes to enforce the rules of the house, which included no women allowed except the performers, no drinks sold to inebriated customers, and no vulgar or profane language. Grimes came on duty about 7:00 p.m. and circulated the premises until the shows started at 8:30, then he posted himself up front where he could keep an eye on the bar and the box office. He shooed out the riffraff and kept an eye peeled for troublemakers in the bar, closing the place down around midnight after the last show ended. Most nights were quiet on both fronts.[5]

Andy was proud to be a member of Fort Worth's finest, even in an auxiliary capacity, and wear his uniform. He had business cards printed up and bought a sterling silver card-holder for his desk at home. The cards read,

Andy J. Grimes
Fort Worth, Texas
Police Officer
Standard Theater[6]

The reality was, Andy was a glorified bouncer, but he was on the career ladder in law enforcement, and that was the whole point. Two years after hiring on with Frank DeBeque, he moved over to the regular force, a day that ranked as the proudest in his life. Officer Grimes received badge no. 13, once worn by Lee Waller and more recently by Bob Rice, who had been severely wounded while on duty in 1895.[7] Grimes did not mind the "history" that went with the badge; he was just happy to be a "real" policeman. At thirty-five, he was one of the oldest members of the force, but he bled blue the same as long-time members of the Department. He even joined the Police Benevolent Society, although the dues were a stretch on his modest salary. In early 1902 he was assigned to beat No. 3 on the south end of town, which covered the area bounded by Irish Town on the eastern edge of "the Acre" down to Front Street and east to the T&P station. Since that beat included the worst part of the Acre and the rail yards, white officers patrolling it had to deal with hoboes and hell-raisers as well as the resentful black population of Irish Town. Violence and death lurked in every alley and dimly lit bar. His partner on that beat was William Logan, a fellow refugee from the Bluegrass State.[8]

Andy Grimes was an old-fashioned policeman, but not just because of his beefy form, Victorian handlebar mustache, and hair parted down the middle. He was old-fashioned in his attitudes about race, women, and authority. He was a firm believer in law and order, imposed with a nightstick when necessary, and that policemen were the first line of defense against the forces of anarchy. What he lacked, however, was training in the finer points of handling weapons and public relations.

In August 1900 the city council received a citizen's complaint against Officer Grimes. J. J. Starr complained that Grimes had arrested him and a friend for "fast driving" on the night of July 20.

The two defendants took the case to trial in corporation court where Grimes was called to testify, and his testimony revealed much about his approach to law enforcement. He requested the court to show leniency to the second defendant but recommended the maximum fine for Starr because he had "shot off his head [mouth]." Grimes had no sympathy for anyone who disrespected the badge or challenged his authority.[9]

Andy Grimes was the city's first (self-styled) traffic cop. His job as he saw it was not just arresting speeders; he considered the hack drivers who swarmed around the Texas and Pacific passenger station jockeying for fares his special mission. Some cabbies treated the streets around the station like the old Roman Circus Maximus, darting across traffic and cutting each other off in the race to grab a fare, plus blocking the streets and sidewalks to get as close as possible. Most of the cabbies adhered to an informal agreement to park their horse-drawn carriages in a parallel line across from the station and wait their turn to pick up the next fare. Even if everybody followed the rules, however, they were still a risk to pedestrian and vehicular traffic and a particular nuisance to the streetcar line that served the station. Whenever cabs blocked the tracks, the streetcars had to wait for them to get out of the way before proceeding, throwing them off schedule and causing occasional confrontations between the cabbies and the motormen.

In 1901 the city council decided to do something about the problem, passing Ordinance No. 803, which prohibited any vehicle from blocking the streets and sidewalks around the station. Hacks were ordered to park around the Al Hayne Triangle west of the entrance, or in a line on the west side of Main where it passed in front of the station. They were also ordered to park single file and not leave their cabs to solicit business. The next year the council passed Ordinance No. 845, which placed the Al Hayne Triangle off-limits. Taken together, the two ordinances put an end to the old free-for-all competition for business. Essentially, the streetcar tracks on Main and Front streets were now a "dead line" that hack drivers could not cross unless specifically hailed by a passenger, and even then they had to take turns with the first in line answering the call; no more mad dashes to the entrance resembling the chariot races in *Ben-Hur*.[10]

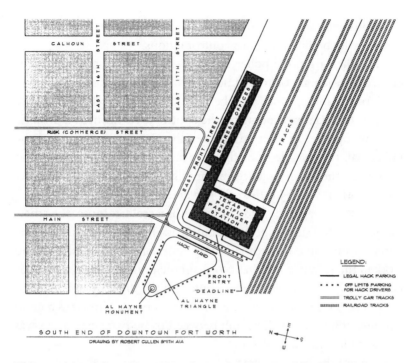

SOUTH END OF DOWNTOWN FORT WORTH

DRAWING BY ROBERT CULLEN SMITH AIA

This graphic of the crime scene shows the Texas and Pacific train station on Front Street with the Al Hayne Triangle and the "dead line" in front of the passenger terminal. It was the dead line that provoked the fatal confrontation with Jeff Vann. (Courtesy of Robert Cullen Smith, AIA)

There were never more than one or two violations of the hack ordinances before police court on any given day, but that did not mean the cabbies liked the new rules. They resented any restrictions on their entrepreneurial freedom, and that was particularly true of the more aggressive drivers who were used to grabbing business wherever and whenever they could. The fact that those same ordinances also placed restrictions on drummers, runners, and others who made their living on the passenger traffic through the train station did not make them any more palatable. The cabbies blamed the cops who enforced the ordinance more than the council that had passed it. The cabbies became convinced that the cops were out to get them because, although the hack ordinance was not a big issue, sixteen cabbies were arrested in a single year for other violations.

Relations between the cops and the cabbies simmered at a slow boil, occasionally boiling over into confrontations.[11]

For their part, the police followed the standard operating procedure of placing violators "under bond" (i.e., "ticketing them" in modern parlance), which was the substitute for custodial arrest. The violator had to sign a bond on the spot that constituted a promise to show up later in court to answer the charge(s). This saved the policeman the trouble of hauling his man off to the hoosegow and the citizen the inconvenience and humiliation of being placed under arrest. Either way, it hit the cabbie where it hurt the most.

Everybody agreed, Andy Grimes was a real hardnose, the strictest on the T&P station beat. He enforced the hack ordinance to the letter, at one time or another citing most of the hack drivers who worked the terminal. He was No. 1 on their "most hated" list. They considered him overbearing and quick on the draw when it came to whipping out his bond book. He preferred to see himself as a good cop just doing his job. The gulf between those two perceptions was a mile wide and a mile deep.

One of the hack drivers Grimes wrote up was thirty-seven-year-old Jeff Vann, two years younger than Grimes and a bantamweight compared to the portly policeman. Vann had lived several years in Fort Worth, working as a driver for a series of livery firms until he finally saved enough money to go into business for himself. He formed a partnership with Jake Stine, a fellow cabbie. Vann was known as a go-getter among the close-knit cabbies and a leader in their union. He had the reputation of being "sober, quiet, industrious, not given to fighting or the use of abusive language." But he also used the alias "Jeff Vance" on occasion, calling into question his reputation as a solid citizen. Still, he had a clean record with the police except for repeated violations of the hack ordinance.[12]

One of those violations was more than a simple mistake. In early 1902 Vann set out to get himself arrested, thereby setting up a test case so the union could challenge the legality of the hack ordinance in court. It was the culmination of a long-running feud between the cabbies and the city. The number of citations handed out had risen to the point where the cabbies decided to more than just grumble. Some among them, the more cautious, considered Vann's approach an unnecessary provocation that would only spur the police to come down harder on them, but the union went ahead with its test case. As luck would have it, the unpopular Andy Grimes was the officer who arrested Jeff Vann, but the court challenge that followed did not go according to script. The case came up in police court and the city lost, leading the drivers naturally to expect that the hated ordinance would be repealed. Instead, the council merely reworked it to avoid future legal challenges. The cabbies were angrier than ever, feeling that they had played by the rules and gotten flimflammed for doing so.[13]

The hack ordinance remained. All that had changed was that Andy Grimes and Jeff Vann were now the personification of the problem. Both men were stubborn and convinced that they were right. Neither was going to back down the next time their paths crossed, and there would be a next time as sure as the sun rose every day because each one had made "threats of a serious nature" against the other.[14]

The day of reckoning came on May 12, a Monday, around six thirty in the morning. Vann's cab arrived and took its usual place on the west side of the driveway in front of the passenger station. The cabbie was looking for his first fare, and the first trains of the day had just unloaded their passengers. People were just coming out the front doors of the station when he started his cab across the street-car tracks, trying to get the jump on the other drivers in line ahead of him. At that moment, Officer Grimes was standing farther down the sidewalk on the west side of the driveway talking to another driver. His regular partner, William Logan, was not present that day or he might have prevented what followed. Seeing Vann pull out of line, Grimes called out, "Jeff, you are going to keep on running over there until you get another case filed against you."[15]

Vann did not drive all the way over to the station side of the street, which would have been a clear violation of the hack ordinance, but backed his cab up until it straddled the streetcar tracks, coming to a stop a good eight-to-ten feet from the line of cabs on the west side of the street. His cab now faced east, blocking traffic in both directions. He was no longer intent on picking up passengers; instead, he was throwing down the gauntlet to Grimes. "File [a case], God damn you," he growled. "File it! You are nothing but a God-damned old jobber," he continued, using the popular slang term for officers with a reputation for trumping up charges against people just to pad their arrest records or make themselves look good.[16]

Up until this moment Grimes was not going to cite Vann for blocking traffic or crossing the dead line. He had turned his back and was walking away when the hack driver started cursing him. With that, Vann had crossed another line, but he did not care; he was just getting warmed up. He was glad when the Officer turned and started back toward him. "That is all you are," he sneered, "a God-damned old jobber, and if you want anything out of me you can get it!"[17]

Grimes approached the right (south) side of the cab and said in a level tone, "I will just place you under bond," as he reached into his pocket to pull out his bond book. He walked up to the cab's boot, took a moment to fill out the form, then held it out saying, "Jeff, sign this bond."

Vann had risen from his seat at the Officer's approach and pulled off one driving glove. Now he stood with the gloved hand holding the reins while with the other he wagged a finger at Grimes. He made no other overtly threatening gesture but continued his rant: "I will sign nothing, God damn you! I will sign nothing!"

The question was no longer whether Grimes would arrest Vann; the cabbie was practically daring the Officer to start something. Still not rising to the bait, Grimes replied steadily, "If you don't sign the bond, you will have to go with me." As he said it, he reached up to stuff the paper in Vann's hand, but the other man jerked away.[18]

At this point, the series of events gets a little muddled. One witness would later testify that Jeff Vann went for his gun, pulling a Colt .45 revolver out of the box under his seat and opening fire. If so, Vann must have been a terrible shot because Grimes was standing right by the front wheel of the cab, at point-blank range, yet the bullet missed completely. However, ten other witnesses would swear under oath that Grimes pulled his gun first and fired two shots at the cabbie. One witness added that the Officer had stepped up onto the wheel hub with gun in hand but did not fire. Only after Vann had jumped off the other side of the cab did the Officer jump down and open fire with his .38 revolver. It all happened so fast, and people caught the action at different times. But all ten witnesses agreed that

Vann fired back after Grimes started shooting. Regardless of who shot first and who shot second, all the shots went wild. The two continued to blaze away at each other in one of the most bizarre gun battles ever to occur on a public street.[19]

Both shooters maneuvered for position keeping the cab between them while trying to gain the advantage. Each decided on the same plan, moving to the rear of the cab to "flank" his opponent. Vann fired a couple more times, ineffectively since neither man had a clear view of the other through the cab's windows. So far, nobody had done any damage. Grimes got to the rear first, firing a shot through the rear window that whizzed harmlessly past Vann's head. Then the cabbie rounded the back of the cab and the two men stood face-to-face separated by only a few feet. They fired simultaneously, but only Vann's shot hit its target, striking the officer in the abdomen "about an inch to the right and a half-inch above the navel," then exiting his right thigh. Grimes got off one more wild shot before crumpling to the ground mortally wounded.[20]

Eyewitnesses would also disagree about what happened next. Two would state under oath that Vann fired another shot at the officer after he was down on his knees. If so, he missed because doctors found only one bullet when they did the postmortem. If Vann did indeed try to administer a coup de grâce, it was an act of coldblooded murder.[21]

In all, eight or nine shots had been exchanged. Neither man deserved any marksmanship medals. Nor had they shown any particular concern for innocent bystanders. One of their wild shots struck an express man in the calf, and two other shots hit horses, but considering the number of humans and animals in the immediate vicinity, it was "miraculous," as one newspaper put it, that there were not more two-legged or four-legged casualties.[22]

The first officers on the scene were Special Policeman John J. Fulford and Police Captain Joe Witcher, both of whom had been inside the T&P station when the shooting erupted. Fulford was in the baggage room when he heard the shots and recognizing them for what they were came running. Witcher just happened to be in the passenger waiting room at the time and also instantly recognized the sound of gunfire. He got to the scene first. The sight that met his eyes was the sort every lawman dreads: someone standing with a smoking gun over the body of a brother officer. By the time Fulford ran up, Witcher had already disarmed the cabbie. While Fulford watched the cabbie, the Captain went to summon help. It took a few minutes to arrive in the form of the police patrol wagon pressed into service as an ambulance. Witcher brought back a stretcher from the station on which they placed Grimes, trying to make him as comfortable as possible. By the time the patrol wagon arrived, Andy Grimes had gone into shock and bled to death.

Officers hustled Jeff Vann off to jail before a gathering crowd could decide to take matters into its own hands. In the next few days, his fellow hack drivers would start a legal defense fund. He spent that night in jail and was brought before Justice of the Peace John Terrell for the standard examining trial the next morning. Four days later the grand jury handed up an indictment for first-degree murder, and the case was set for trial in Judge Irby Dunklin's Forty-eighth District Court.[23]

Marshal William Rea (left) and Captain Joe Witcher (right) were central players in the tragedy that was Andy Grimes' death. Witcher's pusillanimous actions made him an object of scorn among his fellow officers. (Courtesy of Fort Worth Police Historical Association)

Meanwhile, Andy Grimes had to be buried. Lula Grimes left all the arrangements up to the Police Department, and they scheduled the funeral for the day after the shooting. There would be no period of mourning, not even a viewing of the body. There is no explanation for what seems to be an unseemly rush. The service was held at the Grimes' home on the morning of May 13. The turn-out was modest—nothing like the public outpouring of grief that had followed the deaths of other officers in previous years. Even the funeral oration by the minister of the Peach Street Methodist Church was strictly boilerplate. No one had known Andy Grimes all that well. His closest friends had been his fellow officers, and that fact was apparent. Six of them served as pallbearers, and the rest of the Department "attended in a body." Interment was in Oakwood Cemetery.[24]

Jeff Vann's trial got underway two weeks later after minimal pre-trial maneuvering. Thanks to the legal defense fund raised by his fellow cabbies, he was ably represented by Colonel R. M. Wynne, senior partner of the firm of Wynne, McCart & Bowlin. County Attorney Oscar S. Lattimore represented the state. A total of some forty witnesses were subpoenaed by the two sides, and all indications were that it would be a long, grueling trial. As things turned out, however, it was quite short. Jury selection was completed in a single morning, and the jury started hearing testimony that same afternoon. The state called eleven witnesses including Officer Fulford and Captain Witcher. Lattimore also called City Secretary John T. Montgomery to testify that the hack ordinance was legal and proper, an important fact in justifying Officer Grimes' actions that day.[25]

On the second day the defense got its turn. The courtroom was packed with spectators who hung on every word of the twenty-four witnesses called by Colonel Wynne. Most of the defense witnesses were hack drivers and assorted workingmen who testified as character witnesses, painting a picture of Jeff Vann as an average, hardworking Joe. Not a single policeman or public official testified for the defense, nor did Jeff Vann take the stand. Wynne did not want him questioned about the threats he had made against Grimes. Court adjourned late in the afternoon of the second day with more defense witnesses still to be called.[26]

The case went to the jury on the fifth day, a Saturday, following a marathon nine hours of closing arguments. On Sunday at noon the jury of twelve men brought in their verdict. A crowd filled the courtroom to hear Jeff Vann's fate. When the court clerk read the guilty verdict and the sentence of death by hanging, there were murmurs of approval from the spectators. Jeff Vann, standing at the defense table, took the news stoically. Colonel Wynne, without missing a beat, announced he would be filing a motion for a new trial.[27]

On July 11 Judge Dunklin heard defense counsel's oral arguments, which cited a whole raft of exceptions laid out in a thick petition to the Court. Some of the exceptions dealt with the evidence and with the Judge's final charge to the jury, but the heart of the defense's motion was the "spontaneous confession" made by Vann to Officer Fulford right after the shooting, introduced into evidence by the state. That confession, the defense argued, was invalid because Vann had blurted it out "before he had been warned" that anything he said could be used against him. The prohibition against using such a confession was already a well-established principle of American jurisprudence at this date, more than sixty years before the Miranda decision immortalized it.[28]

Judge Dunklin granted the motion for a new trial, and the case moved to Austin and the Texas Court of Criminal Appeals for the next round. Wynne, McCart & Bowlin handed off the appeal to W. P. "Wild Bill" McLean, considered by many to be the finest criminal lawyer in the Southwest, and certainly the most colorful. McLean had been practicing law in Fort Worth only three years but already had a reputation for taking on unpopular clients and hopeless causes. On appeal, he got the conviction overturned. The Court of Criminal Appeals zeroed in on Judge Dunklin's charge to the jury, finding it "too general as to the causes provoking the killing of Grimes." When the case was subsequently retried, McLean stayed on as defense counsel.[29]

Jeff Vann's second trial was in November 1904. Again the hack driver lost, but this time the jury handed down a minimal two-year sentence. McLean appealed that verdict, too, and, like the first, got it reversed. After a third trial with McLean still heading up the defense, and the prosecution in disarray, Jeff Vann walked away a free man. The three trials had been a legal tour de force of the Texas criminal justice system that left many citizens with a much poorer opinion of a system that would let an obviously guilty man get away with murder.[30]

The conclusion of Jeff Vann's journey through the judicial system did not close the book on the affair however. Some loose ends still needed to be tied up. On May 17, 1902, Henry Kaysing, an express-wagon driver whose horse had been one of those wounded during the gun battle, filed a $65 claim with the city council for the animal's injuries. According to the suit, one of Grimes' shots had struck the animal in a hind leg, rendering him permanently "unserviceable." The plaintiff asked for compensation, and the matter was referred to the city's claims committee. There is no record that Kaysing ever received a dime.[31]

The strangest thing about Andy Grimes' case was the attempt to make a connection between his death and his badge number. Much was made of the fact that unlucky no. 13 was the same badge worn by two earlier officers who had been gunned down, Lee Waller and Robert Rice. Officer Waller's death in particular had other eerie similarities: Like Grimes, Waller had been shot just below the navel, and like Grimes, he had been gunned down on Main Street. To the superstitious, three shootings were too many to be a coincidence: badge no. 13 had to be jinxed.[32]

The Grimes case may have claimed one last "victim"—Joe Witcher. The Captain's uncharacteristically passive response as the first officer on the crime scene did not sit well with his fellow officers. Instead of shooting down the man standing, gun in hand, over Grimes, an action that could have been easily justified, Witcher merely disarmed the perp and placed him under arrest. While he may have believed he was exercising admirable restraint, his brother officers took a different view, blaming him for leaving a cop killer's fate up to the notoriously fickle justice system, which ultimately turned him loose. How much better, they thought, if Witcher had dispensed good, old-fashioned street justice on the spot, thus administering well-deserved retribution and saving the state a lot of time and expense. For all practical purposes, Joe Witcher's twenty-four-year career with the FWPD was finished; no officer would ever again give him the respect that his badge and rank deserved. He became a Jonah in a blue serge suit.

When the city council met a week later to make its annual review of the police force, which usually meant rubber-stamping the Police Chief's list, they refused to renew Captain Witcher's commission although he was on the list submitted by Chief Bill Rea. At that same meeting, the council adopted resolutions honoring Officer Andrew Grimes. A few days later, Mayor T. J. Powell repudiated the council's actions by ordering Witcher reinstated. Captain Witcher was back on the job, but he only lasted until the end of Bill Rea's tenure as Chief. As soon as Rea left office in 1905 Witcher was gone, too.[33] The lesson was clear: policemen, like soldiers and firefighters, are a fraternal brotherhood, and brother officers take care of their own. Joe Witcher had violated the first rule of the brotherhood, and his failure was compounded when Jeff Vann subsequently "walked." It may not have been in any book, but it has always been in the policeman's code.

Andy Grimes, the officer as opposed to the victim, represented a new breed of police officer. He was the first FWPD officer to carry his own life insurance policy and put it to use. That was important because the city in 1902 still did not provide death or accident benefits for its officers, and the Police Benevolent Society could not be depended upon apart from a one-time passing of the hat. Andy Grimes' policy paid his widow a modest $2,000. It was not much, but coupled with charitable donations, it allowed her to get a fresh start. But his death and her plight was a reminder that police officers were still poorly compensated by the community that employed them.[34]

The impressive headstone over Andy Grimes' grave in Oakwood Cemetery was paid for by the Police Benevolent Society (later the Police Benevolent Association), which after 1898 filled the gap between what the city provided (nothing) and what the family could afford. (Photograph by Kevin Foster)

This picture of John Nichols was taken not long before his death at the age of forty-three, showing clearly how law enforcement can age a man prematurely. Neatly dressed in civilian clothes, this is a family photograph, not an FWPD photo. Date and photographer unknown. (Courtesy of the Genealogy, History and Archives Unit, Fort Worth Public Library)

SPECIAL OFFICER
JOHN D. NICHOLS, JR.

December 22, 1906

"A good man in every respect"

Not every officer who died in the line of duty was a regular officer. Special police and special deputies were also duly commissioned lawmen who laid their lives on the line to defend law and order. John Nichols was the first "special officer" in Fort Worth history to die in the line of duty.

John Dee Nichols came from a distinguished Fort Worth family. His father, John Nichols, Sr., had made his fortune in the California gold fields before settling in Fort Worth in 1872. The rest of his life followed that same successful arc. In 1876 he was one of the founders of the city's first utility, the Fort Worth Gas Company; later he became vice-president of City National Bank, an alderman on the city council, and the City Secretary. He was also the first fire chief of the combined Panther Engine Company and M. T. Johnson Hook and Ladder Company. Junior never felt any urge to follow his father's path into either business or politics.[1]

John D. Nichols was one of eight children born to John and Elizabeth Nichols. He entered the world on August 6, 1863, in California, which was one of the safest places to be during the Civil War years. He grew up in frontier Fort Worth but, because of his father's social status, life was quite comfortable, and he got the best education available. Growing up and natural attrition whittled the family down until by 1880 there was just John, his father, and one sister, Molly. John could have worn a paper collar and worked in an office, but he chose not to follow in his father's footsteps. His own career choice was to be a policeman. Nor was he cut out to be a family man. He married Kate Brown, but it was a childless marriage, and she left him after several years for unknown reasons. John lived alone the rest of his life.[2]

He dreamed of becoming a policeman for years before finally getting the chance. In 1897 he was hired by the Fort Worth Police Department to fill the lowliest position on the force—turnkey at the city lockup. There was no place to go but up from there yet promotions proved elusive. By 1900 he had risen only to the level of beat cop, assigned to the most undesirable beat in the city, Hell's Half-acre. "The Acre," as it was generally known, had claimed more lives than any other section of the city over the years. The cowboys who were its favored customers in the early years had departed by this time, but murder, muggings, assault, and drug addiction were still the principal activities, and an officer could easily get himself killed if he were not careful.[3]

He could also be forgotten down there. John needed some dramatic accomplishment to kick his career into high gear, and that opportunity seemed to come his way in December 1900 when he assisted Detective James W. Thomason in arresting Jefferson Davis Hardin, younger brother of the infamous gunslinger John Wesley Hardin. Although he tried to emulate his legendary brother, Jeff Hardin was never anything more than a two-bit gambler. When Nichols and Thomason arrested him, he had just held up a poker game at gunpoint because he believed he had been cheated. The two officers relieved him of his pistol and his loot and escorted him to jail.[4]

Unfortunately for John, Jim Thomason got most of the credit. Still that was the high point of the first seven years of John's law enforcement career. He watched as other officers like Tom Maben, Al Ray, and Charlie Scott, who had come onto the force about the same time as he did, move up into the higher ranks while his own career languished. In 1904 he was a forty-year-old bachelor living in a boardinghouse, still walking a beat in the Acre and making the minimum police salary. Not ready to give up on his dream but anxious to find more remunerative work, he quit the Department to become a "special officer." Despite not cutting as wide a swath as his father, John, Jr., had nothing to be ashamed of. As the *Fort Worth Record* put it, he was "widely known, generally liked, and spoken of as a good man in every respect."[5]

His years of experience in the Acre finally paid off. He was hired by saloon man Frank DeBeque in 1903 to be the "special officer" at the Standard Theater (See chapter 7). At that date the Standard had been a landmark in the Acre for nearly a decade, occupying the southeast corner of Rusk and Twelfth. Several of Fort Worth's finest had been employed there in the same capacity over the years, including Andy Grimes and Peyton Maddox, one of Fort Worth's legendary clan of lawmen-brothers. The Standard was what was known as a "variety" or "vaudeville" theater, putting on two or

Lower Rusk Street went unphotographed for the pictorial record because it was the worst street in the worst part of town—a blot on the city's image! The lower end of Main (pictured here pre-1910), looking north from Fourteenth toward the courthouse, gives a fair idea of how lower Rusk looked in the same era. From this view, the Standard Theater would have been one block east and one block north. The touched-up postcard shows streetcar tracks, but the overhead lines have been removed. At this date, horses and wagons still ruled on the streets of Fort Worth. (Postcard courtesy of Dalton Hoffman, Fort Worth)

three shows a night, each consisting of ten to fifteen acts. The theater part of the establishment contained benches for the hoi polloi and elevated boxes for the fancy dans. Its rowdy audiences were not above pelting bad performances with beer bottles and anything else that came to hand. The Standard reflected its surroundings. At least two dozen assaults or killings occurred within a two-block radius between 1892 and 1909.[6]

The boisterous clientele required a full-time officer on the premises every night. John Nichols was merely the latest hired to keep a lid on the place. It was not a job for the timid or faint of heart. Nichols may not have had the intimidating presence of some of his tough, burly predecessors at the Standard, but he was not a man to back down to anybody either. Although it was not by choice, he was house policeman at the Standard longer than any of his predecessors—two years. He stuck it out at first for the money, then in the hope of parlaying it into a return to the regular force and leaving the world of rent-a-cops behind. The regular force was still the ultimate law enforcement job.

Six nights a week (the Standard was closed on Sundays), Officer Nichols was at his post in the lobby wearing a natty blue uniform with shoes polished and pistol holstered at his side. When his boyish charm failed to impress the rowdies, the badge and uniform did because everyone knew that a call from him to the stationhouse would bring the full force of the regular police on the run—with the paddy wagon. That was the last thing management wanted, however. The bantamweight officer was expected to keep out the riffraff, eject obnoxious drunks, and provide security for the ticket office without calling in reinforcements. In two years he never found it necessary to draw his weapon. The job was deceptively easy and paid well, but trouble was never far away at the Standard. This was still the Acre.

His moment of reckoning came at Christmastime, 1906. On Saturday night, December 22, with holiday revelers out in force, the joint was jumping. The first show of the evening was at eight thirty. A second performance would start about ten thirty and run until midnight.[7] Some customers took in both, filling the time in between with drinking and partying. The crowd that night was a mixture of well-heeled "swells" and rough-dressed "countrymen" (i.e., farmers) come to town for a little excitement. Among the latter were a couple of sodbusters, Barney Wise and Dine Wordlaw, from Red River County up on the Oklahoma border. Wise worked as a hand on A. B. Cherry's place near Cunningham, Texas, and was passing through Fort Worth on the way to visit his brother in Brooksville, Texas. Wordlaw's background is a mystery, and the odd spelling of his first name may be a misprint in the records. The two had decided to spend the night in town and start their Christmas celebrating early. Both were in their twenties and not accustomed to the traps and temptations of urban life. They strolled the Acre with their wages stuffed in their pockets, nearly forty dollars in Wise's case, determined to have a high old time on their first visit to the big city. They did not attract much attention because sodbusters and cowboys were still a common sight in Fort Worth, but inside the theater they stood out because they were uncommonly "boisterous" and because Wordlaw never took off his brown slouch hat. Long before the end of the night rolled around, they were well lubricated.[8]

They had bought a few rounds for some of the girls between shows and then bought tickets for the late performance. It had already been a long night before the first act took the stage for the last show. At some point during the show, Wise and Wordlaw decided they wanted a refund on the four bits they had shelled out for admission. Maybe they did not know that the second show would be a repeat of the first, or maybe the tired performers were not up to their personal standards, but, for whatever reason, they got up near the end of the show and made their way unsteadily to the ticket office to demand a refund. The young man behind the window was trying close out his receipts for the night and was taken by surprise. He advised the two customers that it was too late to get a refund and told them to go away. That just made Wise and Wordlaw angrier. Wise went around to the door and barged into the office. Wordlaw tagged along, letting his partner do all the talking. And Wise did plenty of talking, berating the flustered ticket-taker in loud tones. At first it was just the three of them in the office. Frank DeBeque, who was typically present when the receipts were counted at the end of the evening, had not arrived at the box office; he was attending to business elsewhere in the theater. Someone in the lobby, hearing the commotion, went to fetch Officer Nichols. As soon as he entered the box office, the ticket-taker took cover behind a big roll-top desk.

It was getting close to midnight and everyone's nerves were on edge, fueled by liquor and/or adrenaline. Nichols' presence, instead of calming the situation, just made it worse. Here was somebody Wise could jaw at who would jaw back. The inebriated farmer turned his full ire on the officer, and Nichols did not back down: the two troublemakers would have to leave the theater immediately or Nichols would run them in. Their confrontation grew loud enough to attract the attention of people in the lobby and the bar. Nichols had had enough. He told Wise he was under arrest, and the other man told him where he could stick his tin badge. The fuse was lit for a blowup that neither man was trying to avert.

The chronology of what happened next is not entirely clear because, of the two witnesses, one was hiding behind a desk and the other was an "accomplice" to the murderer. The most likely scenario is that as soon as Nichols tried to place Wise under arrest, the latter took exception to being manhandled and pulled a Smith & Wesson .38 revolver. He did not open fire, but used the pistol to crack Nichols over the head—twice. The officer crumpled to the floor with two deep gashes, bleeding profusely but he remained game, going for his own gun, a .45 revolver. Wise had the drop on him, however, and fired two shots at such close range that it seems impossible he could have missed. But he did; only one of the bullets hit its target, striking Nichols in the left side of the chest near the heart. The other shot thudded harmlessly into the wall behind him. Although mortally wounded, Nichols managed to get off three shots, only one of which found its target, hitting Wise in the right side just below the ribs. Propelled by forty-five grains of black powder, it passed all the way through his body. After the third shot, the pistol slipped from Nichols' grasp, and he lapsed into unconsciousness. Wise, severely wounded, was still standing.

It happened so quickly, it was all over before the people in the lobby could react. Altogether, five shots had been fired; it was a miracle more bullets did not find flesh. A panic-stricken Wordlaw picked up Nichols' gun and fled out the door, disappearing into the night. No one made a move to stop him on the way out. He went back at his room, gathered up his stuff, tossed the pistol, and left town.

Back at the theater, Frank DeBeque had come running as soon as he was informed there was trouble in the ticket office. He arrived just in time to see Nichols go down and watch in horror as Wise put a second bullet into his victim. The theater proprietor was unarmed but grappled with Wise, trying to disarm him. He got the gun away from the wounded gunman and kept him covered while someone called for the police. Word that one of their own was down brought the boys in blue running to the scene. Night Captain Ephraim Cone and Officers Denny Lloyd and Sid Waller arrived with the patrol wagon in a matter of minutes. They took Wise into custody, put him in the back of the wagon, and headed for the station as other officers arrived on the scene to begin taking statements. While all that was going on, some of the theater staff gently carried Nichols to a back room and placed him on a cot. Though one newspaper would later report he had died on the spot, the officer was actually conscious for a few minutes before slipping into a coma. There was no such thing as ambulance service at this date; emergency medical treatment still consisted of summoning a physician to the scene. John Nichols died before a physician could reach him.[9] Since neither Nichols nor Wise had made a statement at the scene, it would be up to police later to try to piece together what had happened.

Down at the city lockup, arresting officers showed little compassion for their prisoner. They put him in the infirmary and interrogated him for half an hour before finally sending for the city physician. That gentleman was not to be found, so more time passed before his backup, Dr. George D. Thomas, arrived. Through it all Wise remained stoically silent. He may have been knocking at death's door, but he was not about to incriminate himself. The only thing he would tell them about himself was his name and where he was from. After that, he just kept insisting he was an innocent man. "I'm [being] honest with you, boys," he told his interrogators. "I had a gun on me, but I don't remember having any trouble." He was not so reticent about his recent companion, giving up Dine Wordlaw but claiming he could not remember whether "he was with me at the theater or not." Finally, he said he had no idea how he and Nichols had both ended up shot.

On the surface, Wise's innocent act seems pointless because dying men do not have to worry about incriminating themselves, but it may have been the reflexive response of a lifetime of clamming up whenever being questioned by the authorities. Dr. Thomas finally arrived around 1:00 a.m. and examined the patient, confirming the consensus of the officers present that the prisoner was near death. Nonetheless, he ordered Wise transferred from the jail infirmary to the Fort Worth Medical College hospital to spend his final hours in more comfortable surroundings. The officers would have been happy to let Wise bleed out on the floor of a jail cell.

The next morning, Justice of the Peace Thomas J. Maben held the expected coroner's inquest, examining the corpus delicti and taking the testimony of witnesses. He delivered his verdict in traditional legalese: Officer Nichols "came to his death from effects of a pistol wound in his left breast inflicted by Barney Wise." A complaint charging Wise with murder was sworn out before Maben on December 24. As for Dine Wordlaw, the coroner's verdict let him off the hook calling him a material witness (not an accomplice) pending further investigation. That did not prevent the police from continuing the search for Wise's partner in crime.[10]

John Nichols' funeral was on Monday, and the fact that it was Christmas eve made it all the more tragic for those in attendance. The service was held at the F. S. Boulware residence at Belknap and Grove starting at two o'clock in the afternoon. Six policemen served as pallbearers, yet another indication of the strong bond between the regular force and the special police. Following the service, the body was transported to Pioneers Rest Cemetery for burial in the family plot. Curiously, nobody provided a marker for the grave, but it was no pauper's grave. Nichols simply had to share the marker placed years before by his brother-in-law over the grave of his only sister. Molly Nichols Dawson had died in 1881, and John Dawson had paid a hefty sum for a weeping angel on a tall pedestal, the most prominent marker in that section of the cemetery. In 1885 when John and Molly's father, John Nichols, Sr., died, he was buried beside Molly and his name inscribed on the back side of the angel's pedestal. Now, Officer Nichols was interred with his father and sister, but his name was not inscribed on the marker.[11]

Responding to this latest tragedy, the Police Benevolent Association did what it did best. In an emergency meeting at police headquarters Sunday evening, December 23, an ad hoc committee of Assistant Chief J. A. Allen, Sergeant J. D. Allgood, and Officers A. N. Bills and George Craig tapped the organization's funds for a floral wreath to place on the coffin and, more importantly, a $100 "cash benefit" to help defray funeral expenses. They also drafted "suitable resolutions" for a press release in the *Fort Worth Telegram* the next day:

> *We, the members of the Police Benevolent Association of the City of Fort Worth, feeling keenly the loss of our brother officer, John D. Nichols, who lost his life in the discharge of his duties as an officer of the City of Fort Worth the night of December 22, and,*
>
> *Whereas, we all knew him by his gentlemanly manner and actions, and his fealty to duty, to be a good citizen, and a loyal friend; and*
>
> *Whereas, God in his infinite wisdom, has seen fit to take him from this world in the midst of his usefulness, both as a citizen and as an officer of the police force of the City of Fort Worth; therefore be it*
>
> *Resolved, by the Police Benevolent Association of the City of Fort Worth, in a special meeting assembled, That in the loss of our brother officer the City of Fort Worth has lost a most faithful and efficient officer of the law and each of us has lost a friend, whose fidelity was never questioned; and be it*
>
> *Resolved, That a copy of these resolutions be furnished the press of this city with the request that the same be published.*[12]

The resolutions were the usual boilerplate except the part that called Nichols a "brother officer of the City of Fort Worth." Since he had been only a special officer at the time of this death, this was not strictly accurate, but in the mood of the moment, he was part of the family, regardless of what type of commission he held. No one was going to quibble.

With Officer Nichols in the ground, the full attention of the Department could focus on his killer. To everyone's amazement, Barney Wise survived his gunshot wound. Typically, victims of abdominal wounds, if they did not die quickly of hemorrhaging, died a lingering death from peritonitis and/or sepsis. In Wise's case, he had also been roughly handled and denied emergency medical treatment in the first critical hour after being shot. Fortunately, the bullet had not hit any vital organ, and he had a stout constitution. He spent the next two weeks in the charity ward of the Fort Worth Medical College under constant police guard. His recovery was little short of miraculous. On January 3 his doctors pronounced him "progressing very nicely" and declared he would soon be well enough to stand trial. The officers assigned to guard him wished he would have the decency to die and save everyone a lot of trouble.[13]

As soon as Barney Wise was indicted for first-degree murder and allowed legal counsel, his memory came back. To his original statement, taken down in the jail's hospital ward, he now added a wealth of detail, all calculated to support a legal strategy of self-defense. As he explained things now, he had gone to the ticket office seeking a ticket refund, and Nichols had accosted him without cause, threatening his life. The biggest hole in his defense was that the only other person who might have provided corroboration, Dine Wordlaw, was nowhere to be found. The county attorney finally called off the search for him after discovering that no one except the ticket-taker, who had been behind the desk most of the time, could even place him in the office at the time of the shooting. Not even Frank DeBeque remembered seeing him!

The trial of Barney Wise opened in the Seventeenth District Court of Judge Mike Smith on February 6, 1907. A jury pool of sixty men were summoned, but three-fourths of them did not show up on the appointed day. Judge Smith levied fines, and the next day all sixty were in court. The state had to prove that Wise had made an unprovoked attack on Officer Nichols, shooting him down in cold blood. That would be hard to do, with one witness's view blocked by a desk and the other unavailable. It came down to the word of the defendant against the reputation of a dead officer. County Attorney Jeff McLean, a strict law-and-order man, did his best, but had a hard time painting Farmer Wise as a coldblooded killer to a jury filled with fellow working-class men. The state-appointed defense lawyer, on the other hand, painted the defendant as a simple "country man," in town for a little Christmas celebration, provoked into defending himself by an overly aggressive private cop. The case went to the jury at noon on February 8. Five and a half hours later, jurors still had not reached a verdict. After sleeping on it overnight, however, they brought in a verdict the next morning of "not guilty." They had bought the self-defense argument, believing that Officer

Nichols bore at least some of the responsibility for what occurred. The verdict suggested that there was more to the story than what was being reported in the newspapers. Afterwards, Barney Wise wasted no time getting out of town.[14]

The jury's verdict as much as Nichols' murder outraged a great many good citizens, and one of those most outraged was in a position to do something about it. County Attorney Jefferson Davis McLean believed that the Acre had killed yet another good man and pledged to shut it down once and for all. Other city and county officials before him had made the same pledge to their constituents and proved unequal to the task, but McLean was a man on a mission. He was determined to use the full force of his office to shut down the most brazen vice operators in Fort Worth, not just the sleazy theater owners but the gamblers and barkeepers and all of their minions. Ironically, McLean's commendable resolve would cause the deaths of three more men, two of them law officers.

John Nichols' *first* grave in Pioneers Rest Cemetery was under the same angel statue as his sister, Maggie Dawson, who preceded him in death; his name is inscribed on the south side of the marker. Other family members were in the same plot. Later, the entire family was dug up and moved to Mount Olivet Cemetery. The angel stayed behind because the statuary was considered too fragile to move. Nichols' grave in Mount Olivet remains unmarked to date. (Photograph by Kevin Foster)

The only known picture of Hamil Scott is this one that appeared in the *Fort Worth Telegram* the day after his killing. It is a formal portrait provided to the newspaper by the family, which explains why he is in civilian clothes rather than uniform. The poor quality is because it is taken from newspaper microfilm. (Collections of Kevin Foster)

Memorial, life-sized portrait of Jefferson D. McLean, oil by John W. Alexander. Commissioned by the Tarrant County Bar Association and presented in 1912 to the Carnegie Library. It eventually passed to the Fort Worth Art Association then to the Modern Art Museum then back to the Bar Association (on loan). (Courtesy Collections of the Modern Art Museum of Fort Worth, Gift of the Jefferson Davis McLean Memorial Association).

CHAPTER 9

POLICE OFFICER HAMIL SCOTT & COUNTY ATTORNEY JEFFERSON McLEAN

March 22, 1907

"Fools rush in where angels fear to tread."

After the death of John Nichols, public indignation over the Acre reached new heights. It was a blight on the city and the site of at least two dozen murders over the years. The gamblers seemed the particular objects of the public's fury. The man who was the instrument of that fury was County Attorney Jefferson McLean. In 1907 he launched a war to shut down every gambling house in the Acre and ultimately the whole city. The word went out: Fort Worth was not big enough for both the gamblers and Jeff McLean.

Jefferson Davis McLean was a man with a name that could have been bestowed upon him by all-American moviemaker Frank Capra in a later era, but he was named that by his parents, William P. and Margaret Batte McLean, when he was born in 1871. They came to Texas after Major McLean's service in the Confederate army during the Civil War. The former rebel took up law and devoted his life to public service as a legislator, U.S. Congressman, state railroad commissioner, and judge of the Fifth Judicial District. Jeff was born in Mount Pleasant, Texas, and had three brothers and three sisters, one of whom, W. P. McLean, Jr., grew up to become one of the most distinguished trial lawyers of his day. In 1895 the family moved to Fort Worth.[1]

Jeff McLean was bitten by the political bug early and enjoyed a rapid rise in both law and politics. At the age of twenty-one he was elected mayor of Mount Pleasant, the youngest anyone has ever been elected to that exalted position in Texas. After coming to Fort Worth he became the assistant to crusading County Attorney James Swayne. Like his boss, he was a prosecutor of the first rank, tough, honorable, and knowledgeable in the law. In 1904 when Swayne stepped down, he ran for County Attorney and won. The campaign was a family affair, with his father and younger brother William running things. He made the central issue of his campaign open gambling in Fort Worth, claiming there were twenty to twenty-five places that operated in brazen defiance of the law, but he did not identify any of them. He also vowed he would not stop with prosecuting the gamblers alone. "I am going after the owners of property who are renting to violators of the law."[2]

The new county attorney proved to be as good as his word, taking on the most powerful interests on the local scene, whether the gamblers and liquor dealers who operated in the shadows or the big cattlemen who conducted business at the Fort Worth Livestock Exchange and socialized after hours at the Fort Worth Club. He was hardworking and incorruptible. He also had a flair for the dramatic that garnered headlines, never a bad thing for a man with political ambitions. After his first gambling raid he held a press conference in the lobby of the Delaware Hotel where he waved a money bag holding $3,000 in ill-gotten winnings. It was just the first of many media events he would arrange. And he won statewide fame assisting the attorney general's office successfully prosecuting anti-trust cases against members of the Livestock Exchange.[3]

Jeff took the plunge into marriage in 1895, but the union failed and five years later he was single again and back to living under his father's roof. He did not stay single long. The urbane and handsome young lawyer was introduced to Miss Lena Cogdell, who was the daughter of a prominent Granbury banker and sixteen years his junior. After a brief courtship, they were married in Granbury on October 11, 1905. Two years later, they were still childless.[4]

McLean's first love after his wife was the law. Re-elected in November 1906, he redoubled his efforts against the gamblers and saloon owners. He was the prince of raiders, leading many raids on bars and gambling joints in person. His raids were run like military operations that must have made his father, the former Confederate major, proud. The man who was named for the Confederacy's only president, still a hero to many Southerners, had a flair for show-manship coupled with absolute fearlessness; he was usually the first one in the door when officers had to force their way in. He refused to be a deskbound county attorney. Given his choice he preferred the criminal side of prosecution over the civil; there was more ac-tion and more headlines. While judges, prosecutors, and reformers loved him, he won no friends in the Fort Worth Police Department (FWPD). When the boys in blue proved to be less than willing al-lies in his war on vice, he turned to the Sheriff's Department, even keeping the Police Department in the dark about the precise times and places of his raids. He also suspected the police of being in bed with the gamblers and saloon owners, to the point where they would tip off the targets ahead of time.

In the early part of 1907, McLean planned a series of raids on gambling joints to coincide with the annual National Feeders and Breeders Show (a.k.a. the Fat Stock Show) when the eyes of Texas would be on Fort Worth. D-Day was Friday, March 22, the last day of the event. With thousands of visitors and exhibitors in town, he was assured of maximum publicity. And if, as rumored, he enter-tained larger political ambitions, that publicity would be invaluable in a future run for mayor or even state legislator.[5]

The lives of three men were about to intersect in the biggest gun battle on the streets of Fort Worth since Luke Short and "Longhair Jim" Courtright in 1887. The other two men in this tragic drama were Bill Thomason, a gambler, and Hamil Scott, a special officer. With McLean, they represented the three sides of criminal justice in Fort Worth: the prosecutor, the lawman, and the vice operator.[6]

Hamil Poston Scott had been born in Smith County, Virginia, in 1865 near the end of the Civil War. Growing up, he had four brothers, Charles, William, Edward, and Benton. The family moved to Texas in 1870 and settled near Fort Worth in 1872. The boys grew up on a farm just north of the city watching the cattle herds moving up the Eastern Trail. But they were not attracted to the overly romanticized lifestyle of the cowboy. Three of the brothers eventually made careers with the railroad. Charles and Hamil went into law enforcement, although only Charles made a career out of it. Hamil's first job after leaving the farm was with a railroad, an employer that continued to put food on the table the rest of his life. As an adult, Scott was a respected member of the community, joining the Masons and in 1887 marrying Margaret Campbell, a Fort Worth resident. Twenty years later, the couple was still childless.[7]

Scott got his first taste of law enforcement as an express messenger with the Fort Worth and Denver City Railway. The job came with the responsibility of defending the contents of the express car against all threats. Agent Scott proved to be a nervy fellow, once even holding off Black Jack Ketchum's gang for more than an hour, using the time to hide the valuables in his care so that the gang could not find them when they finally broke in. Even the outlaws were impressed with his spunk. On another occasion, a train wreck derailed the express car he was riding in, causing it to catch fire. He barely escaped with his life that time, too.[8]

Margaret may have persuaded him to quit the railroad and find a less hazardous line of work. In 1902 he was "brokering" real estate, potentially a lucrative business in the booming city, but his heart was not in it. The following year he went back to law enforcement, joining the Tarrant County Sheriff's Department where he worked mostly as an "attaché of the courts" (i.e., bailiff). As a deputy sheriff he earned less than an express agent, but the salary included fees for a variety of extra duties that could increase take-home pay substantially. A deputy sheriff also got to sleep in his own bed at night. In 1903 he participated in raids on Fort Worth's "Bucket of Blood" district, an area of low dives and gambling joints on Thirteenth that was part of the Acre. He became disenchanted with the deputy sheriff's job, however, when Sheriff John T. Honea shorted his salary $15 per month for some unspecified reason and refused to pay him a fee he had earned. Scott resigned in the summer of 1906 but not before suing the Sheriff for his back pay.[9]

Scott's beef was with the Sheriff, not law enforcement. Being a lawman fulfilled him personally and carried on a family tradition. His brother, Charles R. Scott, was Chief of Detectives for the Fort

Worth Police Department. Living in the same community as his highly regarded brother was a constant reminder of the life he desired. When his brother passed away in 1902, he was left to carry on the family tradition in law enforcement alone.[10] Needing a job, he went back to work for the Fort Worth and Denver City, this time as a claims agent. The railroad arranged a special officer's commission from the county that allowed him to carry a pistol and do everything else that regular lawmen did. Seemingly, he now had the best of both worlds: the status of peace officer and the salary of railroad agent. Still, 1907 did not start off well. In February, he was the plaintiff in a lawsuit against the Texas Lumber Yards. When he lost, his legal fees guaranteed he would not be returning to the Sheriff's Department any time soon; he could not afford the pay cut.[11]

The third member of this little drama, Bill Thomason, was a one-armed gambler-cum-saloon-owner with a sour attitude and a bad reputation. He had been run out of more cities then he cared to remember—including Quanah, Texas, and Hays City, Kansas—before landing in Fort Worth in 1883. The Mississippi native was forty-three years old in 1907. He lost his right arm in a hunting accident after coming to Fort Worth. The fact that he survived the accident and the resulting amputation was testimony to his toughness, but the experience had also left him angry at the world. He decided the most remunerative line of work he could go into was gambling, and he quickly acquired a reputation as a brawler whose physical handicap made him, if anything, more dangerous. He had a string of violent confrontations on his rap sheet, all involving gunplay, but had never served any hard time. While living in Quanah, Bill had found time to woo and win Clara Lesley, eight years his junior. He married her in 1890 and brought her to Fort Worth. Seventeen years later they still had no children.[12]

At a time when many gamblers had colorful nicknames such as "Kid Kinney" and "The Bosque Kid," Thomason was simply known as "one-armed Bill." Prior to acquiring his own place, he was a familiar face at the gaming tables in all the city's premier saloons: White Elephant, Board of Trade, and Palais Royal. Among the members of the local gambling fraternity, he was considered a "floater" before taking over the concession upstairs over the Stag Saloon in the 600 block of Main. He did not *own* the Stag Saloon (that was Billy Hornbeck), but he served its clientele, who only had to climb the stairs to find the other favorite activity of saloon patrons. By 1903 he was running the gambling concession at not one but two places: the uptown Stag Saloon and the Crown Saloon in the Acre. In 1900 he had described himself to the census-taker as a common "laborer." Seven years later he was "the well-known gambler and man-about-town." Neither description was entirely accurate. Neither of his operations was on a par with the White Elephant or Palais Royal, but both did plenty of business. On a good night he could pull in $3,000, enough to keep him in diamond stickpins and fancy cigars.[13]

Bill had a complicated relationship with the local representatives of law and order. While he was on a first name basis with the sheriff and his boys, his relationship with the FWPD had a rockier history. For years he had paid off the cops, standard operating procedure among members of the gambling fraternity, but he did not feel like he always got his money's worth. The payments were sometimes called "loans" and other times "fines," which were collected by officers on the spot, supposedly to save him from having to be booked into jail or go to court. Officers regularly dropped by his places to collect their money, and he paid out whatever they demanded "for the benefit of the house," as he put it. In 1903 when Detective James W. Thomason (no relation) became particularly demanding, trying to "shake him down," he first threatened Thomason's life, then complained to the police committee of the city council. The last straw was that his was the only gambling house in the city to be closed down in the previous seven months. The police committee held a hearing but found no evidence of malfeasance, but thereafter Bill found himself targeted by officers in the Department as payback.[14]

By 1907 Big Bill and the police had patched up their relationship, which meant that the gambler was once more back to paying protection money and in return he expected his operations not to be harassed. On Friday afternoon, March 22, when Jeff McLean's office was preparing to raid the Stag Saloon, one of Thomason's courthouse connections tipped him off. Thomason was outraged; being raided was not part of the arrangement. As far as he was concerned, he was being unfairly targeted, just like back in 1903, only now it was the county attorney who had it in for him.[15]

Because the Stag gambling room was not an elite joint and an afternoon raid was unlikely to net any big players, it should have been a routine raid. But the timing, during Fat Stock Show week, was just the sort an ambitious county attorney could parlay into front-page headlines. Bill Thomason's existing arrangements with the police did not concern Jeff McLean, nor did the fact that he had already been raided once that week by said police. By the rules of the game as Thomason understood them, he had every right to expect to be left alone for a while and, if pushed, he would push back. One newspaper called him "cool and self-possessed," but it was more accurate to say he had a short fuse. And like most gamblers, he carried a gun on his person at all times. The one-armed gambler and the "Dudley Do-Right" of Tarrant County represented the two different sides of Fort Worth. At one time those two sides had lived in uneasy peace but no more. Fort Worth was not big enough for both Bill Thomason and Jeff McLean.

It came down about five o'clock on a Friday afternoon, March 22, 1907. That was when the latest chapter of Jeff McLean's anti-gambling offensive commenced. Fat Stock Show week was winding down, and hundreds of participants were heading for the local saloons and honkytonks to start the weekend. The County Attorney's office had just received a tip that games were already in full swing upstairs at 600 Main. Assistant County Attorney W. H. Slay called in Sheriff Tom J. Wood, and they quickly organized a raiding party consisting of themselves plus deputies Joe Witcher, Charles Everett, Charles Evans, Sid Higgins, and Tom Snow. Jeff McLean would only go along on this one as a spectator, but that did not mean he was not calling the shots as he always did. He expected that a dramatic daylight raid on Main Street would generate plenty of publicity for his big cleanup crusade. He even invited his brother Bill, also a lawyer, and County Commissioner Duff Purvis to come along. They rode in Jeff's buggy.

The eight officers in the raiding party piled into the patrol wagon for the quick trip down to the Stag. They pulled up at the front door, jumped out and rushed upstairs where they burst in and placed all those present under arrest—five men playing faro and poker. No high rollers, no stacks of money and chips. Except for the faro wheel, it was a friendly Friday night poker game with the boys. Still, while it was hardly headline-worthy, Jeff's raiders had broken up another gambling operation in the heart of the city. Bill Thomason was nowhere to be seen. While some of the officers began walking the prisoners down to the courthouse, Sheriff Wood and the rest stayed behind to load the gambling equipment into the wagon.[16]

Everything was going smoothly until Thomason arrived on the scene. The timing of his arrival spared him the embarrassment of the long "perp walk" down to the county jail, but he was forced to watch in helpless rage as his place was cleaned out—for the second time in a matter of days. He pulled Wood aside, pleading with him to be reasonable, but the Sheriff just shook his head. "Bill," he told him, "it's no use. If I let the stuff stay in here, it won't be two hours before you're running again, and I'm going to take it all."[17]

Thomason was not used to such treatment. He knew the drill on Main Street gambling raids; they were choreographed performances that satisfied the do-gooders without putting too much of a crimp in the gamblers' operations. This one, however, was Jeff McLean's show, and if there were any doubts, they were laid to rest when the County Attorney put in an appearance. Not only did he have Commissioner Purvis and brother Bill McLean in tow, but he also brought his wife along. It was practically a family outing. The county's top attorney did not need to be there, but he wanted to be present for any newspapermen who might show up to cover the raid. He was also there to deliver a hot tip to the Sheriff that had just come in as he was leaving the office; namely, that there was another gambling operation in full swing just up the street. It might have been the Cabinet Saloon, or the Board of Trade, or the Palais Royal; the record does not say. The important thing was, this was a golden opportunity to shut down two gambling joints with one operation and in the process make an even bigger splash. So McLean parked his buggy across the street, told Lena and the others to wait for him, and went upstairs to find Tom Wood. He surveyed his handiwork, then went back downstairs.

Since all the fun was over and the press was nowhere to be seen, McLean did not intend to hang around. He waved the raiding party off to its next target, then crossed the street to tell his wife and friends he would only be a few more minutes. Then, for reasons unknown, he headed back to the saloon. He had just reached the doorway when Thomason stepped out. The saloon man glared at his nemesis. He was still seething about the raid and, as he told Police Chief Maddox later, "Jim, I was tired of being imposed on, and I couldn't stand it no longer." On top of all that, he could not stand the preening, headline-grabbing county attorney. He sneered loud enough for passersby to hear, "There goes that son-of-a-bitch who always gets in when he ain't got a chance to get a piece of the pie for himself!"[18]

This was a slur on McLean's integrity *and* his courage and in front of witnesses. He could not pretend to ignore it. He raised his hand as if to point a finger at Thomason or even strike him. That was all it took to send Thomason over the edge. Reaching into his hip pocket, he pulled out a .45 caliber revolver and fired a single shot at McLean. He could hardly miss at such a short distance. The bullet struck McLean in the larynx with sufficient force to pass all the way through his neck and smash his spine. It was a mortal wound. The victim never had a chance. He would live only another ten minutes before death took him. As McLean lay on the sidewalk, Thomason coolly walked up and stood over him, then, satisfied, went back into the saloon. Shocked bystanders who had witnessed the shooting stood rooted to the spot. Commissioner Duff Purvis raced across the street. It was he who broke the spell, bellowing, "Bill Thomason has shot Jeff! Catch him!" But it was too late; Thomason had not stopped when he got inside the Stag Saloon but hurried past a few casual drinkers and a puzzled bartender on his way out the back door into the alley. He now had a good head start over the pursuit just getting organized out front.

Meanwhile, others gently picked up the victim and carried him into Anderson's Drugstore, two doors down. McLean, still conscious, managed to gurgle out, "Handle me carefully, boys, I am choking."[19]

They gently laid him out on Anderson's floor, and twenty people crowded around him, uncertain what to do next. Somebody had sent for a doctor so they waited. One of those waiting was Duff Purvis. With a politician's knack for rising to the rhetorical occasion, he composed a statement that he later issued to the press: "[Jeff] looked like a man who had done his whole duty unflinchingly, and he was not ashamed of what he had done."[20]

Outside on the street, all was chaos. People had come running attracted by the gunshot, and others added to the mob as word spread. One bystander, more affected by what had happened than all the others put together, was Lena McLean, who raced across the street, fearing the worst. When she got to the door of Anderson's Drugstore, Duff Purvis was trying to close and lock the door to keep any more gawkers from squeezing in. He tried to keep her out, too, but she forced her way past him. When she saw her husband lying in a pool of blood she screamed. Bill McLean tried to persuade her to leave, but she refused. Jeff McLean died in his wife's blood-covered arms.[21]

On the street, the manhunt for Bill Thomason was just getting underway. It was not an organized action at this point. The police had not arrived on the scene in force, but no one wanted to wait for them either. They set off after their quarry like a pack of baying hounds, their numbers growing as newcomers joined in. In a matter of minutes, hundreds of people were milling about in front of 600 Main Street with just one thought on their minds: catch Bill Thomason and make him pay for what he did. If the mob caught up with him before the police, his life would not be worth a Confederate dollar at one of his faro tables. Uncertain where he was headed, the mob split into smaller groups and fanned out across the business district.

This was all happening right in the backyard of publisher Amon Carter's *Fort Worth Star*, and the *Star* got the jump on its rival, the *Fort Worth Telegram*. By 6:00 p.m., the *Star* already had an "extra" on the street. Carter's newshounds followed up that scoop an hour later with another "extra." It was an impressive publishing triumph that left the larger-circulation *Telegram* in the dust, but in their haste to steal a march, *Star* reporters did not get all their facts straight.[22]

The second act of the drama was unfolding even as the presses were printing the first act. Officer Hamil Scott was on his way home from the Fat Stock Show with his wife when they heard what had happened. Although off-duty, he did not hesitate to join the manhunt. He had his pistol on him, and his lawman's instincts kicked in. He found out where Thomason had last been seen and took off after telling his wife to go home.[23]

The fugitive meanwhile was leading his pursuers on a merry chase. He crossed the alley behind the Stag Saloon and entered through the rear entrance of John Davis' real estate office. Inside, he confronted bookkeeper Ed Hollingsworth and a stenographer, sticking a pistol in Hollingsworth's ribs while frisking him to see if he was armed by anything more deadly than a pencil. Satisfied, he waved the bookkeeper aside and dashed out the front door. He was now heading north on Houston toward Sixth. Hamil Scott had somehow caught up with the pursuing mob and managed to get ahead of them so that he was now leading the chase. Thomason continued to run like a hare before the hounds. He ducked into an alley on the east side of the Elks Club, cut over to Throckmorton, then headed south toward Seventh. Somehow, Scott managed to stay on his trail through all the twists and turns, and was even gaining on him. Just before reaching Seventh, Thomason ducked into a vacant lot and concealed himself among some crates behind a billboard. He was not trying to hide; just the opposite; he planned to ambush his pursuer. He did not have long to wait before Scott came into view. When the officer was just four feet from his hiding place, he fired three shots.

Two hit their mark. The first went through Scott's right forearm, causing him to drop his gun. The second entered his left shoulder, clipped a lung, and lodged against the sixth cervical vertebrae at the base of his neck. Hamil Scott did not die instantly, but he was *hors de combat*, bleeding effusively from the two wounds and paralyzed in his lower body.[24] Thomason would later claim not to have known that the armed man pursuing him was an officer, which might have been true since Scott was not a uniformed policeman but only a special officer with the railroad. But regardless of Scott's status, what Thomason did next was unjustifiable on any grounds. He coolly walked up and pumped two more slugs into the helpless officer; then, because his own pistol was empty, he grabbed Scott's pistol and resumed his flight. In his confession later, Thomason would also attempt to justify shooting Officer Scott after he was already down by saying that Scott had fired first, a transparent lie that was easily disproven once police had Scott's pistol in their possession.[25]

In hindsight, it is obvious that Officer Scott should have exercised more prudence in his pursuit of the suspect, but the same instincts that had once led him to take on the entire Black Jack Ketchum gang singlehandedly would cost him his life this time. Having disposed of one pursuer, Thomason wanted to resume his flight, but now the mob was too close. He crossed the street and slipped into Roe's Lumber Yard, which took up the entire east side of the block between Sixth and Seventh. He hoped the vast sheds with their towering stacks of lumber would provide a good place to hide out or, if necessary, make a last stand. Here, the final act of the drama would play out. The mob saw him duck into the lumberyard and rushed forward to surround the block. They knew they had run him to ground. More importantly, they had sniffed blood.[26]

A new player was about to enter the drama in the last act. Ben U. Bell had been a policeman and volunteer fireman since 1887. When the volunteer fire department was abolished in 1893 in favor of a paid force, Bell went full-time with the FWPD. He was an old-fashioned, hard-nosed cop who literally followed the "take-no-prisoners" approach. On the afternoon of March 22 he was on duty at the Texas and Pacific passenger depot. He did not hear all the shooting but learned about it when someone came in with the news. He left his post and headed uptown where the action was. On his way

This picture of A. J. Roe's lumberyard shows the sprawling complex of sheds that covered an entire city block from Throckmorton to Taylor and Sixth to Seventh. This view, ca. 1906, looks west from Throckmorton with Seventh Street on the left and Sixth on the right, and St. Paul's Methodist Church in the background. One of these sheds is where the manhunt for Bill Thomason came to a bloody end. (Courtesy of the Genealogy, History and Archives Unit, Fort Worth Public Library)

up Main he heard talk of "Let's go to city hall and lynch him!" So he veered over to the municipal building at Tenth and Throckmorton, went in and offered his services to desk sergeant C. W. Newby. That gentleman, whose information was dated, directed Officer Bell to the Stag Saloon. Bell continued north on Throckmorton with the idea of cutting over to Main to reach the saloon. He never arrived because when he got to Throckmorton and Seventh he caught up with the action. Officers were loading Hamil Scott into the police wagon when he walked up. Scott was still alive, just barely. One of the officers whispered to Bell that "death was expected momentarily." Meanwhile, lots of people were pointing at Roe's Lumber Yard saying that was where Thomason was holed up. Subsequent estimates of the number of people present ranged from 3,000 to 5,000. Twenty deputies and policemen were also on the scene by this time. Their greatest fear was not that the mob would attempt to rush the place and take the fugitive, but that they would just set fire to the lumberyard and burn him out. If that happened, the whole business district could go up in flames.[27]

Officer Ben Bell was cut from the same cloth as Hamil Scott: intrepid to the point of recklessness. Don't wait for the criminal to come to you; go find the criminal. Take the initiative! He went around to an alley that cut between Throckmorton and Houston and entered the lumberyard through a gate there. In the darkened interior, he found that Officer Denny Lloyd had preceded him. Lloyd was crouched atop a stack of lumber intently watching something. He waved to get the attention of Bell and wordlessly pointed toward the other end of the stack to show where Thomason was hiding. Just at that moment Thomason raised up and tried to snap off a round at Lloyd but his pistol misfired. He had revealed himself now, and Lloyd opened fire. Bell had his own pistol out and joined in. They had Thomason in a crossfire, and their shots hit home. Thomason was struck three times: one slug pierced his abdomen and lodged against a rib in his back; a second shattered one of his legs just above the knee; and the third broke the shoulder of his good arm. There was no way of telling who fired which shot. Thomason should have gone down, as badly wounded as he was, but he was on his feet stumbling toward the alley entrance—an amazing display of willpower and stamina. He finally collapsed partway out the gate where he lay, unmoving.[28]

Officer Ben U. Bell helped put an end to Bill Thomason's rampage and to Thomason himself the old-fashioned way—by putting a bullet in him, helping to win him a promotion to detective. Dressed here as a plainclothes man for the 1910 "Fort Worth Detectives Department" photo. (Courtesy of Fort Worth Police Historical Association)

Bell and Lloyd cautiously approached and, seeing no signs of life, grabbed the body and dragged it down the alley to Seventh where they tossed it into the patrol wagon that had just returned from taking Hamil Scott to the Medical College, the city's only emergency ward. The crowd stood back and let the wagon through, following all the way to city hall. Everyone breathed a sigh of relief, none more heartfelt than A. J. Roe whose lumberyard was scarcely damaged.

It had been a remarkable series of events, taking less than half an hour from start to finish. This was 1907, and Fort Worth had just witnessed a gun battle in the heart of the city. Three men lay dead or dying. Dodge City had once been notorious for this sort of thing but Fort Worth had never experienced a running gun battle in the streets of downtown. Making it worse: the eyes of Texas were upon the city because of the Fat Stock Show. Fort Worth only thought it had lived down its wild and woolly image.

While the final act was being played out at the lumberyard, a second mob estimated at 500 had gathered in front of city hall, convinced that Thomason was already in custody. They barged inside and confronted the desk sergeant, demanding access to the cells in the basement. Sergeant Newby assured them he did not have the man they were looking for. He even took several of the mob's leaders downstairs to see for themselves. As they were coming back out, the news arrived that Thomason was cornered in the lumberyard, and they all rushed off on a fresh scent. On their way they passed the patrol wagon carrying Thomason going in the opposite direction. A few moments later, those who had stayed behind at city hall saw officers drag Thomason's body out of the wagon and carry it inside. Soon thereafter, the group from the lumber yard arrived, its ranks adding to the city hall mob. The combined mob filled the lawn and spilled out into the streets, showing no sign of leaving any time soon. To hold them at bay, Chief Jim Maddox sent word out that Thomason was dead, but there were few buyers for that story.

If it was an official lie, it was one that was easy to believe. Officers had discovered upon arriving at the jail that Thomason had been "playing 'possum." Although badly wounded, he was far from dead. They put him in a jail cell where they made him as comfortable as possible, administering opiates to ease his pain. When he refused to die, they summoned the official city physician to treat him. That gentleman came and examined the patient, offering the glum diagnosis that there was nothing he could do.

To discourage a lynch mob from storming the jail, the police stuck with the story that Thomason was dead. Meanwhile, they were sorting out the jurisdictional issues. Sheriff Wood let Police Chief Jim Maddox run the show since they were on Maddox's turf. At 8:00 p.m. Wood was on the telephone calling in his men to provide backup to the tired policemen posted around the jail. Every available policeman had been called in to help hold the mob at bay.

Chief Maddox decided more decisive action was needed to avert a lynching. He went out and addressed the mob sternly: "There won't be any call for mob law tonight, boys." He finally conceded that the prisoner was alive but said, "Thomason cannot live."[29] His fatherly admonition backed up by a line of armed officers held the mob off for the time being.

Maddox, a compassionate man, also sent for Clara Thomason to come be with her husband at the end. Officers sneaked her in though the jail's back door. The distraught woman found Thomason surprisingly rational, even solicitous of her feelings. He told her the jail was no place for a lady and ordered her to go home. She departed, but only after imploring Maddox to notify her when the end was nearer, although there was no telling when that might be. Maddox posted a police officer in the cell to maintain a deathwatch.

Thomason continued to defy the odds as well as the sincere wishes of all those watching over him. For a dying man with a lynch mob howling outside for his blood, he displayed remarkable spunk. Through the barred, ground-level windows, he could hear the catcalls of the mob but showed not the least fear. He only asked the guard to roll him a cigarette and light it. When Maddox and Wood tried to interrogate him, he denied responsibility for anything that had happened. They reminded him that he was dying and urged him to come clean—confession is good for the soul—but he stuck to his story. The only remorse he expressed was leaving "my poor wife and children . . . practically in poverty." He told Maddox he had a $75 check in his inside coat pocket and asked him to give it to Clara when he was gone.[30]

To their credit, the boys in blue were determined to do their duty until either nature ran its course or they could hand off their prisoner to the county authorities. The FWPD had never lost a man to a lynch mob to date, and they did not intend to do so now. As night fell, Maddox feared the cover of darkness would embolden the mob, so he called in all special and reserve officers. After he had Winchester-toting officers all around city hall, he assured a newspaper reporter who was waiting for the next act in the drama to unfold, "I don't think there will be any call for mob law [tonight]. Thomason cannot live. He is a dying man."[31]

That night (March 22–23), every beat in the city was uncovered, but the hours passed quietly. About 4:30 a.m. Maddox and Wood decided to risk moving Thomason to the county jail, a more secure lockup with a real infirmary. The transfer was accomplished without incident just before dawn although somehow the word got out and the mob followed. So far the authorities had kept one step ahead of the mob. By the time morning arrived, only a few hardy souls were still camped out on the jailhouse lawn.

Meanwhile, another deathwatch was underway at Hamil Scott's beside. It was a ghoulish race to see which of the two mortally wounded men would expire first. Initially, the Officer had been taken to his home at 611 West Fifth, just two blocks from where he was shot. This was standard practice. Fort Worth had two well-equipped hospitals, one of which was the "emergency department" of the Fort Worth Medical College at Fifth and Calhoun, but the first thought of those at the scene was to get him home. At least let him die surrounded by family. But when he hung on, hopes began to rise. Dr. Bacon Saunders came to the house to treat the victim, and the first thing he saw was the ugly throat wound. He cleared the air passage and administered opiates, and Scott rested comfortably through the night. Saunders was afraid of causing more damage if he probed the wound, but the patient's inert form and cold, clammy extremities had him extremely worried. Fortunately, the city had some of the new X-ray equipment at the medical college, and Scott was a prime candidate for using it to locate the bullet in his neck. Saunders ordered it brought to the house, and on Saturday morning city workers ran an electric line into the house to power it. While waiting for this to be completed, the Doctor issued a wildly optimistic statement to the press.

Mr. Scott's condition is very good and if the bullet has not severed the spinal cord, there is an excellent chance for his recovery. I shall look for the bullet this afternoon with the X-ray machine. He had no fever at all and is perfectly conscious with good pulse, and is cheerful and very pleasant. His condition may be considered very good outside the paralysis.

Hamil Scott was the first Fort Worth police officer and one of the very first Fort Worth citizens to undergo an X-ray examination. Dr. Saunders took pictures of the patient's neck late that afternoon. Two other physicians were present to observe and advise. The X-rays confirmed what Saunders had been afraid of: the bullet had severed the spinal chord. There was no hope. The amazing thing was that he had managed to hang on this long. Saunders ordered his patient transferred to St. Joseph's Hospital to spend whatever time was left to him in hygienic surroundings cared for by trained medical personnel.[32]

Both men hung on through Saturday. Family members who lived out of town rushed to Fort Worth. Scott's sister came down from Denver on the train, and Thomason's sister, a schoolteacher, rushed over from Dallas. As soon as she reached her brother's side, she requested a minister to come and pray over him, but the gambler, a heathen to the end, refused to even talk to the man of God.[33]

Thomason's final hours were anything but easy. He passed in and out of consciousness all day Saturday, gasping for air and begging for water during his waking moments. The authorities decided to keep him in the jail infirmary rather than transferring him to the Medical College although they did permit doctors to come to the jail to treat him. Late Saturday afternoon, Dr. E. L. Stephens and another physician began injecting him with ever-heavier doses of opium to relieve his "terrible agony." The authorities had given up trying to get a useful statement out of him. At one point Stephens asked the patient if he were suffering, to which Thomason moaned, "I am suffering worlds." Although intoxicants were ordinarily prohibited inside the jail, they also allowed some of his friends to bring him wine.[34]

The end came Saturday evening. About 7:20, Thomason rallied briefly and struggled to sit up. Failing, he fell back onto his pillow and slipped into a coma. Ten minutes later he was dead. He had lingered for an excruciating fourteen hours. His wife and sister were beside him at the end with Clara Thomason tenderly holding his hand. Justice of the Peace Richard Bratton, acting as coroner, Chief Maddox, and Sheriff Wood were also present at the end, but not out of any feelings for the dying man. They were still hoping against hope for a deathbed confession or even some expression of regret. He was angry at the world and defiant to the end. In fact, he cursed Jeff McLean with almost his dying breath. His only regret, he gasped, was leaving his poor wife alone and penniless. Afterwards, deputies escorted Clara and her sister-in-law to a waiting carriage. The widow was supported by an officer on either side. Over and over she kept repeating, "I have nothing left." The sheriff sent for undertaker George Gauze to remove the body and see to the burial.[35]

Clara Thomason did not go away quietly either. A week later she wrote a letter to the *Telegram* saying her husband was not the monster everyone was calling him. The newspaper printed her letter in full. She admitted up front that he had been a professional gambler, but, "No man can ever say that Bill Thomason ever deprived them of a dollar wrongfully," she declared. He ran "honest" games, was "liberal to a fault," and had never been run out of any town. "I knew him to be as gentle and considerate of others' feelings as the most peaceable citizen of your community." Readers who had followed the story of the sensational killings must have been mystified who this man was that she was describing. If there was any cause for misunderstanding, she said, it had nothing to do with Bill's character, only their name; it was "Thomason," not "Thompson," or "Tomlinson." She wanted to set the record straight on his character *and* his name. Ironically, the coroner could not get his name right even with all the notoriety; his death certificate was recorded as "William Thomlinson."[36]

On Sunday, March 24, public attention focused on Jeff McLean's funeral. The official mourning had begun on Saturday when the courthouse was draped in black crepe, and all county offices were closed. The mourning was not confined to Fort Worth. Messages of condolence poured over the telegraph from all over the state and, as the news spread, from all over the nation. He was still the center of attention on Sunday. Reverend O. P. Kiker of the Missouri Avenue Baptist Church, McLean's church, preached on "The Enemies to Our Commonwealth: Anarchism, Intemperance, and Gambling," with the emphasis on the last-named. The funeral service got underway that afternoon at three o'clock commencing at the McLean residence on Eighth Avenue. Hundreds of friends and colleagues crowded into the house and spilled out onto the lawn and street. After the sermon and the traditional procession of mourners past the casket, the cortege formed for the trip to Oakwood Cemetery.[37] At its head rode sixteen mounted policemen in full uniform, including Chief Jim Maddox. Scores of carriages followed the hearse on its route down Throckmorton to Sixth, then over to Houston and north across the river. It was reportedly "the longest funeral procession seen in Fort Worth for years," and about 2,000 people were present at the graveside ceremony. A profusion of floral wreaths covered the ground around the grave. One of the largest, from the assistant county attorneys, was in the shape of an open law book with flowers forming the words "Law and Order Shall Prevail." On Monday all state flags in the city were lowered to half-staff.[38]

Bill Thomason's funeral took place that same day, but hardly anyone cared. George Gauze was the undertaker of record for the murderer as he had been for the victim. No one held it against him. Thomason's service was held in the Gauze chapel. Funeral homes were a recent arrival in Fort Worth, and Thomason was one of the first public figures to have his service conducted in one, as opposed to a church or residence. There is no record of anyone else attending besides the widow and sister of the deceased. After a perfunctory service, the remains were interred in a remote section of Oakwood Cemetery and the grave marked with a cheap marker.[39]

In an interview afterwards Clara Thomason lamented that she had "nothing left" after paying for the funeral. She left Fort Worth a few weeks later and settled in Ballinger, Texas, but her fate was tied to the city where her husband died. Six weeks after Bill Thomason died, Clara followed him in death, the victim of a ruptured appendix. On May 4 she was buried beside Bill.[40]

With Jeff McLean and Bill Thomason both in the ground, the public's attention turned to Hamil Scott. The dying officer survived longer than anyone expected. In fact, his will to live was astounding. He lingered between life and death for five weeks. During that time, he was visited by a constant stream of family and friends, although, slipping in and out of consciousness, he was usually unaware of their presence. Newspaper reports of his condition veered between unrealistic hope and fatalism. On Sunday morning, March 24, one newspaper reported "the chances were very favorable toward recovery" because the patient had slept soundly the night before.[41] The truth was the doctors could do nothing but try to make him as comfortable as possible until the end. After April 23 he refused food, and on April 29 he slipped into a coma. Finally, on May 1, 1907, at 8:40 a.m. he passed away.

Scott's funeral the following day was on a just slightly smaller scale than Jeff McLean's. Like McLean's, it was reported in the newspapers as one of the biggest Fort Worth had ever seen, reflecting the public's esteem for him as both a good man and a law officer who had died in the line of duty. The community had closely followed his heroic, five-week battle for life, hoping beyond hope that he would make it. On the day of the funeral, all city and county offices were closed so that officials could attend. The funeral began at the Scott home on West Fifth, which proved far too small to accommodate everyone who showed up. The overflow crowd spilled onto the lawn, the sidewalk, and even into the street for blocks around. The service was an ecumenical affair. Reverend J. A. Whitehurst of Corsicana delivered the oration, assisted by the Reverend P. E. Burroughs of Fort Worth's Broadway Baptist Church, with a series of hymns sung by the First Presbyterian Church choir. Whitehurst's eulogy focused on Scott's indomitable faith and his bravery in those last weeks of suffering.[42]

It took nearly half an hour for all those present to pass by the open coffin and say their farewells. Among those who came to pay their final respects were twenty-two policemen and sheriff's deputies, led by Chief James Maddox and Sheriff Tom Wood. Finally, the coffin was closed and carried outside to the waiting hearse. The pallbearers were a Who's Who of city and county government: Judge W. P. McLean, Sr., the deceased's father; Judge Irby Dunklin of the Forty-eighth District Court; former Sheriff Sterling P. Clark; Assistant County Attorney Hugh Barden; Deputy Sheriff Joe Witcher; and County Tax Collector R. M. Davis. Rev. Whitehurst marched at their head reciting the words of Christ: "I am the resurrection and the life." A detachment of twenty-two mounted officers and deputies from the Sheriff's and Police Departments led the cortege to Oakwood Cemetery. The next day, all flags in the city and county were lowered to half-staff for the second time in five weeks.[43]

In the aftermath of the double homicide, there was a public outcry the likes of which had not been heard even after the shooting of "Longhair Jim" Courtright. It was not just the status of the men who were murdered, it was the brazenness of the whole thing: gamblers who operated with impunity, a running gun battle through the city. The *Fort Worth Star* used words like "hero" and "martyr" to describe the two lawmen-victims, which was to be expected. The newspaper went beyond honoring the dead when it also called for "retribution" against the criminal element in the city since there could be no retribution against Bill Thomason. Instead of retribution there was "rounding up the usual suspects." On Saturday, a coroner's inquest was scheduled in Judge R. E. Bratton's JP court, but it had to be postponed because several witnesses who were supposed to testify were busy with more urgent matters. After Thomason died, Bratton finally handed down a pro forma ruling that McLean had been murdered in cold blood, and after Scott died, it was more of the same. There was no defendant to try and no mystery about what had happened, so justice had to be satisfied with an eye for an eye—except that it was two eyes for one eye.[44]

Without the closure that came from putting a defendant in the dock, the public had to find other outlets for its anger. Newspapers were deluged with letters calling for running the gamblers out of town and shutting down the saloons. McLean's murder was called "an assassination," placing it in the same category as the assassination of President William McKinley and several European heads of state who had died at the hands of anarchists in recent years. The double murder provided grist for countless sermons from the city's pulpits crossing all denominations. The newspapers received sacks of mail. Most of the condolence letters and memorial messages focused on Jeff McLean. The uncertainty for five weeks whether Hamil Scott was going to live or die probably had something to do with it. But Officer Scott was not completely forgotten. This letter from an Arlington writer was printed in Sunday's *Fort Worth Star* while Scott was still battling for his life although the author seemed to think he was already dead:

> We would not fail to remember the official service of Hamil P. Scott in offering, as a sacrifice, his life, in the brave attempt to capture the assassin.[45]

It would be nice to report that the deaths of Hamil Scott and Jeff McLean marked a turning point in the war on vice, and the double tragedy did produce important if limited results. On the same day that Thomason died, rumors circulated that the murder of Jefferson McLean had been part of a conspiracy by the city's gamblers to put an end to the vice raids. The rumors were nonsense, of course, but they sparked a mass meeting at the courthouse on Sunday afternoon, March 23, right after Jeff's funeral. B. B. Paddock presided. Those present first honored McLean's "heroic example" before moving on to more substantive matters. By acclamation they vowed to "give no quarter" to gamblers, to enforce the laws "in the strictest sense," and to fully support law officers. It was heady stuff but nothing that had not been heard before.[46]

Bigger things came out of Austin. The legislature, which was in session at the time of the killings, passed the most stringent set of laws on record against gambling. Sadly, the effect was not to abolish gambling completely but merely to drive it behind closed doors while the other two elements of the vice triad—drinking and prostitution—continued unabated.[47]

Jeff McLean was honored in death as a martyr to law and order. Before the month was out, concerned citizens formed the Jefferson D. McLean Law and Order League, dedicated to shutting down the Acre and putting the city's vice lords out of business for good. The Acre resisted their best efforts, lingering for another decade, but during that time the Law and Order League functioned as a public watchdog over city and county officials. On a more personal level, in 1911 the Tarrant County Bar Association, with the family's approval, commissioned a nearly full-length oil portrait of Jeff by John White Alexander, one of the most respected artists in the country at the time. The Bar Association presented that "memorial portrait" to the Carnegie Public Library in a fancy ceremony on June 14, 1912. It hung in a prominent place in the library for years before eventually being consigned to storage where it remains today.[48]

Far sadder is the fate of Hamil Scott. In death he was virtually forgotten, lost in the penumbra of that day's other victim. His friends and family did not have the resources to commission an oil portrait, nor the influence even if they had to get it exhibited for all to see. By the time Jeff McLean's portrait was hung in the library in 1912, conventional wisdom was that "As a direct result of the killing of McLean, the legislature . . . passed stringent laws that effectually put a stop to gambling that up until then had run more or less openly in this city." Jeff McLean's sacrifice got him martyrdom; Hamil Scott's got him a quiet spot in Oakwood Cemetery.[49]

Credit at least to the FWPD for not forgetting its two living heroes from Bloody Friday—Ben U. Bell and Denny Lloyd. Both officers received recognition for bringing the curtain down on Bill Thomason's reign of terror. Lloyd's commission on the force was renewed pro forma after municipal elections a few weeks later, and he was promoted to mounted patrol. Officer Bell, who had "stood shoulder to shoulder with Lloyd," as the newspapers told it, also had job security and received a promotion—to the detective squad.[50] Good can indeed come out of bad.

Hamil Scott is buried in Oakwood Cemetery. The large marker, one of the most impressive of any fallen officer, has a pedestal and monument of granite and a footstone (not pictured) identifying him as a Mason. (Photograph by Kevin Foster)

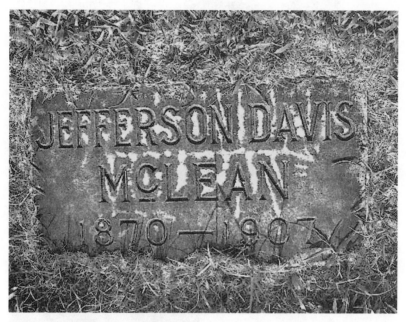

Jeff McLean's grave in Mount Olivet is actually his second resting place; the first was in Oakwood Cemetery (Block 21, Lot 8) in 1907. By mistake, his burial card at Oakwood shows Bill Thomason (his murderer) to be buried in his grave! There wasn't room in the same town for both men, much less in the same grave. McLean was removed to Mount Olivet Cemetery in 1948. The exceedingly modest marker belies his position and his family's status in Fort Worth. (Photograph by Kevin Foster)

Dick Howell, ca. 1906, when he was marshal of the North Fort Worth Police Department (note the old-style badge). Two years later he is out of the Department, a civilian, but still willing to lend a hand in an emergency. From B. B. Paddock, *A Historical and Biographical Record of North and West Texas* (Chicago, 1922). (Courtesy Fort Worth Public Library, Local History & Genealogy Dept.)

Chief Oscar Montgomery, as he appeared in a 1913 Department photograph, probably taken in April. In the group photo, you can tell just how big a man he was by comparing the size of his head and hands to the men on either side of him. (Collections of Kevin Foster)

POLICE OFFICERS DICK HOWELL & OSCAR MONTGOMERY

April 11, 1908

Mamas, Don't Let Your Babies Grow up to Be Lawmen

The deaths of most of the officers in these pages were the direct result of being assaulted in the performance of their duties. It is not that simple with Dick Howell and Oscar Montgomery. Both men were severely wounded in the line of duty and in fact given up to death, but they were too tough to die. Both recovered and lived many more years. It is at least arguable, however, that their lives were ultimately cut short by their wounds, and in Dick Howell's case the medical evidence is so undeniable that the Fort Worth Police and Firefighters Memorial committee had no problem putting him on their monument. Oscar Montgomery did not make the monument, but his story is inseparably tied to Dick Howell's, and but for fate he would have taken the devastating shotgun blast that permanently crippled Howell.

Richard D. Howell and Oscar R. Montgomery worked for the small community of North Fort Worth, just across the Trinity River from Fort Worth. They were lawmen and fast friends. Because of that friendship and the code of the badge, each knew the other would always have his back. In 1908, Montgomery was town marshal of North Fort Worth, and Howell was a special officer for the Fort Worth and Denver City Railway.

Thirty-seven-year-old Oscar Montgomery was born on February

227

24, 1872, in Hico, Hamilton County, Texas, also the hometown of Fort Worth lawmen Lee and Sid Waller (see chapter 6). He had four brothers and sisters growing up and received a limited education in the public school system before leaving Hico to make his mark in the world. He married Rizpah J. Hudson on July 14, 1902, and they had three children: a daughter, Ruth, and two sons, William "Roy" and James Ralph "Sully."[1]

Oscar and Rizpah came to Fort Worth from Comanche County in 1903 so that he could take a job at one of the new packing plants. He worked on the killing floor at Swift and Company; Armour and Company was right across the street. If he had stayed in Comanche all he would have had to look forward to was a life of farming or ranching. The couple bought a house in North Fort Worth not far from his job, but nothing in North Fort Worth was far from the packing plants. North Fort Worth only existed because of the packing plants. As a typical Victorian male, Oscar was a joiner; he belonged to the Woodmen of the World and the Knights of Pythias, which were his retreat from job and family duties.[2]

The first thing everyone noticed about Oscar Montgomery was his size. He was a mountain of a man, standing six foot six inches and weighing more than 200 pounds, none of it fat. Most of the men he worked with were closer to 150 pounds. He had ham-sized hands and an over-large head that a thick black mustache only served to draw more attention to. From the top of his massive head to his similarly proportioned feet he was a formidable presence. He did not intend to slaughter animals and carve up their carcasses for the rest of his life. He could have been the "Strong Man" in a circus but instead joined the North Fort Worth Police Department in 1904. Two years later he was elected marshal, succeeding Dick Howell. Montgomery was well regarded by both his constituents and officers because he enforced the laws fairly and with restraint. His size alone was enough to get drunks and rowdies to come along peaceably. In the spring of 1908, with elections coming up in December, it was assumed he would run for re-election.[3]

Montgomery's pal and fellow lawman was forty-year-old Dick Howell, born in Tennessee in 1868. He came to Texas with his parents in 1881, but when his folks decided to return to Tennessee four years later, he stayed on. He scraped out a living farming, cowpunching, and doing railroad construction. Like so many young men on the frontier, he was not on any career path; he just followed the jobs. In the summer of 1900, he settled in the tiny unincorporated community of North Fort Worth. Two years later North Fort Worth became an incorporated township and on December 2, 1902, the voters elected Howell their first "Marshal and Tax Collector," which was the first time he put on a badge. Twelve-hour days were normal in law enforcement, but he often worked eighteen hours or longer, and he was on call seven days a week.[4]

Howell performed his duties efficiently enough to be re-elected in April 1903 and again in April 1904, after which North Fort Worth went to two-year terms. According to a contemporary, B. B. Paddock, Howell was "a most capable official, justly meriting the trust reposed in him." His second term was marred by the death of Mattie, his wife of twelve years who succumbed to illness on March 11, 1905. Thereafter, his niece Fannie Howell lived with him as his housekeeper and companion. In 1906 he saw a chance to better himself by going to work in the private sector. The railroads were always on the lookout for an experienced lawman to handle security, and they paid a damn sight better than a small municipality. He left a "capable and efficient" department for his successor.[5]

In his new job with the Fort Worth and Denver City, he was "special agent," which meant a railroad detective. The railroad paid his salary, but his peace officer's commission came from the city of North Fort Worth. His duties included chasing down robbers and thwarting union organizers. Besides the fatter paycheck, he got to sleep in his own bed at night. He had the best of both worlds: a job in the private sector and a lawman's badge and authority, like his contemporary, Officer Hamil Scott (see chapter 9).

On the afternoon of April 11, 1908, Dick Howell dropped by the police station on North Main to visit his old friend. Montgomery told him about a call he had just answered to the house of Ike Knight on Lake Street. It was a sad situation, the Marshal said, shaking his head, a domestic dispute that was not going to end happily. But it was a matter for the courts, not law enforcement. Howell thanked his lucky stars he did not have to deal with those things any more and went back to work. He was barely out of sight when Montgomery's phone rang again. It was a Lake Street resident calling to report gunshots at Ike Knight's house. Montgomery grabbed his pistol and headed for the door. He went alone because he did not have the luxury of having officers on call to come along as backup. He did not know what he would find at Ike Knight's, but if there had indeed been gunshots it could not be anything good. North Fort Worth was a small enough community that Dick Howell heard about the trouble almost as soon as the Police Department. He had no reason to involve himself except, like an old fire horse, he could not resist answering the bell one more time. Besides, the former marshal figured Montgomery might need help, and Dick Howell had never been one to shy away from trouble.[6]

The cause of the uproar was one Isaac B. Knight, who had lived in North Fort Worth for six years. Knight was the sort of footloose American male who wandered the West for many years, never settling down anywhere for long and often one jump ahead of the law. Forty-three-year-old Ike had stayed in North Fort Worth longer than anywhere he had lived before. He started out working for the Fort Worth Belt Railroad, then took a job with a moving and storage company on North Main, and most recently worked for North Fort Worth Ice & Cold Storage. None were skilled jobs because Ike had no particular skills, only a strong back. He was never going to be anything more than a menial laborer. He lived with a woman named Florence Bowen and her daughter, Nellie, but it was not the happiest arrangement. Indeed, that was the cause of the frantic April 11 phone call to the North Fort Worth Police Department.[7]

Ike was what they called a "hard case": pugnacious, a scrapper, frequently in trouble with the law. He was born and grew up in rural Tennessee during Reconstruction with two brothers, but with Tennessee recovering slowly from the Civil War, Ike and one sibling headed west. The brother settled in Oklahoma while Ike landed in Harrison, Arkansas, in 1898, then Parsons, Kansas, and finally Texas. After brief stays in Houston and Sherman, he reached Fort Worth in February 1902. His work ethic was to do just enough to get by, which meant at different times driving a jitney and doing odd jobs around a livery stable. Home had always been a boardinghouse as he refused to be tied down in any way. He broke this rule just once when he married briefly and fathered a child, but he left them behind when he moved on. It was different when he met

Flo. She ran the boardinghouse where he stayed in Parsons, Kansas, and had her own string of failed relationships, which included two marriages and a grown daughter, Nellie, who was estranged. Ike and Flo struck up a relationship that was more than landlady and tenant, and when he settled in Fort Worth, she followed. They first lived in a boardinghouse on Belknap, then signed a contract on a house in the Diamond Hill Addition that was part of North Fort Worth. Flo made the down payment on the house while Ike made the ten-dollar monthly payments out of his wages, which were only twenty to twenty-five dollars per month. When he got behind on the payments, the bank foreclosed. By that time they had become a family of three after Nellie moved in with them.[8]

The exact nature of Ike and Flo's relationship is not clear. According to later court testimony, they were never anything more than common-law husband and wife. But according to the records of the Forty-eighth District Court they were properly married "on or about the 10th of April, 1901." They seemed committed to each other, and that even extended to Nellie whom Ike treated like his own daughter. Ike's new family gained another member when Flo's mother came down from Kansas to live with them. Using Flo's and Mama's money they began to move up in the housing market, first to 401 West Central Ave. then 1405 Lake, both places in North Fort Worth. The Lake Street house, which the bank held the mortgage on, was just a little two-bedroom bungalow, but it was only a few blocks from the North Fort Worth Ice & Cold Storage, so Ike could walk to work every day. Per their previous arrangement, Flo signed the contract putting the house in her name, while Ike picked up the twenty-dollar monthly payments out of a paycheck that was still less than $100 per month, and he had to work double shifts to earn that much. Neither worried about the legalities of the arrangement. Nellie came along, taking the second bedroom, and they found a place for Flo's mother next door in Mrs. Azalle Krause's boardinghouse. Ike, who was beginning to feel like a real family man, wanted to bring his own fourteen-year-old daughter down to live with them, but Flo would not permit it. In seven years of marriage, Ike and Flo never had any children of their own.[9]

Those who saw Ike walk down Lake Street every day to and from work could be excused if they didn't notice him. He was of medium height, a solid 185 pounds from a lifetime of physical labor, with dark brown hair and a mustache. But those things do not begin to tell the story. He had lived a hard life and he wore every year of it. His face was coarse with a perpetual sour expression that made others give him a wide berth. His neighbors quickly gave up greeting him when they passed him on the street. He did not socialize. His world was neatly compartmentalized between home and job. He worked six days a week and stayed home on Sunday.

He was more than just unsociable. He carried a chip on his shoulder that had gotten him into more than a few scrapes and helped explain his rootlessness. As he related his past, he had "cut a man all to pieces" in Tennessee, "had a little trouble with another man" in Kentucky, and got into a brawl in Parsons where a barrel to the face "cut his nose in two." There was a warrant out for him in Tennessee, but as long as he stayed on the move there was no chance the law would ever catch up with him. One or more times a year Ike suffered what Flo called "crazy spells" when he behaved "intolerable" toward her and anybody else who crossed him. As a result of his moodiness and erratic behavior, Flo ultimately grew tired of living with him but was not sure how to leave without causing an uproar.[10]

Nellie was the catalyst. She was a "very pretty little woman" by all accounts, and after she moved in with Ike and Flo, suitors began coming around. Handsome, successful Ed Larmon quickly lapped the field. Nellie had her own income, enough to pay Ike two dollars per week in rent. At first, Ike did not mind Ed coming around all the time. After about a year of courtship, Ed and Nellie tied the knot on March 25, 1908, holding the wedding in the Lake Street house. Ike was not there because he was working a double shift that day. When he got home, he learned that the newlyweds were going to be living in his house. That was not the worst of it. They took the master bedroom and Flo took the smaller bedroom, leaving Ike to move into a 7x14-foot "shed room" on the back porch. Not only did he lose his bedroom, he lost conjugal rights. Ed paid a month's rent up front to Flo, who pocketed it. Ike did not say much because he believed the living arrangements were temporary until Ed and Nellie found a place of their own. He did not know that Flo planned on somebody moving out, and it was not the kids.[11]

Before long, the tension in the little house was almost unbearable. Nellie Larmon had little use for her stepfather, and Ed, a cocky sort, shared her contempt. At six foot two, with a handsome face and "striking physique," Ed Larmon represented quite a catch for dear Nellie. He had been a North Fort Worth resident for only three years, clerking in the freight office of the Cotton Belt Railroad. His courtship of Nellie had worn on Ike, who once ordered him off the property, telling him "never to put his foot inside the gate again." When Nellie heard about it, she threatened to wire the authorities in Tennessee and tell them where to find him. Ike backed off, and Ed and Nellie now presumed to do whatever they wanted, including partying half the night. Sometimes they had eighteen or twenty friends over for "frolics," as Ike called them, messing up the place and making it impossible for Ike to get a good night's sleep.[12]

A storm was brewing in the little bungalow. The first storm clouds appeared on April 9, a Thursday, when Ike came home for supper. Ed was there, and Ike asked if he and Nellie had found new quarters yet. That drew a retort from Ed that he had paid rent for the next week, and they would be staying at least that long. Ike ordered them to leave, and Ed told him to drop it or else. It did not take much imagination to know what the "or else" meant. Tennessee authorities would still love to know where Ike Knight was. Ike went back to work. The quiet before the storm lasted until the next day when both men came home for supper again. Ike said something, and Ed told him, "Don't you open your mouth to me again!" When Flo came home later that afternoon and learned of the latest exchange, she blamed Ike. Whether it was the last straw or just the excuse she had been looking for, she informed him that she would be moving out on Saturday. What she did not tell him was that before departing, she intended to transfer the house—lock, stock, and "furnishings"—to Ed and Nellie, writing out a bill of sale to make it legal.[13]

Saturday morning dawned cool and overcast following a downpour the night before. The dreary weather dampened everyone's mood. Ed decided that instead of going to work he would stay home with Nellie all day. Since Ike always worked on Saturdays and Flo was moving out, they could count on having the house all to themselves. Ike got up and went to work as usual that morning, and Nellie

escorted Flo with her bags to the streetcar at two thirty that afternoon. Just before leaving Flo pressed a note into her daughter's hand,
asking her to give it to Ike. She said that she would not be coming
back until Ike was gone for good. Nellie walked over to the Ice &
Cold Storage company to deliver the note but instead of putting it in
his hand, she gave it to a boy there to pass along. What Ike read was
a classic "Dear John" letter shorn of even a shred of tenderness. "I do
not expect to live with you anymore," Flo wrote, and then went on
to specify what items he could have. "[Most of] the furniture in that
house belongs to me. . . . Don't go to the house any more; it will only
buy you trouble." Devastated, he left work without even bothering
to change out of his grimy coveralls. He just jammed his black slouch
hat down on his head and set off for home. It started raining on the
way. When he arrived, he found Ed and Nellie putting his stuff out
on the porch. They told him he was trespassing and ordered him to
leave. Ignoring them, he went inside and called the marshal on the
telephone. The law would protect his interests.[14]

Oscar Montgomery came straightaway, bringing Officer G.
W. Maynor with him. When they got to the house they found Ed,
Nellie, and Ike waiting for them but not with the same expectations all around. Ed was standing on the front porch and ordered
the officers to halt at the gate. Ike was standing right behind him
and pleaded for them to come into the house and place him "in
peaceable possession" of his property. Standing uncertainly in the
drizzle, Montgomery tried to defuse the situation: "Ike, I ain't able
to advise you. . . . Go down and see Mr. [County Attorney R. E. L.]
Roy and find out what legal steps to take. You get the papers, and I
will execute them."

Not the least intimidated, Larmon advised Ike to go with the
policemen. His stuff would be out on the porch when he got back,
or he could "just send for it." Ed added a final blunt warning:
"Don't you come back into this house!"

Retorted Ike, "I'm not through with you yet. I'll fix you!" He
then stormed off the porch, past the officers, and down the street
toward North Main.

As Ike disappeared down the street, Ed and Nellie stood on the
porch taunting him, "Nyah, nyah, nyah!" Maynor and Montgomery
could only sigh and return to headquarters. It was after Montgomery

got back to the station house that Dick Howell showed up and got an earful.[15]

Montgomery was no lawyer or he might have advised all the parties that Ike had the law on his side. It did not matter who had signed the mortgage papers, under Texas law the house and all the furnishings were his to do with as he pleased because his rights as the husband took precedence over Flo's. Ike did not know chapter and verse of the law either, but he knew his son-in-law could not throw him out of his own house. If Montgomery would do nothing, he intended to take it to a higher authority, so he hopped a streetcar that would take him across the river to the Tarrant County courthouse. In those days, courthouses were open for business on Saturdays. Ike stormed into County Attorney Roy's office to file a complaint that would get the Larmons evicted. Assistant Attorney Will Slay took his statement, and looked at Flo's letter. Ike's anger was directed equally at the Larmons and at Flo. He vowed to take legal action no matter the cost. Slay remarked to a clerk in the office, "Knight seems to be game enough about it."

"I am as game as they ever turned out of the Cumberland Mountains!" retorted Ike.

Slay told him the County Attorney's office could do nothing on Saturday afternoon and advised him to be patient. "Let it rest til Monday when we will see what we can do with it," he said. Unmollified, Ike stalked out of the office convinced that there was nothing left but to take matters into his own hands.[16]

After leaving the courthouse, he walked down Main to Arthur Simon's pawnshop where he had hocked a double-barreled shotgun with its case and shells. He paid ten dollars to get them out of hock then hopped a passing streetcar headed back to the North Side. During the ensuing fifteen-minute ride he loaded the shotgun and dropped the remaining eight shells into his coat pocket. Then he sat clutching the scatter-gun tightly in both hands steeling himself for what was to come. He had every intention of "cutting that damn son of a bitch's throat"; the shotgun was insurance. He got off at Fourteenth, then trudged through the mud down Lake, discarding the shotgun case along the way.[17]

The account of what followed would be reported in detail in the pages of the *Record*, Fort Worth's newspaper for those who liked their crime coverage lurid with a dash of racism and sensationalism mixed in.[18] About 5:00 p.m., Ike turned into his front yard to have his reckoning with Ed and Flo. He went around to the rear of the house and through the gate, trampling Flo's potato bed on his way to the back porch. He found the screen door locked, but that did not stop him. He took out his knife, slashed a hole in the screen, reached through and flipped the latch. Then he stepped onto the porch, not bothering to announce his presence.

Nellie and Edwin did not need any announcement. They had been sitting in the front parlor when Ike entered the yard. They jumped up and dashed into the next room where they saw him pass down the side of the house. Nellie screamed, "He's coming and he's got his gun!" As Ike went around to the back of the house, they began frantically locking doors. The house had two back doors onto the porch, one from a hallway and the other from the master bedroom. Ike went right to the bedroom entrance and, finding it locked, kicked it open. In the meantime, Ed had locked the inside bedroom door and was shouting for Nellie to go out the front and get help. Instead she ran into the dining room where the telephone was located to call the police. In her panic she did not wait long enough for "Central" to answer but hung up.

Ike marched through the bedroom past the bed that he and Flo had once shared and kicked open the inside door. He was now in the central hallway and moved toward the front of the house. He kicked in the last door standing between him and Ed and came face-to-face with his son-in-law. Ike kept a pistol at the house, but Ed apparently did not know where it was or else did not think to get it. Now there was no place left for him to run, and he had no way to defend himself. He faced his fate knowing he was about to die but believing Nellie had escaped.

But Nellie was still in the house. She was cowering in the dining room when she heard two shotgun blasts followed by the muffled groan of a man in great pain. A moment later the groaning was terminated by a third blast. The complete silence that followed said all she needed to know. No longer frozen in fear, she fled out the back door, around to the front of the house and down Lake Street screaming for help.

Inside the house, the living room was a bloody shambles. Ike had shot Ed at such close range, there were powder burns on the victim's front and his flesh had been shredded, splattering blood and guts in a wide pattern. The first blast struck him in the hip and groin, the second in the breast with such force that it lifted him off his feet and threw him backward. It was as he lay on the floor, barely alive, that Nellie heard him groaning. As Ike calmly reloaded, Ed pleaded for his life: "Oh, my God, don't kill me!" But his pleading did no good. Ike stood over him "maybe half a minute" before firing the third shot into his belly. The blowback covered Ike with blood and viscera. Later, he could not explain later why he fired the third, unnecessary shot; it was simply the action of a man consumed with rage.

After finishing off Ed, Ike was in no hurry to leave. He was still watching the gathering crowd through the window when Oscar Montgomery came down the street with Nellie tagging along. Someone in the neighborhood had called the police station, and the word was passed on to the Marshal who feared the worst. As he was hurrying up North Main he met the hysterical Nellie coming the other direction. The two of them came back to the house, and now Montgomery was about to enter the lion's den. He came through the front gate and walked up the path to the porch, calling to Ike to "come out and give me the gun." Ike threw open the door and stepped onto the porch leveling his shotgun at Montgomery.

He told the Marshal, "You wouldn't do what I asked you to do this evening, and now I don't need you." When Montgomery kept coming like he intended to enter the house, Ike warned him, "Stop, don't come in here or I will kill you." It was the second time that day Montgomery's life had been threatened, and he was getting tired of it, but he knew better than to push his luck.

Before he could say anything, however, Nellie cried, "Oh, you have killed poor Edwin."

"Yes," retorted Ike, "and I wish I had killed the son of a bitch a year ago. If you come in here you'll go, too."

Trying to avoid further bloodshed, Montgomery spoke in a calm, steady voice: "Ike, come out and give up your gun."

"You wouldn't do what I asked you to do this evening [sic]," he repeated, "and now I don't need you." Then he reiterated his warning as he stepped up to the edge of the porch. Montgomery knew it was no idle threat, but he also had Nellie tugging at his sleeve egging him on. Between the hysterical woman and the murderous Ike, he had his hands full.

"Oh, Mr. Montgomery," she cried, "can't you do something for me?" He knew what she wanted, and that was for him to shoot Knight down where he stood. But that was not going to happen. Instead, he backpedaled out the front gate and went next door where he asked to use the neighbor's telephone to call the Sheriff for backup. On the way he barked at the throng of bystanders, "Clear the street!" However, he made no attempt to enforce the order, so the crowd continued to mill around gawking at Ike who was now waving his gun "wildly" in the air. All witnesses later agreed: Ike was behaving like a "wild man."[19]

By this time, Montgomery had called the Sheriff and come back outside, Ike was on the move, leaving the yard and turning south on Lake Street. Before leaving the yard, however, he caught sight of Mrs. Krause standing on her front porch watching him. He fired a shotgun blast in her direction, which did not strike her but did cause her to swoon in a dead faint. Another neighbor, Will Brown, had been crouching behind a fence armed with a rifle. Thinking Mrs. Krause had been hit, he rose up and fired two rounds at Ike. Both shots missed. With all the lead flying about, however, someone was bound to get hit sooner or later.[20]

Ike headed down Lake toward North Main ordering gawkers to "Clear the street" while pointing his shotgun ominously. Faces disappeared at a few windows, but most of the curious on the street simply fell back as he passed, then joined the crowd following along behind him, albeit at a respectful distance. It was impossible to accurately count the number of people because the crowd kept growing, all tagging along like the children of Hamlin behind the Pied Piper. Ike walked purposefully, occasionally stopping to "snap his gun" at anyone who got too close. Later he would claim that he had been on his way to the courthouse to surrender himself and never intended to shoot anyone but Ed Larmon. The crowd following him came to a different conclusion; they were convinced he was trying to escape into the Trinity River bottom, which was only a few blocks away.[21]

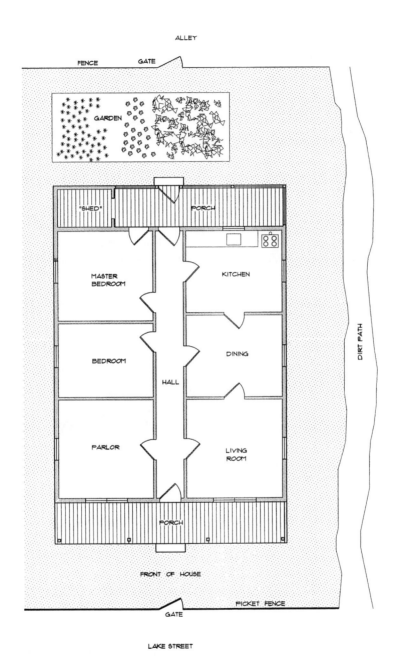

Using this diagram of Ike Knight's house on Lake Street, we can follow his murderous path through the house stalking his "son-in-law" on the afternoon of April 11, 1908. (Courtesy Robert Cullen Smith, AIA)

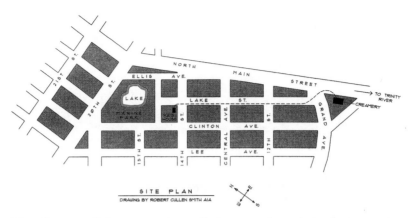

The diagram of the streets shows Ike's route down Lake Street to the creamery on North Main where he made his last stand. The two police officers and a wary mob followed him there. (Courtesy Robert Cullen Smith, AIA)

The crowd swelled steadily as more North Fort Worth citizens came running to the scene. The numbers may have reached 500 before it was all over, but one thing was certain: they filled the street and surrounding yards and sidewalks. Word spread quickly that Ike had murdered someone, but no one knew the details except Nellie, and she had disappeared inside the house as soon as Ike left. Most of the men in the crowd were armed. Some, like P. P. Pritchard, showed up to see what all the excitement was about, then ran back home for their guns. Now all those firearms and the sheer number of persons in the mob gave them the courage to take on the lone armed man they were following. In fact, it was a tossup whether they were following or chasing Knight now. Also among the grim-faced men were women and children treating the whole thing as a lark. What had started out as a gathering of the curious was now a mob on a mission. One newspaper later compared it to the public reaction if "a hostile army had been invading the town." For others, it was a short leap in logic from seeing their quarry as a wild man to seeing him as a mad dog that needed to be put down. Either way, it was bad news for Ike.[22]

Oscar Montgomery was at the front of this mob, but he was not its leader. He was merely hoping to keep things from getting out of hand. He noted with alarm that the mob was "bristling" with shotguns and six-shooters and in a bloodlust. He heard cries of "Shoot him! Shoot him!" interspersed with "Kill him! Kill him! He has murdered a man!" When the fugitive turned and waved his gun threateningly, rather than being intimidated, they started taunting him: "Shoot if you want to!" When he did not, they closed in, more determined than ever not to let him get away.[23]

As the action moved down Lake, some mob members fired in Ike's direction, letting off steam without doing any damage. One man, Frank Kaufman, later admitted to firing "several shots." Even Montgomery joined in the ineffectual shooting. "I fired two shots myself," he later testified. Knight responded with a single blast from his scatter-gun, inflicting a slight scalp wound on J. C. McDonald and striking a boy, Jimmy Hamilton, in the leg. Neither was seriously wounded and stayed in the chase.[24]

Montgomery began to seriously hope the fugitive would reach the river bottoms to avert further bloodshed. A gun battle on North Main was the last thing he wanted. He figured if it were just he and Knight, he could get his man without any further shooting. He was also counting on the sheriff's men showing up sooner rather than later.

They were still on Lake Street when Dick Howell reached the scene. He was unarmed, but Montgomery was nonetheless glad to have his friend as backup. Shoulder-to-shoulder, they tailed Knight waiting for their chance. Howell did not like being unarmed so he confiscated a pistol from a young boy telling him, "Give me that gun, son, and I'll kill him." Less cautious by nature than Montgomery, Howell felt sure he could bring this thing to a close before any more innocent citizens were injured.

Knight had just crossed Twelfth when Howell made his move. He chose to rush Knight rather than shoot him down, an admirable if foolish decision. Howell may have thought he could still take his man alive. If so, it was a bad miscalculation. Without saying a word to Montgomery, he darted forward, seemingly intent on tackling the other man. Knight heard him, whirled and fired a single shotgun blast, catching Howell in the right leg, shattering both large bones and fracturing the kneecap. The officer pitched face forward into the "mud and slush" and lay there writhing in agony. Knight turned and resumed his march toward North Main while a stunned Montgomery knelt at his friend's side to see what he could do. Howell urged him to go on, and Montgomery resumed the chase, catching up with Ike in the next block and ordering him to surrender. His restraint at this point was more puzzling than admirable. Ike had already shot two people and was obviously not about to meekly surrender. That was confirmed when he turned and fired another blast in the general direction of his pursuers. This one caught Montgomery full in the abdomen. Like Howell, he went down and stayed down while Ike paused just long enough to reload his weapon. The score so far: Ike, 3; law and order, 0.

The mob was stunned to see the second officer go down. What had seemed a merry chase before had now turned into something deadly. The quarry had teeth and claws and was not afraid to use them. The self-styled vigilantes could have ended the affair right then and there with a well-aimed volley. Instead, Ike's coldblooded actions took some of the wind out of their sails. More than a few began to reconsider their initial decision to pursue a shotgun-toting crazy man. It was about this time that the Fort Worth Police Department began getting panicked phone calls reporting that "a madman armed with a shotgun" had killed the North Fort Worth chief of police plus several others and was heading for their side of the river. Police headquarters in the bigger city erupted into activity to repel the anticipated armed invasion from north of the river.[25]

As mob and fugitive eyed each other warily, one foolhardy fellow, identified only as "Mr. White," decided he would end it. The would-be hero dashed forward and tried to wrestle the shotgun away from Ike who easily knocked him to the ground and shoved his face into the mud until he quit struggling. Then he finished reloading and continued on his way.[26]

It seemed an eternity since the first shots had rung out on Lake Street; in reality it had been less than half an hour, but the situation was no closer to being resolved. Knight reached the intersection of Lake and North Main and turned right, marching along as if he were on an evening constitutional. The mob stuck stubbornly to his tail making no more efforts to bring him to bay.

Another pursuer, one of the few not armed, was an elderly gentleman named J. F. Bryant, who up to this point had kept well back in the pack. Bryant had been a special officer a few years earlier and though he worked at a desk now, his "steel-grey" eyes were still clear and he had not forgotten how to use a gun. As he passed Montgomery's prone form, he grabbed the Marshal's pistol from its holster and pushed to the front of the crowd. Meanwhile, Dick Howell and Oscar Montgomery lay in the mud, seemingly forgotten.

As soon as Knight turned onto North Main, he made a fateful decision: instead of trying to make it to the river, he turned into the Panther City Creamery on the corner of Lake and North Main, right next door to the Ice & Cold Storage Company. He knew it was built like a fortress with thick stone walls and small windows and additionally that it would be open but virtually empty on a Saturday. He passed under the sign proclaiming "Fancy Jersey Butter, Sweet Milk and Cream" and entered the front door. Then he went up to the second floor.

The mob came around the corner right behind him and halted outside the creamery. They took up positions around the building using whatever cover they could find—bushes, fences, wagons—and waited for their target to show himself. Dozens of rifles were locked and loaded as eager eyes scanned the windows. Knight looked down from his second-floor bastion and fired two blasts from his scatter-gun without hitting anyone. Before the mob could take further action, the Fort Worth Police Department and Tarrant County Sheriff's Department finally arrived on the scene. The Fort Worth police were there because they had received frantic calls from North Fort Worth residents reporting "a madman with a shotgun" loose on the streets and heading for Fort Worth. Fort Worth Police Chief James Maddox ordered "a picket" thrown across the south end of the North Main bridge while other officers hurried to the creamery. The chase had turned into a siege; it would take a miracle to prevent further bloodshed.

That miracle appeared in the form of J. F. Bryant, the bespectacled gentleman who had appropriated Montgomery's pistol. Now he took on the role of peacemaker. Fortunately, the besieged fugitive seemed to have finally come to his senses. Knight hollered down from a window that he wanted to parley, adding that he would sur-render only to a *civilian*, but said civilian must come into the build-ing and escort him out. Bryant accepted those conditions and was soon climbing the stairs to the second floor.

He found Knight standing warily behind a barrel with his shot-gun trained on the door. Bryant assured the other man he was un-armed and entered. Knight let him approach and handed over his shotgun. Bryant noted it was still "loaded full up" and let out a sigh of relief. Following proper police procedure, he ordered Knight to empty his pockets, confiscating the last two unused shells. Bryant then led his prisoner outside and turned him over to North Fort Worth Police Officer G. W. Maynor who hustled the prisoner off to the county jail. Only after it was all over did Maynor learn that Ike had gunned down his boss and friend, Oscar Montgomery, to which news he responded cryptically, "If I had only known, if I had only known."

The mob made no attempt to interfere with Maynor as he led Knight away. They seemed more relieved than inclined to lynch the object of their earlier fury. Most headed home now that the excite-ment was over. A few stayed around, turning their attention to the two downed officers. Compassion replaced fury. Volunteers gently carried Montgomery to the house of Bert Dyer and tried to make him as comfortable as possible. Others took Howell to A. White's house and placed him on the porch until a doctor could be sum-moned. Someone had the presence of mind to apply a tourniquet to Howell's mangled leg while they waited. The two victims' wounds were ghastly. Shotgun pellets don't make clean entry wounds; they obliterate bones and organs. Under the circumstances, neither of-ficer's chances looked good.

With time to reflect, it was hard to believe the whole thing had played out in just forty minutes from the time Ike Knight had walked up to the Lake Street house.[27] Between ten and twenty-five shots had been fired altogether, leaving one man dead, two severely wounded, and another two with minor wounds. It was the bloodiest day in North Fort Worth history, and it was not over yet; there were still loose ends to be tied up. For one thing, there was Ed Larmon's body to be retrieved and somebody needed to inform Flo Knight. When officers went to Ike's house, they found poor Nellie beside her husband's body sobbing. Flo Knight got a phone call from a Lake Street neighbor, hopped the next Stockyards streetcar, and begged the driver to ignore scheduled stops and get her home. While Flo was comforting Nellie, Tarrant County Justice of the Peace Dick Bratton arrived to conduct a coroner's inquest on the spot.

For the next twenty-four hours, Dick Howell and Oscar Montgomery fought for their lives. The latter's prognosis was so dire that the next morning's headline announced "Chief Montgomery Dying."[28] Only one local hospital, All Saints, even had an "emergency ward" for treating trauma cases, and emergency medical treatment was not markedly different from normal treatment.[29] Historically, doctors treated most people either at the office or at the patient's home. A man's survival depended more on having a hardy constitution than on anything medical science could do. After a preliminary examination in Bert Dyer's parlor by the first doctors on the scene, the patient was pronounced as good as dead and transferred to Dr. W. R. Thompson's Lamar Street sanitarium to await death. Dr. Thompson was more of an optimist, however, and decided that immediate surgery might still save the patient. He operated at 7:45 that evening to remove pellets from Montgomery's abdomen, thigh, and foot. The most dangerous wound was just above the navel where buckshot had perforated the stomach and lodged in the muscles of the back, damaging the appendix so severely that it had to be removed. Fortunately, the intestines were not perforated because that would have added septicemia to the other problems and certainly proved fatal. After surgery, the patient was kept heavily sedated and appeared to be resting easily twenty-four hours later.[30]

Howell's prognosis was a little better. He also had been examined and stabilized on the scene before being transported to All Saints Hospital's emergency ward. Surgeons there debated whether to amputate his right leg or not. Their biggest fear was that gangrene would set in, which in the days before antibiotics was the equivalent of a death sentence. On Saturday night, Dr. R. O. Braswell operated on Howell's leg to save it but held out little hope for success. When Monday dawned, Howell still had two legs, and the Doctor guardedly described his condition as "favorable." Ultimately, the patient would walk out of the hospital on crutches and his one remaining leg.[31]

While people on both sides of the river wondered what had gotten into Ike Knight, County Attorney R. E. L. Roy convened the grand jury on April 12. It was a Sunday and their regular session had concluded the week before, but this case was too urgent to wait two months for the next regularly scheduled session. In short order, the gentlemen of the grand jury handed up indictments for first-degree murder in the case of Ed Larmon and two counts of assault to murder in the cases of Dick Howell and Oscar Montgomery. The indictments were officially filed on April 15 with the understanding that if either Howell or Montgomery died subsequently, they would be upgraded to additional counts of murder. Roy also had the option of filing assault-to-murder charges in the cases of Azalle Krause, J. C. McDonald, and "Little Jimmy" Hamilton, but he decided to go with his strongest cases. The public on both sides of the river followed the legal preliminaries closely. Anxious to head off any mob action, Roy and Sixty-seventh District Court Judge Mike Smith both issued statements promising a speedy trial *and* that Ike Knight would stay in jail until that trial. There would be no bail.[32]

Sheriff Tom Wood was anxious enough about a lynch mob storming his jail that he decided to slip Knight out of town. Just before dawn on Sunday, April 12, deputies Bill Rea and Ralph Purvis took the prisoner out the back door and hurried down deserted streets under a light mist to where they could catch the first Interurban train of the day to Dallas. They parked their prisoner in a rear seat of the smoking car and sat down, one right next to their prisoner and the other in the seat directly across the aisle. Knight wore handcuffs but hid them under his coat so that none of the other early-morning passengers would notice. Still, it was impossible not to notice two sheriff's deputies and a scruffy-looking companion. The plan of the Sheriff and County Attorney was to keep Knight in the Dallas jail "until all danger is passed" or his presence was required in court, whichever came first.[33]

On the hour-and-a-half ride, Knight offered the first coherent explanation of his actions the previous day. In fact, he became quite voluble, making a clumsy appeal for sympathy when he told the two deputies it wasn't right to "lock a man's own home against him." He explained that he had only shot at Montgomery and Howell *after* "Monty" had fired at him first, that he was sorry if he had hit either man, that he would have gladly surrendered at any time to a single man but not to a lynch mob, that he never shot at Mrs. Krause or at any other "lady," and finally, that he had not fired more than three shots total. Rea listened, unimpressed. He had heard too many criminals tell too many cock-and-bull stories over the years to buy a word of it, but both he and Purvis related Ike's *mea culpa* in detail later.[34]

When they reached their destination they turned their prisoner over to the jailer at the Dallas County jail and headed home. Knight, who now feared for his life at the hands of either an assassin or a mob, begged the jailor to search any visitors who came to see him.[35]

Knight's stay in the Dallas jail was so brief that Officers Rea and Purvis nearly met themselves coming and going. Before 9:00 p.m. Sunday night they returned to fetch the prisoner back to Fort Worth so he could appear at an examining trial Monday morning in Hugh Bratton's JP court. At his first court appearance on April 13, a subdued and shackled Knight listened as the charges against him were read. The original charges had been amended to one count of murder in the first degree and three counts of assault to murder, adding Azalle Krause to the list. She was a much more sympathetic victim than Dick Howell. This preliminary hearing was a foretaste of the circus to come. The courtroom was packed. The accused stood alone without legal counsel or family present while hundreds of spectators filled the courtroom and spilled out into the hallway.[36] Because the crowd seemed more curious than hostile and there had been no more rumors of mob action, officials decided they did not need to return Ike to Dallas; they could keep him in the Tarrant County jail until his trial.

On Monday, Knight, still without legal counsel, made a jail-house confession, which should have sealed the case against him. It came after County Attorney Roy visited him and offered some free advice: "It will be all the better for you if you make a statement just how this occurred." That was all the encouragement Ike needed to sing like a canary. Roy sent for a recorder who took down "quite a long and voluminous" statement. In addition to Roy, an assistant county attorney and Deputy Sheriff William Rea were also present. After the recorder read the confession back, Ike signed it. Later, courthouse scuttlebutt was that Knight had negotiated some sort of deal or "reward" in return for his "free and voluntary" statement. If so, the rumor was never confirmed, and when he got to trial, there was no deal on the table. The crucial part of his jailhouse confession read:

> *The above and foregoing statement is made by me, after having been warned by Virgil Parker, assistant county attorney of Tarrant County, that I did not have to make any statement at all; that any statement made by me would be used against me in the trial of my cases wherein I am charged with the murder of Ed Larmon, in North Fort Worth, Texas, on the 11th day of April, 1908, and also in cases wherein I am charged with having committed the offense of assault on the persons of O. R. Montgomery and R. D. Howell and Azalle Krause, in North Fort Worth, Texas, on the same date.*

With a confession in hand, the County Attorney went for a first-degree murder indictment, never suspecting that the confession was going to come back and bite him after Ike successfully argued that he had not been properly "warned" of his rights, that the confession had been "induced." His defense counsel, once they were on the job, would make much of that fact, marking the first time in Fort Worth history that a defendant got his conviction overturned by claiming that he had not been duly "Mirandized," as the procedure is described today. They would also encourage the rumor that Ike was not right in the head, setting the stage for an insanity plea if all else failed.[37]

But that was all in the future. First things first. The grand jury handed up an indictment for the murder of Ed Larmon. Roy did not choose to add assault to murder charges for the shootings of Dick Howell and Oscar Montgomery. Knight finally got his defense counsel when the court appointed the Fort Worth firm of Buck, Cummings, Doyle & Bouldin. Trial was set to begin Wednesday, April 29 in the Forty-eighth District Court of Judge Irby Dunklin, a veteran judge with a weak grasp of some of the finer points of the law. On the Sunday before the trial opened, Ike's brother, William A. Knight of Centerville, Tennessee, showed up in town. As luck would have it, he was a lawyer. Brother Bill had first learned about

Ike's troubles from a Nashville newspaper. Only after that did he receive a telegram from Ike's lawyers and a letter from Ike asking him to "come here and aid in the trial." On Monday, William visited Ike in jail, as his brother, not his lawyer, and announced upon emerging, "I will take no active part in the defense of my brother, but will leave the case entirely in the hands of local attorneys, assisting them in any way that they may suggest." He added helpfully that Ike had "always been a peaceful sort of fellow . . . of an even and kindly disposition."[38]

The trial opened on Wednesday, April 29 with a venire of seventy-five men present for jury selection, summoned under the new "jury wheel system."[39] The defense had already gotten off to a bad start by not asking for a change of venue, usually the first order of business in a sensational murder case with an unsympathetic defendant. They did the next best thing, asking for a continuance, a classic ploy of the weaker side in a trial, so that they could "procure material evidence that has lately been discovered" and because one of their key witnesses, Oscar Montgomery, was still in the hospital. Judge Dunklin granted the continuance until May 14, and the venire was sent home.[40]

Come May 14, the trial tried to get underway again with a fresh venire present for jury selection. The April dress rehearsal had not shown either side to be at the top of their game. The respective counsels had changed in the interim with both sides adding legal luminaries to the team. The defense now included W. A. Knight who had decided *not* to leave the case "entirely in the hands of local attorneys," as the newspapers so delicately put it, and so would be sitting at the defense table. On the prosecution's side, the Fort Worth firm of Walter B. Scott and W. P. McLean, Jr., had been hired by Ed Larmon's father, W. W. Larmon, to "assist" County Attorney Roy. Neither move reflected much faith in the abilities of the current counsel.[41]

The defense counsel showed that it knew what it was doing when it opened things by moving for a continuance, for a change of venue, and to quash the venire. The first two motions were routine, but the third was based on the allegation that several veniremen had been selling tickets to the benefit ball held "in aid of the wounded officers." Unimpressed, Judge Dunklin overruled all three motions and ordered the trial to proceed. Jury selection and defense motions took up the whole morning, so things did not really get underway until the afternoon.[42]

Hundreds of would-be spectators crowded into the courtroom, filling the hallways and jostling each other to get as close to the courtroom as possible. Inside the courtroom, they were even sitting inside the rail in the area properly reserved for court officials. Two extra deputies were posted in the rear of the gallery to keep order. The defense was prepared but still failed to exploit a couple of crucial weaknesses in the state's case. They did not challenge the validity of Ike's jailhouse confession or raise questions about Texas marriage and community-property laws. The latter would have gone a long way toward exonerating their client since, under Texas law at that time, "the husband has the legal right to manage and control community property . . . [and] the wife can not without the consent of her husband sell, convey or otherwise dispose of even her separate property."[43]

Fortunately for the defense, Judge Dunklin did the prosecution no favors. His pronouncements from the bench would reveal an appalling ignorance of both the law and his judicial duties. Among his missteps were not instructing the jury properly on the nature of community-property law and common-law marriage in Texas. Such slipups did not seem to matter at the time because everyone from the Judge down to the man in the street considered it an open and shut case. County Attorney Roy turned the prosecution over to Bill McLean, who was as sharp as they come but not a miracle worker.[44]

The prosecution won points with the jury by putting a pale, still-recovering Oscar Montgomery on the stand to testify about how the defendant had shot him down in cold blood. Montgomery did not mention Dick Howell in his testimony, and curiously, Howell was not called to testify because technically, he was not a police officer, so the defense would have painted him as a "vigilante," no better than the mob that was howling after Ike Knight that day. The prosecution called Mrs. Krause, who testified that Knight had fired at her, and Florence Knight, who offered damning testimony against her husband. As his common-law wife, she could have refused to testify, but she was as eager as the prosecutor to see Ike Knight get what was coming to him. Under cross-examination, Flo admitted that she had "no love for [Ike]," but she became evasive when the defense tried to get her to say that she had "ill feelings toward [him]." When defense counsel complained that she was not answering his question about the nature of her feelings for Ike, Judge Dunklin cut him off with the observation that "one was equivalent to the other" [i.e., "no love" and "ill feelings"]. The prosecution also tried to bring up Ike's violent record back in Tennessee, but the Judge instructed the jury to disregard those references.[45]

The defense's case was built on trying to show that a conspiracy existed between Flo Knight and the Larmons "to get rid of the defendant for the purpose of getting his property." With "poor Ed" dead, they had a hard time selling that theory, however. They took the always risky step of putting their client on the witness stand. They had to do something to counter his signed jailhouse confession. Knight testified that the confession had been "induced" because no one had warned him it might be used against him! The jury was obviously not impressed with that argument. And Ike hurt the defense with his surliness and lack of remorse, particularly when he blurted out under oath this stunning statement:

I shot him. I shot him again before he hit the floor. I reloaded my gun and shot him again after he was on the floor.[46]

What was predicted to be an open-and-shut case turned into a nine-day marathon, rare in those days. The proceedings were only adjourned once, on Sunday the seventeenth, so that everyone could attend church services; otherwise, they slogged on all day every day. On Saturday, May 23, the opposing counsels made their closing arguments. Bill McLean and Bob Roy raised the emotional rhetoric so high that the Judge instructed the jury to disregard their most incendiary statements. McLean had raised his own hands as he implored the jury, "Tarrant County holds up blood-stained hands and asks you to wipe out that stain!" Roy, inspired by his colleague, asked the jury to remember "the effect produced by [the news of her son's death] on the grey-haired, crippled mother of Ed C. Larmon!" The defense's rhetoric did not rise to similar levels. The jury got the case late on the afternoon of May 23 after the Judge delivered a lengthy and "comprehensive" charge on the relevant points of law. After the jury filed out, many spectators kept their seats expecting a quick verdict. They were disappointed. The jury was still deliberating at 11:00 p.m. when Judge Dunklin said he was going home to bed but instructed the sheriff to call him if the verdict came back during the night.[47]

The jury was out for eighteen hours, allowing Judge Dunklin to get a good night's rest. They brought in their verdict Sunday morning. The state had made it easy for them; all they had to do was decide whether Ike had killed Ed Larmon in cold blood. They were not asked to determine his guilt or innocence in shooting down Oscar Montgomery and Dick Howell. The twelve men had no trouble deciding Knight was guilty of murdering Larmon; he had admitted as much on the stand. The only debate was over the sentence—death or life in prison. The verdict they finally brought in said it all: "We the jury find the defendant guilty of murder in the first degree . . . and assess his punishment at death." When the verdict was announced, the courtroom was visibly stunned. No one had seen it coming. Most had expected that the defendant would get a long stretch in the penitentiary, fifteen-to-twenty-five years, not get his neck stretched. Ike paled but said nothing until he was back in his cell. Then he lashed out at everybody connected to the state, claiming he had been railroaded. He had sincerely believed he would be acquitted.[48]

The prosecutors did not even have time to celebrate their victory. Ten minutes after the verdict was read, the defense was filing a motion for a new trial even though by law they had two days to file such an appeal. Their amended appeal a few weeks later contained twenty-seven "bills of exception," covering forty-five pages. But the three most important were that the judge had refused to grant a change of venue, that the jury was tainted, and that Ike's jailhouse confession, taken right after the shooting, had been admitted into evidence. The entire trial transcript totaled more than 150 pages, the biggest ever generated by a Fort Worth trial. The appeals court agreed with the defense, citing a "chain of mistakes" in the proceedings. It reversed the conviction and remanded the case back to district court for retrial. The judges found that Knight was the rightful owner of the house and all its furnishings and therefore had the right to arm himself and take possession of either or both with lethal force if necessary. On the day of the shootings, they ruled, the Larmons had no right to "refuse Knight admittance to his home." All other actions of the defendant after that flowed from that initial provocation and therefore constituted self-defense! It was a devastating setback for the state.[49]

The trial had been one of the most expensive in Tarrant County history. Leaving aside the appeal, the nine-day proceeding had cost $650.[50] And now the state faced the prospect of starting all over. Feeling the heat, County Attorney Roy was unwilling to turn Ike Knight loose that easily, so he geared up for another go at him. One difference the second time around was that Irby Dunklin would not be the presiding judge. He had been appointed to the Texas Court of Civil Appeals soon after the first trial ended, thereby avoiding the recriminations that flowed from his mismanagement of those proceedings. R. H. Buck replaced him. The same defense team represented Knight. Their first order of business this time, however, was to ask for a change of venue. Judge Buck, going down the same path as his predecessor, denied the motion citing the wisdom of long-time City Marshal and Police Chief James Maddox who testified thusly against the motion:

> *I am City Marshall of the City of Fort Worth; I mingle right smart with the citizenship of Fort Worth every day . . . and I think I am acquainted with the sentiment generally throughout the city of Fort Worth with regard to this case. I think defendant can get a fair and impartial trial in Tarrant County.*[51]

While he awaited the final decision of the legal system, Ike Knight gave newspaper interviews in jail. Showing what a modern defendant he was, he told reporters that he might write a book. "Before they give me the final jerk," he confided darkly to the men hanging on his every word, "I would like to tell the people something that they don't know."[52]

Before a new judge and jury, the lawyers went through their paces again. For a second time Knight was convicted, but this time he was sentenced to seventy-five years in prison. As in the first go-around, his jailhouse confession was the key piece of evidence.

That was still not the end of it, however. The case was back before the Court of Criminal Appeals in Dallas in February 1910, and the judges reversed the latest verdict, finding that the trial court had committed a serious error when it "improperly admitted the confession of the defendant."[53] With that, the linchpin of the state's case had just been thrown out. The best the state could hope to do now was get a conviction on a charge of manslaughter. The county attorney went back to the grand jury and got an indictment on that charge, and Ike's third trial opened in Judge W. T. Simmons' Sixty-seventh District Court in January 1911. Yet another Tarrant County jury found him guilty a third time and assessed the maximum sentence of five years for manslaughter. This time the prosecution had not made the mistake of introducing the tainted confession, but they still stumbled over procedural matters. To begin with, Sheriff William Rea had disregarded the new jury-wheel system and selected the jury panel the old-fashioned way, by going down the voter rolls and choosing whom he would. If the prosecution's intention was to "stack" the jury, it succeeded. One of the prospective jurymen before being examined stated that he had no opinion on the case, yet during jury deliberations he stated that "any man that would go home and pour money into the lap of such an old hag [as Flo] ought to be hung." That same juror before being selected had stated to other veniremen that if he had been on the previous jury he would have voted to "break Ike's damn neck [since] any man who would live with the parties that he was living with needed his neck broke." Finally, during deliberations he blurted out to his fellow jurors that he could not forget that Knight had gunned down the two officers in addition to Ed Larmon, a fact that had been excluded in testimony. The Appeals Court found in such egregious misconduct grounds to declare yet another mistrial and remand the case back to the district court for yet another go-round.[54]

Once more Tarrant County rolled the dice. On his fourth trip through the system, Ike got the same verdict and same sentence as his previous trial—guilty, five years. His defense team filed yet another appeal, and the case went down to Austin again. While the appeal was pending, Knight was released on bond. He moved to Denton and re-married, thereby opening himself up to a possible charge of "bigamy" if Flo contested it in addition to the other charges against him.[55]

More determined than ever, the state took Ike to trial a fifth time, charging manslaughter once again. The prosecution this time managed to avoid previous missteps, and the jury returned a verdict of guilty with a sentence of five years, the maximum for manslaughter under Texas law. The fifth time apparently was the charm because the Appeals Court subsequently upheld the verdict.

Five years after his first conviction, Ike Knight finally began serving his time in 1913. Apparently, the long, drawn-out proceedings had finally worn down the Tarrant County Attorney's office because on October 29, 1914, they dismissed the assault to murder charges for shooting Oscar Montgomery and Dick Howell, which meant that neither man would ever get his day in court. They could not even draw much satisfaction from Knight's conviction for killing Ed Larmon because, instead of serving the full five years, Ike spent only twenty-one months and seventeen days in the Huntsville penitentiary. By the time he reported to start serving his sentence he was supposedly a reformed man. He had undergone a miraculous conversion to become a "born-again" Christian. Under the skeptical eyes of the prison staff, he spent the next three years witnessing to fellow inmates, saving two souls by his own count. Such a seemingly sincere conversion was sufficient to earn him one of Governor Jim Ferguson's annual Christmas paroles in 1915. Ike was now a free man. He returned to Fort Worth and proclaimed his intention to live an "upright life" henceforward. He never reconciled with Flo and Nellie, but he did become a regular attendee and frequent speaker at the Union Gospel Mission.[56]

The city that had spent so much time and treasure trying to bring Knight to justice showed itself ready to forgive and forget. But the "new" Ike still preferred to pack up and leave Fort Worth for good and go back to his roots in Tennessee. In 1920 he was living quietly in Nashville with his third wife, Donna. Presumably he had waited until his common-law marriage to Flo had been legally dissolved. That occurred in 1926 when she sued to have it terminated on basis of abandonment, telling the court that she did not know where Ike was and asking for the property on Lake Street to be deeded over to her. The court granted the uncontested suit, and Flo was a free woman with the house and lot that previous judicial proceedings had declared belonged solely to Ike. As for the born-again Ike, Donna Knight went to court in Fort Worth in 1929 to end their marriage. There is no evidence that Ike Knight ever committed another crime after April 11, 1908.[57]

During all the courtroom battles, dragging out over six and a half years, Dick Howell and Oscar Montgomery were almost forgotten. Public sympathy peaked in the spring of 1908 when the Police Benevolent Association sponsored a "benefit ball" to raise money to help defray all the medical expenses of the two officers. Since the PBA was an organization of and for Fort Worth officers, it was going beyond the call of duty to extend assistance to the two North Fort Worth officers. Somebody had to do something. The North Fort Worth City Council repeatedly refused to cover the medical bills of either man. Technically, they had no moral or legal obligation in Howell's case because he had not been a city employee at the time, but Montgomery was the chief of the North Fort Worth police force, and still the council felt no sense of obligation! The bills came from four physicians, each of whom submitted bills of fifty dollars, and even appeared before the council to explain why the services were "reasonable and just." But the council was adamant in disallowing payment. In the end, Dick Howell and Oscar Montgomery would be totally dependent on their own resources and the contributions of friends.[58]

Never one to shirk his duty, Oscar Montgomery testified at all five of Ike Knight's trials. Insofar as the record shows, Dick Howell was not called to testify at any of them. Neither man ever spoke out about the inept way the prosecution was handled by the county attorney's office. Whatever frustration or bitterness they felt, they did not express it publicly. Both men returned to work despite their grievous wounds because they were too tough to retire to a rocking chair and because neither could afford to. Howell finally had to have his leg amputated, so the rest of his life he went around on one leg and a pair of crutches. A lesser man would have given up any hope of a law enforcement career, but not Dick Howell. He refused to be either a quitter or a charity case, although he had health problems related to the amputation the rest of his life.

Oscar Montgomery was luckier. He had an almost complete recovery although he too suffered lingering effects of his horrific wounds the rest of his life. Having the constitution as well as the size of a bull helped him come back. After the city of Fort Worth annexed its near neighbor in 1909, he went to work for the Fort Worth Police Department and began a rapid climb through the ranks: Assistant Chief of Police (1912), Chief of Police twice (1913–15 and 1917). In between, he jumped over to the county side of law enforcement to become a detective in the county attorney's office. In August 1917 when Fort Worth Police and Fire Commissioner Ed Parsley was killed, Montgomery was chosen to replace him in a special election a month later. He was re-elected in the next regular election and served until 1921 when he took off the badge for the first time since 1904. He was selling insurance a few years later when Sheriff Carl Smith called him out of retirement to become a deputy sheriff. Montgomery retired from law enforcement for good in 1928, but he was not ready to be put out to pasture yet, so he took a job with the county as "road inspector."[59]

He was on a Sunday drive with his wife on June 14, 1931, when he collapsed, dying en route to St. Joseph Hospital. The medical examiner listed the cause of death as "probably heart failure or apoplexy." He was only fifty-nine years old, with twenty-nine of them spent in law enforcement.[60]

His funeral was held in the same community where he had lived and worked most of his life, now known simply as "the North Side." Dave Shannon's North Fort Worth Undertaking firm prepared the body, but the services on June 15 were held at the North Side Primitive Baptist Church. A large turnout filled every pew, and Chief W. H. Lee sent an honor guard of Fort Worth police to escort him on his last journey—to Mount Olivet Cemetery in Riverside. Lee himself served as one of the pallbearers.

Oscar Montgomery was preceded in death by his old friend. He and Howell had remained close over the years, linked by the badge they wore and by what they had gone through on that terrible day. Montgomery's career was the star that Howell hitched his wagon to for twenty years. Montgomery was instrumental in getting his crippled friend hired on with the FWPD as permanent night sergeant at the North Side substation.[61]

Howell did not want to be put out to pasture, but more to the point, he had to work to support a wife and six stepchildren. Although he suffered chronic pain and other unspecified complications, he reported diligently for duty every evening, stumping into the station house on his crutches. His physical ailments sometimes caused him to miss half the workdays in a given month, and his fellow officers made allowances for him, but although he was short one leg, "Uncle Dick" was no goldbrick. He still had the heart of a policeman as he proved the day after Christmas 1908. He was off-duty when he caught sight of a suspect in a murder investigation. He ordered the man to stop, and when the fellow ran, Howell took off after him, swinging along on his crutches at a rapid clip. It took five blocks, but he caught up with the suspect and put him under arrest. Sgt. Howell's amazing physical feat made him the toast of the town.[62]

Mostly, his life was one long battle against pain, and as if that were not bad enough, he suffered four strokes during the last nineteen years of his life, all of which can be attributed to the gunshot wound and the amputation that followed. After the first three strokes, he returned to work, defying modern-day studies that show that typically only about 50 percent of stroke victims ever regain "functional independence" while another 30 percent remain complete invalids.[63] Uncle Dick beat the odds three times, although the series of strokes left him with a permanent facial "twitch." So unwilling was he to accept his status as an invalid, he ran as an independent for Police and Fire Commissioner in 1921. Americans had not voted en masse for cripples since the post-Civil War era when so many veterans came home missing limbs, and they would not get into the habit again until Franklin Roosevelt's four presidential runs (1932–1944). Just getting on the ballot meant that Dick Howell had beaten long physical *and* electoral odds both. His campaign ads in the newspaper showed him standing tall on one leg and crutches and reminded voters, "He has been faithful, at all times guarding the interests of our city, ever willing and ready to perform his duty." When he lost, he quietly returned to work at the North Side police station where his excellent work eventually got him promoted to captain's rank. He was still in uniform when the fourth stroke took him on September 30, 1927. Those who mourned his passing remembered him not as the physical husk of a man who reported for duty at the North Side station every night but as one who was "fearless, upright and honorable in his daily life as an officer and a citizen, doing his duty without fear or favor."[64]

Dick Howell's death certificate said he died of "apoplexy." Linked in death as in life, it is worth noting that he and Oscar Montgomery both likely even died of the same cause. Both were also fifty-nine years old when they died, and Howell was buried with honors in the same cemetery, Mount Olivet, as his long-time friend.[65]

Dick Howell was the consummate professional. He never publicly bemoaned his fate or expressed regret at having gone to Marshal Montgomery's assistance that April afternoon. The words that were used over and over to describe his career were "faithful service." Over the last nineteen years of his life, the Fort Worth Police Department and city fathers did all they could to help him even when it meant bending the rules. They were motivated by more than just compassion; men with that kind of grit were few and far between and provided good role models for the young bucks on the force. Giving him a desk job was the least they could do. What is known today as "light duty" was simply "doing the right thing" back then. In 1911, after the city financial officer tried to dock his pay for the six days he had missed in August due to health problems, Mayor W. D. Davis wrote a personal letter to commissioners asking them to restore the money as a "moral obligation of the city." They did.[66]

The same cannot be said of North Fort Worth. No officers were ever more shabbily treated by city government than Oscar Montgomery and Dick Howell by North Fort Worth. The city re- fused even to come up with $200 to pay their medical expenses. Many more years would pass before either Fort Worth or Tarrant County began providing disability and retirement benefits for their officers. The twin tragedies of Oscar Montgomery and Dick Howell were a cautionary tale to other officers about how dangerous and thankless police work could be. They had sacrificed so much, yet the system let them down. If someone had written a country-western song about it, they might have called it, "Mamas, Don't Let Your Babies Grow up to Be Lawmen."

Oscar Montgomery's marker in Mount Olivet Cemetery memorializes both the officer and his wife, Rizpah. It is first-class, from the granite pedestal to the highly engraved (front and back) granite headstone. Montgomery was such a big man, it took one-and-a-half plots to bury him, as cemetery records show. (Photograph by Kevin Foster)

"Uncle Dick," finally "at rest" in Mount Olivet Cemetery after enduring years of chronic pain and other health issues. His marker is not far from that of lifetime pal Oscar Montgomery on the north side of the cemetery. A big man, like Montgomery, it took one-and-a-half plots to bury him. Curiously, Mount Olivet had no record that Howell even had a marker until it was pointed out to them in 2010. (Photograph by Kevin Foster)

The youthful looking William "Ad" Campbell was anything but meek and mild; he was a terror to the lowlifes of the Acre. This is the only known photograph of him, passed down in the family and shared with the FWPD for the Department's Memorial Room. It is not dated. (Courtesy of Vicky Campbell Underhill, Fort Worth)

CHAPTER 11

POLICE OFFICER
WILLIAM ADDISON CAMPBELL
August 12, 1909

"The Clean-up Policeman"

Not until 1908 did the Fort Worth Police Department finally get around to drawing up a list of qualifications for men seeking to join the force. With the sweep of a pen, a new era had dawned. Henceforward, all would-be policemen must be between the ages of 25 and 45, able to read and write, have resided in the city for at least two years, and never been convicted of a crime (any crime). Physical qualifications included being at least five-feet-ten inches tall, weighing no less than 160 pounds, and being "of good health and sound body." Finally, candidates must possess "steady habits and moral character." That last alone would have eliminated half the police force in the early days![1]

William Campbell was one of the first officers hired under the new standards. When he started in April 1909 he was one of the new breed of more professional Fort Worth policemen. Unfortunately, he never got a chance to make a lasting impact on the culture of the FWPD because he was a policeman for just four months. He was murdered on August 12, 1909, a month shy of his thirtieth birthday and just sixteen months after the shootings of Oscar Montgomery and Dick Howell.

Campbell had been born in Kentucky on September 17, 1878, and come to Texas as a boy with his family when they moved to Fannin County. He grew up there, acquiring the nickname "Ad" along the way. When he was old enough, he took a job with the Honey Grove Police Department. Later he joined the long list of lawmen who traded in their badges for jobs with the railroad, finding the pay and prospects of living to a ripe old age much better. It was the railroad job that brought him to Fort Worth in 1906, but after three years he returned to law enforcement because he missed the excitement and respect that came with the badge. Bypassing the usual procedure, he applied directly to Police Commissioner George Mulkey for a place on incoming Chief L. J. "June" Polk's force.

His first assignment might have made him reconsider his career move: his beat was Hell's Half-acre, where a man could get laid, rolled, and killed all in the same night. He might have accepted the Acre as a force of nature and contented himself with keeping a lid on the district, but that was not his way. He was determined to clean up the Acre, something that a host of district attorneys, mayors, and police chiefs before him had been unable to accomplish in more than thirty years. Not the least discouraged, he set about making things hot for the lowlifes on his beat. In less than two months he was on the way to making a record number of arrests, albeit for misdemeanor offenses such as carrying a weapon, drunkenness, and vagrancy. Unfortunately, for every one he ran in or ran out of town, there were two more to replace him or her. Campbell went after the big fish as well as the small, targeting saloon owners and gamblers. And he was incorruptible: he did not drink, keep company with the ladies of the evening, or accept payoffs from gamblers and saloon men to look the other way. Captain Tom Blanton applauded his rookie as "one of his most fearless and trustworthy men" he had ever known, a shining example for all the men in blue. Others, however, worried that, among the denizens of the Acre, Blanton's golden boy was also "the most hated man" on the force. That is how Ad Campbell happened to acquire his own bodyguard just two months into the job. The death threats against him were unrelenting and not the idle mutterings of jailbirds. He was warned by people on his beat that "his life was in jeopardy every hour that he worked in the Acre." The easy thing to have done would have been to reassign Campbell to some other beat, but that would have been caving in to pressure. Instead, Captain Blanton took the unprecedented step of assigning protection to shadow the Department's rookie with a bull's-eye on his back. It was ironic that the Captain had to pull officers off other beats in the city to provide protection for Campbell. Theoretically, police were supposed to protect the public, not each other. Nonetheless, for several nights running in early July, officers with Winchesters were posted in the shadows on Campbell's beat, just in case.[2]

When several nights passed and nothing happened, Blanton pulled the protection, but that did not mean he was no longer worried. One night he took Assistant Chief Ed Parsley with him, and they did a little unofficial sleuthing in the dark corners of the Acre. What they heard were rumors of a new assassination plot. A gang of cutthroats, it seemed, were planning to bushwhack Campbell as he walked his beat. Alarmed, Blanton sent men to raid a favorite hangout of the plotters, and they turned up further evidence that the threat was legitimate even though no arrests were subsequently made. The Captain reinstated the protection detail. Meanwhile, Ad Campbell continued to work his shift every night never knowing when a blast from the darkness might cut him down. The young Galahad grew tense and jumpy.[3]

Why did the Department virtually dare the anonymous conspirators to kill Campbell? It might have been that they were trying to send a message that they would not be stampeded by back-shooters and other lowlifes. But it also had something to do with the fact that Officer Campbell was the hero of every upstanding citizen in Fort Worth. In July the grand jury even took time out from its regular work to write an unsolicited letter to Police Commissioner George Mulkey commending the exemplary work of Patrolman Campbell "in reporting and prosecuting bootleggers and other law violators along his beat." Jury members did more than just write a letter of commendation; they suggested that an additional officer be assigned to "assist" Campbell. Mulkey gritted his teeth and passed the word down the chain of command, and Captain Blanton assigned veteran cop Tom Jones as Campbell's partner. Ad Campbell was now the only officer in FWPD history to have his own personal bodyguard. Jones was a good choice; he was not as gung-ho as the rookie, and he knew the players in the Acre. His assignment was to keep Ad Campbell alive.[4]

While the Department tried to find a happy middle ground between coddling their golden boy and supporting him, Ad Campbell
even managed to make a new enemy, Robert Hammond, proprietor of a hole-in-the-wall saloon on Thirteenth. Hammond seems
to have been a special target of Officer Campbell. He was the worst
of the worst among the Acre's saloon-keepers. He had a chip on his
shoulder and more brass than a Kansas City fire engine. He seldom
stepped outside unarmed, sometimes toting a Winchester in brazen
defiance of city gun ordinances. His record for disorderly conduct,
criminal assault, and general mayhem was unmatched in the Acre,
and that was saying a lot. More astounding, he had accomplished
most of it in less than two years.

Robert P. Hammond was born in Tarrant County in January
1876 to J. K. and Annie Hammond. He grew up as the oldest in
a house full of kids, where, by 1900, there was a twenty-one-year
difference between the oldest and the youngest. Until May 1898
he was content to be a farmer on his father's farm at Azle, but the
Spanish-American War changed all that. He enlisted in the army
and after a very brief training was assigned to Company H, Second
Texas Infantry. His army service did not go well; in November he
received a medical discharge in Dallas, Texas, due to a hernia. He
promptly packed up and moved to Los Angeles, California, but he
was back in Tarrant County by 1900, living under his father's roof
and working on the farm.[5]

He was an undistinguished man, standing five foot ten and
weighing less than 170 pounds, medium-built with brown hair and
gray eyes. He had a ruddy, wind- and sunburned complexion from
a life of following a mule up one furrow and down another. He
might have lived out the rest of his life in anonymity had he not
decided to leave the farm and make a better life for himself in the
city. With only the most perfunctory schooling and few marketable
skills, his options were limited. He was lucky that in October 1907
the FWPD was looking for a few good men to refill positions that
had been axed while the city was facing a budget crunch. Now the
budget crunch had passed, and Bob was able to parlay his war veteran's status into a patrolman's job. He bought a house in town at
808 East Seventeenth, definitely the wrong end of town but close
to his job. Enduring twelve-hour days on his feet and nursing a

hernia, barely squeaking by on the pay, he lasted only five months. On March 26, 1908, he quit the force, giving as a reason that he planned to "enter business in Fort Worth." That business turned out to be the Dew Drop Inn, at the corner of East Thirteenth and Crump. It was that saloon that Officer Campbell was trying to shut down.[6]

Hammond's personal life was as unsettled as his career. He married for the first time in 1908 when he was thirty-two and his bride twenty-two years old. Anna Williams also had a five-year-old son, Daine, when she married Hammond. Their marriage lasted less than two years before she divorced him, possibly because her husband's legal troubles brought out her own embarrassing past life in court, or perhaps because four months into their marriage Bob had left town one step ahead of the law without so much as a word to her about when or even if he might return. Whatever the reason, he would be a free man again in 1910, but he did not remain single long, marrying a woman named Margaret who became his partner in more ways than one: in September 1910, they were indicted on six counts of selling liquor without a license. They posted bond but skipped out before the cases went to trial.[7]

Whether alone or with a partner, Bob Hammond had managed to acquire a rap sheet longer than that of many men doing time in Huntsville. His crimes started with operating his saloon with no license and selling liquor on Sunday, then escalated to assault to murder. On July 22, 1908, he got into a dispute with Will Chadwick, former proprietor of the Dew Drop Inn and tracked him to the Arizona barroom on Twelfth where he pulled a gun and tried to shoot him. Chadwick got away unscathed, but a sheriff's deputy who heard the shots came running up and opened fire on Hammond as he fled. Hammond, too, got away, but some bystanders were not so lucky: a woman sitting on her front porch was severely wounded, another man had his clothes "perforated," and a neighborhood dog was killed. Hammond was blamed for all the damage and charged with two counts of assault to murder on August 11. After the heat died down, he turned himself in and was released on bond pending trial.[8]

Bob Hammond may have been violent and venal, but he was no fool. On the contrary, he possessed a creative streak. He would receive a patent in 1910 for inventing a "coin controlled slide," which, roughly translated, was an improved mechanism for push- ing coins into a slot machine. The invention would never make him rich, but it did earn him a place among the nation's amateur inven- tors somewhere below Thomas Alva Edison and Alexander Graham Bell.[9]

When Ad Campbell came onto the force in the spring of 1909, he decided that Hammond had to go. It was not unusual for the police to run undesirables out of town without the benefit of due process. Usually those targeted were vagrants, prostitutes, or blacks. Hammond was an ex-policeman, but that did not keep Campbell from turning up the heat, by citing the saloon man for every viola- tion, including operating without a license and selling liquor on Sunday. Every time Hammond looked up, Campbell was in his place "jobbing" him.

On Saturday, July 10, 1909, the saloon man had to appear in county court and pay a twenty-five dollar fine for his latest violation of the Sunday closing ordinance. Fed up with the harassment, he swore aloud to get even, and the threat got back to Campbell. That night, around ten thirty, Hammond and his nemesis ran into each other near the intersection of Rusk and Twelfth. When Campbell saw Hammond coming up Twelfth towards him, the officer was still thinking of Hammond's threat, plus his nerves already on edge. He overreacted. As Hammond passed by and glared at him, Campbell thought he saw him reaching into his coat. He whirled, pulling his own piece as he did, and opened fire. The thoroughly surprised saloon man took off running but did not get far. Just before he reached the other side of the street, two of Campbell's bullets caught up with him: one pierced his left hip, and the other passed through his right thigh. Hammond cried out and stumbled but managed to stay on his feet until he could duck inside the Standard Theater. Campbell had fired at least three shots on a crowded street, but Hammond was the only one injured.[10]

Two officers, H. M. Lively and N. F. Turner, who had been on the protection detail that night, raced up to find out what had hap- pened. Later they would support Campbell's version of the incident that Hammond had acted threateningly and was going for a gun when Campbell opened fire. They could not say why Campbell had continued to blaze away at a man running for his life. Both officers did state unequivocally that Hammond was armed even if none of the civilians at the scene reported seeing a weapon in the victim's hand at any time. Later, Lively admitted under oath that Hammond was not carrying a weapon that night. It is ironic that Hammond had not been armed the one time he should have been—and would have been justified in returning fire.[11]

Accompanied by his two bodyguards, Campbell went to police headquarters and turned himself in. He was charged with assault "with intent to commit murder" and suspended from duty pending an investigation. But things were not as serious as they looked. A justice of the peace released him that same night on $500 bond. Meanwhile, Hammond was not doing so well. Some of his friends took him to the Medical College, which doubled as a hospital, just a few blocks away where newspaper reporters, sniffing a front-page story, tracked him down. They interviewed the physicians treating him and their stories appeared in the next morning's newspapers, but it is hard to believe they all talked to the same doctors. The *Fort Worth Star-Telegram* reported the victim's wounds to be "not of a very serious nature." The *Dallas Morning News* described his condition as "extremely critical." Like so much else in this case, agreement on the so-called facts was hard to come by.[12]

Bob Hammond limped out of the hospital two weeks later, glad to be alive although the doctors told him he would be crippled for life. While he was convalescing, he got more bad news: he had been charged by County Attorney R. E. L. Roy with carrying a concealed weapon. Roy really wanted to make the charge assault with intent to kill, but the police had no weapon in their possession so he settled for a lesser charge of unlawfully carrying a weapon, logic be damned. Without a weapon, the state did not have a case, only the word of the three policemen that there had ever been a weapon. Nevertheless, the County Attorney decided to prosecute the misdemeanor charge.

Being shot had not mellowed Bob Hammond any. Out of bed just one day, on July 25 he assaulted Special Officer Will Purdy, kicking and punching Purdy in the face and ripping off his badge. Hammond believed that the officer had gotten his landlord to evict him while he was in the hospital and sought out Purdy at his place of employment. He flashed a revolver just before lighting into his victim with feet and fists. After pummeling Purdy, he left but was arrested the next day. Hammond told the police he did not know Purdy was a special policeman when he took the badge away from him. Purdy filed an assault charge in municipal court but failed to appear when the case was called so the charge was dismissed.[13]

That left the concealed-weapon charge unresolved from his run-in with Ad Campbell. It came to trial on August 4. Officer Campbell took the witness stand in his full uniform to tell his side of the story, and Hammond, who made a sympathetic witness, got his chance to tell his side of it. Typically, juries tend to give the benefit of the doubt to officers of the law, but this time they found Hammond innocent. He was a free man again and as angry at the world as ever. If anything, his brush with death had given him more reason to feel persecuted.

While all this was going on, the story took a bizarre turn. On July 28, the victim-defendant announced himself a candidate for Tarrant County sheriff although the elections were more than a year away in November 1910, and nobody ever announced this far ahead. He said he would enter the Democratic Party primaries but in the meantime got the ball rolling by passing out printed cards soliciting votes. To inquiring newspaper reporters he offered no platform, just that he was running "strictly on my merits." He did not bother to specify what those "merits" were. The *Star-Telegram* did not comment on his candidacy but did remind voters that just the year before Hammond had shot "a man, a woman, and a dog, all with one bullet"—possibly the first, but certainly not the last, "magic bullet" in American history.[14]

Hammond was not one to let things slide. If he had not had good reason to kill Ad Campbell before being shot, he did now. He had often gone about armed previously; now he never stepped outside the house without his automatic. He was determined to defend himself the next time he crossed paths with any of Fort Worth's finest, but more than that he wanted payback against Ad Campbell. He told a friend that the Officer was "his meat and he would get him."[15]

It was just one week after Hammond's trial for the "crime" of being shot by Ad Campbell that the Officer himself was bushwhacked.

The end came on Thursday night, August 12. Officers Campbell and Jones were walking their beat, proceeding east on Fourteenth. The bodyguards had been pulled, so it was just the two of them. It had rained that afternoon, so the usually sultry summer temperatures were cooler than normal and, making their rounds, they had to step around puddles in the street. It was an unusually quiet night in the Acre with not many folks on the street. The two officers were between Rusk and Calhoun just passing the Jockey Club Saloon when the quiet was shattered by a shotgun blast. It came from somewhere above and behind them, catching Campbell in the neck and upper back with a full load of buckshot. He pitched forward onto his face and lay there moaning, too badly injured to even roll over. His stunned partner, uninjured, stood for a moment, making him an easy target for another blast if the shooter had been so inclined, but only silence followed. The shooter, whoever he was, had hit his target. Jones drew his pistol and turned in every direction, scanning the nearby doorways and windows. He did not know exactly where the shot had come from; he could only look around helplessly. The only people he saw were a handful of panicked citizens scattering in all directions. He knelt down at his partner's side to provide whatever aid he could and saw that Campbell's upper torso had been turned into hamburger meat. When he rolled him over, he could see where several pellets had passed all the way through the body and come out the chest.

Tom Jones yelled for somebody to call police headquarters, hoping that someone within earshot had a telephone and would place the call. The crowd inside the Jockey Club had come to the windows to see what was going on. Bert McGuire heard footsteps clattering down the stairs and looked around just in time to see someone disappearing out the back of the saloon. On the street, Jones decided not to wait for the patrol wagon but commandeered a private conveyance to take his partner to the hospital. Of course there was no emergency medical treatment en route, but it really did not matter. Will Campbell was beyond help.[16]

As always, the report of an officer down brought the swiftest possible response. In a matter of minutes, mounted officers were on the scene, and they were soon joined by four foot cops, plus Detective W. J. Williams, and Assistant Chief Ed Parsley who had been at headquarters when the call came in. The preliminary conclusion as they tried to reconstruct the crime was that the fatal shot had come from a second-story window over the Jockey Club. They sealed off the building and started a room-to-room search. They found only one person on the second floor, a "floozy" named Grace Hemmings who was recovering from recent "surgery" (likely an abortion). Grace was hardly "innocent," in any sense of the word, but she was no killer either. Still, she was the closest thing they had to a suspect, so they forced her to get dressed and come with them down to the police station for questioning. For good measure, they also took along bartender Will Spradley and customer Charley Kent who happened to be in the saloon at the time.[17]

Assistant Chief Parsley took personal charge of the investigation and at headquarters put Grace through the wringer. He allowed newspaper reporters to be present and even ask a few questions of their own. No one had forgotten the trouble between Campbell and Bob Hammond, and attention immediately focused on him. Hammond certainly had the motive, and after it was learned from the owner of the Jockey Club that he had been in the bar that evening, it was clear he had the opportunity. Grace insisted she knew nothing about the shooting although she admitted knowing Hammond. She also gave them the name of a friend of his, another unsavory character named Stokes Clark. Police were well acquainted with Clark. The Fort Worth resident was a bar fly whose day job was conductor for the Northern Texas Traction Co. He was also a loud-mouth and self-styled pistolero who had a run-in with Texas Ranger Homer White in Weatherford on February 4, 1908. The encounter left White dead and Clark with two bullet holes in his leg. He was subsequently convicted of murder but was out on bail more than a year later while his case was being appealed. He still walked with a limp. That gave him two things in common with Bob Hammond besides a fondness for bars: a limp and a virulent hatred of lawmen. Now police had a second person of interest, as they say today, and a dragnet was launched to bring in the two suspects. Parsley also charged Grace with vagrancy so he could keep her locked up while the investigation continued.[18]

Back at the crime scene, Detective Williams was doing more to develop the case than all the interrogations at city hall. He made a careful search of the entire second floor and was able to identify the room used by the assassin. It was empty except for a dirty mattress lying on the floor with an old suit coat tossed on top of it. When Williams stood at the window, the first thing he observed was that the distance from the window down to where Campbell had been standing was only about fifteen to twenty feet, which explained the horrific wounds caused by the shotgun blast. Continuing his examination of the room, he noticed a pile of cigarette butts just beneath the window and right beside them an empty glass and a whiskey flask, likewise empty. He deduced from this evidence that the shooter had sat at the window for some time, smoking and drinking, while waiting for his victim. He estimated that no more than an hour had elapsed judging by the number of cigarette butts on the floor. The fact that the killer had sat patiently waiting also suggested that he knew the officers' routine. Williams came up with the first theory of the crime: this had been premeditated ambush, not a crime of opportunity.[19]

Detective Williams next lifted the mattress to look underneath where he found a 12-gauge, double-barreled shotgun. It was obviously the murder weapon because it still contained a spent shell casing, and the barrel was still warm. The second barrel held an unfired shell, which would support the theory that Campbell had been the only target. The shells were No. 7 shot, which would match the pellets subsequently dug out of Campbell's body. After going over the room from top to bottom, Williams next checked out the alley behind the saloon, hoping to find fresh footprints in the damp earth, but there were none. Perhaps the killer had walked out the front door of the saloon. Williams' sharp-eyed work would prove to be the best part of the investigation that followed.[20]

Outside, gawkers were gathering at the crime scene like moths drawn to a flame. Word traveled fast in the Acre, and murder on a public street, even in the Acre, was extraordinary enough to attract a crowd. The fact that the victim was a policeman made it that much more exciting. Some in the crowd who had had dealings with Officer Campbell in the past were happy he was dead, but others, including a few well-dressed, sporting types, expressed outrage. There were even a few calls for vigilante justice to save the state the time and expense of a trial. The problem was, nobody knew who the killer was.[21]

Still, if he were not caught, it would not be for lack of effort. For the boys in blue, there would be no rest until they caught the man who had killed one of their own—dead or alive. Even mounted officers, who never worked at night, were called in. Assistant Chief Parsley ordered his men to fan out across the city and bring in all suspicious characters for interrogation. Even the tiny North Fort Worth Police Department was asked to be on the lookout in case he headed across the river. The word even went out by telephone and telegraph. Fort Worth District Judge James W. Swayne heard about it in Mineral Wells and raced back to "take such action as I deemed it my duty to take." Police Commissioner George Mulkey was also out of town, on a fishing trip down on the Rio Concho. The San Angelo marshal had to come out and find him. He traveled all night Sunday to get back to town Monday morning and immediately went into closed-door sessions with officers and officials.[22]

Meanwhile, on the night of the killing, the manhunt for Hammond and Clark came up aces. Forty minutes after the shooting, Hammond strolled into the police station and surrendered. He was unarmed and as calm as a deacon. He explained that he had been down in the Acre in Tom Bradley's saloon when the shooting occurred and knew nothing about it until the bar owner told him Officer Campbell had been killed. "Then," replied Hammond, "I guess they will be looking for me, and I had just as well go to city hall and give myself up." Stokes Clark was not so obliging. Police had to bring him in, but he offered no resistance.[23]

Hammond was correct to assume he would be the No. 1 suspect, and not just because of his history with Campbell. The proprietor of the Jockey Club, Frank Ghouldson, had remembered serving Hammond shortly before the murder. That definitely placed Hammond at the scene of the crime. The police were overjoyed, but their case was far from being made. The investigation continued. Later that night, while Hammond was still in the city jail, Ed Parsley came downstairs to question him. The ex-policeman was too wily to confess but more than willing to defend his innocence even when confronted with damning evidence against him. He had a statement already prepared when Parsley came in:

The only cause of my arrest is prejudice and because Campbell shot me, which fact furnishes a good reason for charging me with this killing, claiming that I killed Campbell for revenge. That's all there is about it and that's all I wish to say.

Ike Knight who happened to be in jail on one of his periodic returns to custody while waiting for his own murder case to wend its way through the criminal justice system (see chapter 10), had been listening. Now he leaned over and told Hammond, "Bob, keep quiet." As the newspaper reported it, Hammond became "as dumb as an oyster" after that. Parsley gave up trying to get anything out of him and ordered him transferred to the county lockup.[24]

Parsley next grilled Stokes Clark, but he initially proved as tightlipped as his pal. Like Hammond, Clark had been to the dance before and was too smart to do the cops' job for them. Parsley ordered Stokes transferred to the county along with Hammond. Besides putting his prisoners in a more secure facility, he could now use the space in the city jail for all the "persons of interest" being processed—eleven more before the night was over. Each and every one of them had to be questioned. Parsley, Captain A. N. Bills, and County Attorney Virgil Parker all participated in the interrogations, and they were none too gentle. The next day a source within the FWPD told a reporter that the suspects had all been "subjected to a taste of the third degree." Not a single voice was raised publicly in protest. Some of these suspects would remain in jail for the next fifteen days with no charges filed against them and with no access to a lawyer.[25]

Chief June Polk did not participate personally in the investigation that first night because he was sick in bed, but he was kept apprised of every development by telephone. His principal contribution was ordering the Department's full-court press that put every available man on the street looking for the murderer(s). By Friday morning the police had squeezed every useful bit of information from those in custody and interviewed all the regulars on Fourteenth Street. Bob Hammond was still their No. 1 suspect but proving it was not going to be easy. If they had possessed modern ballistics and DNA testing, their job would have been easy. They had the shotgun recovered at the crime scene. They also had cigarette butts smoked by

Police Chief June Polk (1909–1911) as he appeared in a 1910 photograph of the "Fort Worth Detective Department." Polk was old school, but he was also MIA in the manhunt for the killer of Officer Campbell. In fact, he stayed home! (Courtesy of Fort Worth Police Historical Association)

the killer and a whiskey flask and glass he had been drinking from. That evidence was lousy with fingerprints and saliva, but the technology did not exist to match them to a suspect.

The urgency of the investigation was almost unprecedented. Not since Lee Waller's murder seventeen years earlier had the FWPD been so determined to catch a felon. In Lee Waller's case, race had been the additional incentive. With Ad Campbell it was something else. Police Commissioner George Mulkey spoke for every man on the force when he said, "While Campbell was the man killed, the shot that killed him was aimed at the entire police department." The authorities were convinced this had not been a lone gunman, but a criminal "conspiracy" that amounted to a war on the forces of law and order. The enemy was the Acre and all of its loathsome denizens. This was why the Police Department would not let up until they got to the bottom of it. Curiously, the Sheriff's Department and County Attorney's Office both stayed in the background during the investigation. The case was built almost entirely by the police.[26]

One of those the police interrogated most intensely was the proprietor of the Jockey Club Saloon. Not only was he one of the last people to see Bob Hammond before the killing, but his answers seemed suspiciously vague. Sure, he knew Hammond. He'd been in the saloon either once or twice that evening, the last time at ten before nine or maybe a little earlier. No, he did not see him come in or go out. No, he did not remember what he had said. However, under hard questioning, Ghouldson began to remember more. Hammond did not buy a drink because he had his own whiskey flask. He had requested "a goblet" of ice water as a chaser for his whiskey and took that with him when he left. Where Hammond went after that, he did not know, but when showed the flask and glass found at the crime scene, he identified them as the ones he had seen Hammond with. This was critical testimony for the state's case, although without matching fingerprints or DNA to support Ghouldson's testimony, it was hardly decisive.[27]

Under further questioning, Stokes Clark provided another crucial link in the chain of evidence: the shotgun recovered at the scene belonged to his brother and prior to the shooting was being held as collateral for his brother's bar tab at Brantley's, a dive in the Acre. Clark had asked Hammond to get it "out of pawn," and Hammond did so, paying $2.50. Clark had not yet gotten the weapon back at the time of the murder and did not know where it was. Questioned on the same subject, Hammond admitted getting the gun out of pawn, but said he did not know where the gun was now and he had no way of knowing if it was the same weapon used to kill Ad Campbell. Absent ballistics testing, not available at that date, there was no way to tie him to the murder weapon. It was simply more circumstantial evidence.[28]

Forty-eight hours into the investigation, police told reporters the case was coming together nicely. The whiskey flask, the water glass, and the shotgun had all been linked (circumstantially) to Bob Hammond. They even found an employee at A. J. Anderson's gun shop who, with only a little encouragement, identified Hammond as the man who had recently bought a box of No. 7 shotgun shells. The salesclerk had paid particular attention at the time of the sale because "he feared that they were intended to be used for murder." And thanks to fine work by the Sheriff's Department, they knew that Hammond had a suspicious bruise on his left shoulder—the kind that might be caused by the powerful kickback of a shotgun discharging. A strip search revealed it, and a doctor had confirmed it.[29]

Hammond started his latest journey through the criminal justice system on August 13. In the next three weeks he would face an "examining trial" and a habeas corpus hearing, but first he would be charged. On that Friday, the day after the shooting, County Attorney Roy announced he would be filing first-degree murder charges. As far as Roy was concerned, the defendant could sit in jail until he rotted or his trail came up, but Hammond had lawyers, too, who were looking out for his interests. Hammond's first appearance in court came six days after he was charged when he went before Justice of the Peace Richard Bratton for his "examining trial" (a.k.a. preliminary examination) That was a formality that would decide whether there was enough evidence to hold him over until the grand jury met. It would also influence whether he was released on bond. News of the examining trial spread through town like wildfire, and an overflow crowd attended the proceedings, which started out in a basement courtroom so stifling that Judge Bratton ordered them moved upstairs to the larger and better-ventilated Seventeenth District courtroom. Even in the larger venue, the crowd still occupied every available seat, jammed the aisle, and spilled out into the hallway. A pair of the County Attorney's best assistants, Virgil Parker and Tom Valentine, represented the state, while Hammond was represented by the Fort Worth firm of William R. Parker and Richard C. Parker.[30]

The hearing quickly turned into a full-blown dress rehearsal for the trial. The state put "a half dozen or more" witnesses on the stand to testify about Hammond's movements that night, showing that he had the opportunity. They also introduced the shotgun as the "murder weapon" and tried, with limited success, to link the defendant to both the beer schooner and the whiskey flask. The proceedings were exceedingly casual. Some of the state's witnesses sat in the courtroom while waiting their turn on the stand; others were held in basement cells until called. A court recorder was present, but he took down only the testimony of selected witnesses.

Nonetheless, the hearing dragged on all day, with only a break for lunch. After lunch, the state picked up where it had left off presenting its case. Finally at 4:00 p.m. Thursday, exhausted prosecutors asked for a continuance until the following day so that all their witnesses could be heard. Justice Bratton agreed to a recess until 9:00 a.m. Friday.

When court reconvened on Friday morning, three more state witnesses remained to be heard before the defense attorneys got their turn. When they did, they presented few witnesses and were careful not to reveal their strategy for the coming trial. They did request bail for Hammond, which Justice Bratton denied, to no one's surprise.

The hearing had reached the foregone conclusion that there was sufficient evidence to bind Bob Hammond over to the grand jury. The question was why such a lengthy and involved preliminary hearing since all the evidence would have to be presented again to the grand jury. The answer was that the prosecution wanted to be sure Hammond did not get out on bail and skip town.

A trial may have been in his future, but in the court of public opinion Bob Hammond had already been found guilty. The fury directed against him smeared everyone and everything associated with him. Even the Retail Liquor Dealers' Association, of which Hammond was a member, was accused of complicity. In response, forty-two of the city's respectable barmen offered a $500 reward for "the apprehension and conviction of the [assassin]." Few citizens doubted that the authorities already had that man in custody, making the reward appear to be a publicity stunt.[31]

County Attorney Roy intended to show not just that Bob Hammond had murdered Ad Campbell in cold blood but that the murder had been a conspiracy involving not just Hammond and Stokes Clark as co-conspirators but every lowlife character in the Acre who had knowledge of it and said nothing or openly assisted the man who pulled the trigger. This was the theory of the FWPD from Commissioner Mulkey down to the greenest beat cop. To support their theory they pointed to May Ferguson. May was a bawd who happened to be the last person Campbell arrested that night, right after nine o'clock. As he was putting her in the patrol wagon, she taunted him, "You'll be a dead man before I get back from city hall [on bond]!" Less than an hour later, he was dead. The only connection among the so-called conspirators, however, was that they were all habitués of the Acre. The conspiracy theory was given credence by Judge Swayne in his charge to the grand jury: "This man lost his life simply and solely because he was trying to enforce the law. . . . If there had been no Hell's Half-acre, Ad Campbell would be alive today." The problem was, Swayne did not provide details or connect the dots to prove a conspiracy, just the "hint of a conspiracy." He could only vaguely suggest that the lords of the Acre, whoever they might be, were the perpetrators.[32]

The case against Stokes Clark began to unravel soon after he was arrested. He could not be placed at the scene of the crime, he had never been heard to utter threats against Ad Campbell, he had no obvious motive for wanting Campbell dead. His only connection to the murder, besides his friendship with Bob Hammond, was the shotgun. The police also mishandled his arrest. The night of the murder he was taken into custody without so much as a warrant or complaint and held without being allowed to see his lawyer, B. D. Shropshire, for the next two days. On Saturday, Shropshire filed a writ of habeas corpus with Judge Swayne for his client's release. County Attorney Roy left Bob Hammond's hearing to come to Swayne's court and plead for more time to gather evidence. The attorneys settled on a compromise that if Roy could not present his evidence by Tuesday, Clark would be freed and, if he could, then Clark would be released on his own recognizance pending an indictment from the grand jury. The conspiracy theory was unraveling.[33]

While the wheels of justice turned, Ad Campbell was laid to rest. His nearest kin wanted him buried in their hometown of Honey Grove, Texas. On Saturday morning his brother came on the train to Fort Worth to collect the body and escort it home. But first the city had to pay its final respects to the golden boy of the FWPD. It could easily have been one of the grandest public funerals in Fort Worth history, but there was no time to plan anything appropriate. Instead, a short service was conducted in the chapel of the Fort Worth Undertaking Company. City offices were not closed, but the entire police force was reported in attendance plus "a number of citizens." An honor guard of officers then escorted the casket to the train station. Officer Jones, Campbell's partner the night he was murdered, was one of the pallbearers. At the station, the brother took over, and he was accompanied back to Honey Grove by Assistant Police Chief Ed Parsley. William Addison Campbell was buried in the family plot in Oakwood Cemetery, Honey Grove, Texas.[34]

The legal proceedings now held the public's undivided attention. On August 23, the grand jury convened but even with Judge Swayne's charge ringing in their ears, they were not about to rush to judgment. Assistant County Attorneys Virgil Parker and Tom Valentine had put together the state's case and took the lead in presenting it while County Attorney Roy left town on an extended fishing trip just a few days before the grand jury convened. It was not that Roy had such unshakeable faith in his two young assistants; it was that he was experienced enough to know that the state's case was in serious trouble. He could not prove conspiracy, he could not tie Stokes Clark to the crime, and all of his evidence against Bob Hammond was circumstantial. At this crucial point in the proceedings. Roy wanted to put as much distance between himself and the case as possible in the event the whole thing fell apart. He was not about to embarrass himself in front of the grand jury trying to sell a half-baked case.[35]

Sure enough, the grand jury took two weeks to consider the state's evidence. Roy returned from his fishing trip while they were deliberating, but he remained strangely silent about the most important case his office was prosecuting. Almost reluctantly, the grand jury returned an indictment against Bob Hammond for first-degree murder. It said nothing about any purported conspiracy, leaving that for the prosecution to demonstrate at trial. Case No. 18891 was set for trial on October 4 in the Forty-eighth District Court, Judge R. H. Buck presiding. In the weeks following, the state's supposedly open-and-shut case began to evaporate like the morning mist over the Trinity River. First, the county attorney was unable to produce enough evidence to hold Stokes Clark, much less indict him. That did not mean he would walk, however. Roy was able to get his bond forfeited in his murder appeal. The Parker County sheriff came and picked him up. Stokes Clark would stay in jail one way or another for the foreseeable future.[36]

Bob Hammond would stand trial alone in the death of Ad Campbell. William Parker was his lead defense attorney, which might easily have been construed as a conflict of interest since his brother Virgil Parker was an assistant county attorney working on the case, but such things were seldom considered important in those days. On September 4 the defense filed a writ of habeas corpus to get their client released on bond. The hearing on that petition took place before Judge Buck in the Forty-eighth District Court on Tuesday, September 7. Both sides gave a good account of themselves, sending a parade of witnesses to the stand and conducting spirited cross-examinations. The defense put Anna Hammond on the stand to testify as to the sterling quality of her husband's character and to swear that he was at home on the night of the murder. She also dropped a bombshell when she claimed that Campbell had "insulted and threatened" her after shooting her husband on July 12. She had not informed Hammond when it happened, however, not until the morning of the day Campbell was killed. That last portion of her testimony nullified any previous statements she had made attesting to her husband's good character and giving him an alibi. Even her credibility as a character witness was destroyed when, on cross-examination, her own character was thoroughly besmirched. Bob Hammond, it turned out, was her third husband following two divorces, and she could not remember the given name of one of those husbands though she did remember his last name was Williams. In the end, Judge Buck denied the request for bail and remanded Hammond to jail to await trial. The final nail in the defense motion was that defendant was already under indictment for "assault to murder" three persons the previous year.[37]

Will Campbell's family had been watching all these developments with growing concern. Two days after the habeas corpus hearing, they brought in an outside prosecutor to assist the state. Perhaps they were concerned with County Attorney Roy's fishing trip right on the eve of his office making its pitch to the grand jury for a murder indictment. The family never said, but it spoke volumes that they brought in a legal "hired gun" in the person of former Red River County District Attorney Dave Watson. Absent an explanation, his hiring did not reflect well at all on the County Attorney and his team.[38]

When October 4 arrived, it quickly became apparent just how much trouble the state's case was in. Prosecutors could not locate all of their witnesses and some of those who were on their list did not want to testify. Nine reluctant witnesses were being held in custody until the trial, what court papers called "witness attachment." Roy got the court to grant a continuance on October 4 while the Sheriff tried to round up the rest of his witnesses, and then had to ask for a second continuance a week later. With all the continuances threatening to drag out the proceedings indefinitely, the witnesses in custody had to be released, whereupon they promptly disappeared. In the middle of October, Hammond's lawyers petitioned for the case to be transferred to Judge W. T. Simmons' Sixty-seventh District Court, ostensibly so that their client, who had already been sitting in jail two months, might receive "a speedy trial." The prosecution opposed the petition because they wanted to keep it in Judge Buck's court where it would not come up for trial until at least December. Simmons heard the two sides' arguments, but in the end denied the motion because his docket was already "badly crowded" and he anticipated the trial would take "at least a week." Hammond's case would stay in Judge Buck's Forty-eighth District Court, where he was already facing charges for the brouhaha with Will Chadwick in July 1908.[39]

On December 9 the case came up on the docket again. A venire of a hundred men was present for jury selection, and a "big crowd" filled every remaining seat in the courtroom and spilled out into the hallway anticipating an exciting trial. They were disappointed. Missing five of his "material witnesses," Robert Roy was forced to ask for yet another continuance; this made three. Judge Buck dismissed the venire and ordered the defendant released on $7,500 bond, "which he readily made." At four o'clock that afternoon, Bob Hammond was a free man for the first time since August 13. His father met him and escorted him home.[40]

So far, the defense team had benefited from the state misplaying its hand. It remained to be seen how they would do when they had to make their case in court. William R. Parker was a veteran criminal defense lawyer who had made a reputation defending unpopular, high-profile defendants. Another one of his clients at this same time was Ike Knight, now facing a third trial for murdering Ed Lamont (see chapter 11).[41]

Bob Hammond's case would wind up spending years in the system. Three times the state tried to bring him to trial, and three times they shot blanks. The first two times its principal witnesses could not be located, leaving County Attorney Roy with no other recourse than to delay while he put out an "all-points bulletin" for them. Ironically, the authorities were victims of their own zeal because in the aftermath of Campbell's murder, they had launched an offensive to clean up the Acre, and the state's witnesses were among those who packed up and left town. Saloonkeepers, bawds, and gamblers were not eager to see the inside of a courtroom and even less eager to have their lives placed under a microscope on the witness stand, so they skipped out leaving no forwarding addresses. Without witnesses, with no confession and dubious circumstantial evidence, the state's case began to look more and more like a lost cause. On March 1, 1910, the original indictment was "quashed" by Judge Buck on a defense motion that went unchallenged by the County Attorney. Justice N. M. Maben promptly ordered Hammond released on bond pending a new examining trial. Since the grand jury of the Forty-eighth District Court was already in session, Roy's office hoped for a quick re-indictment. He tried to put the best face on things by saying that the interval between the indictment and the new trial would allow the state to build a stronger case. The fact was, Bob Hammond had won his first round with the judicial system.[42]

Hammond's second round had already started. He was re-indicted for murder on March 1, 1910 (Case No. 19019). A trial date was set in Judge Buck's court again, but legal maneuvering kept pushing it back. In the meantime, Hammond was sprung on another writ of habeas corpus. He wasted no time getting into trouble again, this time for fishing in the Trinity River with dynamite instead of a fishing pole. During the trial in county court things just got worse. The chief witness against him was a twelve-year-old boy, Barnum Thompson. After testifying, he was waylaid in the basement of the courthouse by Hammond and his fourteen-year-old brother-in-law. Hammond himself did not throw any punches, but he egged on his brother-in-law, saying, "Don't hit him in the back; hit him in the face!" To the dynamiting charge was now added an aggravated assault charge. It took two trials on the dynamiting charge—the first trial ended in a hung jury—to get a conviction. Hammond's defense was that it was a lit stogie he threw into the river, and his fishing companion had then fired at it with a pistol. He was fined $100. Tried the same day on the aggravated assault charge, he was found guilty and ordered to pay a fine of $25. Speaking in his own defense, he complained that the police were "jobbing" him again. The jury was unmoved—and Bob Hammond was unrepentant. After the trial he confronted S. M. Gross, the state's witness to the attack on the boy, and "pulled his nose." That brought another assault charge. For those keeping score, Bob Hammond was now charged with murder (Ad Campbell), assault to murder (William O. Chadwick and Sophia Wolfe), simple assault (S. M. Gross), and selling liquor on Sunday and without a license.[43]

The murder trial, of course, was the biggest charge hanging over his head. Both sides finally assured Judge Buck they would be ready to start the trial on December 8, 1910. When December 8 arrived, the defense was present and ready to proceed as was a venire of 100 men for jury selection. But it was another false start. The state was represented by a new county attorney, John W. Baskin, who had been elected in the November elections. The first words out of his mouth to Judge Buck were a request for another continuance. An exasperated Judge granted the motion, pushing the case into the next year. Case No. 19019 ultimately fell apart just like the first case had. The cause was the same old problem: the state could not produce its witnesses. For the next four years John Baskin tried to hold the case together but with no more success than his predecessor. The County Attorney finally ran out of time and legal arguments to keep postponing the trial, and Judge Buck ran out of patience. Baskin was forced to concede defeat in 1914 because "the witnesses have moved beyond the jurisdiction of the State." On October 29, the murder charge against Bob Hammond was dismissed, and a little more than a week later, John Baskin turned over his office to the new County Attorney, Marshall Spoonts.[44]

Bob Hammond's guilt or innocence would never be determined in a court of law. He had beaten the system for five years, during which time he spent a grand total of eight months behind bars. He had beaten two county attorneys who had all the resources of the state behind them. Neither R. E. L. Roy nor John W. Baskin was ever able to bring him to trial. To all appearances, it was a classic miscarriage of justice. The fact that the accused was such a despicable character made the failure all the worse. While awaiting trial, Hammond seemed to be deliberately baiting the authorities and doing everything he could to help the state. In the summer of 1912 he jumped bail, and before he could be re-arrested he was indicted for "burglary and theft" on December 20. Still, he seemed to live a charmed life. The latest charges hung over him with all the rest until August 31, 1914, when all but the murder charge were dismissed. Two months later the murder charge, too, was dismissed. Bob Hammond celebrated the end of his ordeal. He was a completely free man for the first time in five years. Unable to bring him to justice, the authorities did the next best thing: they threatened to make his life a living hell if he stayed in Fort Worth. County Attorney Baskin persuaded him to "leave the county and not return any more." In old English law this was known as "outlawry," and has always been unconstitutional in the United States, but in 1914, Fort Worth authorities did it anyway as the only practical solution for the Man They Couldn't Bring to Trial.[45]

The cold-blooded murder of Policeman William A. Campbell and the failure of the authorities to bring his murderer to justice aroused a sense of outrage among law-abiding citizens directed as much at Hell's Half-acre as at Bob Hammond. The fires of reform that had been stoked by the murders of Jefferson McLean and Hamil Scott grew white-hot. Three days before Campbell was gunned down, one of the city's leading newspapers had carried a half-page editorial denouncing the Acre as "the lowest, basest, rottenest plague spot of the municipal life of the United States . . . [one] that shames the name and endangers the peace of the whole city." This bit of journalistic hyperbole might have been quickly forgotten had it not been followed by the death of Ad Campbell in the district. After the Acre claimed its latest victim, citizens recalled the editorial and vowed to take action. At a mass meeting on September 3, one speaker after another got up to decry the Police Department's feeble response to lawlessness on the streets of Fort Worth. One of those speakers, Jordan Cummings, predicted correctly that Campbell's killer would "never be hung."[46] The question naturally followed, "What then is to be done?"

Ad Campbell's grave in Oakwood Cemetery, Honey Grove, Texas. Campbell may have lived in Fort Worth and worked as a Fort Worth policeman, but Fort Worth was not "home." His family claimed the body and took it home to Honey Grove. (From collections of Kevin Foster)

CONCLUSION:
THE END OF THE TRAIL

By 1909 the Progressive era was running at full tide. Reformers angling for a thorough house-cleaning of American society did not overlook law enforcement. There was a new emphasis on professional standards, on modernizing the Fort Worth Police Department's (FWPD's) organization, and on using the new forensic science to help catch criminals. The old cowboy ways were now frowned upon, although they were not so easy to eliminate. The Police Department might have its eye on the future, but the sheriffs and their men in particular clung to the old ways longer, although even they were being forced to change with the times.

In the new order, public image was very important. Buffaloing and bracing citizens on public streets was out. The third degree was no longer something that police officials bragged about using when they needed to squeeze a confession out of a prisoner. The embarrassing fee system of old, which put law enforcement on a piece-work basis, had been replaced by a decent living wage. Both the police force and sheriff's men were still all white, but at least it was acknowledged that black citizens had rights, too. And in the next few years, Hispanics would become an increasingly significant segment of the population necessitating some changes in attitude and procedure (such as hiring Spanish-speaking cops). People were still treated according to their reputations by the men with the badge. This meant "known" prostitutes and vagrants could still be harassed and even ordered out of town without due process being invoked.

While women were still divided into two categories—ladies and all others—the modest progress achieved by women in this era was reflected in law enforcement. In 1907 the FWPD hired its first jail matron to supervise female prisoners. But there were still no female officers on the street, just like there were no black officers. "Longhair Jim" Courtright or Sam Farmer would not have felt that out of place in the Fort Worth of 1910 even though the old title "city marshal" was now reduced to being only the chief of police, reporting to a police commissioner.

The basic structure of local law enforcement was in transition. As the city expanded, new ways had to be found to cover the growing area. This is what drove the city to begin replacing its horses with motorcycles and, soon, bicycles and automobiles. The special officer still had an important role to fill because demands on law enforcement were growing faster than budgets. The special officer, paid for by a private employer, helped stretch limited forces. In the new era, however, special officers were held to higher standards, which included more oversight from the entities that granted their commissions. As crime became more sophisticated, more organized, and more random, both the city and county added detectives to the force. In the years to come, the detective force became the fastest-growing element of law enforcement. That was a long way from 1884 when Marshal William Rea appointed the city's first detective, his nephew-in-law, and there was not enough to keep the young man busy. Aside from detectives, officers in the new force were outfitted with billy clubs, helmets, and automatic weapons. The helmets were an English affectation that soon became passé, but the nightsticks and automatic weapons were here to stay in the policeman's arsenal. The sheriff's boys hung onto their horses, their Winchesters, and six-shooters longer.

By 1909, the Acre was on its way to becoming a historic footnote. It still existed on the south end of town, but it was more of a slum neighborhood than a wide-open vice district as it had been in its heyday thirty years earlier. Prostitution and gambling had not been wiped out; they had just gone behind closed doors. In another year the former main axis of the Acre, Rusk Street, would undergo a name change (to Commerce Street) in an official effort to change its image. The days when the cowboy reigned supreme in the Acre were over. Derelicts and social outcasts now populated the district.

The FWPD still had its share of problem officers and no procedure for getting rid of them. Any officer dismissed by the chief could still appeal to the police commissioner or even the full city commission with a good chance of getting reinstated. The police force still operated on the patronage principle. Officers were reappointed after municipal elections every year and their politics was the most important qualification, trumping factors like on-the-job experience or schooling. Bad apples like James Kidwell Yates and Sid Waller would cause the Department much embarrassment in the next few years.

Officers still worked twelve-hour days six days a week, and it did not appear that was likely to change any time soon. They had no vacation time, no health benefits, no retirement or disability pension. If they did not work, they did not get paid. The Police Benevolent Association provided some help to officers who were injured in the line of duty or to their families if they were killed. But the PBA was a far cry from being a labor union. The sheriff's men did not even have the equivalent of the PBA.

Until 1909, local law enforcement jurisdiction had stopped at the Trinity. North of the river, the North Fort Worth Police Department took responsibility; south of the river, the Fort Worth Police Department had responsibility. In 1909 that distinction disappeared as North Fort Worth was annexed by Fort Worth and the NFWPD was absorbed by the FWPD. In another year, Nile City, on the north side of the river, would be chartered and have its own tiny police department. Of course, the sheriff was still responsible for the county as a whole. Constables, one per precinct, had less and less law enforcement responsibility. They were little more than process servers.

One sign that modern times had arrived was the "drug problem." Ever since selling or distributing dangerous drugs had been made a federal crime in 1906, law officers were spending more and more time dealing with "cocaine fiends" and "opium-eaters." By contrast, cattle rustling and horse stealing were no longer major problems for the sheriff and his men. Crime, like the nation in general, was becoming urbanized.

Another sign of the new order was that law enforcement was increasingly motorized. In 1909, the Department purchased a pair of Indian motorcycles, little five-horsepower machines to be used in chasing down speeding automobiles. The first motorcycle cop was nineteen-year-old Henry Lewis who issued the first speeding ticket that same year. The new squad was so successful, the following year the Department added two more motorcycle cops. The motorcycle squad quickly became the last refuge of the "cowboy cop"—daring young men on their two-wheeled machines. Showing that the new order was not that far removed from the old days, when Officer Ad Campbell was killed in 1909, the first officer on the scene arrived on horseback. Underscoring how slowly fundamental change comes, Officer Lewis in 1910 pursued a car full of joy riders, and when they wouldn't pull over, he shot out their tires. The cowboy culture was not completely dead!

In the next three years, the FWPD would add an automobile to its transportation stable, but horses and officers walking beats were still the norm. In the meantime, the chief concession to a growing city was establishing substations in the Polytechnic and the Southside neighborhoods. Telephones tied the substations to headquarters. Sheriff's deputies still rode the county's back roads and made regular visits to small communities such as Mansfield and Euless.

The problems associated with race, drugs, and criminals-on-wheels that law enforcement had to deal with in 1909 were too big for the cowboy-booted cops of old. These were problems that could not be solved by cracking a troublemaker over the head and locking him up for the night or ordering him out of town. In a city of more than 73,000 people, the lawman no longer knew every citizen by name and reputation. He needed new, less personal methods for dealing with lawbreakers. Fingerprinting, photo files, and networking with other agencies were the future of law enforcement. Uniformity in dress and procedure, rules and regs governing behavior, these were the order of the day. The "cowboy cop" would have to change or be put out to pasture with his horse. Still, the years after 1909 would not live up to the Progressive dream of thoroughly modern, efficient police and sheriff's departments. Just the opposite in fact. The next decade would prove to be the deadliest in the history of the Fort Worth Police Department. And its sister agency, the Tarrant County Sheriff's Department, would have its share of troubles, too, as it struggled to enter the twentieth century.

The Fort Worth Police and Firefighters Memorial, dedicated on June 5, 2009, after nine years of laboring to transform the dream into reality. Located in the beautiful arboreal setting of Trinity Park just off West 7th Street. (Photograph by Kevin Foster)

ENDNOTES

Notes to Introduction

1. As Officer Joe Witcher did. Witcher, "1879 Policeman Tells How It Was," in Mack Williams, ed. *The* News-Tribune *in Old Fort Worth,* A Bicentennial Memory Book (Fort Worth: privately printed by Mack Williams and Madeline Williams, 1975).

2. Quoting President Craig Floyd in Siobhan Morrissey, "A Surge in Cop Killings," *Time Magazine* online, September 28, 2007, www.time.com/time/printout/0,8816,1666750,00.html, accessed October 16, 2007.

3. John Moritz, "Data Sought on Officer Deaths," *Fort Worth Star-Telegram*, July 10, 2008, p. 2B.

4. That total includes sixty-four police officers, six Tarrant County constables, eight Tarrant County sheriff's deputies, two Tarrant County special deputies, and four Fort Worth special officers. Figures compiled by Sgt. Kevin Foster.

5. The special issue comes out every October, naming the officers by name and describing the exploits that led to their recognition; e.g., Larry Smith, To Protect and to Serve," *Parade*, October 21, 2007.

6. Moritz, "Data Sought."

7. Terry Baker, "Texas Finding the Forgotten: Police Officers Killed in the Line of Duty," *National Academy Associate: The Magazine of the FBI National Academy Associates* 4, no. 4 (July/August 2002): 21–23.

8. For *San Francisco Chronicle* quotation, see Kevin J. Mullen, *The Toughest Gang in Town: Police Stories from Old San Francisco* (Novato, CA: Noir Publications, 2005), p. 167. The death of Officer Wood was the subject of filmmaker Errol Morris' scathing docudrama *The Thin Blue Line* (1988). See Richard K. Sherwin, "Framed," in John Denver, ed., *Legal Reelism: Movies as Legal Texts* (Urbana: University of Illinois Press, 1996), p. 74.

9. *Fort Worth Record*, August 13, 1909.

10. Interview with Mr. and Mrs. Steve Elwonger, authors and veteran Dallas Police Officers. *Dallas Morning News*, December 23, 2002.

Notes to Part I Introduction

1. Meeting of October 4, 1887, in Fort Worth City Council Minutes, vol. F (October 4, 1887-November 1, 1887), deposited in Genealogy, History and Archives Unit, Central Library, Fort Worth Public Library.

Notes to Chapter 1

1. Mack Williams, ed., *The* News-Tribune *in Old Fort Worth,* p. 35.

2. See John B. York in the TXGenWeb Project, http://www. tarrantcounty.com/esheriff/view.asp, modified February 5, 2004, accessed July 22, 2006.

3. For background on John York and the small community on the prairie north of the river, see Julia Kathryn Garrett, *Fort Worth: A Frontier Triumph* (Fort Worth: Texas Christian University Press, 1996 reprint of 1972 ed.), pp. 88–89. Note: John York was Seaborne Gilmore's son-in-law, not vice versa as Garrett says. See also "John B. York," in Seventh United States Federal Census (1850), Navarro/Tarrant counties, TX, Microfilm Roll No. M432_910, p. 140; "Julia A. York," in Tenth United States Federal Census (1880), Precinct 1, Tarrant County, TX, Microfilm Roll No. T9_1328; and "John B. York" on Family Genealogy website, http://freepages.genealogy.rootsweb.com/~allyorks/ badguy.htm.

4. There is some confusion about the children because census records show the first William was ten months old in October 1850 while the second William was reportedly born in July 1849. All that can be stated for certain is that a child, William J. York, grew to manhood celebrated as the first white male child born at Fort Worth. His cousin, Martha Ellen Gilmore, was the first white girl born at Fort Worth. William was still alive and living with his mother and siblings in Tarrant County in 1880.

For first boy and girl, see Garrett, *Frontier Triumph,* pp. 88–89. For York children see "John B. York" in 1850 Census; "Julia A. York" in 1880 Census; and "John B. York" on Family Genealogy website. What began as the York-Gilmore family plot acquired the first part of its current name from Eli Mitchell, a later owner of the property. John York and Seaborne Gilmore are both buried there. The site got a Texas historical marker in 1984. It is located behind the Fort Worth Grain Exchange at 2707 Decatur Ave. near the intersection with Northeast 28th. Mary Daggett Lake, "Rugged Frontiersmen Buried in Tarrant County Graves," undated newspaper clipping in "Ripley Arnold" file of Mary Daggett Lake Papers, Series II, Box 4, Genealogy, History and Archives Unit, Central Library, Fort Worth Public Library hereafter cited as MDL Papers. See also Bill Fairley, "A Historic North Side Cemetery is Getting a Cleanup," *Fort Worth Star-Telegram*, March 24, 2004, p. 6B.

5. "Comptroller's Plat Book and Plat Map of Birdville—1851," in *Footprints: The Magazine of the Fort Worth Genealogical Society* 18, no. 4 (November 1975): 155–159.

6. Tucker Hill, for instance, was a residential district on the south side of town. B. B. Paddock, ed., *A Twentieth Century History and Biographical Record of North and West Texas* (Chicago: Lewis Pub. Co., 1906), vol. 2, pp. 102–03.

7. Paddock, *Twentieth Century History*. Paddock says, erroneously, that William Tucker was Tarrant County's second sheriff. He was the third; John B. York was the second. See also Mack Williams, ed., *The* News-Tribune *in Old Fort Worth*, p. 39.

8. Garrett, *Frontier Triumph*, p. 134.

9. Other signatories to the bond were William B. Tucker, M. T. Johnson, Carroll M. Peak, and E. M. Daggett. Bill Fairley, "South Side Founder Made Mark," *Fort Worth Star-Telegram*, December 15, 2004.

10. The modern historical accounts are Julia Kathryn Garrett's, Oliver Knight's, J'Nell Pate's, Ty Cashion's, and Vivian A. Castleberry's. The first four show a preconceived Fort Worth bias; the fifth represents the Dallas or Peak-Fowler version of events. Garrett's book is considered the bible of early Fort Worth history; Knight's version is derived entirely from an old newspaper account; Pate's retells the familiar story; Cashion's is a mis-telling of the Oliver Knight account; and Castleberry offers the most detailed account but her knowledge of the people and events stops at the eastern edge of the Trinity River. Garrett, *Frontier Triumph*, p. 144; Knight, *Fort Worth: Outpost on the Trinity* (Norman: University of Oklahoma Press, 1953), pp. 42-43; Pate, *North*

of the River: A Brief History of North Fort Worth (Fort Worth: Texas Christian University Press, 1994), pp. 2-3; Cashion, *The New Frontier: A Contemporary History of Fort Worth and Tarrant County* (San Antonio: Historical Publishing Network, 2006), p. 16; Castleberry, *Daughters of Dallas: A History of Greater Dallas Through the Voices and Deeds of Its Women* (Dallas: Odenwald Press, 1994), pp. 63-65.

11. For Fowler family background, see "Archibald Fowler, Sr.," in Fifth United States Federal Census (1830), Greenville, SC, Microfilm Roll No. 172 (available online at AncestryLibrary.com); and "Archibald Fowler, Jr.," in Seventh United States Federal Census (1850), Northern Division, Marshall, MS, Microfilm Roll No. M432_377 (online). See also Willie Flowers Carlisle, *History of the Old Cemetery, Dallas* (Dallas: privately printed, 1948), p. 10; and the will of Archibald Fowler, Sr., 1840, *Upper South Carolina Genealogy and History* 14, no. 4 (November 2000) (available online at HeritageQuest Online); *(Austin) Texas State Gazette* 12, no. 2, August 18, 1860.

12. Like so much else in this story, there are two versions of Juliette Fowler's name. She was christened Juliet Abbey Peak but as a teenager adopted the French spelling, "Juliette," and thus she was known the rest of her life even in her will. Castleberry, *Daughters of Dallas*, p. 63. For "May Queen," see her obituary in *Dallas Herald*, June 17, 1889; and Castleberry, *Daughters of Dallas*, p. 63. For additional background on Juliette Fowler, see "Application for Official Texas Historical Marker" for Juliette Abbey Peak Fowler's grave, Pioneer Cemetery, Dallas, TX, prepared by Bill Southwell, 1987, Texas Historical Commission, Austin (hereafter cited as Historical Marker Application; Willie Carlisle, *History of the Old Cemetery, Dallas*, p. 10; obituary in *Dallas Morning News*, June 27, 1889; and Sam Acheson, "Juliette Fowler, Philanthropist," *Dallas Morning News*, November 21, 1966. For their marriage, see Historical Marker Application.

13. A copy of Fowler's business card has been handed down in the family. It and additional details of Fowler family history come from George Parrish, Rohmer Park, CA, in correspondence with Kevin Foster, various dates, 2002 (hereafter cited as Parrish-Foster correspondence). Mr. Parrish kindly passed along copies of several

helpful documents as well as family lore. Reference to the Fowlers' Fort Worth residence comes from Khleber M. Van Zandt, *Force without Fanfare: The Autobiography of K. M. Van Zandt*, Sandra L. Myres, ed. (Fort Worth: Texas Christian University Press, 1968), p. 115, and from the *Fort Worth Star-Telegram*, July 18, 1915. For information on Carroll Peak, see biographical essays prepared by Olive Peak, June 20, 1924, and April 14, 1942, in "Carroll Peak and Family" vertical file, Genealogy, History and Archives Unit, Central Library, Fort Worth Public Library. For Fowler as newspaper agent, see *Dallas (Weekly) Herald*, July 13, 1859. For advertising, see *Dallas (Weekly) Herald*, various dates, 1859–1860.

14. For Fort Worth quote, see letter of Mrs. William H. Crawford in open letter to the *Waseca (MN) Citizen*, n.d., reprinted in the *(Boston) Liberator*, April 5, 1861.

15. Would-be lawyers in Texas before 1939 did not have to pass a bar exam to practice law. They could either go to law school or "read law" under an established lawyer, but they could hang out their shingle whenever they decided they were ready. Neither law nor medicine were the highly regulated professions they are today.

16. Both Willie Carlisle (*History of the Old Cemetery, Dallas*, pp. 7 and 10) and the *Dallas Weekly Herald* of September 11, 1861, confirm that Fowler was a Mason. In September, the members of Fort Worth Lodge no. 148 passed a resolution mourning the death of "our brother, A. Y. Fowler." For Smith-Fowler relationship, see Kristi Strickland, "Smith, John Peter" entry in Ron Tyler *et al.*, eds., *The New Handbook of Texas* (Austin: Texas State Historical Association, 1996), vol.5, p. 1104. For Fort Worth's population and number of lawyers, see *Dallas Morning News*, July 22, 1893 (quoting Dr. Carroll Peak's "History of the City" written in 1860 [*sic*]). For Smith, see Mack Williams, "The Frontier Lawyer [John Peter Smith] Who Built Fort Worth"; and Mack Williams, ed., "John Peter Smith's Own Story," in *The News-Tribune in Old Fort Worth*, A Bicentennial Memory Book, p.5. (Smith's memoir hereafter cited as "Smith's Own Story")

17. *Dallas Herald*, May 1, 1861; *(Boston) Liberator*, April 5, 1861.

18. *Dallas Herald*, December 5, 1865; Garrett, *Frontier Triumph*, p. 186; Knight, *Outpost on the Trinity*, p. 50.

19. Charles Ellis Mitchell, "Biography," "Federal Writers'
Project, Research Date: Fort Worth and Tarrant County, Texas"
(Fort Worth: Fort Worth Public Library Unit, 1941), vol. 6, pp.
2011–2012 (hereafter cited as Mitchell Reminiscences. Mitchell's
reminiscences are also reprinted in "When Every Man Carried
a Six-shooter," in Mack Williams and Madeline Williams, eds.,
In Old Fort Worth, Texas Centennial ed. (Fort Worth: Mack H.
Williams and Madeline C. Williams, 1986), p. 46. Fowler family
history comes from Parrish-Foster correspondence; Julia Kathryn
Garrett, *Frontier Triumph*, p. 144. Supporting the 1856 date
are *Fort Worth Star-Telegram*, December 15, 1912, and Leonard
Sanders, *How Fort Worth Became the Texasmost City* (Fort Worth:
Amon Carter Museum of Western Art, 1973), p. 12. Cf. long-time
resident and local historian Mary Daggett Lake gives August 21 as
the date ("Rugged Frontiersmen Buried in Tarrant County Graves
without Identifying Marks," an undated newspaper clipping in
MDL Papers). Cf. July 1861, Pinkney Holt, "Early Recollections
of Fort Worth and Tarrant County," *Footprints: The Magazine
of the Fort Worth Genealogical Society* 36, no.1 (February 1993):
p. 2. (hereafter cited as Holt Recollections). Cf. Willie Carlisle,
History of the Old Cemetery, Dallas, p. 10, gives August 26, 1861
as Fowler's death date. The August 24, 1861, date comes from
the *Dallas Weekly Herald* of September 11, 1861, which carried a
resolution by Fort Worth Masonic Lodge no. 148 mourning the
death of their brother A. Y. Fowler. Cf. the usually reliable Sammy
Tise, *Texas County Sheriffs* (Albuquerque, NM: privately printed,
1989), p. 43, says York left office August 6, 1860.
20. Eddins, Andrew Evyonne, Betty Porter, and David
Voorhees, *Birdville, Texas: Frontier Wilderness, County Seat and
Beyond* (privately printed, 2005), p. 15; Capt. J. C. Terrell,
Reminiscences of the Early Days of Fort Worth (Fort Worth: Texas
Printing Company, 1906), p. 14.
21. Various Fort Worth accounts over the years have
incorrectly attributed the "tragedy" of John York's killing to the
county-seat fight. See Mary Daggett Lake, MDL Papers; *Fort
Worth Star-Telegram*, December 15, 1912; Garrett, *Frontier
Triumph*, p.145; Knight, *Outpost on the Trinity*, p. 43; and Bill
Fairley, "South Side Founder Made His Mark, *Fort Worth Star-*

Telegram, December 15, 2004.

22. Howard W. Peak was the son of Dr. Carroll Peak and the nephew of Juliette Peak Fowler. His recollections from 1934 are cited in Federal Writers' Project, "Research Data: Fort Worth and Tarrant County, Texas," series I, vol. 3, pp. 888-89.

23. The barbecue and military "drill" are described in the *Dallas Herald,* July 24, 1861. And every detailed version of the affair says it began at the Cold Spring on the day of the big barbecue.

24. The story is pieced together by comparing and combining various Fort Worth and Dallas sources, trying to filter out obvious family biases, fanciful details, and dime-novel elements. Peak-Fowler family tradition concerning Willie comes from the account of Olive Peak in Castleberry, *Daughters of Dallas,* and from Parrish-Foster correspondence. It has the stamp of authenticity because it is supported by a contemporary, Susan Anna Good, in a letter to her husband, Captain John Jay Good. See Good to "My Dear Husband," September 1, 1861 (Letter No. 39), and September 23, 1861 (Letter No. 49), in *Cannon Smoke: The Letters of Captain John J. Good, Good-Douglas Texas Battery, CSA,* compiled and edited by Lester Newton Fitzhugh (Hillsboro, TX: Hill Junior College Press, 1971), pp. 60–61, 78.

25. Fitzhugh, *Cannon Smoke,* August 28, 1861 (Letter No. 38); September 1, 1861 (Letter No. 39); and September 23, 1861 (Letter No. 49), pp. 59–61, 78.

26. James Marten, *Texas Divided* (Lexington: University Press of Kentucky, 1990), pp. 103–04, 203 n. 42).

27. The little family plot eventually became the Mitchell Cemetery, Tarrant County's oldest white (cf. Indian) burial ground, and it is still there today beside the old Fort Worth and Denver City railroad tracks, just west of Decatur Avenue and south of Northeast 28th. In 1890 the railroad tried to get the Gilmore and York families to remove the remains of their ancestors so that the railroad could use the property, but the families adamantly refused. Today, John York's gravesite can no longer be identified because the cemetery has been vandalized so many times over the years. For dispute between the railroad and Gilmore-York families, see *Dallas Morning News,* March 5, 1890. For probate,

see *Dallas Weekly Herald*, May 16, 1868. The Fowlers' final resting place, Pioneer Memorial Cemetery, is located on South Akard in Dallas. For a listing of all occupants of the "Fowler Lot," see Willie Carlisle, *History of the Old Cemetery, Dallas*, p. 10.

28. Information on Juliette Fowler comes from Castleberry, *Daughters of Dallas*, and Fitzhugh, *Cannon Smoke*, Letter No. 49, p. 78. Information on Julia York derived from 1870 and 1880 U.S. Census reports, which show Mary A. York as eight years old on September 1, 1870, and eighteen years old on October 4, 1880, living in the household of Julia A. York.

29. Her bequest eventually became the Fowler Homes for Children and the Aged. Today, Juliette Peak Fowler is regarded as Dallas' first philanthropist of note. *Dallas Morning News*, June 12 and 27, 1889; and November 21, 1966. "The Founder of Fowler Homes," *The Christian Courier* (a publication of the Disciples of Christ), March 8, 1923. For additional information on Juliette Fowler, see Historical Marker Application.

30. Mitchell Reminiscences; Holt Recollections; "Smith's Own Story"; Van Zandt, *Force without Fanfare*.

31. Holt Recollections.

32. For Susan Good, see Fitzhugh, *Cannon Smoke*, pp. 59 and 78. Cf. modern accounts that have Fowler dying either July 4 or August 26, referenced in Castleberry, *Daughters of Dallas*, p. 65. For Olive Peak, see Peak to "Dear Florence," January 24, 1941, in possession of Brian Fowler, LaGrange, TX, which the owner has generously shared with the authors of this book. Portions of Olive Peak's letter reprinted in Castleberry, *Daughters of Dallas*, p. 65.

33. Garrett, *Frontier Triumph*, p. 144; and "Smith's Own Story." This is also the version supported by the unofficial historian of the Tarrant County Sheriff's Department, Chief Deputy Hank Pope. It is part of Department lore.

34. For Peak-Fowler family history, see Castleberry, *Daughters of Dallas*; Parrish-Foster correspondence; and Thomas W. Spalding, ed., *Descendants of Jane Owsley Gregg, Daughter of Major Thomas Owsley (1658–1700): The Gregg, Peak (e), Jacobs, Moseley and Related Families* (Springfield, VA: Owsley Family Historical Society, 2002), p. 69 (also available on the website www.owsleyfamily.com). The document that forms the basis

of family traditions was Olive Peak's 1941 letter to her cousin Florence. Until descendants of the York-Gilmore families get busy and publish an official family history, all the advantage goes to the Peak-Fowler version on this one. For Fowler obituary, see *Dallas Morning News*, June 27, 1889. For "Dallas Masonic records," see Willie Flowers Carlisle, *History of the Old Cemetery: City—Masonic—Odd Fellow* (Dallas: privately printed, 1948).

Notes to Chapter 2

1. *(Austin) Daily State Journal*, August 16, 1870.

2. Mack Williams, ed., *The* News-Tribune i*n Old Fort Worth*, p. 39.

3. There is some question about exactly when Fitzgerald arrived in Fort Worth. The *Fort Worth Democrat* of August 28, 1877, says that as of that date, he had been living in the city for two years, which would place his arrival in 1875 not 1874. Yet the record is clear that he becomes town marshal in December 1874. Fitzgerald's sudden elevation to the marshal's office is recorded in Record of Bonds, Book A (1873–1888), City Secretary's Office, Records of the City of Fort Worth, Series 1, Mayor and Council Proceedings, Genealogy, History and Archives Unit, Central Library, Fort Worth Public Library (hereafter referred to as Bond Records).

4. Julia Kathryn Garrett, "Fort Worth: A Frontier Triumph," unpublished MS, Box 142, p. 428, Special Collections, University of Texas at Arlington Library.

5. *Dallas Daily Herald*, February 2, 1875, p. 7.

6. "Federal Writers' Project," vol. 1, p. 218; vol. 3, p. 1091; vol. 16, p. 6083; and Bud Kennedy, "Pawing around for the True Panther," *Fort Worth Star-Telegram*, February 19, 2005.

7. The TXGenWeb Project, Tarrant County, List of Registered Voters for 1867, p. 2, http://www.rootsweb.com/~txtarran/tax/1867vote2.htm; and Fort Worth City Directory for 1877 ("Rev. A. Fitsgerald [*sic*]").

8. Cemetery records at Pioneers Rest Cemetery incorrectly list his birthdate as 1859, cutting a decade off his life, which, if correct, would have made him interim town marshal at the tender age of fifteen! For his correct age and other family information, see

Seventh United States Federal Census (1850), Floyd County, GA, Microfilm Roll No. M432_69; and Eighth United States Federal Census (1860), Whitefield County, Dalton, GA, Microfilm Roll M653_141. Cf. Weldon Hudson and Barbara Knox, compilers, *Pioneers Rest Cemetery, Fort Worth, Tarrant County, Texas* (Fort Worth: Genealogical Society, 2001), p. 32.

9. The newspaper reported that Fitzgerald, along with Captain Sam Evans and "Tuck" Boaz, were called to Tyler to answer the charges. There were no subsequent reports of how it was resolved. *Fort Worth Democrat*, May 3, 1873.

10. Fort Worth newspapers of the day often used the despicable term in their pages as shorthand to distinguish between blacks who were welcome in the community and those who were not. See, for example, the *Fort Worth Daily Democrat* on the day after Fitzgerald was shot, August 26, 1877.

11. Hagar Tucker's appointment can be found in Mayor and Council Proceedings, Minutes of the City Council, April 23, 1873, Box A, Genealogy, History and Archives Unit, Central Library, Fort Worth Public Library. The KKK quote comes from Charles Mitchell, "When Every Man Carried a Six-shooter," in Mack Williams, ed., *The* News-Tribune *in Old Fort Worth*, p. 46. Julia Kathryn Garrett's research notes say the incident happened on a Sunday night, but in 1874 Sunday fell on January 29. Garrett, "Fort Worth: A Frontier Triumph," p. 428, Special Collections, University of Texas at Arlington Library.

12. Fort Worth City Council Minutes, vol. A, for November 18, 1874; September 28, 1875; and February 8, 1876; in collections of Genealogy, History and Archives Unit, Central Library, Fort Worth Public Library; *Fort Worth Democrat*, December 12 and 19, 1874; October 23, 1875; and February 19, 1876; *Fort Worth Standard*, February 10, 1876.

13. The other candidates in the marshal's election were J. I. Peters, John Stoker, and D. S. Covert. *Fort Worth Democrat*, April 8, 1876.

14. *Fort Worth Standard*, April 27, 1876.

15. *Fort Worth Standard*, April 27, 1876.

16. *Fort Worth Daily Democrat*, July 20, 1876.

17. *Fort Worth Daily Democrat*, September 19, 1876.

18. *Fort Worth Daily Democrat*, August 28, 1877.

19. For Pendery's, see *Fort Worth Star-Telegram*, September 22, 1915. For Davis, see "Washington Davis" in Ninth United States Federal Census (1870), McLennan County, TX, Microfilm Roll No. M593_1598.

20. For Shannon and Elson, see Fort Worth City Directory, 1877 (on microfiche), Genealogy, History and Archives Unit, Central Library, Fort Worth Public Library. For Quarles, see *Dallas Weekly Herald*, November 21, 1874.

21. The newspaper says he "happened to be present at the stable when the party arrived." *Fort Worth Daily Democrat*, August 26, 1877.

22. *Fort Worth Daily Democrat*, August 26, 1877.

23. The *Democrat* incorrectly refers to Officer J. W. O'Connell as "McConnell." *Fort Worth Daily Democrat*, August 26, 1877.

24. All three incidents are reported in Sunday's newspaper, the *Fort Worth Daily Democrat*, August 26, 1877.

25. The firemen would repeat this ritual upon the death of T. I. Courtright ten years later because Courtright was another (former) lawman-fireman. By 1887 the city would be accustomed to the tolling of the main fire bell to commemorate a fallen officer. See *Fort Worth Daily Gazette*, February 10, 1887, and *Dallas Morning News*, February 10, 1887.

26. *Fort Worth Daily Democrat*, August 28, 1877.

27. *Fort Worth Daily Democrat*, August 29, 1877.

28. *Daily Fort Worth Standard*, August 28 and 29, 1877.

29. *Fort Worth Daily Democrat*, September 1, 1877.

30. *Fort Worth Daily Democrat*, September 2, 1877.

31. See Davis, Washington, in Ft. Smith Criminal Case Files, 1866–1900, Control No. NRFF-21-3W51-46982, online at Ancestry.com.

32. For deserting his wife, see *Fort Worth Daily Democrat*, August 29, 1877. For involvement in the strike, see *Dallas Morning News*, March 8, 1886.

33. For Quarles, see *Dallas Morning News*, March 6, 1886.

34. *Fort Worth Press*, July 20, 1938.

35. *Fort Worth Daily Democrat*, July 11, 1878; and September 11, 1879; U.S. Federal Census Mortality Schedules, 1850–1880

Record, Tarrant County, Fort Worth, TX, 1880, Microfilm Roll T1134_60.

36. His grave is in block 2, lot 76, at Pioneers Rest. The granite marker is obviously not a circa 1879 tombstone. It had to have been placed by descendants much later, in the twentieth century. Compounding the error, the information on the marker conflicts with information in the official cemetery guide, which states that Fitzgerald was the "First City *Fire* Marshal of Fort Worth." Hudson and Knox, *Pioneers Rest Cemetery*, p. 32.

Notes to Chapter 3

1. There is some confusion over the details of George White's life, specifically his birthdate, birthplace, and even his full name. Records of Fort Worth's Pioneers Rest Cemetery, where he is buried (block 2, lot 47), incorrectly give his birthdate as 1857 and birthplace as Franklin County, Georgia. Weldon Hudson and Barbara Knox, compilers, *Pioneers Rest Cemetery, Fort Worth, Tarrant County, Texas* (Fort Worth: Genealogical Society, 2001), p. 27. Cf. Eighth United States Federal Census (1860), Eastern Division, Pike, AL, Microfilm Roll No. M653_21; and Ninth United States Federal Census (1870), Upshur, TX, Microfilm Roll No. M593_1607. The 1860 Census gives his middle initial as "D," while the Fort Worth "bond book" for 1879 gives his middle initial as "M"; both are incorrect. The "bond books" are in the Records of the City of Fort Worth, Records of the City Secretary's Office, Series I, Mayor and Council Proceedings, City Secretary's Record Book, 1873–1888, Box 1, Genealogy, History and Archives Unit, Central Library, Fort Worth Public Library.

2. United States Federal Census records for 1850, 1860, and 1870; and Tenth United States Federal Census (1880), Rusk County, Henderson, TX, Microfilm Roll No. T9_1325, Enumeration District 73. See also "George H. [*sic*] White" in Fort Worth City Directory, 1877.

3. R. C. McPhail testifies at the trial of George White's murderer as George's "step-father" despite the fact that there was no legal basis for the claim. The 1880 Census also lists George ("killed") as the "step-son" of R. C. and P. A. McPhail. See Tenth United States Federal Census (1880), Tarrant County, Fort Worth,

TX, Microfilm Roll No. T9_1328; and *George Alford v. State of Texas*, Court of Criminal Appeals of Texas, 8 Tex. Ct. App. Case No. 545, 1880 Tex. Crim. App.

4. *Fort Worth Democrat*, August 3 and 10, 1879.

5. Testimony of J. M. Henderson in *George Alford v. State of Texas*, Case No. 545. For information on Tenth Judicial District, see "County Government" section of Fort Worth City Directory, 1878-79

6. *Fort Worth Democrat*, August 3 and 10, 1879.

7. *Fort Worth Democrat*, September 25, 1876.

8. Details of this case come from District Court records, Texas Court of Appeals records, and newspapers. *State of Texas v. Thomas Alford*, Case No. 1823 (for "Theft of a Mare"), Seventeenth District Court, Tarrant County District Clerk's Office, Criminal Section, Tarrant County Justice Center, Fort Worth, TX; and *George Alford v. State of Texas* (for Murder), no case number given in original, Court of Appeals of Texas, 8 TX. Ct. App. 545; 1880 Tex. Crim. App. *Fort Worth Democrat*, August 3 and 6, 1879. The authors are also indebted to J. J. Johnson of Tampa Bay, FL, for sharing the fruits of his research into the Alford cases. Johnson to Kevin Foster via e-mail, August 20, 2002. Note: In original court papers, Storm's name is misspelled "Strum." Information on the McCafferty brothers (Charles, J. J., and Anthony) comes from correspondence with Donna Donnell, a descendant of another branch of the McCafferty clan. Donnell to Selcer via e-mail, November 3 and 8, 2008.

9. The record does not indicate why Storm, the reputed owner of the horse, did not swear out the complaint himself. Re the complaint: The custom of the time was to refer to an unknown party in public papers by the generic "John Smith" rather than "John Doe" as we do today. Re Charlie McCafferty's violent nature, see the *Columbia (SC) State Newspaper*, January 5, 1893; *Chicago (IL) Inter Ocean*, November 9 and 10, 1893, November 23, 1895; and *Columbus (GA) Daily Enquirer*, November 12, 1893.

10. The scanty family background comes from *George Alford v. State of Texas*, Appeals Case No. 545. For "desperadoes" see *Fort Worth Democrat*, August 3 and 6, 1879.

11. *George Alford v. State*, Case No. 545.

12. The two sides of the exchange between White and Alford come from *Fort Worth Democrat*, August 3, 1879; and *George Alford v. State*, Case No. 545.

13. *George Alford v. State*, Case No. 545.

14. Elias J. Beall (1835–1914) was not the only doctor in Fort Worth, but he was the best at this time. He had been a physician in Fort Worth since 1868. During the Civil War he was a highly respected surgeon in the Confederate army. He married K. M. Van Zandt's sister Fanny in 1860. Later he was one of the founders of the Fort Worth Medical College. See Beall's obituary in *Fort Worth Star-Telegram*, October 21, 1914. See also Van Zandt, *Force without Fanfare*, p. 120, and *Fort Worth Democrat*, August 3, 1879.

15. *Fort Worth Democrat*, August 3, 1879.

16. For background on Beall, see *Fort Worth Star-Telegram*, October 21, 1914.

17. *George Alford v. State*, Case No. 545.

18. *George Alford v. State*, Case No. 545.

19. *Fort Worth Democrat*, August 5 and 6, 1879.

20. The medical postmortem is based on the analysis of Dr. R. D. Caldroney of a similar case in *Military History Magazine* (May 2006): 10-16. Naturally, without any actual medical records, it is an educated guess.

21. The date of death comes from White's tombstone in Fort Worth's Pioneers Rest Cemetery. Later published accounts get the date wrong. Cravens' bill to county officials is contained in the minutes of the Tarrant County Commissioners Court meeting of November 1879, Tarrant County Courthouse, Old Records Office.

22. *Fort Worth Democrat*, August 7 and 9, 1879.

23. *Fort Worth Democrat*, August 10, 1879.

24. *George Alford v. State of Texas*, Case No. 545.

25. Judge W. B. Dunham for Texas Court of Criminal Appeals in *George Alford v. State*, Case No. 545.

26. *State of Texas v. Thomas Alford*, Case No. 1823, Minute Book E, p. 564, Seventeenth District Court, Tarrant County District Clerk's Office, Criminal Section, Tarrant County Justice Center, Fort Worth, TX.

27. *State of Texas v. George Alford* (for "theft of property over the value of $20"), Case No. 2837, and *State of Texas v. Tom Alford*, Case No. 2838, Minute Book D-4, p. 20 C, Seventeenth District Court, Tarrant County District Clerk's Office, Criminal Section, Tarrant County Justice Center, Fort Worth, TX; and Johnson to Foster, August 20, 2002.

28. The history of the Alfords' battles with the law are found in *State of Texas v. George Alford*, Case No. 2837 and *State of Texas v. Tom Alford*, Case No. 2838.

29. Although he never practiced law in Texas, Buckley Paddock had been a member of the bar in Mississippi, so he was not without some legal expertise. *Fort Worth Weekly Democrat*, May 27, 1876 (quoted in Robert DeArment, *Jim Courtright of Fort Worth: His Life and Legend* [Fort Worth: Texas Christian University Press, 2004], pp. 28–29).

Notes to Chapter 4

1. From "The Ballad of Dock Bishop," by Dottie Moore of Pontotoc County, MS, ca. 1886. Reprinted in *The Calhoun County (MS) Journal*, January 2, 1997. Bishop's name is variously written as either "Doc" or "Dock." It is not known whether there was some medical connection with the nickname, such as was the case with John Henry "Doc" Holliday, and therefore the "k" was merely a misspelling, but that is the most reasonable explanation. To be consistent, this work will use the "Doc" spelling.

2. Meeting of October 7, 1884 (Tuesday), City Council Minutes, Volume E, November 6, 1884-December 16, 1884, on deposit at Genealogy, History and Archives Unit, Central Library, Fort Worth Public Library; and *Fort Worth Daily Gazette*, October 8, 1884.

3. All birthdates come from family Bible. Dora gave birth to a girl in 1885 whom she named "Willie" in honor of her father. Family background comes from e-mails and correspondence between Mrs. Monte K. Smith (descendant) and Kevin Foster, January 1, 2006; and Marian Rea (descendant) to Foster, February 19 and 26, 2004, and May 4, 2006. According to family lore, Dora's father, James Berry Boydston, personally tracked down James' killer and "brought him to justice." Willie Wise is

incorrectly listed in the 1890 Census (Ellis County, Township 6 fragment) as a "male."

4. "The Ballad of Dock Bishop."

5. City directories were being published every other year at this point. They contained, besides an alphabetical listing of all citizens, their home addresses, race, occupation, and sometimes even marital status. Unfortunately, Bill Wise did not live long enough to bask in the glow of his new title; he was dead when it came out.

6. James Gillett, *Fugitives from Justice: The Notebook of Texas Ranger Sergeant James B. Gillett* (Austin: State House Press, 1997), p. 178. Swofford and Marksbury were finally captured in Texas in 1896. *Dallas Morning News*, September 2, 1896.

7. That was what happened when a pair of Texas lawmen showed up in Florida in 1877 to arrest the notorious John Wesley Hardin. They "kidnapped" him and hustled him out of the state, killing Hardin's companion in the process. Jesse Earle Bowden and William S. Cummins, *Texas Desperado in Florida: The Capture of Outlaw John Wesley Hardin in Pensacola, 1877* (Pensacola, FL: Pensacola Historical Society, 2002).

8. For details on Courtright's New Mexico escapades and the subsequent attempt to extradite him back to Albuquerque, see Robert K. DeArment, *Jim Courtright of Fort Worth* (Fort Worth: Texas Christian University Press, 2004), pp. 127–172.

9. *New Orleans Daily Picayune*, July 4, 1886.

10. Doc Bishop's first trial was carried as a brief, four-line item in the local newspapers (*Dallas Morning News*, October 3, 1885). For more details of Bishop's journey through the legal system, see *New Orleans Daily Picayune*, July 4, 1886.

11. *Calhoun City (MS) Monitor-Herald*, June 21, 1923.

12. *Calhoun City (MS) Monitor-Herald*, June 21, 1923; *New Orleans Daily Picayune*, July 4, 1886.

13. *Calhoun City (MS) Monitor Herald*, April 9, 1942.

14. *New Orleans Daily Picayune*, July 4, 1886.

15. *Oxford (MS) Eagle*, July 8, 1886.

16. *Calhoun City (MS) Monitor Herald*, April 9, 1942.

17. *Calhoun City (MS) Monitor Herald*, April 9, 1942.

18. *New Orleans Daily Picayune*, July 4, 1886; and *Calhoun City (MS) Monitor Herald*, April 9, 1942.

19. This story has been handed down in the family for four generations. Diane Smith to Kevin Foster in an e-mail, January 1, 2006.

20. *Dallas Morning News*, July 5, 1886.

21. *Mississippi: The WPA Guide to the Magnolia State*, pp. 472–473.

22. *Fort Worth Gazette*, June 2, 1888; and *Dallas Morning News*, September 2, 1896.

23. *Calhoun City (MS) Monitor-Herald*, June 21, 1923.

24. The 1900 Census shows Willie living in Johnson County, Precinct 8, not with her mother. That fact is confirmed in the family's history. Diane Smith to Kevin Foster, e-mail, January 1, 2006 and in documents mailed to Foster by Marian Rea, May 4, 2006.

25. Dennis Murphree, "The Hanging of Dock [*sic*] Bishop," *Calhoun City (MS) Monitor-Herald*, April 9, 1942.

26. *Fort Worth Star-Telegram*, June 30, 2002.

Notes to Chapter 5

1. Born Timothy Isaiah Courtright "around 1848," somewhere along the way he picked up the name "Longhair Jim," which is how he was known during his Fort Worth years, roughly 1875–1887.

2. The minimum fine until 1877 was $10 "plus costs"; after that it went up to $25 plus costs. DeArment, *Jim Courtright of Fort Worth*, p. 61.

3. See "James T. Townsend" in Eighth United States Federal Census (1860), Logan County, KY, Microfilm Roll No. M653_383; and Ninth United States Federal Census (1870), Tarrant County, TX, Microfilm Roll No. M593_1605. See "J. T. Townsend" and "R. W. Townsend" in Tenth United States Federal Census (1880), Fort Worth, Tarrant County, TX, Microfilm Roll No. T9_1328. See "James F. [*sic*] Townsend" in Twelfth United States Federal Census (1200), Fort Worth, Tarrant County, TX., Microfilm Roll No. T623_1671; and Fort Worth City Directories, 1883–1886.

4. For Townsend, see *Dallas Morning News*, June 9, 1929. For Courtright's dramatic escape from custody on October 19, 1884, see DeArment, pp. 153–172.

5. V. V. Masterson, *The Katy Railroad and the Last Frontier* (Norman: University of Oklahoma Press, 1952); Ruth Allen, *Chapters in the History of Organized Labor in Texas*, University of Texas's Bureau of Research in the Social Sciences, Publication No. 4143 (Austin: University of Texas, 1941), pp. 20–21; and *Dallas Morning News*, November 21, 1885.

6. The exact date of the *Gazette* quote is unknown, but it is cited in a history of the strike that appeared in the *Dallas Morning News*, June 9, 1929. See also *Dallas Morning News*, April 5, 1886.

7. Firsthand accounts of the strike are hard to come by. It is mentioned in the memoirs of Jesse G. Smith, a policeman at the time and later Fort Worth judge. Sam Smith, "Things I Remember about Early Days in the History of Fort Worth" (Fort Worth: privately printed, [circa 1965]), p. 8. Note: Jesse G. Smith was Sam Smith's father.

8. *Fort Worth Gazette*, April 6, 1886.

9. *Fort Worth Gazette*, April 6, 1886.

10. Will Rushing was initially charged, but the charges were dismissed. Witcher and Jim Rushing were never even charged. *Dallas Morning News*, April 27, 1886.

11. Paddock, *A Twentieth Century History and Biographical Record of North and West Texas*, p. 103; and obituary from *Fort Worth Record*, June 7, 1920, p.1.

12. James W. Thomason (sometimes misspelled "Thompson") was born April 30, 1854. A long and mostly distinguished career in law enforcement saw him rise to the rank of detective in the FWPD in 1900. He came to a tragic end on April 24, 1905, when he drowned while fishing in the Trinity River. *Dallas Morning News*, April 25, 1905. For payola, see *Fort Worth Telegram*, September 16, 1903.

13. *Dallas Daily Herald*, December 2, 1880; Fort Worth Police Department Rosters, 1880 and 1881, in FWPD Miscellaneous Materials, Archive Holdings, Genealogy, History and Archives Unit, Central Library, Fort Worth Public Library; Fort Worth City Directories, 1882–1886; Weldon I. Hudson, "Tarrant County, TX, Marriage Records, 1876–1885" (privately printed, 1984), vol. 1, p. 70; DeArment, *Jim Courtright of Fort Worth*, pp. 194–96.

14. *Fort Worth Daily Gazette*, April 4, 1886, p. 2.

15. The *Fort Worth Gazette* of December 31, 1893, carried a feature story on the Fort Worth Fire Department, which included biographical sketches of all regular firemen. By this date, Charlie Sneed had been a fireman for fifteen years.

16. Officer William Hale, quoted in *Fort Worth Daily Gazette*, August 4, 1886.

17. Testimony of witnesses at the habeas corpus hearing for Henry Henning on January 15, 1887, reported in the *Dallas Morning News*, January 18, 1887.

18. *Dallas Morning News*, April 4, 1886.

19. *Dallas Morning News*, April 4, 1886.

20. ".45-60" describes a cartridge specifically manufactured for the 1876 Winchester Centennial Model rifle. The numbers mean a .45 caliber cartridge with a powder charge of 60 grains—way too much shell for any revolver. William Hale is either misquoted here, or else ".45-60" is a misprint by the newspaper. Interview with William Hale in *Fort Worth Daily Gazette*, August 4, 1886.

21. For Courtright quote, see *San Antonio Daily Express*, October 21, 1884.

22. Details of injuries come from *Dallas Morning News*, April 4, 1886; and *H. Henning v. State of Texas*, No. 2616 Court of Criminal Appeals, 24 TX. Court of Appeals 315; 6 S.W. 137; 1887 TX. Criminal Appeals.

23. The number of shots comes from an unidentified participant, cited in *Dallas Morning News*, April 4, 1886.

24. *Dallas Morning News*, April 4,1886.

25. The Fort Worth newspaper calls Nace a "former hostler [stableman]" at the Missouri Pacific roundhouse, which does not make sense because that is not a place where horses were kept, and goes on to say that he was living "near Union Depot." The Dallas newspaper correctly identifies Nace's employment, but locates his residence "near Polk Stockyards," which was just south of the Texas and Pacific railroad reservation. *Fort Worth Daily Gazette*, April 4, 1886; *Dallas Morning News*, March 7 and April 4, 1886. Fort Worth City Directories show only Dalton, of the five, living in Fort Worth prior to the events of 1886, and none living there afterwards; thus the conclusion that they were "outsiders."

26. *Fort Worth Daily Gazette*, April 4, 1886.

27. *Dallas Morning News*, October 13, 1886.

28. For Hardin's role, see *Dallas Weekly Times Herald*, July 12, 1890. For Pierce, see *Dallas Morning News*, April 5, 1886; and *Dallas Weekly Herald*, April 5, 1886.

29. *Dallas Morning News*, April 4, 1886.

30. *Dallas Morning News*, April 4, 1886; *Fort Worth Daily Gazette*, April 4, 1886; and Sam Smith, "Things I Remember," p. 8.

31. Wilburn King, *With the 18th Texas Infantry: The Autobiography of Wilburn Hill King*, ed. by L. David Norris (Hillsboro, TX: Hill College Press, 1996), pp. 105–06.

32. Dallas Morning News, April 4, 1886.

33. There is no indication in contemporary newspaper accounts that artillery was deployed in Fort Worth. If the big guns had been sent in, surely this would have drawn comment, and if so, it was the only time in Fort Worth history that artillery was actually deployed on the streets of the city. *Dallas Morning News*, April 5, 1886; Report of the Adjutant General of the State of Texas, December, 1886 (Austin: Triplett & Hutchings, State Printers, 1886), p. 11, Texas State Library and Archives, Austin.

34. *Dallas Morning News*, April 5, 1886; *Fort Worth Daily Gazette*, April 5, 1886; and Report of Adjutant General of Texas, pp. 10–11.

35. *Dallas Morning News*, April 5, 1886.

36. For his leadership of local union, see *Dallas Morning News*, January 1, 1888. For "master workman" and "accessory," see *Dallas Morning News*, April 5 and 6, 1886.

37. *Dallas Morning News*, April 6 and 9, August 1, 1886.

38. *Fort Worth Daily Gazette*, April 5, 1886; *Dallas Morning News*, April 5, 1886.

39. Officially, Dick Townsend still lies in an unmarked grave at Pioneers Rest Cemetery (Samuels Avenue, Fort Worth). The fragmentary cemetery records do not even show him in the family plot. However, the evidence is practically undeniable. There are seven Townsend graves in block 3, lot 38. The last space on the south end is marked by a simple rock with no inscription, but is probably the grave of James T. Townsend, the father. Going north, there are two unmarked spaces, then the grave of James T.

Townsend, Jr., Dick's brother, then two more unmarked spaces, then Walter B. Townsend, another brother. On the north end is the marked grave of W. Frank Turk, a family friend who served with the two brothers in the Confederate army during the Civil War. One of the unmarked graves contains the remains of L. L. Townsend, wife of James Townsend, Jr.—probably the empty spot next to him. The unmarked spot beside Walter Townsend is probably occupied by his son, Walter, Jr., who died a week after his father. One unmarked spot beside James Townsend, Jr., is probably his son. That leaves one unmarked spot between the markers of James Townsend, Jr., on the north end and the rock on the south end. That spot, we believe, holds the remains of Dick Townsend. In the summer of 2009, a little sleuthing by Kevin Foster discovered the Townsend family plot and filled in the blank spaces in the historical record. Pioneer Rest Cemetery Assoc. Records, Box 2 of 2, records of Block 3, Genealogy, History and Archives Unit, Central Library, Fort Worth Public Library; and e-mail correspondence between Foster and J. M. Myrick, president of the Pioneer Rest Cemetery Association, August 24, 2009.

40. *Dallas Morning News,* April 5, 1886.

41. Murray Klein, *The Life and Legend of Jay Gould* (Baltimore, MD: Johns Hopkins University Press, 1986), p. 362.

42. *Fort Worth Daily Gazette,* April 6 and 7, 1886; Report of Adjutant General of Texas, p. 11.

43. None of the men named as bushwhackers appear in city directories for the four years before the strike, nor can any relatives be identified as Fort Worth residents by last names. See Fort Worth City Directories, 1882–1886. For Rowland see *Dallas Morning News,* April 5, 1886.

44. *Dallas Morning News,* August 1, 1886.

45. *Dallas Morning News,* January 17 and 18, 1887.

46. *Dallas Morning News,* January 18, 1887.

47. *Dallas Morning News,* June 15, 1887.

48. Remember, in this era before sentencing guidelines, juries had the last word, deciding not just guilt or innocence but in the case of the latter, the appropriate punishment. *Dallas Morning News,* June 19, 1887.

49. *Dallas Morning News,* June 25, 1887.

50. *Dallas Morning News*, November 21 and December 22, 1887. The Court of Criminal Appeals spent three months of the year in Tyler, three months in Dallas, and three months in Austin.

51. *Dallas Morning News*, October 13, 1886.

52. *Dallas Morning News*, October 5, 1887.

53. *Dallas Morning News*, January 1, 1890.

54. *Dallas Morning News*, October 4 and 8, 1887; April 2, May 21, and May 31, 1889; January 1, March 25, and March 27, 1890. For "honorably acquitted," see *Dallas Weekly Times-Herald*, July 12, 1890.

55. *Dallas Weekly Times Herald*, July 12, 1890.

56. *Dallas Morning News*, April 10 and 11 and June 27, 1886; January 1, 1888.

57. *Dallas Morning News*, July 13, 1894.

58. *Dallas Morning News*, March 20, 1888.

59. *New York Times*, March 14, 1888; *Dallas Morning News*, March 14 and 20, 1888; April 2, 18, and 19, 1889.

60. *Dallas Weekly Times Herald*, July 12, 1890; *Dallas Morning News*, April 17, 1891.

61. *Dallas Morning News*, June 4, 1886; Sneed's obituary is in the *Fort Worth Star-Telegram*, October 20, 1921; *Fort Worth Gazette*, April 4, 1886.

62. *Dallas Weekly Times-Herald*, July 12, 1890.

63. For Courtright's precipitous decline in the eyes of his fellow citizens, his hearing and trial testimony, and his spectacular death, see Richard Selcer, "Legendary Marshal Timothy Isaiah Courtright" in *Fort Worth Characters* (Denton: University of North Texas Press, 2009), pp. 52–56.

64. When Coker refused to resign, Rea could not rally support among his officers for an arbitrary dismissal, so the Marshal backed down. Coker was able to retire with honor in 1916. In April 2000, the Fort Worth Police Association placed a commemorative headstone on his grave in Fort Worth's Greenwood Cemetery (*Fort Worth Star-Telegram*, April 28, 2000). For Rea's original accusation, see *Dallas Morning News*, April 24, 1886.

Notes to Part II Introduction

1. The Kerner Commission, named for Illinois Governor Otto Kerner, was appointed by the Federal government after the "long hot summer" of bloody race riots in 1967. Its report, issued on February 29, 1968, was a watershed in making white Americans aware of the problems in law enforcement.

2. In the popular mind, all Latinos were lumped together as "Mexicans," which based on country of origin, was pretty accurate. Statistics come from *Fort Worth Daily Gazette*, September 28, 1890. For Mexicans' standing under Texas law, see Eric Foner, *Give Me Liberty! An American History*, 2nd ed. (New York: W. W. Norton, 2009), vol. 2, p. 615. For more on Fort Worth's Hispanic population through its history, see Carlos E. Cuéllar, *Stories from the Barrio: A History of Mexican Fort Worth* (Fort Worth: Texas Christian University Press, 2003), pp. 5–9.

3. "Federal Writers Project," vol. 11, p. 4083.

4. "Facts about Fort Worth and Adjacent Country," Columbian Souvenir edition, author unknown, 1893, collections of Amon Carter Museum, Fort Worth; *Fort Worth Telegram*, February 10, 1906.

5. The only black special officers on record prior to this were Hagar Tucker in 1874 and Sam Higgins in 1885. Records of the City of Fort Worth, Mayor and City Council Proceedings, April 20, 1896, Series I, Box 2 of 3, Genealogy, History and Archives Unit, Central Library, Fort Worth Public Library; *Dallas Morning News*, May 20, 1896.

6. Webster's "Police Regulations" were published in the *Dodge City Times* on June 22, 1882. That list of fourteen directives is reprinted in full in Nyle H. Miller and Joseph W. Snell, *Why the West Was Wild* (Norman: University of Oklahoma Press, 2003), pp. 48–49. Note: The Eastern Cattle Trail first came through Fort Worth, connecting to the Chisholm Trail at the Red River before continuing on up to Abilene, Kansas. The Western Trail was opened subsequently, connecting Fort Worth to Dodge City.

7. Henceforward, opium, morphine, or cocaine could only be dispensed by pharmacists to persons with a doctor's prescription. The fine for anyone else caught selling the drug was set at "not less than $5 nor more than $100." *Dallas Morning News*, January

18, 1902. William Rea's quote comes from *Fort Worth Register,* ca. 1901. Photocopy of same, n.d., is in "Hell's Half-acre" vertical file, Genealogy, History and Archives Unit, Central Library, Fort Worth Public Library.

8. For example of Chinese stereotyping, see *Dallas Morning News,* December 18, 1897. For examples of black stereotyping, see *Dallas Morning News,* April 16, 1897, and August 20, 1911.

9. *Dallas Morning News,* March 19, 1897; and August 31, 1913.

10. *Dallas Morning News,* April 11, 1891.

11. *Dallas Morning News,* April 11, 1891. For Sam Farmer in particular, see *Fort Worth Daily Democrat,* August 14, 1879; February 25, 1881; February 25, 1882; and September 4, 1890.

12. The historic changeover of Fort Worth from the city council form of government to the commission form has been covered in only one source: Russell B. Ward, "Panther City Progressives: Fort Worth and the Commission Form of Government" (thesis in U.S. history, 1900–1940, Texas A&M University, fall 1995).

13. Trial testimony in *State of Texas v. Ike Knight,* Case No. 18416, Forty-eighth District Court, Tarrant County District Clerk's Office, Criminal Section, Tarrant County Justice Center, Fort Worth, TX.

14. *Dallas Morning News,* December 31, 1905, and February 28, 1906.

15. *Dallas Morning News,* January 14, 1907.

16. "The First 100 Years," Fort Worth Police Department Annual, 1973, p. 4 (in authors' collections).

17. The rest of the story is that Waller was forced to shoot one of the combatants when the man grappled with him over the officer's pistol. *Dallas Morning News,* May 27, 1906.

18. J'Nell Pate, *North of the River: A Brief History of North Forty Worth* (Fort Worth: Texas Christian University Press, 1994), p. 48.

19. B. B. Paddock, *A Historical and Biographical Record of North and West* Texas (Chicago: Lewis Publishing Company, 1906), p. 246.

20. The story of Howell, Montgomery, and Claypool comes

from Howell's obituary in the *Fort Worth Star-Telegram*, October 1, 1927. There is practically no detailed information of North Fort Worth's days as an independent "township." Its newspaper of record and various city records were lost or destroyed long ago.

21. *Fort Worth Star-Telegram*, October 1, 1927.

Notes to Chapter 6

1. *Fort Worth Gazette*, June 30, 1892. Additional family history is also found in Sid Waller's obituary, *Fort Worth Star-Telegram*, July 13, 1912.

2. Even discounting the postmortem hyperbole, it is clear that Lee Waller was highly regarded around the FWPD. *Fort Worth Gazette*, June 29 and 30, 1892.

3. Lou Davis was not the sort of person to show up in city directories and census records at the time. She may have been the same person as "Lulu Davis," a "colored" woman with no stated occupation who appears in the Fort Worth City Directory of 1892–93, or "Louise Davis," a "colored" woman also with no stated occupation living in Dallas in 1900. Twelfth United States Federal Census (1900), Dallas County, Dallas, Ward No. 1, Microfilm Roll No. T623_1624. The Waller-Davis relationship comes out at the time the state Board of Pardons takes up the case of Jim Burris in November 1895. The board heard testimony from E. H. Weaver of Henrietta, Texas, about a conversation he overheard between Waller and his policeman partner on the night of June 28, 1892. The relationship is also cited in Governor Joseph D. Sayers' pardon of Jim Burris in 1902. See *Fort Worth Gazette*, December 7, 1895; and "Proclamation by the Governor of the State of Texas" regarding Jim Burris, alias Jim Toots, December 18, 1902, in Executive Record Books, Texas Secretary of State Executive Clemency Records, Archives and Information Service Division, Texas State Library and Archives Commission, Austin.

4. Governor Blease wrote, in one of his official pardons, "I have . . . very serious doubt as to whether the crime of rape can be committed upon a negro." Douglas A. Blackmon, *Slavery by Another Name* (New York: Doubleday, 2008), p. 305. Lee's brother Sid followed in his footsteps as a racial bigot; both were

notorious among their contemporaries. See obituary of A. S. "Sid" Waller, Jr., *Fort Worth Star-Telegram*, July 13, 1912; and *Dallas Morning News*, July 1, 1892.

5. For "disgrace," see *Dallas Morning News*, June 30, 1892, quoting a Fort Worth citizen. Personal information on Henry C. Townes from Twelfth United Stated Federal Census (1900), Tarrant County, Fort Worth, TX, Microfilm Roll No. T623_1671, Enumeration District 103; and Fort Worth City Directories, 1890–1900.

6. In the account that follows, the particulars including direct quotations and movements of various parties come from four sources: *State of Texas v. Jim Burris*, alias Jim Toots, Case No. 7179, Forty-eighth District Court trial record, Tarrant County Justice Center, District Clerk's Office, Criminal Section (hereafter cited as *State of Texas v. Jim Burris*); *Jim Burris, alias Jim Toots v. The State*, Case No. 613, Court of Criminal Appeals of Texas, 34 Tex. Crim. 387; 30 S.W. 785; 1895 Tex. Crim. App. LEXIS 112 (Hereafter cited as *Jim Burris v. The State* on appeal); *Fort Worth Gazette*, December 22, 1895; and *Dallas Morning News*, various issues, 1892. Where details diverge, the authors go with the version cited by more than one source or choose sworn testimony over newspaper accounts.

7. Details of the confrontation recounted here come from eyewitness testimony at Jim Burris' trial. They differ significantly from newspaper accounts provided by police sources that appeared in the days following and during Burris' trial. Specifically, eyewitnesses suggest that Waller entered Tom Curry's Saloon looking for Davis, whereas the newspaper accounts (police version) say that Waller and Townes heard a "disturbance" while making their rounds and investigated, and the whole affair occurred on the street. For testimony, see *State of Texas v. Jim Burris*. For police version, see *Dallas Morning News*, December 22, 1895; and *Fort Worth Gazette*, June 29 and 30, 1895.

8. The descriptive details for Burris come from his admission record at the time he entered Huntsville State Prison, January 4, 1896. See Jim Burris (Prisoner No. 13548) in Huntsville Penitentiary Records, 1848–1954, Texas Department of Criminal Justice, Convict Record Ledgers, 1849–1970, Microfilm Reel

No. 4, vol. 1998/038—154 "B" Series (hereafter cited as Burris convict record). The prison measurements differ from those given in the newspaper two days after the shooting. The newspaper's measurements were only an estimate.

"Cigarette dude" was the descriptive term for any African American with a defiant attitude or elevated view of himself. "Zip Coon" was the historical stereotype of the black urban prankster or con man. Both were definitely hostile stereotypes, unlike "Uncle Tom." Blackmon, pp. 300–01. There is no explanation for the "Toots" nickname, although no positive spin can possibly be put on it, whether drugs, gaseousness, or whatever. *Fort Worth Gazette*, June 29 and 30, 1892; and *Fort Worth Star-Telegram*, August 13, 1909.

9. From testimony at the Board of Pardons hearing for Jim Burris, cited in *Fort Worth Gazette*, December 7, 1895. Since Burris is identified as "Toots" in all newspaper accounts and trial testimony, that is what we will call him henceforward.

10. From written testimony of "Sec. Prince"[?] and Henry Lynch in *State of Texas v. Jim Burris.*

11. All quotes come from the trial testimony, the appeals record, or the state Board of Pardons hearing. See *State of Texas v. Jim Burris*, testimony of E. H. Weaver at pardons hearing, cited in *Fort Worth Gazette*, December 7, 1895; and lawyer James H. Swayne's letter to Governor Culberson, cited in *Fort Worth Gazette*, December 22, 1895.

12. Townes subsequently changed his story that Toots pulled the first gun when confronted with contradictory eyewitness testimony, but he still insisted under oath that the black man had provoked the affair by threatening to assault Waller. *Dallas Morning News*, June 30, 1892. For conflicting testimony, see *State of Texas v. Jim Burris*, testimony of E. H. Weaver at pardons hearing, cited in *Fort Worth Gazette*, December 7, 1895; and lawyer James H. Swayne's letter to Governor Culberson, cited in *Fort Worth Gazette*, December 22, 1895.

13. Such a self-incriminating admission by a uniformed officer today would get him immediately suspended and probably fired, but it was business as usual in 1892. *Fort Worth Gazette*, June 29, 1892; and testimony of Henry Townes, *Jim Burris v. State of Texas.*

14. "Hugging the negro woman" was newspaper codespeak for solicitation, and back-talking a white policeman constituted an actionable affront to law and order everywhere. *Fort Worth Gazette*, June 29, 1892.

15. Testimony of E. H. Weaver, a visitor to the city that night, heard for the first time at a Board of Pardons hearing for Burris three years later (December 1895). Cited in *Fort Worth Gazette*, December 7, 1895.

16. *Fort Worth Gazette*, June 29 and 30, 1892. In the *Dallas Morning News*, Horace Bell is incorrectly identified as "George Bell." *Dallas Morning News*, March 8, 1893. For additional information on Burris' two accomplices, see *Jim Burris v. State* on appeal; and convict records of Horace Bell (Convict No. 10340) and Will Campbell (Convict No. 10341), Texas Department of Criminal Justice, Convict Record Ledgers, 1849–1970, Microfilm Reel No. 3, vol. 1998/038—152, "B" Series (hereafter cited as Bell convict record and Campbell convict record).

17. *Fort Worth Gazette*, June 30, 1892.

18. Ridgeway's had been more than just the usual low dive ever since it was the site of a very public marriage in 1887 by a couple of its regulars. See *Dallas Morning News*, November 30, 1887. Both Snow and Rushing testified at the trial, and the state subpoenaed the pistol as evidence. There was no question that it was the weapon used to murder Lee Waller; the challenge for the prosecution was explaining how it came into Toots' possession. *State of Texas v. Jim Burris*.

19. The chronologies from Burris' account of the evening and the police account do not match up in every detail, but a rough timeline can still be constructed from the different accounts. This incident comes from jailhouse interview with Jim Burris, *Fort Worth Gazette*, July 9, 1892. Police quote comes from opinion of Appeals Judge J. M. Hurt in *Jim Burris v. State* on appeal.

20. Testimony of Hill Deering in *Jim Burris v. State* on appeal.

21. Testimony of Lou Overton and Appellate Judge J. M. Hurt's summary of the facts in *Jim Burris v. State* on appeal.

22. Details of gun battle come from *Fort Worth Gazette*, June 29 and 30, 1892, and from *State of Texas v. Jim Burris*. Officer Frank Bryant testified that Toots' first shot struck Waller. Witness

Henry Lynch testified that he heard shots coming from the livery stable. Lou Overton said nothing about shots from the livery stable. For Bryant and Lynch, see *State of Texas v. Jim Burris.* The authors have attempted to reconcile and rationalize obvious contradictions, and also to filter out the blatant racism that taints the newspaper coverage.

23. The *Dallas Morning News* of June 30, 1892, reports that one or more bullets passed through his body. Not true. Cf. *Fort Worth Gazette*, June 29, 1892.

24. "Irish Town" was the longstanding name for the black residential district on the southeastern edge of town. At one time it had been filled with Irish railroad workers but had long since been taken over by blacks. It was also known to police as "Little Africa" and "the Negro District." Officer Charles R. Scott's written testimony in *State of Texas v. Jim Burris.* For Toots' escape, see *Fort Worth Gazette*, June 29, 1892.

25. Henry Lynch's written testimony in *State of Texas v. Jim Burris. Fort Worth Gazette*, June 29, 1892.

26. "Nigger" quote is from a Dallas newspaper. The *Fort Worth Gazette* reported the slightly less racially charged "Partner, I'm done for—Go an' get the Negro." *Dallas Morning News*, June 30, 1892. Cf. *Fort Worth Gazette*, June 29, 1892. The other two quotations here are also from the *Gazette,* June 29, 1892. All of the *Gazette*'s quotations seem to have been manufactured or at least cleaned up for public consumption. Even if one hundred percent accurate, however, statements such as these would not be considered nuncupative or dying declarations in a court of law for the reasons given. For a discussion of dying declarations, see Michael A. Crane, "Dr. Goodfellow: Gunfighter's Surgeon," *Quarterly of the National Association for Outlaw and Lawman History* 27, no. 4 (Oct.–Dec., 2003), p. 34 n. 1.

27. *Fort Worth Gazette*, June 29, 1892.

28. Initial reports were that Waller's mother was in town that night and rushed to the firehouse with his sister. Those reports were wrong; she did not arrive until the next afternoon. *Fort Worth Gazette*, June 29 and 30, 1892. For Garfield analogy, see *Fort Worth Gazette*, June 29, 1892. For Duringer's background, see his trial testimony in *State of Texas v. Frank Fossett*, Seventeenth

District Court, Case No. 14415, 1899, Tarrant County District Clerk's Office, Criminal Section, Tarrant County Justice Center, Fort Worth, TX, trial transcript, pp. 92–93 (hereafter cited as *Texas v. Frank Fossett*, Case No. 14415).

29. *Fort Worth Gazette*, June 30, 1892.

30. *Fort Worth Gazette*, June 30, 1892.

31. *Fort Worth Gazette*, June 30, 1892.

32. *Dallas Morning News*, June 30, 1892; *Fort Worth Gazette*, June 30, 1892.

33. *Dallas Morning News*, June 30, 1892.

34. *Fort Worth Gazette*, June 30, 1892; *Dallas Morning News*, June 30, 1892.

35. *Fort Worth Gazette*, June 30 and July 9, 1892.

36. *Dallas Morning News*, July 1, 1892.

37. All details of his death and funeral arrangements, in this and succeeding paragraphs, come from the *Fort Worth Gazette*, July 1, 1892, and the *Dallas Morning News*, July 1, 1892.

38. *Fort Worth Gazette*, July 1, 1892; *Dallas Morning News*, July 1, 1892.

39. *Fort Worth Gazette*, July 1 and 9, 1892.

40. *Fort Worth Gazette*, July 1, 1892.

41. *Fort Worth Gazette*, July 9, 1892.

42. *Fort Worth Gazette*, July 1 and 2, 1892; *Dallas Morning News*, July 1, 1892.

43. *Fort Worth Gazette*, July 2, 1892.

44. *Dallas Morning News*, July 9, 1892; *Fort Worth Gazette*, July 9, 1892.

45. All details in the above account come from Jim Burris' interview in the Big Spring jail while awaiting Fort Worth officers to come for him. *Fort Worth Gazette*, July 9, 1892.

46. *Dallas Morning News*, July 10, 1892.

47. See Maddox's testimony for the prosecution in *Jim Burris v. State* on appeal. *Dallas Morning News*, July 10, 1892.

48. Not only was Toots the number one target of the mob outside, but if they did break into the jail and all three black men were together, there might be a free-for-all should they choose to put up a fight, or a mass lynching if the mob took all three. Better to keep them separated. *Dallas Morning News*, July 12, 1892.

49. *Dallas Morning News*, February 14, 1893.

50. *Dallas Morning News*, March 10 and 12, 1893.

51. *Dallas Morning News*, March 12 and 15, 1893. The Campbell verdict is found not in the newspapers but in Campbell's Huntsville convict record.

52. *Jim Burris v. State*, No. 613; *Dallas Morning News*, February 14, 1893.

53. *Jim Burris v. State*, No. 613; *Dallas Morning News*, March 24, 1893.

54. *Dallas Morning News*, March 24, 1893.

55. Dallas Morning News, March 25, 1893; *Fort Worth Star-Telegram*, August 13, 1909.

56. "Death Warrant," *State of Texas v. Jim Burris.*

57. Bell convict record and Campbell convict record.

58. Motion for a new trial (filed December 4, 1895), *State of Texas v. Jim Burris.*

59. Burris convict record. *Dallas Morning News*, November 23 and December 22, 1895; *Fort Worth Gazette*, December 22, 1895.

60. Culberson was appointed to the U.S. Senate in 1899 where he served for the next twenty-four years, building a reputation as a moderate progressive. He is buried in Fort Worth's Oakwood Cemetery. Kenneth B. Hendrickson, Jr., *Chief Executives of Texas* (College Station: Texas A&M University Press, 1995), pp. 131–34.

61. *Ibid.*, p. 140.

62. "Proclamation by the Governor of the State of Texas . . ." December 18, 1902, Executive Record Books, Secretary of State, Archives and Information Services Division, Texas State Library and Archives Commission, Austin.

63. "Proclamation by the Governor of the State of Texas . . ." December 18, 1902.

64. *Fort Worth Gazette*, December 7, 1895.

65. *Fort Worth Star*, January 8, 1903; *Fort Worth Star-Telegram*, August 14, 1909.

66. *Fort Worth Star-Telegram*, July 13, 1912.

67. *Fort Worth Star-Telegram*, August 14, 1909.

68. Bell convict record and Campbell convict record.

69. *Dallas Morning News*, July 27, 1892; December 22, 1898; and June 7 and 8, 1902.

70. First quotation from *Fort Worth Star-Telegram,* July 13, 1912; second from *Dallas Morning News,* July 13, 1912.

Notes to Chapter 7

1. The two Dallas officers were C. O. Brewer, killed on May 24, and William H. Riddell, killed on June 17. See "The Officer Down Memorial Page, Inc.," Dallas Police Department, at www. odmp.org. For Garrett interview, see *Fort Worth Gazette,* June 30, 1892.

2. Another Fort Worth officer, Robert J. Rice, came very close to becoming a casualty after he was severely wounded while pursuing some perps through the railroad yards in 1895. Fortunately, Rice lived and even returned to work after a long recovery.

3. See "Aud J. Grimes" [*sic*] in Ninth Federal Census of the United States (1870), Wayne County, TN, Microfilm Roll No. M593_1569 (available online at Ancestry.com). Additional details of family history provided by Roy T. Grimes, grandson of Andy Grimes, in e-mail correspondence, Grimes to Foster, June 28, July 4 and 16, 2008. Ellen Katie Grimes is buried in Pioneers Rest Cemetery, in the Grant family plot. *Dallas Morning News,* May 13 and November 15, 1902.

4. In 1934, the passing of the old theater occasioned a walk down memory lane in both the *Fort Worth Press,* October 12, 1934, and *Fort Worth Star-Telegram,* October 12, 1934. Reporters interviewed old-timers who recalled the operations of the Standard in its heyday. After it was torn down, the site was turned into a used car lot.

5. Frank DeBeque interview, 1922, in "Hell's Half-Acre" vertical file of Genealogy, History and Archives Unit, Central Library, Fort Worth Public Library.

6. Roy Grimes to Kevin Foster, e-mail July 17, 2008.

7. The "bloody career" of badge no. 13 is related in the *Fort Worth Register,* May 19, 1902.

8. *Dallas Morning News,* May 13, 1902; *Dallas [Daily] Times Herald,* May 12, 1902.

9. J. J. Starr to "the Honorable Mayor and City Council," August 1900, in Records of the City of Fort Worth, Mayor and

City Council Proceedings, Series I, Box 2, Genealogy, History and Archives Unit, Central Library, Fort Worth Public Library.

10. For the text of the two ordinances, see *Fort Worth Register*, May 15, 1901, and *Fort Worth Mail Telegram*, July 4, 1902. The Al Hayne Triangle was a little sliver of land at the intersection of Houston, Main, and Front (now Lancaster) streets where a memorial to the hero of the Spring Palace fire had been built in 1893. The triangle was surrounded by curbing. The streetcar tracks on Main were about twenty-five yards from the west-facing entrance to the station. It was the cabbies who came up with the name "dead line." *Dallas Morning News*, May 30, 1902.

11. More than one driver was cited under the new hack ordinances in 1901 and 1902. One of them (not Jeff Vann) challenged the ordinance in county court, and it was "declared void" on May 12, 1903, too late to do Jeff Vann or Andy Grimes any good. *Jeff Vann v. State*, No. 2759, 45 Tex. Crim. 434; 77 W.E. 813; 1903 Tex. Crim. App. For relations between police and cabbies, see "Police Department Report" of 1904, Records of City of Fort Worth, Series I, Mayor and Council Proceedings, Box 2 of 5, Genealogy, History and Archives Unit, Central Library, Fort Worth Public Library.

12. No reason was ever given why Jeff Vann used an alias. *Dallas Morning News*, June 3, 1902; *Fort Worth Telegram*, October 31, 1904.

13. *Fort Worth Register*, May 13, 1902; and *Dallas Morning News*, May 13 and June 3, 1902.

14. From testimony given at the trial of Jeff Vann, quoted in *Dallas Morning News*, May 29, 1902.

15. Logan is missing in action during what follows, and his absence is surprising. On this day, it would seem, Grimes was working their beat alone. *Dallas Morning News*, May 13, 1902.

16. Western etymologists do not agree on the definition of "jobbing" or "jobber." William Dale Jennings says it meant joshing or kidding. Ramon F. Adams goes with "coddling." All examples from local history suggest an entirely different meaning: an epithet for someone trying to cheat or take advantage of another. William Dale Jennings, *The Cowboys* (New York: Stein and

Day, 1971), p. 233. For "dead line," see *Dallas Morning News,* May 30, 1902.

17. *Fort Worth Register,* May 31, 1902.

18. *Fort Worth Register,* May 31, 1902. *Dallas Morning News,* May 30, 1902.

19. Trial testimony is quoted in *Dallas Morning News,* June 3, 1902.

20. The movements of the two principals in the gun battle come from *Jeff Vann v. State,* quoted in *Dallas Morning News,* June 3, 1902. The description of Grimes' wound comes from *Dallas Morning News,* May 13, 1902.

21. *Dallas Morning News,* May 14, 1902.

22. The number of shots exchanged is based on a count of the empty chambers in each man's pistol after the fight. The Dallas newspaper, which otherwise did a good job reporting the shootout, was incorrect on this particular point when it stated, in a headline, "Each Man Discharged Every Chamber in His Revolver Except One." *Dallas Morning News,* May 13, 1902.

23. *Dallas Morning News,* May 13 and June 3, 1902.

24. *Dallas Morning News,* May 14, 1902.

25. *Dallas Morning News,* May 13 and 30, 1902; July 12, 1902.

26. *Dallas Morning News,* May 30, 1902.

27. *Dallas Morning News,* June 3, 1902.

28. *Dallas Morning News,* July 12, 1902.

29. Since there was no money changing hands in this case, and since a hack driver obviously could not afford top-drawer legal talent, it is likely that Vann's fellow drivers contributed substantially to a legal defense fund. In the end, the Vann case became one of William Pinckney McLean's most remarkable in a long career of remarkable cases. In thirty-five years of practicing law in Fort Worth, McLean's firm successfully defended seventy-five clients charged with murder. See McLean's obituaries in *Fort Worth Star-Telegram,* Nov. 19, 1941, AM and PM editions. For appeals verdict, see *Fort Worth Telegram,* October 31, 1904.

30. *Fort Worth Telegram,* October 31, 1904.

31. *Fort Worth Register,* May 17, 1902.

32. *Dallas Morning News,* May 13, 1902.

33. *Dallas Morning News*, May 17, 18, 20, and June 7, 1902.

34. *Dallas Morning News*, May 13, 1902.

Notes to Chapter 8

1. Information on Nichols family from "Historical Notes on the Fort Worth Fire Department," compiled by Jim Noah; from Nichols family genealogy compiled by Elton Harwell of Dallas and shared with authors in telephone conversations and correspondence over several years, 1996ff.

2. *Fort Worth Record*, December 23, 1906; and Twelfth United States Federal Census (1900), Tarrant County, Fort Worth, TX, Microfilm Roll No. T623_1671.

3. *Fort Worth Record*, December 23, 1906.

4. *Fort Worth Register*, December 16, 1900; Leon Metz, *John Wesley Hardin: Dark Angel of Texas* (El Paso, TX: Mangan Books, 1996), pp. 137, 279–80.

5. 1904–05 Fort Worth City Directory; *Fort Worth Record*, December 23, 1906.

6. The Standard Theater was opened in 1897 by John M. Moore, bought by Frank DeBeque the next year, and closed for good in 1914 after a memorable seventeen-year run. The building was torn down in 1934 to be replaced by a used car lot. *Fort Worth Star-Telegram*, October 12, 1934; *Fort Worth Press*, October 12, 1934. Re the Maddoxes. They were not quite on a par with the Earps, but the Maddox brothers, Peyton, James, Walter, Edward, and Sebe, served three decades in the FWPD and Tarrant County Sheriff's Department. Former policeman Peyton was one of the first special officers employed at the Standard. See Frank DeBeque letter to Police Chief W. M. Rea, April 7, 1897, Records of City of Fort Worth, Series I, Mayor and Council Proceedings, 1911, Box 5 of 5. Genealogy, History and Archives Unit, Central Library, Fort Worth Public Library.

7. *Fort Worth Star-Telegram*, October 12, 1934.

8. All details of the events of that night come from the *Fort Worth Record*, December 23, 24, and 25, 1906; the *Fort Worth Telegram*, December 23 and 24, 1906; and the *Fort Worth Star-Telegram*, August 13,1909.

9. The headline in *Fort Worth Telegram*, December 23, 1906

said, "John Nichols . . . Instantly Killed."

10. *Dallas Morning News*, December 25, 1906.

11. In February 1912, after Pioneers Rest had sunk into disrepair, the family had the remains of all three disinterred and moved to the new Mount Olivet Cemetery. The angel monument was left behind, either because it was too fragile or too expensive to move. At the new site, the family did not put any marker over Officer Nichols' grave, and no marker was placed later. John Dee Nichols' grave remains unmarked today.

12. *Fort Worth Telegram*, December 24, 1906; and *Dallas Morning News*, January 1, 1907.

13. *Fort Worth Star-Telegram*, January 3, 1907. Dr. Joseph Lister's invention of "antisepsis surgery," using diluted carbolic acid, had been known in the medical profession since 1865, but while it dramatically increased the rate of survival for surgical patients, it was far from a sure thing, and there is no indication that Barney Wise was treated with the Lister method. He was initially lodged in the hospital ward of the jail and considered a hopeless case. It seems doubtful, therefore, that he received first-rate medical treatment at any time. See Michael A. Crane, "Dr. Goodfellow: Gunfighter's Surgeon," *Quarterly of the National Association for Outlaw and Lawman History* 27, no. 4 (Oct.–Dec., 2003), p. 32.

14. *Fort Worth Star-Telegram*, February 7, 1907; *Dallas Morning News*, February 9 and 10, 1907.

Notes to Chapter 9

1. See "Jeff D. McLean" in Twelfth United States Federal Census (1900), Fort Worth, Ward 6, Tarrant County, TX, Microfilm Roll No. T623_1671; Obituary, *Fort Worth Star-Telegram*, March 23, 1907; Obituary for W. P. McLean, Jr., *Fort Worth Star-Telegram*, November 19, 1941.

2. Quoted in *Fort Worth Telegram*, January 20, 1904, reprinted in *Fort Worth Chronicle* 2, no.1 (1994).

3. *Dallas Morning News*, March 23, 1907; *Fort Worth Star-Telegram*, March 23, 1907.

4. For McLean, Twelfth United States Federal Census (1900), Tarrant County, Fort Worth, TX, Microfilm Roll No. T623_1671;

and for Cogdell, Hood County, Granbury, TX, Microfilm Roll No. T623_1645. *Dallas Morning News*, October 15, 1905; and *Fort Worth Record*, March 24, 1907.

5. The Fat Stock Show had been held annually in the stockyards district north of the river since 1896. It would not move indoors until the North Side Coliseum was built in 1908. But as an outdoors event, it was just as big as it would be later when moved into its own venue. North Fort Worth was an independent township from 1902–1909. Everybody knew Jeff McLean had political ambitions for higher office with his father as a role model and mentor; it was just a question of how high.

6. On the night of February 8, 1887, "Longhair Jim" Courtright came to the White Elephant Saloon looking for Luke Short to settle old scores. Courtright called him out, and after a few words Short pulled a pistol and emptied it into the ex-marshal. W. M. "Bill" Thomason's name is often misspelled in the historical records as "Thompson" or "Thomlinson." The 1900 Census compounds the errors by giving his name as "W. H. [*sic*] Thomason." After his death, his wife of ten years made a point of informing the Fort Worth Telegram that his name was Thomason, which is why we are going with this spelling in the present work. Fort Worth Telegram, March 31, 1907. Cf. "William Thomlinson" [*sic*], Tarrant County, Certificate No. 54924 in Texas Death Indexes, 1903-2000, Texas Dept. of Health, State Vital Statistics, Austin; "Interview with John W. Renfro" in Federal Writers' Project, "Research Data: Fort Worth and Tarrant County, Texas," vol. 2, p. 498; "Early History of Fort Worth" in Federal Writers' Project, "Research Data: Fort Worth and Tarrant County, Texas," vol. 11, p. 4054; *Fort Worth Record and Register*, March 23, 1907; and Twelfth United States Federal Census (1900), Fort Worth, Ward 2, Tarrant County, TX, Microfilm Roll No. T623_1671.

7. The family background is very sketchy, mostly pieced together from Hamil's and Charles' obituaries. *Fort Worth Morning Register*, April 8, 1902; *Fort Worth Star-Telegram*, May 2, 1907.

8. This story is impossible because the Black Jack Ketchum Gang did its dirty work at the tail-end of the century, by which time Hamil Scott was no longer working for the railroad. Scott

may well have faced down train robbers during his years with the Fort Worth & Denver, but they were not "the noted Blackjack [*sic*] Gang." Both of these stories come from Scott's obituary and cannot be verified in the historical record. This does not necessarily mean they did not occur, just that they were not recorded by Scott's contemporaries. As far as the record shows, Ketchum never held up a train near Clayton, New Mexico. He was hanged there, however, on April 25, 1901. For the only biography of Black Jack Thomas Ketchum, see Ed Bartholomew, *Black Jack Ketchum: Last of the Hold-up Kings* (Houston: Frontier Press of Texas, 1955). For Scott's obituary, see *Fort Worth Telegram*, May 1, 1907.

9. *Fort Worth Morning Register*, April 8, 1902; *Fort Worth Telegram*, August 2, 1903. Scott's civil case came to trial in March 1906, and he won half a loaf, getting the salary but not the fee. *Dallas Morning News*, March 23, 1906; and May 2, 1907.

10. C. R. Scott was one of the first detectives on the FWPD, after starting out as a beat cop in 1879. He finally had to retire for health reasons about a month before he died in April 1902. Fort Worth Police Department Annual, 1901, Special Collections, University of Texas at Arlington Library. See obituary in *Fort Worth Register*, April 8, 1902.

11. *Dallas Morning News*, March 23, 1907; *Fort Worth Telegram*, February 12, 1907 (available online through www. GenealogyBank.com).

12. W. H. Thomason in Twelfth United States Federal Census (1900), Fort Worth, Tarrant County, TX, Microfilm Roll No. T623_1671. *Fort Worth Record*, March 24 and 25, 1907, AM eds. Details of Thomason's background also come from his testimony in *State of Texas v. Frank Fossett*, Case No. 14415, Seventeenth District Court, Tarrant County, TX, 1899, trial transcript, p. 89, archived in Tarrant County District Clerk's Office, Criminal Section, Tarrant County Justice Center, Fort Worth, TX (hereafter cited as *Texas v. Frank Fossett*, Case No. 14415).

13. For "laborer," see 1900 Census. For "man-about-town," see *Fort Worth Telegram*, March 23, 1907. The $3,000 take is based on a raid on the Stag Saloon. *Dallas Morning News*, March 23, 1907; *Fort Worth Telegram*, September 17, 1903.

14. *Fort Worth Star-Telegram*, September 16 and 17, 1903.

15. *Fort Worth Star*, March 23, 1907; *Dallas Morning News*, March 23, 1907. Testimony of Bill Thomason in *Texas v. Frank Fossett*, Case No. 14415, trial transcript, p. 89.

16. There are some discrepancies between the Dallas and Fort Worth accounts of the raid. Both Fort Worth newspapers said that no gambling paraphernalia was found on the site, while the Dallas newspaper says poker and faro equipment were confiscated. The Dallas paper says that Thomason was not present during the raid; the *Fort Worth Star* has him present and watching the raid in considerable agitation. There is no consistent bias in any of the three papers, either pro- or anti-Thomason or pro- or anti-authorities. We have attempted to let common sense and the weight of the evidence guide us in telling the story. *Dallas Morning News*, March 23, 1907. Cf. *Fort Worth Star*, March 23, 1907.

17. *Fort Worth Star*, March 23, 1907.

18. For Thomason to Maddox, see *Dallas Morning* News, March 23, 1907. For other details, see Federal Writers' Project, "Research Data: Fort Worth and Tarrant County, Texas," 1941, pp. 13, 125–132, Genealogy, History and Archives Unit, Central Library, Fort Worth Public Library. See also *Dallas Morning News*, March 23, 1907; and *Fort Worth Record*, March 24, 1907, AM ed.

19. *Dallas Morning News*, March 23, 1907.

20. Caleb Pirtle, *Fort Worth, The Civilized West* (Tulsa, OK: Continental Heritage Press, 1980), p. 90.

21. *Fort Worth Star*, March 23, 1907 (also reprinted in Mack Williams, ed., *The* News-Tribune *in Old Fort Worth*, p. 72).

22. See sidebar in *Fort Worth Star*, March 23, 1907, p. 1 (reprinted in Mack Williams, ed., *The* News-Tribune *in Old Fort Worth*, p. 72). Cf. *Dallas Morning News*, March 23, 1907.

23. Scott's commission from Tarrant County gave him broad powers to enforce the law anywhere inside the county. Who paid his salary did not change that, which is why special officers were considered an adjunct to the regular law enforcement agencies.

24. The *Record* initially reported that Scott was shot in the right shoulder and right forearm. This was corrected the next day and confirmed by the Dallas newspaper. *Fort Worth Record*, March 23 and 24, 1907, AM ed.; *Dallas Morning News*, March 23, 1907.

25. When recovered from Thomason's possession later, Officer Scott's pistol was found not to be working; it had not been fired by either Scott or Thomason. The failure of the gun to work properly probably saved others from being shot that day because Thomason had clearly shown he would not go down without a fight. When cornered at the lumberyard, he tried to continue the gun battle. When Thomason finally gave his version of events, he was in police custody and dying. Why he chose to continue the charade at that point can only be attributed to sheer meanness or a lifetime of lying. *Dallas Morning News*, March 23, 1907; *Fort Worth Record*, March 24, 1907, AM ed.

26. For descriptions of chase and the route it followed, see *Fort Worth Telegram*, March 23, 1907 and *Fort Worth Record*, March 24, 1907, AM ed.

27. The first account of the episode to appear in the *Fort Worth Record*, March 23, 1907, would put the size of the mob at 1,000, 3,000, and 5,000—all in the same story. The reporter made no attempt to reconcile the discrepancy. The March 24 edition of the same newspaper would settle on 3,000 as the size of the mob. Cf. the *Dallas Morning News*, March 23, 1907, placed it at 5,000 people. For Bell's background, see *Dallas Morning News*, February 20 and 21, 1912

28. *Fort Worth Record*, March 23 and 24, 1907.

29. *Dallas Morning News*, March 23, 1907.

30. *Dallas Morning News*, March 23, 1907; *Fort Worth Star*, March 23, 1907.

31. *Dallas Morning News*, March 23, 1907.

32. *Fort Worth Star*, March 23, 1907; *Fort Worth Telegram*, March 23, 1907.

33. *Fort Worth Record*, March 24, 1907, AM ed.

34. *Fort Worth Record*, March 24, 1907, AM ed.

35. *Fort Worth Record*, March 24, 1907, AM ed.

36. *Fort Worth Telegram*, March 31, 1907; "Wm. Thomlinson" [*sic*], Certificate No. 54924, Tarrant County, Texas Death Indexes, 1903-2000, Texas Dept. of Health, State Vital Statistics, Austin.

37. Years later he was moved to Mount Olivet Cemetery, located in the Riverside section of town at 2205 North Sylvania.

Mount Olivet opened the same year McLean was killed as the city's third public cemetery after Pioneers Rest and Oakwood. There is a McLean family plot at Mount Olivet today, which also holds the remains of Jefferson McLean's father, William Pinkney McLean, who died in 1915.

38. By protocol, the national flag could not be lowered since Jeff was not a civil or military official. *Fort Worth Telegram*, March 23, 1907; *Fort Worth Record*, March 25 and 25, 1907, AM eds.; and *Fort Worth Star*, March 23, 1907 (reprinted in Mack Williams, ed., *The* News-Tribune *in Old Fort Worth*, p. 73).

39. *Fort Worth Record*, March 24 and 25, 1907, AM eds.

40. She had been rushed to a Fort Worth hospital to be operated on, but the shock of the surgery was too much. She suffered another two days before dying. *Dallas Morning News*, May 5, 1907.

41. *Fort Worth Record*, March 24, 1907, AM ed.

42. This and subsequent descriptions of the funeral ceremony on May 1 come from *Fort Worth Star*, May 2, 1907.

43. *Fort Worth Star*, March 23, 1907 (reprinted in Mack Williams, ed., *The* News-Tribune *in Old Fort Worth*, p. 73).

44. *Fort Worth Star*, March 23, 1907 (reprinted in Mack Williams, ed., *The* News-Tribune *in Old Fort Worth*, p. 73); *Fort Worth Telegram*, March 23, 1907.

45. *Fort Worth Star*, March 24, 1907, AM ed. (for flags); *Fort Worth Record*, March 24, 1907 AM ed. (for memorials).

46. *Fort Worth Record*, March 24, 1907, AM ed.

47. *Fort Worth Star-Telegram*, June 14, 1912.

48. For Law and Order League, see *Fort Worth Record*, March 24, 1907, AM ed. For painting, see *Fort Worth Star-Telegram*, June 14, 1912. The McLean portrait is currently in the collections of the Modern Art Museum of Fort Worth, in storage because it does not fit in with their other works. The museum inherited the painting along with many other eclectic pieces from the original Modern Art Museum.

49. *Fort Worth Star-Telegram*, June 14, 1912.

50. This was before official commendations came in, and the FWPD has never had a bonus system. *Dallas Morning News*, May 14, 1907.

Notes to Chapter 10

1. Both boys followed in their father's footsteps as lawmen, a family tradition that also included Oscar's cousin, George W. Montgomery. Details of Oscar Montgomery's life come from obituary in *Fort Worth Star-Telegram*, June 15, 1931 (evening ed.); and *The Book of Fort Worth* (*Fort Worth Record*, 1913), collections of Genealogy, History and Archives Unit, Central Library, Fort Worth Public Library (hereafter cited as *Book of Fort Worth*). Cf. his obituary, with information furnished by his son W. R. Montgomery, says he was born February 17, 1872, in Comanche County, and that his mother's maiden name was "Read." Death Certificate for O. R. Montgomery (No. 36716), June 14, 1931, Texas State Board of Health, Bureau of Vital Statistics, Austin (available on microfilm, "Texas Deaths, 1890–1876").

2. *Book of Fort Worth*, p. 116.

3. According to a 1913 newspaper interview with his Police Commissioner, Montgomery was the biggest among a group of "big boys" on the FWPD. *Dallas Morning News*, May 10, 1913; Obituary in *Fort Worth Star-Telegram*, June 15, 1931, PM ed.; *The Book of Fort Worth* (*Fort Worth Record*, 1913), in Genealogy, History and Archives Unit, Central Library, Fort Worth Public Library.

4. Most of the information on Howell comes from his press bios many years later when he ran for office and from his obituary. *Fort Worth Star-Telegram*, April 4, 1921, and October 1, 1927, AM ed.

5. B. B. Paddock, *A Historical and Biographical Record of North and West Texas* (Chicago: Lewis Publishing Company, 1906), p. 246; Howell obituary, *Fort Worth Star-Telegram*, October 1, 1927, AM ed.

6. Lake Street is North Houston today. These details and all those in the following story unless otherwise noted come from the *Fort Worth Record*, April 12, 1908, AM ed.

7. *Fort Worth Record*, April 12, 1908, Part One, p. 1f.

8. Ike's background is pieced together from census records, court testimony, and newspaper reports. See "Isaac Knight" and "Florence Knight" in Thirteenth United States Federal

Census (1910), Fort Worth, Tarrant County, TX, Microfilm Roll T624_1591; Ike's testimony at May 1914 trial, *State of Texas v. Ike S. Knight*, Case No. 18416, Forty-eighth District Court, Tarrant County District Clerk's Office, Criminal Section, Tarrant County Justice Center, Fort Worth, TX (hereafter cited as *Texas v. Knight*, Case No. 18416); and *Fort Worth Telegram*, May 12 and 25, 1908.

9. Background on Flo and Nellie comes from Ike's testimony at his May 1914 trial, *Texas v. Knight*, Case No. 18416. See also *Ike S. Knight v. State*, Case No. 1694, Court of Criminal Appeals of Texas, 66 Tex. Crim. 335; 147 S.W. 268; 1912 Tex. Crim. Appeals, April 24, 1912 (hereafter cited as *Knight v. State*, Appeals Case No. 4474). For their marriage, see *Ex parte Florence B. Knight*, Case No. 74090, September 21, 1926, Minutes of the Forty-eighth District Court of Texas, Book No. 34, p. 171, on microfilm in Tarrant County Justice Center, District Clerk's Civil and Family Records, Fort Worth (hereafter cited as *Ex parte Florence B. Knight*, Case No. 74090).

10. Ike's background comes from his own testimony in *Texas v. Knight*, Case No. 18416. Additional information comes from *Knight v. State*, Appeals Case No. 4474.

11. *Fort Worth Record*, April 12, 1908. *Texas v. Knight*, Case No. 18146; and *Knight v. State*, Appeals Case No. 4474.

12. *Fort Worth Record*, April 12, 1908.

13. *Texas v. Knight*, Case No. 18416; and *Knight v. State*, Appeals Case No. 4474.

14. *Texas v. Knight*, Case No 18416.

15. This entire exchange comes from *Texas v. Knight*, Case No. 18416.

16. All quotes and Ike's movements come from Ike's testimony and cross-examination in *Texas v. Knight*, Case No. 18416; and *Knight v. State*, Appeals Case No. 4474.

17. See Ike's testimony in *Texas v. Knight*, Case No. 18416; and *Knight v. State*, Appeals Case No. 4474.

18. The movements and actions of the principals, described in the following paragraphs, are taken from the statements of Nellie Larmon, Ike Knight, and Oscar Montgomery, as they appeared in the *Fort Worth Record*, April 12 and 13, 1908.

19. *Ike Knight v. State*, Appeals Case No. 4474. Testimony about a wild-looking Ike comes from *Fort Worth Record*, April 12, 1908, Part One.

20. *Fort Worth Record*, April 12, 1908.

21. Ike's claim that he was on the way to surrender himself is, of course, impossible to verify, but highly unlikely. *Texas v. Knight*, Case No. 18416.

22. *Fort Worth Record*, April 12, 1908, Part One.

23. Both quotations from appeals trial transcript, *Knight v. State*, Appeals Case No. 4474.

24. *Fort Worth Record*, April 12, Part One, and 13, AM ed., 1908.

25. *Fort Worth Record*, April 12, 1908, Part One.

26. *Fort Worth Record*, April 13, 1908, AM ed.

27. *Fort Worth Record*, April 12, 1908, Part One.

28. *Fort Worth Record*, April 12, 1908, Part One.

29. The Emergency Hospital operated by All Saints Hospital Association opened its doors in 1904 as a teaching hospital for the Fort Worth Medical College next door. *Dallas Morning News*, March 7, 1904; *Fort Worth Star-Telegram*, March 23, 2006.

30. *Fort Worth Record*, April 13, 1908, AM ed.

31. *Fort Worth Record*, April 13, 1908, AM ed. The date the amputation was performed is unknown, although there is no doubt the leg was amputated based on pictures and descriptions of Howell later in life. *Dallas Morning News*, June 17, 1909.

32. The indictments are listed as Case No. 18415, "assault to murder"; No. 18416, "manslaughter" [*sic*]; and No. 18417, "assault to murder," in the Criminal Index ledger, felony cases, Tarrant County District Clerk's Office, Criminal Section, Tarrant County Justice Center, Fort Worth, TX. *Fort Worth Record*, April 12 and 13, 1908, AM eds.

33. *Fort Worth Record*, April 13, 1908, AM ed.

34. *Fort Worth Record*, April 13, 1908, AM ed.

35. *Fort Worth Record*, April 13, 1908, AM ed.

36. *Fort Worth Record*, April 14, 1908, AM ed.

37. Strictly speaking, there was no such thing as a "Miranda warning" at this time, but there was legal precedent that a confession must be "freely and voluntarily made," and that the

defendant must be advised that it might be used as evidence against him. Apparently, the County Attorney's Office was remiss on this occasion. *Knight v. State*, Appeals Case No. 4474. The insanity defense was already being tested when it was mentioned, without attribution, in the newspaper on April 27. *Fort Worth Star-Telegram*, April 27, 1908.

38. *Fort Worth Star-Telegram*, April 27, 1908.

39. Recently enacted by the state legislature, the jury wheel system provided for a random selection of veniremen lottery-style. Under the old system, the sheriff summoned a venire from the voter rolls using his own judgment. Having to locate and summon selected men placed more pressure on the sheriff but theoretically made for a more representative venire. *Fort Worth Telegram*, May 12, 1908.

40. *Fort Worth Telegram*, April 17 and 27, 1908.

41. *Fort Worth Telegram*, May 12, 1908; *Dallas Morning News*, May 15, 1908.

42. *Dallas Morning News*, May 15, 1908.

43. *Fort Worth Telegram*, May 15, 1908; *Knight v. State*, Appeals Case No. 4474.

44. *Knight v. State*, Appeals Case No. 4474.

45. *Knight v. State*, Appeals Case No. 4474; *Fort Worth Telegram*, May 24, 1908.

46. *Texas v. Knight*, Case No. 18416.

47. *Fort Worth Telegram*, May 24, 1908.

48. *Texas v. Knight*, Case No. 18416; *Knight v. State*, Appeals Case No. 4474; *Fort Worth Telegram*, May 24 and 25, 1908.

49. *Fort Worth Telegram*, May 25 and June 25, 1908; *Knight v. State*, Appeals Case No. 4474.

50. *Fort Worth Telegram*, May 24, 1908.

51. *Texas v. Knight*, Case No. 18416.

52. *Fort Worth Telegram*, May 25, 2908.

53. *Knight v. State*, Appeals Case No. 4474.

54. *Knight v. State*, Appeals Case No. 1694. The Court of Criminal Appeals met in Dallas from January through March very year.

55. *Fort Worth Star-Telegram*, January 2, 1916.

56. The ultimate disposition of the three original indictments

against Ike Knight are listed in the Criminal Index ledger, felony cases, Tarrant County District Clerk's Office, Criminal Section, Tarrant County Justice Center, Fort Worth, TX. For Ike's miraculous conversion, see *Fort Worth Star-Telegram*, January 2, 1916.

57. Fourteenth United States Federal Census (1920), Davidson County, Nashville, TN, Microfilm Roll No. T625_1735. For Ike's marital woes, see *Ex parte Florence B. Knight*, Case No. 74090; and *Ike Knight v. Donna Knight*, Case No. 76907, May 6, 1929, Forty-eighth District Court, on microfilm in Tarrant County Justice Center, District Clerk's Civil and Family Records, Fort Worth.

58. *Fort Worth Telegram*, May 15 and June 10, 1908.

59. *Fort Worth Star-Telegram*, June 15, 1931, PM ed.; O. R. Montgomery death certificate.

60. O. R. Montgomery death certificate; *Fort Worth Star-Telegram*, June 15, 1931, PM ed.

61. "Night sergeant" was a desk job that did not require walking a beat. Although not on the front lines, night in and night out, he was the busiest man at the stationhouse. It was his job to admit prisoners, keep a record of all persons incarcerated with "their final disposition," and "to enter every bit of money that came in from fines or bonds." For the position, see Walter J. Hurst, "A Paper on 'Fort Worth's Finest': the Fort Worth Police Department," term paper submitted for Sociology 24, Texas Christian University, May 23, 1929 (in collections of Dalton Hoffman, Jr.), p. 24. For Howell's service, see *Fort Worth Star-Telegram*, April 4, 1921.

62. *Fort Worth Telegram*, December 27, 1908; *Fort Worth Star-Telegram*, April 4, 1921.

63. Statistics compiled by American Stroke Association, published in *Fort Worth Star-Telegram*, July 10, 2004, p. 14B.

64. See campaign ad in *Fort Worth Star-Telegram*, April 4, 1921; and obituary in *Fort Worth Star-Telegram*, October 1, 1927, AM ed.

65. See obituary in *Fort Worth Star-Telegram*, October 1, 1927, AM ed. Death Certificate for R. D. Howell (No. 29183), September 30, 1927, Texas State Board of Health, Bureau of Vital Statistics, Austin (on microfilm, "Texas Deaths, 1890–1976").

66. Mayor W. D. Davis to "the Honorable City Commission", October 4, 1911, Records of the City of Fort Worth, Series I, Mayor and Council Proceedings, 1911, Box 5 of 5, Genealogy, History and Archives Unit, Central Library, Fort Worth Public Library.

Notes to Chapter 11

1. Fort Worth Police Rules and Regulations, 1908. An original copy is in collections of Fort Worth Police Association, Fort Worth Police Academy. A copy is in Fort Worth Police Department Miscellaneous Materials, Archive Holdings, Genealogy, History and Archives Unit, Central Library, Fort Worth Public Library.

2. *Fort Worth Star-Telegram*, July 11 and August 15, 1909.

3. *Fort Worth Record*, August 13, 1909.

4. Why the grand jury singled out Campbell and not his partner is unknown, but Campbell definitely was getting all the publicity for putting the squeeze on the Acre's denizens. *Dallas Morning News*, July 14, 1909.

5. See "Robt. P. Hammond" in Twelfth United States Federal Census (1900), Tarrant County, Justice Precinct 3, TX, Microfilm Roll No. T623_1671. 6. For physical characteristics, see "Robert P. Hammond" in U.S. National Homes for Disabled Volunteer Soldiers, 1866–1938," Record Group 15, Microfilm Roll No. M1749, National Archives and Records Administration, Washington, DC, available online at Ancestry.com; and *Fort Worth Telegram*, October 5, 1907. For FWPD tenure, see *Fort Worth Telegram*, October 5, 1907, and March 27, 1908. Some newspapers give the location of his saloon at Thirteenth and Calhoun, but it was Thirteenth and Crump. See *Fort Worth Telegram*, July 29, 1909. For residence, see *Fort Worth Telegram*, December 10, 1909.

7. *Fort Worth Star-Telegram*, September 3, 1910.

8. *Fort Worth Telegram*, July 23, 1908. *Fort Worth Star-Telegram*, May 11, 1913.

9. *Palestine (TX) Daily Herald*, September 22, 1910.

10. *Fort Worth Star-Telegram*, July 11, 1909. For Hammond's fine, see p. 24; for the shooting, see p. 11. It was purely coincidence that the two stories appeared on the same date.

11. *Dallas Morning News*, July 11, 1909; *Fort Worth Star-Telegram*, September 5, 1909.

12. *Fort Worth Star-Telegram*, July 11, 1909; *Dallas Morning News*, July 11, 1909.

13. *Fort Worth Star-Telegram*, July 27, 1909.

14. *Fort Worth Record*, August 13, 1909; *Fort Worth Star-Telegram*, August 5, 1909.

15. *Dallas Morning News*, July 11, 1909; *Fort Worth Record*, August 13, 1909; *Fort Worth Star-Telegram*, August 5 and September 8, 1909.

16. *Fort Worth Star-Telegram*, September 5, 1909.

17. *Fort Worth Star-Telegram*, August 14, 1909.

18. *Fort Worth Telegram*, February 5 and 6, 1908; *Dallas Morning News*, April 7, November 24 and 29, 1908; *Weatherford Daily Herald*, February 7, 1908.

19. Details of the crime scene and Detective Williams' investigation come from the *Fort Worth Record*, August 13, 1909, and the *Dallas Morning News*, August 19, 1909. Where there are discrepancies, we have gone with the later version reasoning that there was more time for the reporter to check out his facts.

20. Another slipup by the killer: the mattress would have acted as insulation, slowing down the cooling of the barrel. *Fort Worth Record*, August 13, 1909; *Dallas Morning News*, August 19, 1909.

21. *Fort Worth Record*, August 13, 1909.

22. *Fort Worth Star-Telegram*, August 14 and 16, 1909.

23. Bradley later testified that Hammond also said, "Whoever killed Campbell did a good thing." Hammond denied ever saying that. *Fort Worth Star-Telegram*, August 15 and September 7, 1909.

24. *Fort Worth Star-Telegram*, August 14 and September 7, 1909.

25. For "third degree," see *Fort Worth Record*, August 13, 1909. For progress of investigation, see *Fort Worth Star-Telegram*, September 7, 1909.

26. For Mulkey, see *Fort Worth Star-Telegram*, August 25, 1909. For "conspiracy," see *Fort Worth Star-Telegram*, August 15, 1909.

27. *Fort Worth Star-Telegram*, August 15, 1909.

28. *Fort Worth Star-Telegram*, August 15, 1909.

29. For shotgun shells, see *Fort Worth Record*, August 14, 1909. For bruise, see *Fort Worth Star-Telegram*, September 5 and 8, 1909.

30. *Dallas Morning News*, August 19, 1909.

31. *Dallas Morning News*, August 19, 1909.

32. For May Ferguson, see *Fort Worth Star-Telegram*, August 14, 1909. The complete text of Judge Swayne's charge to the grand jury is found in *Fort Worth Star-Telegram*, August 23, 1909.

33. *Fort Worth Star-Telegram*, August 15, 1909.

34. *Fort Worth Star-Telegram*, August 14, 1909.

35. *Fort Worth Star-Telegram*, August 21, 1909.

36. *Fort Worth Star-Telegram*, August 29, 1909.

37. Sophia Wolfe, W. R. Hunt, and Will Chadwick, on July 22, 1908; *Fort Worth Star-Telegram*, July 23, 1908; September 7 and 8, 1909; *State of Texas v. Bob Hammond*, Case No. 18891, Forty-eighth District Court, Tarrant County District Clerk's Office, Criminal Section, Tarrant County Justice Center, Fort Worth, TX (hereafter cited as *Texas v. Bob Hammond*, Case No. 18891).

38. *Fort Worth Star-Telegram*, September 11, 1909.

39. *Fort Worth Star-Telegram*, October 17 and December 29, 1909.

40. *Fort Worth Star-Telegram*, December 10, 1909.

41. Petition of W. R. Parker (November 8, 1909) and record of subpoenas, *State of Texas v. Bob Hammond*, Case No. 18891.

42. *Dallas Morning News*, March 2, 1910; *State of Texas v. Bob Hammond*, Case No. 18891.

43. *State of Texas v. Bob Hammond*, Case No. 19019, Forty-eighth District Court, Tarrant County District Clerk's Office, Criminal Section, Tarrant County Justice Center, Fort Worth, TX (hereafter cited as *Texas v. Bob Hammond*, Case No. 19019). For dynamite trials, see *Fort Worth Star-Telegram*, April 22, 27, and 28, 1910.

44. *State of Texas v. Bob Hammond*, Case No. 19019. Chronology of county officials in Oliver Knight, *Fort Worth: Outpost on the Trinity* (Norman: University of Oklahoma Press, 1953), pp. 252–53.

45. *State of Texas v. Bob Hammond*, Case Nos. 19019 and

20131. Final resolution of each of Hammond's cases (Nos. 18891, 19019, and 20131) is found in Criminal Index, Felony Cases, January 15, 1876–September 30, 1932, A–Z Volume, in Tarrant County District Clerk's Office, Criminal Section, Tarrant County Justice Center, Fort Worth, TX. For dismissal of "assault to murder" charges, see *Fort Worth Star-Telegram*, May 11, 1913. For "outlawry" order, see notation written and signed by John W. Baskin in the file for *State of Texas v. Bob Hammond*, Case No. 20131.

46. *Fort Worth Record*, August 14, 1909; *Fort Worth Star-Telegram*, September 4, 1909.

BIBLIOGRAPHY

Primary Source Documents and Unpublished Works

Adjutant General of Texas. "Reports of the Adjutant General of the State of Texas." Texas State Library and Archives, Austin.

"American Valley Murders: An Overview." Author unknown. Unpublished MS. History File No. 21. State Records Center and Archives, Santa Fe, NM.

Book of Fort Worth, The. Fort Worth: *Fort Worth Record*, 1913. Genealogy, History, and Archives Unit, Central Library, Fort Worth Public Library.

Bowden, Jesse Earl, and William S. Cummins. *Texas Desperado in Florida: The Capture of Outlaw John Wesley Hardin in Pensacola, 1877.* Pensacola, FL: Pensacola Historical Society, n.d.

Carlisle, Willie Flowers (Mrs. George F.). *History of the Old Cemetery: City—Masonic—Odd Fellow.* Dallas: privately printed, 1948. Booklet in collections of Dallas Public Library.

———. *History of the Old Cemetery, Dallas.* Dallas: privately printed, 1948. Booklet in collections of Dallas Public Library.

Carlton, Dora, compiler. Scrapbook of Fort Worth Police Department clippings. Genealogy, History, and Archives Unit, Central Library, Fort Worth Public Library.

Colcord, C. F. *Autobiography of Charles Francis Colcord.* Tulsa, OK: privately printed, 1970.

Convict Record Ledgers with Indexes, 1849–1970. "A" and "B" series. Microfilm, 20 reels. Texas Department of Criminal Justice. Texas State Library, State Records Center, Records Management Division, 2002.

Dallas County Marriage Records, 4 vols. 1846–1877. Genealogy Department, J. Erik Jonsson Central Library, Dallas Public Library.

Facts about Fort Worth and Adjacent Country, Columbian Souvenir Ed. Author unknown. Fort Worth: publisher not known, 1893. Collections of Amon Carter Museum, Fort Worth.

Federal Writers' Project. *Mississippi: The WPA Guide to the Magnolia State.* 1938. Reprint, University Press of Mississippi, 1988.

———. "Research Data: Fort Worth and Tarrant County, Texas." Series I and II. 77 vols. Fort Worth: Texas Writers' Project, Fort Worth Public Library Unit, 1941. Genealogy, History, and Archives Unit, Central Library, Fort Worth Public Library.

Fort Worth "Bond Books." Records of the City of Fort Worth. Records of the City Secretary's Office. Series I. Mayor and Council Proceedings. City Secretary's Record Book, 1873–1888. Genealogy, History, and Archives Unit, Central Library, Fort Worth Public Library.

Fort Worth City Council. City Council Minutes, April 1873–present. Vols. A–Z (on microfiche). City Secretary's Office, City Hall.

Fort Worth City Council. Records of the City of Fort Worth. Series I. Mayor and Council Proceedings, 1895–present. Genealogy, History, and Archives Unit, Central Library, Fort Worth Public Library.

Fort Worth City Directories, 1877–1928. On microfiche. Genealogy, History, and Archives Unit, Central Library, Fort Worth Public Library.

Fort Worth Police Department Annual, 1901. Special Collections, University of Texas at Arlington Library.

Fort Worth Police Department Miscellaneous Materials, Archive Holdings, Genealogy, History, and Archives Unit, Central Library, Fort Worth Public Library.

General Statute Laws of the State of Texas, 1859–2007. 137 vols. Austin: The Legislature. Central Library, Fort Worth Public Library.

Gillett, James. *Fugitives from Justice: The Notebook of Texas Ranger Sergeant James B. Gillett.* Austin, TX: State House Press, 1997.

Gooch, J. A. "100 Years: Cantey, Hanger, Gooch, Munn & Collins." Fort Worth: privately printed, n.d.

Good, John J. *Cannon Smoke: The Letters of Captain John J. Good, Good-Douglas Texas Battery, CSA.* Compiled and edited by

Lester Newton Fitzhugh. Hillsboro, TX: Hill Jr. College Press, 1971.

Greenwood Cemetery Records, Greenwood Funeral Home, 3100 White Settlement Road, Fort Worth, TX.

"Historic Oakwood Cemetery with Cavalry Cemetery and Old Trinity Cemetery of Fort Worth, Texas." Compiled by Helen McKelvy Markgraf and Robert G. Yoder. Fort Worth: Fort Worth Genealogical Society, 1994.

History of Texas together with a Biographical History of Tarrant and Parker Counties. Author unknown. Chicago: Lewis Publishing Co., 1895. Genealogy, History, and Archives Unit, Central Library, Fort Worth Public Library.

Hudson, Weldon I., compiler. *Tarrant County, Texas Marriage Records, 1876–1885.* Two vols. Privately printed, 1984.

Huntsville Penitentiary Records, 1848–1954. Texas Department of Criminal Justice, Convict Record Ledgers, 1849–1970. On microfilm. Genealogy, History, and Archives Unit, Central Library, Fort Worth Public Library.

King, Wilburn Hill. *With the 18th Texas Infantry: The Autobiography of Wilburn Hill King,* edited by L. David Norris. Hillsboro, TX: Hill College Press, 1996.

Lake, Mary Daggett. MDL Papers. Series II: State and Local History. 2 boxes. Series 3: Genealogical Notes and Manuscripts. 3 boxes. Genealogy, History, and Archives Unit, Central Library, Fort Worth Public Library.

Pioneers Rest Cemetery, Fort Worth, Tarrant County, Texas. Weldon I. Hudson and Barbara Knox, compilers. Fort Worth: Fort Worth Genealogical Society, 2001.

Report of the Adjutant General of the State of Texas, 1886. Austin: Triplett & Hutchings, State Printers, 1886.

Rich, Harold Wayne. "Twenty-five Years of Struggle and Progress: The Fort Worth Police Department, 1873–1897." Master of Arts Thesis submitted to AddRan College of Arts and Sciences, Texas Christian University, May 1999.

Schrag, Zachary Moses. "Nineteen-nineteen: The Boston Police Strike in the Context of American Labor." Undergraduate Honors Thesis in History for B.A. Degree, Harvard University, 1992.

Sextons Record. Pioneers Rest Cemetery, Fort Worth, Texas (copy, 1982). Genealogy, History, and Archives Unit, Central Library, Fort Worth Public Library.

Shannon Funeral Chapels. "Index of Archive Records." December 1906–December 1930. Fort Worth: privately printed, 1991.

Shannon's Funeral Chapel and Home. Records. 36 microfilm rolls. Fort Worth, TX, 1990. Genealogy, History, and Archives Unit, Central Library, Fort Worth Public Library.

Spalding, Thomas W., ed. Descendants of Jane Owsley Gregg, Daughter of Major Thomas Owsley (1658–1700): The Gregg, Peak, Jacobs, Moseley and Related Families. Springfield, VA: Owsley Family Historical Society, 2002.

Tarrant County, TX, Civil and Criminal District Court Records. Tarrant County Justice Center, Fort Worth.

Tarrant County, TX, Criminal Docket, County Court, 1878–1879. Special Collections, University of Texas at Arlington.

Tarrant County, TX, Marriage Records. Weldon I. Hudson, compiler. Vol. 1, 1876–1885. Vol. 2, 1885–1892. Vol. 3, November 16, 1892–November 2, 1901. Fort Worth Genealogical Society, 1992.

Terrell, Capt. J. C. *Reminiscences of the Early Days of Fort Worth.* Fort Worth: Texas Printing Company, 1906.

Texas Birth Indexes, 1903–1976. Texas Department of Health. Bureau of Vital Statistics. On microfilm. Genealogy, History, and Local Archives Unit, Central Library, Fort Worth Public Library.

Texas Death Records, 1903–1940. Texas Department of Health. Bureau of Vital Statistics. On microfilm. Genealogy, History, and Local Archives Unit, Central Library, Fort Worth Public Library.

Texas Masonic Deaths with Selected Biographical Sketches. Michael Kelsey et al., eds. Bowie, MD: Heritage Books, 1998.

Texas Rangers. Adjutant General Records. Service Reports. Frontier Battalion. Record No. 401-154. Austin: Texas State Library and Archives.

———. Frontier Battalion Muster Rolls, Record No. 401-750. Austin: Texas State Library and Archives.

Texas Secretary of State. Executive Record Books. Texas
Secretary of State Executive Clemency Records. Archives and
Information Service Division, Texas State Library and Archives
Commission, Austin.
United States Federal Censuses, Seventh (1840)–Fifteenth (1930),
on microfilm.
United States Federal Mortality Census Schedules, 1850–1880,
and Related Indexes in the Custody of the Daughters of
the American Revolution. Record Group 29. On microfilm,
30 reels. National Archives and Records Administration.
Washington, DC: National Archives Microfilm Publications.
U.S. National Homes for Disabled Volunteer Soldiers, 1866–
1938. Record Group 15 (Records of the Dept. of Veterans
Affairs). On microfilm, 282 rolls. Washington, D.C.: National
Archives and Records Administration. Available online at
Ancestry.com.
Vertical files (various). Genealogy, History, and Archives Unit,
Central Library, Fort Worth Public Library.
Ward, Russell B. "Panther City Progressives: Fort Worth and the
Commission Form of Government." Thesis for U.S. history,
1900–1940, Texas A&M University, Fall 1995.

Secondary Works

Allen, Ruth. Chapters in the History of Organized Labor in Texas.
Publication No. 4143. Austin: University of Texas, Bureau of
Research in the Social Sciences, 1941.
"American Valley Murders: An Overview." Author unknown.
Unpublished Manuscript in History. File No. 21. Santa Fe,
New Mexico: State Records Center and Archives.
Anderson, Ken. *Crime in Texas: Your Complete Guide to the
Criminal Justice System.* Revised ed. Austin: University of
Texas Press, 2005.
Arnold, Ann. *A History of the Fort Worth Legal Community.*
Austin: Eakin Press, 2000.
———. *A History of the Fort Worth Medical Community.*
Arlington, TX: Landa Press, 2001.
Bartholomew, Ed. *Black Jack Ketchum: Last of the Hold-up Kings.*
Houston: Frontier Press of Texas, 1955.

Blackmon, Douglas A. *Slavery by Another Name: The Re-enslavement of Black People in America from the Civil War to World War II.* New York: Doubleday, 2008.

Bullis, Don. *New Mexico's Finest: Peace Officers Killed in the Line of Duty, 1847–1996.* Santa Fe: New Mexico Dept. of Public Safety, 1996.

Castleberry, Vivian A. *Daughters of Dallas: A History of Greater Dallas Through the Voices and Deeds of Its Women.* Dallas: Odenwald Press, 1994.

Coerver, Don M. "Plan of San Diego." See entry for *New Handbook of Texas, The.*

Cuéllar, Carlos E. *Stories from the Barrio: A History of Mexican Fort Worth.* Fort Worth, TX: Texas Christian University Press, 2003.

DeArment, Robert K. *Jim Courtright of Fort Worth: His Life and Legend.* Fort Worth, TX: Texas Christian University Press, 2004.

DeLord, Ronald, ed. *The Ultimate Sacrifice: Trials and Triumphs of the Texas Peace Officer, 1823–2000.* Austin, TX: Peace Officers Memorial Foundation, 2000.

Denver, John, ed. *Legal Reelism: Movies as Legal Texts.* Urbana: University of Illinois Press, 1996.

Duffin, Jacalyn. *History of Medicine: A Scandalously Short Introduction.* Toronto, Canada: University of Toronto Press, 1999.

Egerton, John. *Speak Now against the Day: The Generation before the Civil Rights Movement in the South.* New York: Knopf, 1994.

A Family History of Limestone County. Author unknown. Dallas, TX: Taylor Publishing Co., 1984.

"The First 100 Years." Fort Worth Police Department Annual, 1973. (In authors' collections.)

Fitzhugh, L. N., ed. *Cannon Smoke.* Hillsboro, TX: Hill Jr. College Press, 1971.

Flexner, Stuart Berg. *I Hear America Talking.* New York: Simon & Schuster / Touchstone Books, 1976.

Foner, Eric. *Give Me Liberty! An American History.* Vol. 2: From 1865. 2nd ed. New York: W. W. Norton, 2009.

Freeman, G. D. *Midnight and Noonday*. Norman, OK: University of Oklahoma Press, 1984.

Garrett, Julia Kathryn. *Fort Worth: A Frontier Triumph*. Fort Worth: Texas Christian University Press, 1996 (reprint).

Gournay, Luke. *Texas Boundaries: Evolution of the State's Counties*. College Station, TX: Texas A&M University Press, 1995

Hendrickson, Kenneth B., Jr. *Chief Executives of Texas*. College Station: Texas A&M University Press, 1995.

Hinz, Dale. *History of the Fort Worth Police Department*. Fort Worth: privately printed, 2007.

Hurst, Walter J. "A Paper on 'Fort Worth's Finest': The Fort Worth Police Department." Term paper submitted for Sociology 24, Texas Christian University, May 23, 1929. Copy in author's collections.

Jackson, Kenneth T. *The Ku Klux Klan in the City, 1915–1930*. Chicago, IL: Ivan R. Dee Publisher, 1992 (reprint).

Jary, William E., ed. *Camp Bowie, Fort Worth, 1917–1918*. Fort Worth, TX: B. B. Maxfield Foundation, 1975.

Klein, Murray. *The Life and Legend of Jay Gould*. Baltimore: Johns Hopkins University Press, 1986.

Knight, Oliver. *Fort Worth: Outpost on the Trinity*. Norman: University of Oklahoma Press, 1953.

Laning, Jim, and Judy Laning, eds. *Texas Cowboys: Memories of the Early Days*. College Station: Texas A&M University Press, 1984.

Marten, James. *Texas Divided: Loyalty and Dissent in the Lone Star State, 1856–1874*. Lexington: University Press of Kentucky, 1990.

McIntire, Jim. *Early Days in Texas: A Trip to Hell and Heaven*. Norman: University of Oklahoma Press, 1992 (reprint of 1902 ed.).

McKenzie, Phyllis. *The Mexican Texans*. College Station: Texas A&M University Press, 2004.

Miller, Nyle H., and Joseph W. Snell. *Why the West Was Wild*. Norman: University of Oklahoma Press, 2003.

Mullen, Kevin J. *The Toughest Gang in Town: Police Stories from Old San Francisco*. Novato, CA: Noir Publications, 2005.

New Handbook of Texas, The. Ron Tyler et al., eds. 6 vols. Austin: Texas State Historical Association, 1996.

O'Connor, Richard. *Iron Wheels and Broken Men.* New York: G. P. Putnam's Sons, 1973.

Paddock, B. B., ed. *History of Texas: Fort Worth and the Texas Northwest Edition.* 4 vols. Chicago: Lewis Publishing Co., 1922.

————. *A Twentieth Century History and Biographical Record of North and West Texas.* 2 vols. Chicago: Lewis Publishing Co., 1906.

Pate, J'Nell. *North of the River: A Brief History of North Fort Worth.* Fort Worth: Texas Christian University Press, 1994.

Phares, Ross. *The Governors of Texas.* Gretna, LA: Pelican Publishing Company, 1976.

Pirtle, Caleb. *Fort Worth: The Civilized West.* Tulsa, OK: Continental Heritage Press, 1980.

Porter, Roy. *The Greatest Benefit to Mankind: A Medical History of Humanity.* New York: W. W. Norton, 1997.

Reeves, L. H. The *Medical History of Fort Worth and Tarrant County: One Hundred Years, 1853–1953.* Fort Worth: privately printed, 1955.

Riegel, Robert Edgar. *The Story of the Western Railroads.* Bison ed. Lincoln: University of Nebraska Press, 1967.

Sanders, Leonard. *How Fort Worth Became the Texasmost City.* Fort Worth: Amon Carter Museum of Western Art, 1973.

Selcer, Richard. *Fort Worth Characters.* Denton: University of North Texas Press, 2009.

————. *Hell's Half Acre: The Life and Legend of a Red-Light District.* Fort Worth: Texas Christian University Press, 1991.

Sherwin, Richard K. "Framed," in John Denver, ed. *Legal Reelism: Movies as Legal Texts.* Urbana: University of Illinois Press, 1966, pp. 70–92.

Shogan, Robert. *The Battle of Blair Mountain: The Story of America's Largest Labor Uprising.* Boulder, CO: Westview Press, 2004.

Smith, Sam. "Things I Remember about Early Days in the History of Fort Worth." Fort Worth: privately printed, [ca. 1965].

Stanley, F. *Longhair Jim Courtright: Two-Gun Marshal of Fort Worth*. Denver, CO: World Press, 1957.

Stemtiford, Barry M. *The American Home Guard: The State Militia in the Twentieth Century*. College Station: Texas A&M University Press, 2002.

Stephens, Robert W. *Bullets and Buckshot in Texas*. Dallas: privately printed, 2002.

Tise, Sammy. *Texas County Sheriffs*. Albuquerque, New Mexico: privately printed, 1989.

Walter, Ray A. *A History of Limestone County*. Austin: Von Boeckmann-Jones, 1959.

Periodical Literature

Newspapers

Albuquerque Morning Journal, 1885.

Arlington Journal, 1897–1916 (in transcribed form only, online at www.ArlingtonLibrary.org).

Atlanta Constitution, 1886 (on microfilm).

Austin Daily State Journal, 1870 (on microfilm).

Dallas Herald / Times Herald (Weekly and Daily), 1855–1885 (on microfilm and online).

Dallas Morning News, 1885–2002 (on microfilm).

Fort Worth Democrat (Daily), 1871–1881 (on microfilm).

Fort Worth Advance / Democrat-Advance, 1880–1882 (on microfilm)

Fort Worth Gazette, 1883–1896 (on microfilm).

Fort Worth News-Tribune (see Williams, Mack, and Williams, Mack, and Williams, Madeline, below).

Fort Worth Press, 1921–1975 (on microfilm).

Fort Worth Record, 1903–1925 (on microfilm).

Fort Worth Record-Telegram, 1925–1931 (on microfilm and online).

Fort Worth Register / Morning Register, 1896–1905 (on microfilm).

Fort Worth Standard, 1873–1878 (only a few issues on microfilm).

Fort Worth Star, 1906–1909 (on microfilm).

Fort Worth Star-Telegram, 1909–1995 (on microfilm and online).

Fort Worth Telegram, 1897–1909 (archived as *Fort Worth Star-Telegram*, on microfilm and online).
Galveston (Daily) News, 1855–1884 (on microfilm and online).
Houston Chronicle, 2004 (on microfilm).
The Liberator (Boston), 1861 (online).
New Orleans Picayune, 1886.
New York Times, 1888 (on microfilm and online).
San Antonio Light, 1886 (on microfilm).
Santa Fe Daily New Mexican, 1883.
Williams, Mack, ed. *The* News-Tribune *in Old Fort Worth*. A Bicentennial Memory Book (collected newspaper columns). Fort Worth: privately printed by Mack Williams and Madeline Williams, 1975.
Williams, Mack, and Williams, Madeline, eds. *In Old Fort Worth*. Texas Centennial Edition (bound and indexed collection of newspaper columns). Fort Worth: privately printed by Mack and Madeline Williams, 1986.

Magazine and Journal Articles

Baker, Terry. "Finding the Forgotten: Texas Police Officers Killed in the Line of Duty." *National Academy Associate: The Magazine of the FBI National Academy Associates* 4, no. 4 (July/August 2002): 21–24f.
Caldroney, R. D. "What Killed Stonewall Jackson? A 21st–century Physician Offers a Historical 'Autopsy'." *Military History Magazine* 23, no. 3 (May 2006): 10–16.
Crane, Michael A. "Dr. Goodfellow: Gunfighter's Surgeon." *Quarterly of the National Association for Outlaw and Lawman History* 27, no. 4 (October–December, 2003): 31–35.
Ellis, Ann Wells. "A Crusade against 'Wretched Attitudes': The Commission on Interracial Cooperation's Activities in Atlanta." *Atlanta Historical Journal* 23 (Spring 1979): 21–44.
Fairbanks, Robert B. "Making Better Citizens in Dallas." *Legacies Journal* 11, no. 2 (Fall 1999): 26–36.
Fairley, Bill. Various subjects. Weekly columns on Fort Worth History, *Fort Worth Star-Telegram*, 1990–2007.
Footprints: The Quarterly Publication of the Fort Worth Genealogical Society, 1958–1984. Vols. 1–27 with Index.

Harris, Charles H., III, and Louis R. Sadler, "The Plan of San Diego and the Mexican-United States War Crisis of 1916: A Re-examination." *Hispanic American Historical Review* 58, no. 3 (August 1978): 381–408.

Morrissey, Siobhan. "A Surge in Cop Killings." *Time Magazine* online. September 28, 2007. www.time.com/time/print-out/0,8816,1666750,00.html.

Penn, Chris. "Gunfire in Dodge City: The Night Ed Masterson Was Killed." *Wild West Magazine* 17, no. 4 (December 2004): 48–53.

Sandos, James A. "The Plan of San Diego: War and Diplomacy on the Texas Border, 1915–1916. *Arizona and the West Quarterly* 14, no. 1 (Spring 1972): 5–24.

Schulz, David A. "Old Red Court House, Dallas, Texas." *American History Magazine* 40, no. 3 (August 2005): 26–28f.

Signal 50: The Newsletter for the Fort Worth Police Officers Association. Issued monthly. Archives, Fort Worth Police and Fire Academy.

Smith, Larry. "To Protect and Serve." *Parade (Sunday) Magazine* (October 21, 2007): 6–7.

Websites

Ancestry genealogy database. http://www.ancestry.com.

Family Genealogy website. http://freepages.genealogy.rootsweb.com/~allyorks/badguy.htm.

HeritageQuest genealogy database. http://persi.heritagequeston-line.com/hqoweb/library/do/index.

LexisNexis law database for Texas Court of Appeals cases (access by case number). https://www.lexis.com/research/retrieve.

Officer Down Memorial Page, Inc., of the Dallas Police Department. www.odmp.org.

Correspondence

Donnell, Donna, of Fort Worth, TX, and Richard Selcer, e-mails, November 3 and 8, 2008.

Grimes, Roy T., of Lubbock, TX, and Kevin Foster, e-mails, June–July, 2008.

Harwell, Elton, of Dallas, TX, and Richard Selcer, correspondence, 1996ff.

Myrick, J. M. (Pres. Pioneers Rest Cemetery Association) to Kevin Foster, e-mail, August 24, 2009.

Parrish, George, of Rohmer Park, CA, and Kevin Foster, e-mails, various dates, 2002.

Rea, Marian, of Johnson County, TX, and Kevin Foster, e-mails, Feb. 19 and 26, 2004; May 4, 2006.

Smith, Mrs. Monte K. (Diane), of Flint, TX, and Kevin Foster, e-mails and correspondence, January 1 and 15, 2006.

INDEX